D1267193

An
Introduction
to
NURBS

With Historical Perspective

An Introduction to NURBS

With Historical Perspective

David F. Rogers

Professor of Aerospace Engineering
United States Naval Academy, Annapolis, MD

MORGAN KAUFMANN PUBLISHERS

AN IMPRINT OF ACADEMIC PRESS
A Harcourt Science and Technology Company

SAN FRANCISCO   SAN DIEGO   NEW YORK   BOSTON
LONDON   SYDNEY   TOKYO

Executive Editor Diane D. Cerra
Director of Production and Manufacturing Yonie Overton
Senior Production Editor Cheri Palmer
Editorial Coordinator Belinda Breyer
Cover Design Ross Carron Design
Cover Images (l. to r.)
  Top row: Courtesy of John C. Dill and David F. Rogers;
       © Dunwell Photography, Steve/The Image Bank; © David Chasey/PhotoDisc
  Center row: © Rob Magiera/The Image Bank/Picture Quest
  Bottom row: Courtesy of CGI: R/GA Digital Studios
Back Cover Images Courtesy of John C. Dill and David F. Rogers
Back Cover Photo Courtesy of Ken Mierzejewski
Copyediting, Text Design and Indexing NAR Associates
Composition NAR Associates using TEX
Illustration Windfall Software and the author
Proofreader Jennifer McClain
Printer Courier Corporation

ACADEMIC PRESS
A Harcourt Science and Technology Company
525 B Street, Suite 1900, San Diego, CA 92101-4495, USA
http://www.academicpress.com

Academic Press
Harcourt Place, 32 Jamestown Road, London, NW1 7BY, United Kingdom
http://www.academicpress.com

Morgan Kaufmann Publishers
340 Pine Street, Sixth Floor, San Francisco, CA 94104-3205, USA
http://www.mkp.com

Library of Congress Cataloging-in-Publication Data

Rogers, David F., date
    An introduction to NURBS : with historical perspective / David F. Rogers.
        p. cm.
    Includes bibliographical references and index.
    ISBN 1-55860-669-6
    1. Spline theory--Data processing. 2. Computer-aided design. I. Title.

QA224.R64 2001
511'.42--dc21

                                                        00-039119

This book is printed on acid-free paper.

Dedicated to

Pierre Bézier for his fundamental contribution
Robin Forrest for his insight
Bill Gordon for his mathematical contributions
Carl de Boor and Maurice Cox for the Cox–de Boor algorithm
Steve Coons for his mathematical genius
Rich Riesenfeld for B-splines
Elaine Cohen, Tom Lyche and Rich Riesenfeld for the Oslo Algorithms
Lewie Knapp for rational B-splines
Ken Versprille for NURBS

and all those great and small
who advance the state of the art

Contents

List of Examples

Chapter 4   Rational B-spline Curves

Chapter 5   Bézier Surfaces

Chapter 6   B-spline Surfaces

Chapter 7   Rational B-spline Surfaces

List of Algorithms

Chapter 4 Rational B-spline Curves

Chapter 5 Bézier Surfaces

Chapter 6 B-spline Surfaces

Chapter 7 Rational B-spline Surfaces

Preface

NonUniform Rational B-Splines, or NURBS, grew out of the pioneering work of Pierre Bézier's development of Bézier curves and surfaces in the late 1960s and early 1970s. Because of their increased power and flexibility, B-spline curves and surfaces rapidly followed. Rational and nonuniform rational B-spline curves and surfaces added both greater flexibility and precision. Especially important is the ability of NURBS to represent conic curves and surfaces precisely. Thus, with NURBS a modeling system can use a *single* internal representation for a wide range of curves and surfaces, from straight lines and flat planes to precise circles and spheres as well as intricate piecewise sculptured surfaces. Furthermore, NURBS allow these elements to easily be buried within a more general sculptured surface. This single characteristic of NURBS is key to developing a robust modeling system, be it for computer aided design of automobiles, aircraft, ships, shoes, shower shampoo bottles, etc., or for an animated character in the latest Hollywood production or computer game, or even as the motion path for that character. As a result, NURBS are the standard of much of the computer aided design and interactive graphics community.

NURBS often appear mysterious to many people who use them daily. They appear mathematically complex and hence beyond the reach of even professional computer scientists, engineers, graphic artists and animators, to name just a few. To the average student in a computer science or engineering program, they appear to be a deep, dark mathematical puzzle. This

need not be true. Yes, there is some mathematics required to truly understand NURBS. It is the purpose of this book to demystify it. Many books
and papers on NURBS are replete with theorems, lemmas and corollaries,
along with all those weird symbols. Yes, even though I am an aeronautical
engineer, they still turn me off. You won't find any in this book. So, how
are we going to demystify NURBS? We do this by clearly and simply stat-
ing the underlying mathematics, very heavily illustrating the results of that
mathematics, and presenting a large number of detailed worked examples.
However, having said that, this is no "NURBS for Dummies" book. The
objective is for you to end up with a fundamental understanding of NURBS.

First-year college-level mathematics is a sufficient prerequisite. The
book is suitable for the working professional with a grounding in college-
level algebra and a first course in calculus (derivatives). The large number
of detailed worked examples makes it quite suitable for self-study. The book
can easily serve as the basis for a single-semester course on NURBS at the
senior or first-year graduate level.

Because NURBS are parametric curves and surfaces, the first chapter
briefly addresses some fundamental properties of parametric curves and
surfaces. The second chapter begins the discussion of NURBS by looking at Bézier curves, which laid the original foundation for NURBS. The
third chapter introduces nonrational (or standard) B-spline curves and thor-
oughly discusses two very important aspects of B-splines—knot vectors and
basis functions, an understanding of which is fundamental to understanding B-splines and NURBS. Chapter 3 continues by presenting some fundamental tools, specifically degree elevation, degree reduction, knot insertion
and curve subdivision, knot removal and reparameterization considerations.
Chapter 4 completes the discussion of curves with a thorough presentation of
rational B-spline curves, i.e., NURBS. Representation of the conic sections,
i.e., circles, ellipses, parabolas and hyperbolas using NURBS, is included.

The discussion of surfaces begins in Chapter 5 with Bézier surfaces, including a short discussion of transformation between surface descriptions.
Chapter 6 contains a discussion of nonrational B-spline surfaces, including
surface derivatives, fitting, subdivision and fairness using Gaussian curvature. NURBS surfaces are covered in depth in Chapter 7, including bilinear,
sweep and blending surfaces. Surfaces of revolution, e.g., cylinders and
spheres, are also discussed. The chapter ends with a detailed discussion of
a fast B-spline surface algorithm that efficiently allows dynamic real-time
manipulation of a single control polygon vertex or even the homogeneous
weighting factor at a single control polygon vertex.

The book concludes with three appendices, including a detailed description of a B-spline surface file format, problems illustrating additional aspects of Bézier and B-spline curves and surfaces, and finally more than two dozen pseudocode algorithms for generating Bézier and B-spline curves and surfaces. These algorithms form the basis of a library for calculating Bézier, B-spline and NURBS curves and surfaces.

A note about the choice of pseudocode vice working code in some language: First, the working professional wants working code. However, the academic frequently does not, because s/he prefers to have students learn by implementing the pseudocode in some language of choice. Second, what language should we use—C, C^{++}, Java, BASIC or the current fashionable language, whatever that is? The compromise is a website with C code that can be reached by a link from *http://www.mkp.com/NURBS/nurbs.html*. By using a website, the code is fresh, mistakes can be corrected, and hopefully you, the user, will produce even more efficient code than my sometimes lame attempts. 'Nuff said.

No book is ever written without the assistance of many individuals. A very special thanks to each of those who contributed to the historical perspectives—Robin Forrest, Rich Riesenfeld, Elaine Cohen, Tom Lyche, Lewie Knapp, Ken Versprille and Al Adams. My thanks to John Dill who, as usual, read several parts of the manuscript in very rough form. Special thanks to Wayne Tiller, who patiently straightened me out on knot removal: I really did not mean to be quite so dense. My thanks to Paul Kry, who read the entire manuscript looking for those typical author's bloopers. Any that still remain are mine and not Paul's.

A very special thanks to Diane Cerra, my editor at Morgan Kaufmann. Her courage is without par. When I walked up to her at SIGGRAPH and without preamble said "I have an introductory book on NURBS, 'ya want it?" she did not even blink, but said "Yes, and can I buy you a coffee?" All I can say is that she really did not know what she was agreeing to.

After forty years of marriage during which she has understood my need to write, has copyedited and proofed my messy manuscripts, learned TEX so that she could typeset them, and done it all with patience well above and beyond the call of duty, there are not enough thanks to even come close to my appreciation of my wife and partner, Nancy A. (Nuttall) Rogers.

David F. Rogers, Annapolis, May, 2000
introbook@nar-associates.com
www.mkp.com/NURBS/nurbs.html

Chapter 1

Curve and Surface Representation 1

NURBS, or NonUniform Rational B-Splines, are the standard for describing and modeling curves and surfaces in computer aided design and computer graphics. They are used to model everything from automobile bodies and ship hulls to animated characters in the latest feature length film. To fully exploit the flexibility of NURBS, a thorough working knowledge of the underpinning mathematics is necessary.

Frequently, NURBS are considered a very mathematical subject beyond the means of many working professionals and students. On one level that is true. Many papers and books are replete with theorems, proofs, lemmas and corollaries. On another level, the working level, this deep mathematical understanding is not necessary. This is the approach taken in this book. You will not find any theorems, proofs, lemmas or corollaries in the book. What you will find is the mathematics necessary for you to understand NURBS, along with detailed worked examples and illustrations to help you understand that mathematics.

Before we begin our discussion of NURBS, we briefly touch on curve and surface description in general, and on parametric curve and surface description specifically.

1.1 Introduction

Curves and surfaces are mathematically represented either explicitly, implicitly or parametrically. Explicit representations of the form $y = f(x)$, although useful in many applications, are axis dependent, cannot adequately represent multiple-valued functions, and cannot be used where a constraint involves an infinite derivative. Hence, they are little used in computer graphics or computer aided design.

Implicit representations of the form $f(x, y) = 0$ and $f(x, y, z) = 0$ for curves and surfaces, respectively, are capable of representing multiple-valued functions but are still axis dependent. However, they have a variety of uses in computer graphics and computer aided design. Bloomenthal [Bloo97] and his colleagues provide a useful discussion of the details of implicit surfaces and their use.

Here, we are concerned with parametric curve and surface representations, because rational and nonrational B-spline curves and surfaces and their antecedents, Bézier curves and surfaces, are parametrically represented.

1.2 Parametric Curves

Parametric curve representations of the form

$$x = f(t); \qquad y = g(t); \qquad z = h(t)$$

where t is the parameter, are extremely flexible. They are axis independent, easily represent multiple-valued functions and infinite derivatives, and have additional degrees of freedom compared to either explicit or implicit formulations. To see this latter point, consider the explicit cubic equation

$$y = ax^3 + bx^2 + cx + d$$

Here, four degrees of freedom exist, one for each of the four constant coefficients a, b, c, d.

Rewriting this equation in parametric form, we have

$$x(t) = \alpha t^3 + \beta t^2 + \gamma t + \delta \qquad c_1 \le t \le c_2$$
$$y(t) = \bar{\alpha} t^3 + \bar{\beta} t^2 + \bar{\gamma} t + \bar{\delta}$$

Here, eight degrees of freedom exist, one for each of the eight constant coefficients α, β, γ, δ, $\bar{\alpha}$, $\bar{\beta}$, $\bar{\gamma}$, $\bar{\delta}$. Although not necessary, the parameter range is frequently normalized to $0 \le t \le 1$.

The derivative of y with respect to x is given by

$$\frac{dy}{dx} = \frac{dy/dt}{dx/dt}$$

where, for example, from the equation above we have

$$\frac{dy}{dx} = \frac{3\bar{\alpha}t^2 + 2\bar{\beta}t + \bar{\gamma}}{3\alpha t^2 + 2\beta t + \gamma}$$

Here, the derivative is infinite when the denominator is zero. Note that simply testing if the denominator is zero shows that the derivative is infinite. Conversely, setting the denominator to zero imposes the constraint of an infinite derivative. One example is the requirement that the derivative be infinite for a circular arc tangent to a vertical edge.

In practice, curves and surfaces are generally bounded. When either an explicit or implicit representation is used, imposing the boundaries is awkward. In contrast, the parameter range bounds a parametrically represented curve or surface. The parameter range for a parametric curve also specifies a natural traversal direction along the curve.

Although very powerful, the parametric form is not a panacea. Some typical operations are more difficult, e.g., determining the intersection of two parametric curves, finding the distance from a point to a curve or specifying an unbounded geometry.

Extension to Three Dimensions

The parametric form easily extends to three dimensions (or more) by specifying $z = z(t)$, where again t is the parameter. An example of a simple three-dimensional parametric space curve is the circular helix shown in Fig. 1.1. The circular helix is represented by the parametric equations

$$x(t) = r\cos t; \qquad y(t) = r\sin t; \qquad z(t) = bt$$

or any point on the helix is given by the vector-valued function, i.e., the function has x, y, z components. Thus, we write

$$P(t) = [\,x(t) \quad y(t) \quad z(t)\,] = [\,r\cos t \quad r\sin t \quad bt\,]$$

for r and $b \neq 0$ and $-\infty \leq t \leq \infty$. This curve lies on the surface of a right circular cylinder of radius $|r|$. The effect of the equation $z = bt$ is to move the points of the curve infinitely in the z direction. After each 2π interval in the parameter t, the variables x and y return to their initial values; but z increases or decreases by $2\pi|b|$, depending upon the sign of b. This change in z is called the pitch of the helix.

Parametric Line

The simplest 'curve' is a straight line. We use the line to illustrate several characteristics of parametric representations. The general parametric equation for a straight line segment is

$$P(t) = P_1 + (P_2 - P_1)t \qquad 0 \le t \le 1$$

where P_1 and P_2 are vector-valued functions typically called position vectors and t is the parameter.

A position vector has components in some coordinate system. The values of the components are specified with respect to the origin of the coordinate system. Here in this book, a Cartesian (xyz) coordinate system with origin at $(0,0,0)$ is implied. We write the position vector in row matrix form as $P\begin{bmatrix} x & y & z \end{bmatrix}$ or $P = \begin{bmatrix} x & y & z \end{bmatrix}$ or even just $\begin{bmatrix} x & y & z \end{bmatrix}$. For example, the origin of a typical Cartesian coordinate system is $P\begin{bmatrix} 0 & 0 & 0 \end{bmatrix}$ or $P = \begin{bmatrix} 0 & 0 & 0 \end{bmatrix}$ or $\begin{bmatrix} 0 & 0 & 0 \end{bmatrix}$.

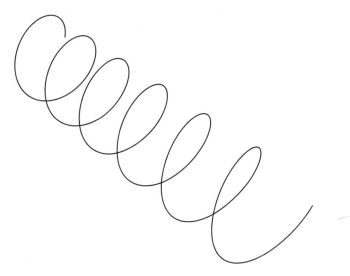

Figure 1.1   Circular helix for $r = 1$, $b = .7$, $0 \le t \le 12\pi$.

Each component of the position vector also has a parametric representation, i.e.

$$x(t) = x_1 + (x_2 - x_1)t \qquad 0 \le t \le 1$$
$$y(t) = y_1 + (y_2 - y_1)t$$
$$z(t) = z_1 + (z_2 - z_1)t$$

An example illustrates these characteristics.

Example 1.1 Parametric Line

Determine the parametric representation for the line segment between the position vectors $P_1 [\, x_1 = 1 \quad y_1 = 1 \quad z_1 = 1 \,]$ and $P_2 [\, x_2 = 20.1 \quad y_2 = 5.6 \quad z_2 = 10.8 \,]$. Calculate the point on the line halfway between P_1 and P_2.

Recalling the general parametric representation of a line with

$$P_1 [1 \quad 1 \quad 1] \qquad \text{and} \qquad P_2 [20.1 \quad 5.6 \quad 10.8]$$

we have

$$P(t) = [1 \quad 1 \quad 1] + ([20.1 \quad 5.6 \quad 10.8] - [1 \quad 1 \quad 1])t$$

Performing the subtraction of the components of P_1 and P_2 yields

$$P(t) = [1 \quad 1 \quad 1] + [19.1 \quad 4.6 \quad 9.8]t$$

Because this is a straight line and the parameterization is linear (see Ex. 1.2 and Sec. 3.16), the midpoint of the line occurs for a parameter value $t = 1/2$. Thus

$$P(1/2) = [1 \quad 1 \quad 1] + 1/2 [19.1 \quad 4.6 \quad 9.8] = [10.55 \quad 3.3 \quad 5.9]$$

Recalling that each component of the position vector also has a parametric representation, we have

$$x(t) = 1 + (20.1 - 1)t = 1 + 19.1t$$
$$y(t) = 1 + (5.6 - 1)t = 1 + 4.6t$$
$$z(t) = 1 + (10.8 - 1)t = 1 + 9.8t$$

and for $t = 1/2$ we have

$$x(t) = 1 + 1/2(19.1) = 10.55$$
$$y(t) = 1 + 1/2(4.6) = 3.3$$
$$z(t) = 1 + 1/2(9.8) = 5.9$$

which, of course, yields the same result.

Although it is common to normalize the parameter range to $0 \leq t \leq 1$, the parameterization is not unique. A simple example illustrates this point.

Example 1.2 Reparameterization

Reparameterize the line segment defined in Ex. 1.1 to the range 0–2.

First, let the new parameter be u. The conditions or constraints on the new parameter are

$$t = 0 \quad u = 0; \qquad t = 1 \quad u = 2$$

Assuming a linear form of the reparameterization function, i.e.

$$u = a + bt$$

and imposing the constraints yields

$$u = 2t \qquad 0 \leq t \leq 1$$

Thus, the new equation of the line segment is

$$P(u) = P_1 + {}^1\!/{}_2(P_2 - P_1)u \qquad 0 \leq u \leq 2$$

Exactly the same line segment is generated as in Ex. 1.1.

Additional discussion of reparameterization is given in Sec. 3.16.

1.3 Parametric Surfaces

Specifying a surface parametrically requires two parameters, e.g.

$$x = x(u, w) \qquad y = y(u, w) \qquad z = z(u, w)$$

The surface is said to be biparametric. An example of a biparametric surface is shown in Fig. 1.2. If one of the parameter values is held constant while the other is varied, an isoparametric curve is formed on the surface. Figure 1.2 shows both $u = $ constant and $w = $ constant isoparametric curves. If both parameters are held constant, then a point on the biparametric surface results, as shown in Fig. 1.2. The edges of the surface are formed by holding the minimum or maximum value of one of the parameters constant and varying the other parameter; e.g., for a surface bounded by $0 \leq u \leq 1$ and $0 \leq w \leq 1$, the edges are formed for $u = 0$, $0 \leq w \leq 1$; $u = 1$, $0 \leq w \leq 1$; $w = 0$, $0 \leq u \leq 1$; $w = 1$, $0 \leq u \leq 1$. Specifying one of the parameters as a

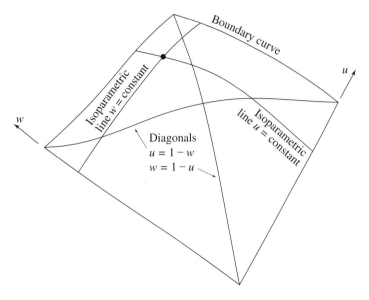

Figure 1.2 Parametric surface.

function of the other also yields a curve on the surface. For example, for a surface bounded by $0 \leq u \leq 1$ and $0 \leq w \leq 1$, the functions $w = 1 - u$ and $u = 1 - w$ yield diagonals of the surface.

The normal at a point on a biparametric surface is given by the cross product of the derivatives at the point; specifically, given a surface $Q(u, w) = Q(x(u, w), y(u, w), z(u, w))$ with partial derivatives specified by $Q_u(u, w) = Q(x_u(u, w), y_u(u, w), z_u(u, w))$, $Q_w(u, w) = Q(x_w(u, w), y_w(u, w), z_w(u, w))$, the unit normal vector at the point u, w on the surface is

$$\mathbf{n} = \frac{Q_u \times Q_w}{|Q_u \times Q_w|} \qquad |Q_u \times Q_w| \neq 0 \qquad (1.1)$$

where $Q_u = \partial Q / \partial u$ and $Q_w = \partial Q / \partial w$.[†] The normal vector is a property of the surface independent of the actual form of the parameterization of the surface, as is the associated tangent plane to the surface.

[†]Here, the notation $Q_u(u, w) = Q(x_u(u, w), y_u(u, w), z_u(u, w))$ means that the derivative in xyz space is a function of the derivatives in parametric (uw) space through the transformation (or mapping) from parametric, uw, space to xyz space. For compactness we will simplify the notation to Q_u.

1.4 Piecewise Surfaces

Although many surfaces can be represented analytically, there are also many surfaces for which analytical descriptions do not exist. Typical examples are automobile bodies, aircraft fuselages and wings, ship hulls, sculpture, bottles, shoes, etc. These surfaces are represented in a *piecewise* fashion, i.e., similar to a patchwork quilt. The intention is to join individual patches together along the edges to create a complete surface. Interestingly enough, our discussion begins by using a portion or patch of an analytical surface, specifically the sphere, to illustrate several basic concepts.

The boundaries of a spherical surface patch on a unit sphere are formed by four planes, two cutting planes that pass through the axis connecting the poles, which is the z-axis in Fig. 1.3, and two cutting planes perpendicular to the axis connecting the poles. The vector-valued parametric equation for the resulting surface patch $Q(\theta, \phi)$ is

$$Q(\theta, \phi) = [\cos\theta\sin\phi \quad \sin\theta\sin\phi \quad \cos\phi] \qquad \theta_1 \le \theta \le \theta_2, \ \phi_1 \le \phi \le \phi_2 \quad (1.2)$$

where θ and ϕ are the parameters. In this particular case θ and ϕ have angular interpretations, as shown in Fig. 1.3. The resulting surface patch is a biparametric function.

The parametric representation of the Cartesian coordinates of a point on the spherical patch of the unit sphere is

$$x(\theta, \phi) = \cos\theta\sin\phi$$
$$y(\theta, \phi) = \sin\theta\sin\phi$$
$$z(\theta, \phi) = \cos\phi$$

The patch shown in Fig. 1.3 is defined for $0 \le \theta \le \pi/2$ and $\pi/4 \le \phi \le \pi/2$. The boundaries or edges of the patch are defined by the curves AB, BC, CD and DA. For the spherical patch of Fig. 1.3, these curves are circular arcs. Each curve is defined by two end points and the tangent vectors at the ends. Consequently, the four patch boundary curves are defined by the four position vectors at the corners and eight tangent vectors, two at each corner.

For the spherical patch of Fig. 1.3, the tangent vectors are given by the parametric derivatives of $Q(\theta, \phi)$, i.e.

$$Q_\theta(\theta, \phi) = \frac{\partial Q}{\partial \theta}(\theta, \phi) = [-\sin\theta\sin\phi \quad \cos\theta\sin\phi \quad 0] \qquad (1.3)$$

and
$$Q_\phi(\theta, \phi) = [\cos\theta\cos\phi \quad \sin\theta\cos\phi \quad -\sin\phi] \qquad (1.4)$$

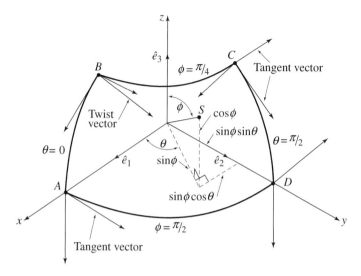

Figure 1.3 Spherical surface patch.

The tangent vectors at each corner are shown in Fig. 1.3.

The shape of the interior of the surface near each corner is controlled by the twist vector, or cross derivative, at the corner. For the spherical surface patch given in Fig. 1.3, the cross derivative or twist vector is

$$Q_{\theta\phi}(\theta, \phi) = \frac{\partial^2 Q}{\partial\theta\partial\phi} = \frac{\partial^2 Q}{\partial\phi\partial\theta} = [-\sin\theta\cos\phi \quad \cos\theta\cos\phi \quad 0] \qquad (1.5)$$

Evaluation at the corners of the patch yields the twist vectors at the corners. The interior of the patch is given by Eq. (1.2). Equation (1.2) is a spherical *blending* function. Thus, a quadrilateral surface patch is described by

the four position vectors at the corners;

the eight tangent vectors, two at each corner;

the four twist vectors at the corners;

a blending function.

Recall that the normal to a surface patch at any point is given by the cross product of the parametric derivatives (see Eq. 1.1). For a spherical surface, we have

$$Q_\theta \times Q_\phi = \begin{vmatrix} \mathbf{i} & \mathbf{j} & \mathbf{k} \\ -\sin\theta\sin\phi & \cos\theta\sin\phi & 0 \\ \cos\theta\cos\phi & \sin\theta\cos\phi & -\sin\phi \end{vmatrix}$$

$$= [-\cos\theta\sin^2\phi \quad \sin\theta\sin^2\phi \quad -\sin\phi\cos\phi] \qquad (1.6)$$

On the spherical surface patch, isoparametric lines, i.e., lines of constant parameter values, are orthogonal. Consequently, the dot product of the parametric derivatives is zero. For example, for a spherical surface

$$Q_\theta \cdot Q_\phi = [-\sin\theta\sin\phi \quad \cos\theta\sin\phi \quad 0] \cdot [\cos\theta\cos\phi \quad \sin\theta\cos\phi \quad -\sin\phi] = 0$$

$$= [-\sin\theta\sin\phi \quad \cos\theta\sin\phi \quad 0][\cos\theta\cos\phi \quad \sin\theta\cos\phi \quad -\sin\phi]^T = 0$$

$$= [-\cos\theta\sin\theta\cos\phi\sin\phi \quad \cos\theta\sin\theta\cos\phi\sin\phi \quad 0] = 0 \qquad (1.7)$$

This discussion shows that specifying the position vectors, tangent vectors and twist vectors at the corners of a surface patch, along with a blending function for the interior of the patch, allows generating the patch. This concept, called a Coons patch (see [Coon67; Roge90a]), was the basis of the earliest computer aided design systems. However, because the position vectors, tangent vectors and twist vectors are all of different magnitudes, specifying them correctly and accurately is both difficult and nonintuitive. A clever French engineer, Pierre Bézier, developed a technique for indirectly and intuitively specifying and controlling these parameters (see [Bezi68, 70, 71, 72; Forr68]). The result was Bézier curves and surfaces. Bézier curves and surfaces were followed by B-spline curves and surfaces, and eventually by NURBS curves and surfaces, in the search for greater flexibility and precision. B-spline and NURBS curves and surfaces are generalizations of Bézier curves and surfaces. They are manipulated in similar ways to Bézier curves and surfaces. Because of the greater flexibility and precision of NURBS, they have become the standard in much of the computer aided design and interactive graphics community and are the topic of this book.

1.5 Continuity

There are two kinds of continuity, or smoothness, associated with parametric curves and surfaces—geometric continuity and parametric continuity. Simplistically, you can think of geometric continuity as physical and parametric continuity as mathematical. Geometric continuity is less restrictive than parametric continuity.

Geometric Continuity

If two curve segments are joined together at respective end points, the resulting curve is said to have G^0 continuity, i.e., zeroth-order or positional continuity, *at the join.* The curve segments may have a higher degree of continuity internally. Here, we are only concerned with the continuity at the join.

If the tangent vectors at the join for both curves *point* in the same direction, i.e., their *geometric* slopes are equal, then G^1 continuity exists at the join. The *magnitudes* of the tangent vectors at the join *do not* have to be equal; they only need to be scalar multiples of each other, i.e., $|V_{T_1}| = \alpha|V_{T_2}|$ for $\alpha > 0$.

Parametric Continuity

Like geometric continuity, if two curve segments are joined together, the resulting curve is said to be C^0 continuous. Again, the curve segments may internally have a higher degree of continuity. Clearly, C^0 continuity implies G^0 continuity, and vice versa.

If the tangent vectors at the join have *both* the same direction (slope) *and* the same magnitude, then the curve is said to be C^1 continuous in the parameter t. This is a more restrictive condition than G^1 continuity. Clearly, C^1 continuity implies G^1 continuity. However, the inverse is not necessarily true; i.e., a curve may be G^1 continuous and may *not* be C^1 continuous. If the nth derivatives of a curve, $d^nP(t)/dt^n$, at the curve segment join are equal in both direction and magnitude, then the curve is said to have C^n parametric continuity at the join.

Figure 1.4 illustrates the difference between geometric and parametric continuity. The vectors indicate the length of the tangent vector at the join indicated by the dot. The tangent vector at the end of the left-hand curve segment is equal in length to the longer tangent vector shown for the right-hand curve segment. Thus, the curve labeled C^1 has parametric continuity,

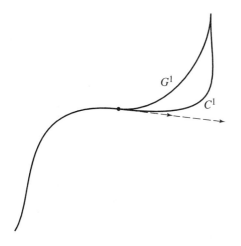

Figure 1.4 Comparison of C^1 and G^1 continuity.

because both the direction and magnitude of the tangent vectors where the curve segments join are equal. The magnitude of the tangent vector for the curve labeled G^1 is half that of the curve labeled C^1. Notice the significant difference in the shape of the curves.

A physical analog serves to clarify the fundamental difference between geometric and parametric continuity. Given a parametric vector-valued function, $P(t)$, over some parameter range describing a curve, then any given value of t represents a specific point on the curve. The derivative, $P'(t)$, represents the velocity of a point as it moves along the curve; and $P''(t)$ represents the acceleration. If the curve is C^1 continuous at a join, then both the direction and magnitude of the tangent vector are equal across the join; and the point smoothly transitions from one curve segment to the next.

If, however, the curve is only G^1 continuous at the join, then as the point transitions across the join the direction of motion does not change; but there is an *instantaneous* change in speed (magnitude of the velocity) that represents an *instantaneous* acceleration as the point transitions across the join. If the curve, for example, represents a camera path or is used for inbetweening in animation, the abrupt velocity change is quite disconcerting.

Although many applications find G^1 continuity adequate, for applications that depend on the fairness or smoothness of a curve or surface, especially those that depend on a smooth transition of reflected light, e.g., automobile bodies, G^1 or even G^2 continuity is not adequate. For these applications, at least C^2 continuity is required to achieve the desired results.

Robin Forrest

In the early days of the development of surfaces for computer-aided design, there were relatively few players, scattered mainly around the United States and the United Kingdom. Information was available largely through technical reports, since there was no recognised place to publish such material. Fortunately, enthusiasm meant that papers and views were readily exchanged and commercial confidentiality did not intrude.

My own work started in Cambridge University in October 1965. I had intended to work on control theory, but changed my mind after a seminar by Ivan Sutherland and the suggestion that I join the fledgling CAD Group headed by Charles Lang in the Mathematical Laboratory. I soon became familiar with the work of Steve Coons, and after a trawl by regular mail I obtained copies of reports on the early work on interpolatory parametric spline surfaces by Ferguson at Boeing (1963), the rational parametric form of the conic section (Roberts, MIT Lincoln Labs, 1965), and the combination of parametric cubics and rational conics derived by Rowin at Boeing (1964). A summer spent at MIT Project MAC working with Steve Coons at the time of the writing of his celebrated "little red book" led to my own thesis on rational cubic curves (including curve splitting) and extensions of Coons surfaces at Cambridge in the summer of 1968. Ted Lee, whom I met at Harvard (Coons being on sabbatical there, working with Sutherland), completed his thesis on rational bicubic surfaces in 1969. The external examiner for my Ph.D. thesis was Malcolm Sabin, whose Numerical Master Geometry system using interpolatory bicubic surfaces was first documented in 1968.

In 1969, following a visit to General Motors Research Laboratories where I was shown "the crazy way Renault design surfaces," I recast the Bézier definition of curves and surfaces in terms of polygon vertices rather than polygon sides. This led to the discovery of the Bernstein basis for Bézier curves and surfaces, which is now the standard definition. I also developed curve-splitting and degree-raising/-lowering methods, which subsequently became important in the development of practical B-spline techniques. Coons, who had moved from MIT to Syracuse University, decided that it was a good idea to send research students abroad for a few months. On this basis, Rich Riesenfeld came to work with me at Cambridge in the summer of 1970.

Bill Gordon from General Motors, having read my reworking of Bézier, realised that B-splines were the spline analogues of Bernstein polynomials. Gordon was on leave at Syracuse in early 1971 and suggested that Riesenfeld investigate the use of B-splines for computer aided design. Subsequently, I went to Syracuse in 1971–1972 as a Visiting Professor to work with Coons and help supervise Riesenfeld, Gordon having returned to General Motors.

At that stage, whilst mathematically interesting, the algorithms for B-spline computation were numerically unstable. But, by a stroke of good fortune, shortly after I arrived I was sent a copy of Maurice Cox's paper on B-splines, which contained the now familiar de Boor–Cox algorithm enabling, which provided stable and accurate numerical evaluation of B-splines. I believe a copy of Carl de Boor's paper arrived shortly afterwards.

Riesenfeld completed his thesis in the summer of 1972. Among the graduate students at Syracuse to whom I taught a course on curves and surfaces was Ken Versprille, who embarked on a thesis on rational B-splines (1975). Coons sent another Syracuse student, Lewie Knapp, to work with me at Cambridge in the summer of 1973, when we cut probably the first B-spline surfaces by numerical control on the CAD Group's foam cutter, which was based on Bézier's milling machine at Renault. (I am holding two of these surfaces in the picture). This machine was driven as a graphics peripheral by the GINO device-independent graphics package developed at Cambridge, a precursor of GPGS, ACM CORE and PHIGS.

Knapp's thesis on nonuniform B-splines appeared in 1979. Riesenfeld, by then at Utah, was responsible for unification in terms of the nonuniform rational B-spline or NURBS curves and surfaces. My final contribution to the history was to act as host for Jeff Lane from Utah in 1975, following my move to the University of East Anglia. Lane's thesis on B-spline methods appeared in 1976.

A.R. (Robin) Forrest
Norwich, January 2000

Cambridge University Computer Aided Design Group's Mark II foam cutter (circa
1973). (Courtesy of Robin Forrest).

Robin Forrest was responsible for the mechanical design and construction of
the Cambridge CAD Group's Mark II foam-cutting machine, with Charles
Lang and David Wheeler responsible for the electrical and electronic design.
The machine was controlled along each of the three xyz-axes, with two additional rotational axes (one about the center of the cutter). The cutting
volume was approximately $20 \times 14 \times 10$ inches. The start–stop speed was
0.6 in/sec, with a maximum speed of 16 in/sec on all three axes. The machine was used to cut rigid foam, wood and rigid, high-density polyethylene
models, two examples of which, produced on the earlier Mark I machine,
are held by Robin Forrest in the picture on page 13. A PDP11/45, running
the GINO-F software, was used as the controller. (David F. Rogers)

Chapter **2**

Bézier Curves 2

We begin our discussion of NURBS (NonUniform Rational B-Spline) curves and surfaces by looking at their antecedents, specifically Bézier curves. First, some comments about curve and surface design are appropriate.

There is a class of shape description design problems in which the basic shape is arrived at by experimental evaluation or mathematical calculation. Examples of this class of shape are aircraft wings, engine manifolds, mechanical and/or structural parts. For this class of shape design problems, excellent results are frequently obtained using a curve or surface 'fitting' technique. In this context, 'fitting' means that the resulting curve or surface is required to pass through each and every previously defined data point. Examples of such techniques are cubic spline or parabolically blended interpolation, and Coons linear or bicubic surfaces (see [Roge90a] and the references therein for details).

However, there is another class of shape design problems that depends on *both* aesthetic *and* functional requirements. These problems are frequently termed ab initio design. Examples of ab initio design problems are the 'skin' of car bodies, aircraft fuselages, ship hulls, furniture and glassware.

Ab initio design problems cannot be formulated entirely in terms of quantitative criteria but must be resolved by a judicious combination of computational and heuristic methods.

A method of shape description suitable for ab initio design of free-form curves and surfaces was developed by a very clever French engineer, Pierre Bézier, at Renault Automobile. Bézier not only used his curves and surfaces to describe automobile bodies but also used them to design aircraft wings (see Fig. 2.1), yacht hulls and even common products such as a seat for the French railway system.

Although Bézier originally derived the mathematical basis of the technique from geometrical considerations [Bezi68, 70, 71], Forrest [Forr72] and Gordon and Riesenfeld [Gord74] showed that the result is equivalent to the Bernstein basis or polynomial approximation function.

2.1 Bézier Curve Definition

A Bézier curve, which is a special case of a NURBS curve, is determined by a control polygon, such as shown in Fig. 2.2. Because the Bézier basis is also the Bernstein basis, several properties of Bézier curves are immediately known. For example:

The basis functions are real.

The degree of the polynomial defining the curve segment is one less than the number of control polygon points.

The curve generally follows the shape of the control polygon.

The first and last points on the curve are coincident with the first and last points of the control polygon.

Figure 2.1 An aircraft wing described by Bézier surfaces, as seen in 1975 in Bézier's laboratory.

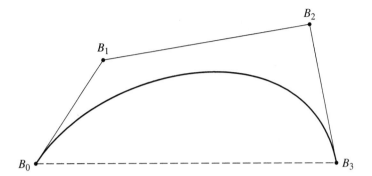

Figure 2.2 A Bézier curve and its control polygon.

The tangent vectors at the ends of the curve have the same direction as the first and last polygon spans, respectively.

The curve is contained within the convex hull of the control polygon, i.e., within the largest convex polygon defined by the control polygon vertices. In Fig. 2.2, the convex hull is shown by the polygon and the dashed line.

The curve exhibits the variation-diminishing property. Basically, this means that the curve does not oscillate about any straight line more often than the control polygon.

The curve is invariant under an affine transformation.

Several four-point Bézier polygons and the resulting cubic curves are shown in Fig. 2.3. With just the information given above, a user quickly learns to predict the shape of a curve generated by a Bézier polygon.

Mathematically, a parametric Bézier curve is defined by

$$P(t) = \sum_{i=0}^{n} B_i \, J_{n,i}(t) \qquad 0 \le t \le 1 \qquad (2.1)$$

where the Bézier, or Bernstein, basis or blending function is

$$J_{n,i}(t) = \binom{n}{i} t^i (1-t)^{n-i} \quad (0)^0 \equiv 1 \qquad (2.2)$$

with
$$\binom{n}{i} = \frac{n!}{i!(n-i)!} \quad 0! \equiv 1 \qquad (2.3)$$

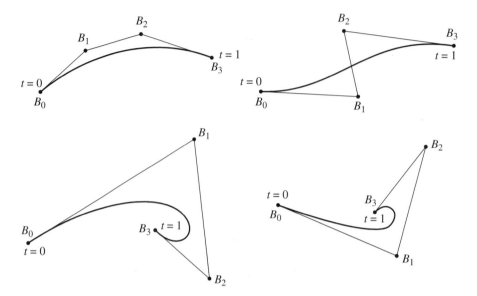

Figure 2.3 Bézier polygons for cubics.

where, as indicated, we define $(0)^0 \equiv 1$ and $0! \equiv 1$. $J_{n,i}(t)$ is the ith nth-order Bernstein basis function. Here, n, the degree of the Bernstein basis function and thus of the polynomial curve segment, is one less than the number of points in the Bézier polygon. The vertices of the Bézier polygon are numbered from 0 to n, as shown in Fig. 2.2.[†]

Figure 2.4 shows the blending functions for several values of n. Notice the symmetry of the functions. Each of the blending functions is of degree

---

[†]This notation and control polygon numbering scheme is chosen to be consistent with the vast body of existing literature on Bézier curves and Bernstein basis functions. For programming purposes, an alternate formulation may be somewhat more convenient, i.e.

$$P(t) = \sum_{I=1}^{N} B_I J_{N,I}(t)$$

where

$$J_{N,I} = \binom{N-1}{I-1} t^{I-1}(1-t)^{N-I}$$

and

$$\binom{N-1}{I-1} = \frac{(N-1)!}{(I-1)!\,(N-I)!}$$

The control polygon vertices are numbered from 1 to N. The transformations $n = N - 1$ and $i = I - 1$ convert between the two notations.

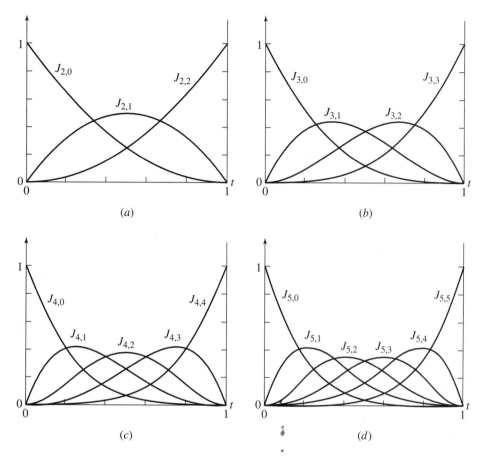

Figure 2.4 Bézier/Bernstein blending functions. (a) Three polygon points, $n = 2$; (b) four polygon points, $n = 3$; (c) five polygon points, $n = 4$; (d) six polygon points, $n = 5$.

n. For example, each of the four blending functions shown in Fig. 2.4b for $n = 3$ is a cubic. The maximum value of each blending function occurs at $t = i/n$ and is given by Forrest [Forr72] as

$$J_{n,i}(i/n) = (n/i) \frac{i^i (n-i)^{n-i}}{n^n} \tag{2.4}$$

for example, for a cubic $n = 3$. The maximum values for $J_{3,1}$ and $J_{3,2}$ occur at $1/3$ and $2/3$, respectively, with values

$$J_{3,1}(1/3) = 4/9 \qquad \text{and} \qquad J_{3,2}(2/3) = 4/9$$

Figure 2.4b illustrates this result.

Examining Eqs. (2.1)–(2.3) for the first point on the curve, i.e., at $t = 0$, shows that

$$J_{n,0}(0) = \frac{n!\,(1)(1-0)^{n-0}}{n!} = 1 \qquad i = 0$$

and

$$J_{n,i}(0) = \frac{n!\,(0)^i(1-0)^{n-i}}{i!\,(n-i)!} = 0 \qquad i \neq 0$$

Thus

$$P(0) = B_0 J_{n,0}(0) = B_0$$

and the first point on the Bézier curve and on its control polygon are coincident, as previously claimed.

Similarly, for the last point on the curve, i.e., at $t = 1$

$$J_{n,n}(1) = \frac{n!\,(1)^n(0)^{n-n}}{n!\,(1)} = 1 \qquad i = n$$

$$J_{n,i}(1) = \frac{n!}{i!\,(n-i)!}t^i(1-1)^{n-i} = 0 \qquad i \neq n$$

Thus

$$P(1) = B_n J_{n,n}(1) = B_n$$

and the last point on the Bézier curve and the last point on its control polygon are coincident. The blending functions shown in Fig. 2.4 illustrate these results.

Furthermore, it can be shown that for any given value of the parameter t, the summation of the basis functions is precisely one; that is

$$\sum_{i=0}^{n} J_{n,i}(t) = 1 \qquad\qquad (2.5)$$

An example illustrates the technique for determining a Bézier curve.

Example 2.1 Bézier Curve

Given the vertices of a Bézier polygon (see Fig. 2.5)

$$B_0\,[1 \quad 1],\ B_1\,[2 \quad 3],\ B_2\,[4 \quad 3],\ B_3\,[3 \quad 1]$$

determine seven points on the Bézier curve.

Recall Eqs. (2.1)–(2.3)

$$P(t) = \sum_{i=0}^{n} B_i J_{n,i}(t)$$

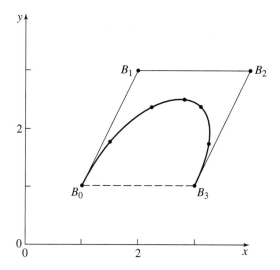

Figure 2.5 Results for Bézier curve segment for Ex. 2.1.

where

$$J_{n,i}(t) = \binom{n}{i} t^i (1-t)^{n-i}$$

and

$$\binom{n}{i} = \frac{n!}{i!\,(n-i)!}$$

Here, $n = 3$, because there are four vertices. Hence

$$\binom{n}{i} = \binom{3}{i} = \frac{6}{i!\,(3-i)!}$$

and

$$J_{3,0}(t) = (1)\,t^0(1-t)^3 = (1-t)^3$$

$$J_{3,1}(t) = 3t(1-t)^2$$

$$J_{3,2}(t) = 3t^2(1-t)$$

$$J_{3,3}(t) = t^3$$

Thus

$$P(t) = B_0 J_{3,0} + B_1 J_{3,1} + B_2 J_{3,2} + B_3 J_{3,3}$$

$$= (1-t)^3 B_0 + 3t(1-t)^2 B_1 + 3t^2(1-t)B_2 + t^3 B_3$$

Values of $J_{n,i}$ for various values of t are given in Table 2.1 The points on the curve are then

$$P(0) = B_0 = \begin{bmatrix} 1 & 1 \end{bmatrix}$$

$$P(0.15) = 0.614 B_0 + 0.325 B_1 + 0.058 B_2 + 0.003 B_3 = \begin{bmatrix} 1.5 & 1.765 \end{bmatrix}$$

Table 2.1

t	$J_{3,0}$	$J_{3,1}$	$J_{3,2}$	$J_{3,3}$
0	1	0	0	0
0.15	0.614	0.325	0.058	0.003
0.35	0.275	0.444	0.239	0.042
0.50	0.125	0.375	0.375	0.125
0.65	0.042	0.239	0.444	0.275
0.85	0.003	0.058	0.325	0.614
1	0	0	0	1

$$P(0.35) = 0.275B_0 + 0.444B_1 + 0.239B_2 + 0.042B_3 = \begin{bmatrix} 2.248 & 2.367 \end{bmatrix}$$

$$P(0.5) = 0.125B_0 + 0.375B_1 + 0.375B_2 + 0.125B_3 = \begin{bmatrix} 2.75 & 2.5 \end{bmatrix}$$

$$P(0.65) = 0.042B_0 + 0.239B_1 + 0.444B_2 + 0.275B_3 = \begin{bmatrix} 3.122 & 2.367 \end{bmatrix}$$

$$P(0.85) = 0.003B_0 + 0.058B_1 + 0.325B_2 + 0.614B_3 = \begin{bmatrix} 3.248 & 1.765 \end{bmatrix}$$

$$P(1) = B_3 = \begin{bmatrix} 3 & 1 \end{bmatrix}$$

Notice that the basis functions, $J_{n,i}$, determine how much of each polygon vertex is used to construct a point on the curve. The results are shown in Fig. 2.5.

Bézier Curve Algorithm

Using Eqs. (2.1)–(2.3) and Ex. 2.1, the basic algorithm for calculating points on a Bézier curve is

> **for** each value of the parameter t
> $\quad P(t) = 0$
> $\quad$**for** each value of i
> $\quad\quad$ determine the Bernstein basis function $J_{n,i}(t)$
> $\quad\quad P(t) = P(t) + B_i J_{n,i}(t)$
> $\quad$**loop**
> **loop**

Notice that the summation sign in Eq. (2.1) corresponds to the inner loop over $i, 0 \le i \le n$. The outer loop calculates individual points on the curve based on the parameter value t. It is important to remember that $P(t)$ is a vector-valued function. Thus, in practice

$$P(t) = P(t) + B_i J_{n,i}(t)$$

is

$$x(t) = x(t) + B_{i_x} J_{n,i}(t)$$

$$y(t) = y(t) + B_{i_y} J_{n,i}(t)$$

$$z(t) = z(t) + B_{i_z} J_{n,i}(t)$$

where the B_{i_x}, B_{i_y}, B_{i_z} are the x, y, z components of the vector-valued control polygon vertices $B_i [\, x_i(t) \quad y_i(t) \quad z_i(t) \,]$.

2.2 Matrix Representation of Bézier Curves

The equation for a Bézier curve is expressed in matrix form as

$$P(t) = [T][N][G] = [F][G] \tag{2.6}$$

Here
$$[F] = [\, J_{n,0} \quad J_{n,1} \quad \cdots \quad J_{n,n} \,]$$

and the matrix

$$[G]^T = [\, B_0 \quad B_1 \quad \cdots \quad B_n \,]$$

contains the geometry of the curve.

The specific matrix forms for low values of n are of interest. For four control polygon vertices $(n = 3)$, the cubic Bézier curve is given by

$$P(t) = [\, (1-t)^3 \quad 3t(1-t)^2 \quad 3t^2(1-t) \quad t^3 \,] \begin{bmatrix} B_o \\ B_1 \\ B_2 \\ B_3 \end{bmatrix}$$

Collecting the coefficients of the parameter terms allows rewriting this as

$$P(t) = [T][N][G] = [\, t^3 \quad t^2 \quad t \quad 1 \,] \begin{bmatrix} -1 & 3 & -3 & 1 \\ 3 & -6 & 3 & 0 \\ -3 & 3 & 0 & 0 \\ 1 & 0 & 0 & 0 \end{bmatrix} \begin{bmatrix} B_o \\ B_1 \\ B_2 \\ B_3 \end{bmatrix} \tag{2.7}$$

Similarly, the quartic $(n = 4)$ Bézier curve corresponding to five Bézier polygon points is

$$P(t) = [\, t^4 \quad t^3 \quad t^2 \quad t \quad 1 \,] \begin{bmatrix} 1 & -4 & 6 & -4 & 1 \\ -4 & 12 & -12 & 4 & 0 \\ 6 & -12 & 6 & 0 & 0 \\ -4 & 4 & 0 & 0 & 0 \\ 1 & 0 & 0 & 0 & 0 \end{bmatrix} \begin{bmatrix} B_o \\ B_1 \\ B_2 \\ B_3 \\ B_4 \end{bmatrix} \tag{2.8}$$

Cohen and Riesenfeld [Cohe82] generalized this representation to

$$P(t) = [T][N][G]$$

where here

$$[T] = [t^n \quad t^{n-1} \quad \cdots \quad t \quad 1]$$

$$[N] = \begin{bmatrix} \binom{n}{0}\binom{n}{n}(-1)^n & \binom{n}{1}\binom{n-1}{n-1}(-1)^{n-1} & \cdots & \binom{n}{n}\binom{n-n}{n-n}(-1)^0 \\ \binom{n}{0}\binom{n}{n-1}(-1)^{n-1} & \binom{n}{1}\binom{n-1}{n-2}(-1)^{n-2} & \cdots & 0 \\ \vdots & \vdots & \vdots & \vdots \\ \binom{n}{0}\binom{n}{1}(-1)^1 & \binom{n}{1}\binom{n-1}{0}(-1)^0 & \cdots & 0 \\ \binom{n}{0}\binom{n}{0}(-1)^0 & 0 & \cdots & 0 \end{bmatrix} \tag{2.9}$$

$[G]^T$ is again $[B_0 \quad B_1 \quad \cdots \quad B_n]$. The individual terms in $[N]$ are given by

$$\left(N_{i+1,j+1}\right)_{i,j=0}^n = \begin{cases} \binom{n}{j}\binom{n-j}{n-i-j}(-1)^{n-i-j} & 0 \leq i+j \leq n \\ 0 & \text{otherwise} \end{cases}$$

Equation (2.9) can be decomposed into a sometimes more convenient form

$$[N] = [C][D] \tag{2.10}$$

where

$$[C] = \begin{bmatrix} \binom{n}{n}(-1)^n & \binom{n}{1}\binom{n-1}{n-1}(-1)^{n-1} & \cdots & \binom{n}{n}\binom{n-n}{n-n}(-1)^0 \\ \binom{n}{n-1}(-1)^{n-1} & \binom{n}{1}\binom{n-1}{n-2}(-1)^{n-2} & & 0 \\ \vdots & \vdots & \ddots & \vdots \\ \binom{n}{1}(-1)^1 & \binom{n}{1}\binom{n-1}{0}(-1)^0 & & 0 \\ \binom{n}{0}(-1)^0 & 0 & \cdots & 0 \end{bmatrix}$$

$$[D] = \begin{bmatrix} \binom{n}{0} & & \cdots & & 0 \\ \vdots & \binom{n}{1} & & & \vdots \\ & & \ddots & & \vdots \\ 0 & & \cdots & & \binom{n}{n} \end{bmatrix}$$

Equation (2.10) is more convenient to evaluate for arbitrary values of n. Notice that for each value of n the matrix $[N]$ is symmetrical about the main diagonal, and that the lower right triangular corner is all zeros.

2.3 Bézier Curve Derivatives

Although it is not necessary to numerically specify the tangent vectors at the ends of an individual Bézier curve, maintaining slope and curvature continuity when joining Bézier curves, determining surface normals for lighting or numerical control tool path calculation, or local curvature for smoothness or fairness calculations requires a knowledge of both the first and second derivatives of a Bézier curve.

Recalling Eq. (2.1), the first derivative of a Bézier curve is

$$P'(t) = \sum_{i=0}^{n} B_i J'_{n,i}(t) \tag{2.11}$$

The second derivative is given by

$$P''(t) = \sum_{i=0}^{n} B_i J''_{n,i}(t) \tag{2.12}$$

The derivatives of the basis function are obtained by formally differentiating Eq. (2.2). Specifically

$$J'_{n,i}(t) = \binom{n}{i}\left(i\,t^{i-1}(1-t)^{n-i} - (n-i)t^i(1-t)^{n-i-1}\right)$$

$$= \binom{n}{i}t^i(1-t)^{n-i}\left(\frac{i}{t} - \frac{n-i}{1-t}\right)$$

$$= \frac{i-nt}{t(1-t)}J_{n,i}(t) \tag{2.13}$$

Similarly, the second derivative is

$$J''_{n,i}(t) = \left(\frac{(i - nt)^2 - nt^2 - i(1 - 2t)}{t^2(1 - t)^2} \right) J_{n,i}(t) \qquad (2.14)$$

At the beginning and the ends of a Bézier curve, i.e., at $t = 0$ and $t = 1$, *numerical* evaluation of Eqs. (2.13) and (2.14) creates difficulties.[†]

An alternate evaluation for the rth derivative at $t = 0$ is given by

$$P^r(0) = \frac{n!}{(n - r)!} \sum_{i=0}^{r} (-1)^{r-i} \binom{r}{i} B_i \qquad (2.15)$$

and at $t = 1$ by

$$P^r(1) = \frac{n!}{(n - r)!} \sum_{i=0}^{r} (-1)^i \binom{r}{i} B_{n-i} \qquad (2.16)$$

Thus, the first derivatives at the ends are

$$P'(0) = n(B_1 - B_0) \qquad (2.17)$$

and

$$P'(1) = n(B_n - B_{n-1}) \qquad (2.18)$$

This illustrates that the tangent vector for a Bézier curve at the initial and final points has the same direction as the initial and final polygon spans.

Similarly, the second derivatives at the ends are

$$P''(0) = n(n - 1)(B_0 - 2B_1 + B_2) \qquad (2.19a)$$

and

$$P''(1) = n(n - 1)(B_n - 2B_{n-1} + B_{n-2}) \qquad (2.19b)$$

Thus, the second derivative of the Bézier curve at the initial and final points depends on the two nearest polygon spans, i.e., on the nearest three polygon vertices. In general, the rth derivative at an end point or starting point is determined by the end or starting point and its r neighboring polygon vertices. An example provides a more explicit illustration.

Example 2.2 Derivatives of Bézier Curves

Consider a four-point Bézier polygon as shown, for example, in Figs. 2.5 and 2.6. Recall that the Bézier curve is given by

$$P(t) = B_0 J_{3,0}(t) + B_1 J_{3,1}(t) + B_2 J_{3,2}(t) + B_3 J_{3,3}(t)$$

[†]Algebraic evaluation of $J_{n,i}(t)$ and substitution *before* numerical evaluation yields correct results (see Ex. 2.2).

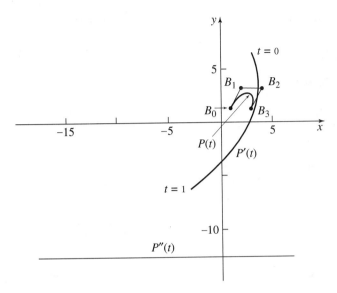

Figure 2.6 Bézier curve and its derivatives. (a) $P(t)$; (b) $P'(t)$; (c) $P''(t)$.

Hence, the first derivative is

$$P'(t) = B_0 J'_{3,0}(t) + B_1 J'_{3,1}(t) + B_2 J'_{3,2}(t) + B_3 J'_{3,3}(t)$$

Recalling Ex. 2.1 and differentiating the basis functions directly yields

$$
\begin{aligned}
J_{3,0}(t) &= (1-t)^3 & \Rightarrow\quad & J'_{3,0}(t) = -3(1-t)^2 \\
J_{3,1}(t) &= 3t(1-t)^2 & \Rightarrow\quad & J'_{3,1}(t) = 3(1-t)^2 - 6t(1-t) \\
J_{3,2}(t) &= 3t^2(1-t) & \Rightarrow\quad & J'_{3,2}(t) = 6t(1-t) - 3t^2 \\
J_{3,3}(t) &= t^3 & \Rightarrow\quad & J'_{3,3}(t) = 3t^2
\end{aligned}
$$

Evaluating these results at $t = 0$ gives

$$J'_{3,0}(t)(0) = -3 \qquad J'_{3,1}(t)(0) = 3 \qquad J'_{3,2}(t)(0) = 0 \qquad J'_{3,3}(t)(0) = 0$$

Substituting these values into the equation for the first derivative yields

$$P'(0) = -3B_0 + 3B_1 = 3(B_1 - B_0)$$

Thus, the direction of the tangent vector at the beginning of the curve is the same as that of the first polygon span (see Fig. 2.6). In Fig. 2.6 draw a line *from* the origin to any point on the $P'(t)$ curve. That line is the tangent vector at the first point on the curve. In fact, a line from the origin to any point on $P'(t)$

represents the tangent vector at the corresponding point (parametric value) on the curve.

At the end of the curve, $t = 1$ and

$$J'_{3,0}(t)(1) = 0 \qquad J'_{3,1}(t)(1) = 0 \qquad J'_{3,2}(t)(1) = -3 \qquad J'_{3,3}(t)(1) = 3$$

Again, substituting these values into the equation for the first derivative yields

$$P'(1) = -3B_2 + 3B_3 = 3(B_3 - B_2)$$

Thus, the direction of the tangent vector at the end of the curve is the same as that of the last polygon span. Again, see Fig. 2.6 and draw the line from the origin to the end of the $P'(t)$ curve. Notice in this case that the direction of the tangent vector is somewhat counterintuitive.

The basis functions given above, along with Eqs. (2.13) and (2.14), are used to evaluate the derivatives along the curve. Specifically, the first derivatives are

$$J'_{3,0}(t) = \frac{0 - 3t}{t(1-t)}(1-t)^3 = -3(1-t)^2$$

$$J'_{3,1}(t) = \frac{1 - 3t}{t(1-t)}3t(1-t)^2 = 3(1-3t)(1-t) = 3(1-4t+3t^2)$$

$$J'_{3,2}(t) = \frac{2 - 3t}{t(1-t)}3t^2(1-t) = 3t(2-3t)$$

$$J'_{3,3}(t) = \frac{3(1-t)}{t(1-t)}t^3 = 3t^2$$

Notice that there is no difficulty in evaluating these results at either $t = 0$ or $t = 1$. Substituting into Eq. (2.11) yields the first derivative at any point on the curve. For example, at $t = 1/2$

$$P'(1/2) = -3(1 - 1/2)^2 B_0 + 3(1 - 3/2)(1 - 1/2)B_1 + (3/2)(2 - 3/2)B_2 + 3/4 B_3$$

$$= -3/4 B_0 - 3/4 B_1 + 3/4 B_2 + 3/4 B_3 = -3/4(B_0 + B_1 - B_2 - B_3)$$

Complete results for B_0, B_1, B_2, B_3 given in Ex. 2.1 are shown in Fig. 2.6.

Similarly, the second derivatives are

$$J''_{3,0}(t) = \frac{\{(-3t)^2 - 3t^2\}}{t^2(1-t)^2}(1-t)^3 = 6(1-t)$$

$$J''_{3,1}(t) = \frac{\{(1-3t)^2 - 3t^2 - (1-2t)\}}{t^2(1-t)^2}(3t)(1-t)^2 = -6(2-3t)$$

$$J''_{3,2}(t) = \frac{\{(2-3t)^2 - 3t^2 - 2(1-2t)\}}{t^2(1-t)^2}(3t^2)(1-t) = 6(1-3t)$$

$$J''_{3,3}(t) = \frac{\{(3-3t)^2 - 3t^2 - 3(1-2t)\}}{t^2(1-t)^2}t^3 = 6t$$

Using Eq. (2.12) for $t = 1/2$, these results yield

$$P''(1/2) = 6(1 - 1/2)B_0 - 6(2 - 3/2)B_1 + 6(1 - 3/2)B_2 + 3B_3$$
$$= 3B_0 - 3B_1 - 3B_2 + 3B_3 = 3(B_0 - B_1 - B_2 + B_3)$$

Complete results for B_0, B_1, B_2, B_3 given in Ex. 2.1 are also shown in Fig. 2.6. Recall that a vector from the origin to any point on each of these curves represents the direction and magnitude of the position, tangent and approximate curvature, respectively, of that point on the curve.

2.4 Continuity Between Bézier Curves

Continuity conditions between adjacent Bézier curves are simply specified. If one Bézier curve, $P(t)$ of degree n, is defined by vertices B_i and an adjacent Bézier curve, $Q(s)$ of degree m, by vertices C_i, then first-derivative geometric continuity at the point where the curves join is given by

$$P'(1) = gQ'(0)$$

where g is a scalar. Using Eqs. (2.17) and (2.18) yields

$$C_1 - C_0 = 1/g\,(n/m)\,(B_n - B_{n-1})$$

Because positional continuity is implied at the joint, $C_0 = B_n$ and

$$C_1 = 1/g\,(n/m)\,(B_n - B_{n-1}) + B_n$$

Thus, the tangent vector directions at the join are the same if the three vertices B_{n-1}, $B_n = C_0$, C_1 are colinear; i.e., B_n need only lie somewhere on the line between B_{n-1} and C_1. If both direction *and* magnitude of the tangent vectors at the join are to be equal, then $g = 1$. In this case, parametric continuity is also achieved.

For equal degree curves $(n = m)$, $B_n = C_0$ must be the midpoint of the line joining B_{n-1} and C_1, i.e.

$$C_1 - C_0 = B_n - B_{n-1} = C_0 - B_{n-1}$$

or
$$C_1 + B_{n-1} = 2C_0 = 2B_n$$

Figure 2.7 illustrates this for $n = m = 3$, i.e., for two cubic Bézier curves.

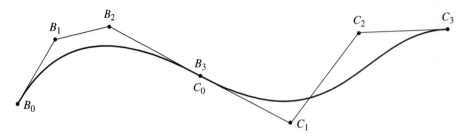

Figure 2.7   First-derivative continuity between cubic Bézier curves.

Second-derivative parametric continuity between adjacent Bézier curves is given by

$$m(m-1)(C_0 - 2C_1 + C_2) = n(n-1)(B_{n-2} - 2B_{n-1} + B_n)$$

Using the conditions for C^0 and C^1 continuity at the join given on page 31 yields

$$C_2 = \frac{n(n-1)}{m(m-1)} B_{n-2}$$

$$- 2\left(\frac{n(n-1)}{m(m-1)} + \frac{n}{m}\right) B_{n-1} + \left(1 + 2\frac{n}{m} + \frac{n(n-1)}{m(m-1)}\right) B_n$$

Thus, the position of the third defining vertex in the *second* control polygon is given in terms of the last three vertices in the *first* control polygon. This result shows that the polygon vertices B_{n-2}, B_{n-1}, $B_n = C_0$, C_1, C_2 must either form a convex polygon or be colinear to maintain C^2 continuity across the join. For cubic Bézier curves ($n = m = 3$) the general equation given above reduces to

$$C_2 = B_{n-2} - 4(B_{n-1} - B_n) = B_1 - 4(B_2 - B_3)$$

If n and m are not equal, e.g., $n = 3, m = 4$, then

$$C_2 = \tfrac{1}{2}(B_{n-2} - 5B_{n-1}) + 3B_n = \tfrac{1}{2}(B_1 - 5B_2) + 3B_3$$

A few minutes' work with pencil and paper shows that this requirement places significant restrictions on overall piecewise curve design. Consequently, practical design using Bézier curves results in higher-degree polynomial curves when second-derivative continuity is required. An example of second-derivative continuity is shown in Fig. 2.8 for two five-point adjacent Bézier curves.

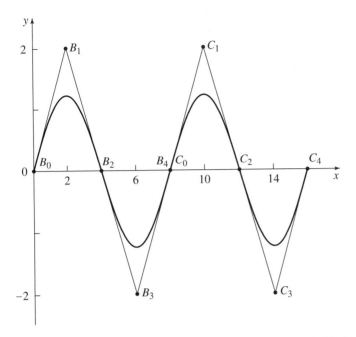

Figure 2.8 Second-derivative continuity between quartic Bézier curves.

2.5 Increasing the Flexibility of Bézier Curves

Degree Elevation

If a Bézier curve with additional flexibility is required, the degree of the defining polynomial can be increased by increasing the number of control polygon points. For every point on a Bézier curve with n control polygon vertices $B_0, \cdots, B_n$, the same point on a new Bézier curve with $n+1$ control polygon vertices $B_0^*, \cdots, B_{n+1}^*$ is given by

$$P(t) = \sum_{i=0}^{n} B_i J_{n,i}(t) = \sum_{i=0}^{n+1} B_i^* J_{n+1,i}(t) \qquad (2.20)$$

where
$$B_0^* = B_0$$
$$B_i^* = \alpha_i B_{i-1} + (1 - \alpha_i) B_i \qquad \alpha_i = \frac{i}{n+1} \qquad i = 1, \cdots, n$$
$$B_{n+1}^* = B_n$$

This technique, given by Forrest [Forr72], can be applied successively. In the limit, the polygon converges to the curve.

Subdivision

Additional flexibility is also obtained by subdividing a Bézier curve into two new Bézier curves that, combined, are identical to the original curve. The task is to determine the control polygons for the two new curves in terms of those for the original curve. Barsky [Bars85] and Bartels et al. [Bart87] show that a Bézier curve can be divided at any parameter value in the range $0 \leq t \leq 1$. The simplest choice is at the midpoint, i.e., $t = 1/2$. Here, the results for midpoint subdivision are derived for the special case of cubic Bézier curves.

A cubic Bézier curve (see Ex. 2.1) is given by

$$P(t) = (1 - t)^3 B_0 + 3t(1 - t)^2 B_1 + 3t^2(1 - t)B_2 + t^3 B_3 \qquad 0 \leq t \leq 1$$

with the control polygon given by B_0, B_1, B_2, B_3. The polygon C_0, C_1, C_2, C_3 then defines the Bézier curve $Q(u)$, $0 \leq u \leq 1$, which corresponds to the first half of the original curve; i.e., $P(t)$, $0 \leq t \leq 1/2$. Similarly, the polygon D_0, D_1, D_2, D_3 defines the Bézier curve $R(v)$, $0 \leq v \leq 1$, which corresponds to the second half of the original curve; i.e., $P(t)$, $1/2 \leq t \leq 1$. The new control polygon vertices C_i and D_i are obtained by equating the position and tangent vectors at $u = 0$, $t = 0$; $u = 1$, $t = 1/2$ and $v = 0$, $t = 1/2$; $v = 1$, $t = 1$. Using Eqs. (2.1) and (2.11) yields

$$C_0 = B_0$$

$$3(C_1 - C_0) = 3/2(B_1 - B_0)$$

$$3(C_3 - C_2) = 3/8(B_3 + B_2 - B_1 - B_0)$$

$$C_3 = 1/8(B_3 + 3B_2 + 3B_1 + B_0)$$

Solution of these equations gives

$$C_0 = B_0$$

$$C_1 = 1/2(B_1 + B_0)$$

$$C_2 = 1/4(B_2 + 2B_1 + B_0)$$

$$C_3 = 1/8(B_3 + 3B_2 + 3B_1 + B_0)$$

Similarly
$$D_0 = \tfrac{1}{8}(B_3 + 3B_2 + 3B_1 + B_0)$$
$$D_1 = \tfrac{1}{4}(B_3 + 2B_2 + B_1)$$
$$D_2 = \tfrac{1}{2}(B_3 + B_2)$$
$$D_3 = B_3$$

These results generalize to

$$C_i = \sum_{j=0}^{i} \binom{i}{j} \frac{B_j}{2^i} \qquad i = 0, 1, \cdots, n \qquad\qquad (2.21a)$$

$$D_i = \sum_{j=i}^{n} \binom{n-i}{n-j} \frac{B_j}{2^{n-i}} \qquad i = 0, 1, \cdots, n \qquad\qquad (2.21b)$$

Applied successively, the polygons converge to the Bézier curve itself.

(a) (b)

Pierre Bézier. (a) A formal picture; (b) explaining his ideas. (Courtesy of C. Bézier.)

Pierre Etienne Bézier (1910–1999) made lasting contributions to computer aided design and manufacturing and to mathematics. Bézier was the son and grandson of engineers and his sons are engineers, five generations of engineers. Forty-six years after receiving his degree in mechanical engineering from the Ecole des Arts et Métiers, he was awarded a Doctor of Science in mathematics from the University of Paris. Bézier joined the ranks of academia in 1968 as Professor of Production Engineering at the Conservatoire National des Arts et Métiers, a position he held for 11 years. He wrote numerous papers and four books and received numerous honors and awards.

After university, he joined Renault and remained with them for 42 years until his retirement in 1975. He started as a toolsetter and eventually became managing staff member for technical development, a position that he held for 15 years. Bézier's interest in CADCAM began in the early 1960s. The result was his UNISURF system, which was founded on his invention of Bézier curves and surfaces. That system is still in use today. As with any new idea, there was initial resistance, particularly from management. Bézier was fond of quoting a managing director of Renault who remarked to Bézier after a conference, "If your system were that good, the Americans would have invented it first!" (June 1971, SOFERMO, Meudon). As history shows, the reverse is quite the case.

Dave Rogers
Annapolis, May 2000

Rich Riesenfeld

By spring 1970 I had finished most of the course work required for a Ph.D. in mathematics at Syracuse University, transferred to the new program in Systems and Information Science (SIS), completed course requirements for the doctoral degree there, and aligned with a major professor—a guy called Steve Coons. I was delighted to be affiliated with Coons, and most enthusiastic about the possibilities ahead but, first—well, I needed a break!

When I went to Coons and mentioned to him I wanted to take a break for the summer, maybe knock around Europe, he suggested that instead of waiting tables or such, I might join the Computer Aided Design Group in the Computer Laboratory at Cambridge University. Steve wrote to Robin Forrest, who quickly responded that he and the group head Charles Lang would welcome my visit. Like Steve, Robin and Charles were mechanical engineers, so their research often drew on examples taken from this field. As a student of mathematics for most of my life, exposure to a mechanical engineering perspective was new to me and instilled a continuing interest that has remained undiminished for three decades. Robin was my mentor; Charles was the head of the group. Ian Braid was calmly finishing up his landmark thesis, Malcolm Sabin stopped by several times, Fred Brooks (Turing Award '00) had recently gone back from a sabbatical visit to the laboratory, and Maurice Wilkes (Turing Award '67), head of the computer laboratory, often inquired about new developments.

At Cambridge during the summer of 1970, I realized that I had joined a close-knit international family of researchers largely connected through Steve. In Europe I learned much about Steve's greatness and influence. Before he joined the faculty at Syracuse, he had been at MIT. Charles and

Robin had visited him to gain insights on this new field coined CAD. In some sense, my visit to Cambridge was a reciprocal one. Nearly daily, Robin and I had lunch in a pub by the river Cam, where we talked about computer geometry problems and the emerging field over a couple of pints. I still remain grateful for the warmth, kindness and formative instruction shown to me by Robin and Charles.

Partly through that summer, Elaine Cohen and I visited Pierre Bézier at Renault. His intuitive way of controlling the shape of a curve was quite the topic of discussion in CAD research communities, because the curve, defined by a user-specified "control polygon," gracefully mimicked its shape. This was a completely novel idea that had set the CAD world abuzz trying to understand what was fundamentally going on. In this first of many meetings and communications, Bézier was gracious and kind and demonstrated his new system on the graphics output of the time, a large flatbed plotter. Robin Forrest later showed that these curves were parametric polynomials in the Bernstein basis. As an engineer and a leader, Bézier profoundly inspired me and, of course, had a similar effect on many a community of other researchers.

As part of a serious commitment to establish a presence in graphics, Syracuse recruited Bill Gordon from General Motors Research Lab. Gordon was a mathematician who worked in approximation theory and numerical methods and was famous for his spline "Gordon Surfaces." He was scheduled to arrive for spring semester 1971, so I spent fall 1970 studying spline and approximation theory literature and Gordon's papers on the "theory of projectors," an elegant characterization of surface interpolation schemes in a lattice hierarchy. When Bill arrived, he and I went for coffee and spent several hours talking about research. Thus went the first day of my apprenticeship under the master who spent so much time imparting the trade. He was interested in what I had learned about Bézier and his method. Beginning my research in Bernstein-Bézier methods of curve design, Bill felt that Robin's result relating the Bézier method to Bernstein approximation could open interesting research directions.

At the time, approximation methods for splines were principally interpolation based, which tended to introduce undesired undulations. Spline curve representation methods largely used piecewise power basis representations, "plus function" bases, or divided difference formulations. In early 1971 Bill went to a math meeting where he interacted with other leaders (probably including de Boor) about new directions in spline theory. He learned of a new result of de Boor's on an attractive method for evaluating splines by using an unusual basis, the B-spline basis. Cox in England had produced a similar formula. Bill had the insight that working with spline *approximations* for CAD would be a fruitful research direction. Theoretically, using a spline representation for a curve would allow much more general curves than was possible with polynomials.

Bill and I targeted the goal: find the spline analog to Bézier's method. We wanted to find a Bézier-like scheme that used a "control polygon" to produce well-controlled, smooth spline shapes of prescribed (low) degree. Although Bill had decided to return to General Motors Research and left Syracuse after only one semester, he offered to continue as my primary thesis advisor. Even though we worked long distance, he was nurturing and meticulous in teaching me the profession. By fall 1971 we had found the appropriate generalization, which included Bézier curves as a special case. The graphics results were gratifying, and I was headed toward a doctorate degree. The relationship of this formulation to Schoenberg's variation-diminishing spline approximation paralleled the relationship of the Bézier curve to Bernstein approximation. Exploring the characteristics and consequences of this method and the corresponding spaces of functions with applications to design, rendering, analysis and manufacturing is still a major research topic.

Steve Coons liked matrix formulations. The general case of the B-spline curve method that I was developing for my thesis did not easily fit that formulation. However, by considering only the special case of floating uniform knots, Steve was able to derive a matrix formulation. His efforts had the effect of making B-spline curves much easier to grasp and therefore more popular to use. However, this was a double-edged sword, for only the uniform floating B-splines lent themselves to this approach. So it had the effect of promulgating the uniform floating case and leaving largely unexploited the much more powerful and general nonuniform case. It was not until several years later that the Oslo Algorithm and subdivision interacted to focus attention on nonuniform B-splines and their importance.

On a visit to Ivan Sutherland at the University of Utah, Steve presented the B-spline method for curves and surfaces that I was developing. It inspired one of Ivan's graduate students, a fellow by the name of Jim Clark (SGI, Netscape, etc.), to modify his dissertation to include the first real-time, augmented reality (!), implementation of an interactive design system using the B-spline method for uniform floating surfaces. He used Sutherland's famous Head Mounted Display for superimposing a B-spline surface in space over a view of the environment.

Curve and surface activity continued for a while longer at Syracuse. Although Bill returned to GM Research, Robin Forrest visited Syracuse for the academic year 1971–1972. Lewis Knapp, whom I had met when I taught a systems class, became interested in this area. Since my visit to Cambridge had been so inspiring, I convinced Lewie to have Steve Coons arrange for him to visit Robin at the Cambridge CAD Group as well. Lewie had a similarly beneficial time. His Ph.D. thesis focused on building a design system using the B-spline surface representation and Boolean sum operators. Ken Versprille, another graduate student who had gravitated toward the Coons community, was slightly more than two years behind me. By the time he was looking for a research topic, Steve had become excited about the B-spline method and its possibilities. Coons viewed rational curves, particularly rational conics, and their perspective relationships, as very elegant, but they had not yet been encompassed into this new approach. Paralleling my thesis by defining an analogous scheme for rational nonuniform B-splines, Ken made the important contribution of combining rationals and B-splines. These curves have since become known as NURBS. Ken went on to take a job at Computervision, where he persuaded his company to be the first to adopt NURBS as a fundamental representation in a CAD system.

A few years later when I was on the faculty at Utah, I asked Robin, who had migrated to East Anglia, to host a gifted graduate student of mine named Jeff Lane for a summer. In an effort to abstract and generalize some of the desirable properties of B-spline and related methods, Jeff did an impressive thesis involving total positivity and convolutions. Later we collaborated on some fundamental B-spline papers. B-splines were not fully exploited until years later, when subdivision and the Oslo Algorithm became available and they became a commodity. Today they have probably become the most common surface representation in modern CAD systems.

Rich Riesenfeld
Salt Lake City, January 2000

Chapter 3

B-spline Curves 3

From a mathematical point of view, a curve generated by using the vertices of a control polygon is dependent on some interpolation or approximation scheme to establish the relationship between the curve and the control polygon. This scheme is provided by the choice of basis function. As noted in Sec. 2.1, the Bernstein basis produces Bézier curves generated by Eq. (2.1). Two characteristics of the Bernstein basis, however, limit the flexibility of the resulting curves. First, the number of specified polygon vertices fixes the order of the resulting polynomial that defines the curve. For example, a cubic curve must be defined by a polygon with four vertices and three spans. A polygon with six vertices always produces a fifth-degree curve. The only way to reduce the degree of the curve is to reduce the number of vertices, and, conversely, the only way to increase the degree of the curve is to increase the number of vertices.

The second limiting characteristic is due to the global nature of the Bernstein basis. This means that the value of the blending function $J_{n,i}(t)$ given by Eq. (2.2) is nonzero for all parameter values over the entire curve. Because any point on a Bézier curve is a result of blending the values of all control vertices, a change in one vertex is felt throughout the entire curve. This eliminates the ability to produce a local change within a curve.

For example, because the end slopes of a Bézier curve are established by the directions of the first and last polygon spans, it is possible to change the middle vertex of a five-point polygon without changing the *direction* of the end slopes. However, the shape of the total curve is affected due to the global nature of the Bernstein basis. This lack of local control is detrimental in some applications.

There is another basis, called the B-spline basis (from Basis Spline), which contains the Bernstein basis as a special case. This basis is generally nonglobal. The nonglobal behavior of B-spline curves is due to the fact that each vertex B_i is associated with a unique basis (support) function. Thus, each vertex affects the shape of a curve only over a range of parameter values where its associated basis function is nonzero. The B-spline basis also allows changing the order of the basis function, and hence the degree of the resulting curve, without changing the number of control polygon vertices. The theory for B-splines was first suggested by Schoenberg [Scho46]). A recursive definition useful for numerical computation was independently discovered by Cox [Cox71]) and by de Boor [deBo72]). Riesenfeld [Ries73] and Gordon and Riesenfeld [Gord74] applied the B-spline basis to curve definition.

3.1 B-spline Curve Definition

Letting $P(t)$ be the position vector along the curve as a function of the parameter t, a B-spline curve is given by

$$P(t) = \sum_{i=1}^{n+1} B_i N_{i,k}(t) \qquad t_{\min} \le t < t_{\max}, \quad 2 \le k \le n+1 \qquad (3.1)$$

where the B_i are the position vectors of the $n + 1$ control polygon vertices, and the $N_{i,k}$ are the normalized B-spline basis functions.

For the ith normalized B-spline basis function of order k (degree $k - 1$), the basis functions $N_{i,k}(t)$ are defined by the Cox–de Boor recursion formulas. Specifically

$$N_{i,1}(t) = \begin{cases} 1 & \text{if } x_i \le t < x_{i+1} \\ 0 & \text{otherwise} \end{cases} \qquad (3.2a)$$

and

$$N_{i,k}(t) = \frac{(t - x_i)N_{i,k-1}(t)}{x_{i+k-1} - x_i} + \frac{(x_{i+k} - t)N_{i+1,k-1}(t)}{x_{i+k} - x_{i+1}} \qquad (3.2b)$$

The values of x_i are elements of a knot vector satisfying the relation $x_i \leq x_{i+1}$ (see Sec. 3.3). The parameter t varies from $t_{\min}$ to $t_{\max}$ along the curve $P(t)$.[†] The convention $\%_0 = 0$ is adopted.

Formally, a B-spline curve is defined as a polynomial spline function of order k (degree $k - 1$), because it satisfies the following two conditions:

$P(t)$ is a polynomial of degree $k - 1$ on each interval $x_i \leq t < x_{i+1}$.

$P(t)$ and its derivatives of order $1, 2, \cdots, k - 2$ are all continuous over the entire curve.

Thus, for example, a fourth-order B-spline curve is a piecewise cubic curve.

Properties of B-spline Curves

Because a B-spline basis is used to describe a B-spline curve, several properties in addition to those already mentioned are immediately known:

The sum of the B-spline basis functions for any parameter value t is (see [deBo72] and [Gord74])

$$\sum_{i=1}^{n+1} N_{i,k}(t) \equiv 1 \tag{3.3}$$

Each basis function is positive or zero for all parameter values, that is, $N_{i,k} \geq 0$.

Except for first-order basis functions, $k = 1$, each basis function has precisely one maximum value.

The maximum order of the curve equals the number of control polygon vertices. The maximum degree is one less.

The curve exhibits the variation-diminishing property. Thus, the curve does not oscillate about any straight line more often than its control polygon oscillates about the line.

The curve generally follows the shape of the control polygon.

Any affine transformation is applied to the curve by applying it to the control polygon vertices; i.e., the curve is transformed by transforming the control polygon vertices.

The curve lies within the convex hull of its control polygon.

[†]Here, note that, in contrast to the Bézier curve, the control polygon vertices or points are numbered from 1 to $n + 1$.

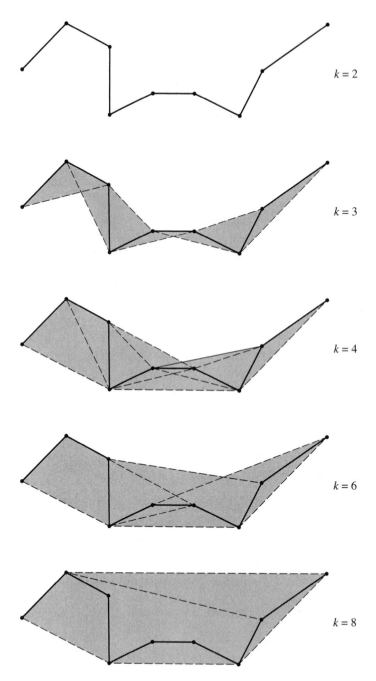

$k = 2$

$k = 3$

$k = 4$

$k = 6$

$k = 8$

Figure 3.1 Convex hull properties of B-spline curves.

3.2 Convex Hull Properties of B-spline Curves

The convex hull properties of B-spline curves are stronger than those for Bézier curves. For a B-spline curve of order k (degree $k-1$), a point on the curve lies within the convex hull of k neighboring points. Thus, all points on a B-spline curve must lie within the union of *all* such convex hulls formed by taking k successive control polygon vertices. Figure 3.1, where the convex hulls are shown shaded, illustrates this effect for different values of k. Notice in particular that for $k = 2$ the convex hull is just the control polygon itself. Hence, the B-spline curve is also just the control polygon itself.

Using the convex hull property, it is easy to see that if all the control polygon vertices are colinear, then the resulting B-spline curve is a straight line for all orders k. Furthermore, if ℓ colinear polygon vertices occur in a noncolinear control polygon, then the straight portions of the curve (if any) start and end at least $k-2$ spans from the beginning and end of the series of colinear polygon vertices. If the series of colinear polygon vertices is completely contained within a noncolinear control polygon, then the number of colinear curve spans is at least $\ell - 2k + 3$. If the series of colinear polygon vertices occurs at the end of a noncolinear control polygon, then the number of colinear curve spans is at least $\ell - k + 1$. Figure 3.2 illustrates these results.

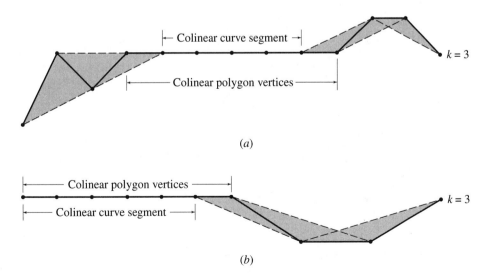

(a)

(b)

Figure 3.2 B-spline convex hull properties for colinear curve segments. (a) Within the control polygon vertices; (b) at the end of the control polygon vertices.

If at least $k - 1$ coincident control polygon vertices occur, i.e., $B_i = B_{i+1} \cdots = B_{i+k-2}$, then the convex hull of B_i to B_{i+k-2} is the vertex itself. Hence, the resulting B-spline curve must pass through the vertex B_i. Figure 3.3 illustrates this point for $k = 3$. In addition, because a B-spline curve is everywhere C^{k-2} continuous, it is C^{k-2} continuous at B_i.

Finally, note that because of these continuity properties B-spline curves smoothly transition, with C^{k-2} continuity, into embedded straight segments, as shown in Fig. 3.4.

3.3 Knot Vectors

Equations (3.2) clearly show that the choice of knot vector has a significant influence on the B-spline basis functions $N_{i,k}(t)$ and hence on the resulting B-spline curve. The only requirement for a knot vector is that it satisfy the relation $x_i \leq x_{i+1}$; i.e., it is a monotonically increasing series of real numbers. Fundamentally, two types of knot vector are used, periodic and open, in two flavors, uniform and nonuniform.

In a *uniform* knot vector, individual knot values are evenly spaced. Examples are

$$\begin{bmatrix} 0 & 1 & 2 & 3 & 4 \end{bmatrix}$$

$$\begin{bmatrix} -0.2 & -0.1 & 0 & 0.1 & 0.2 \end{bmatrix}$$

In practice, uniform knot vectors generally begin at zero and are incremented by 1 to some maximum value, or are normalized in the range between 0 and 1, i.e., equal decimal intervals; for example

$$\begin{bmatrix} 0 & 0.25 & 0.5 & 0.75 & 1.0 \end{bmatrix}$$

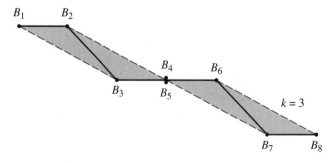

Figure 3.3 Convex hull for coincident polygon vertices, $k = 3$.

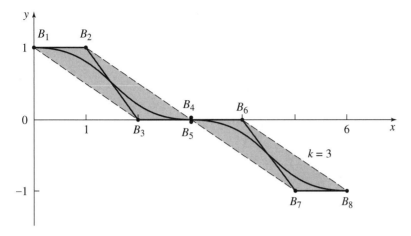

Figure 3.4 Smooth (C^{k-2}) transition into straight segments.

For a given order k, *periodic uniform* knot vectors yield periodic uniform basis functions for which

$$N_{i,k}(t) = N_{i-1,k}(t-1) = N_{i+1,k}(t+1)$$

Thus, each basis function is a translate of the other, as Fig. 3.5 illustrates.

An *open uniform* knot vector has multiplicity of knot values at the ends equal to the order k of the B-spline basis function. Internal knot values are evenly spaced. Some examples using integer increments are

$$k = 2 \qquad \begin{bmatrix} 0 & 0 & 1 & 2 & 3 & 4 & 4 \end{bmatrix}$$
$$k = 3 \qquad \begin{bmatrix} 0 & 0 & 0 & 1 & 2 & 3 & 3 & 3 \end{bmatrix}$$
$$k = 4 \qquad \begin{bmatrix} 0 & 0 & 0 & 0 & 1 & 2 & 2 & 2 & 2 \end{bmatrix}$$

or for normalized increments

$$k = 2 \qquad \begin{bmatrix} 0 & 0 & \tfrac{1}{4} & \tfrac{1}{2} & \tfrac{3}{4} & 1 & 1 \end{bmatrix}$$
$$k = 3 \qquad \begin{bmatrix} 0 & 0 & 0 & \tfrac{1}{3} & \tfrac{2}{3} & 1 & 1 & 1 \end{bmatrix}$$
$$k = 4 \qquad \begin{bmatrix} 0 & 0 & 0 & 0 & \tfrac{1}{2} & 1 & 1 & 1 & 1 \end{bmatrix}$$

Formally, an open uniform knot vector is given by

$$x_i = 0 \qquad 1 \le i \le k$$
$$x_i = i - k \qquad k+1 \le i \le n+1$$
$$x_i = n - k + 2 \qquad n+2 \le i \le n+k+1$$

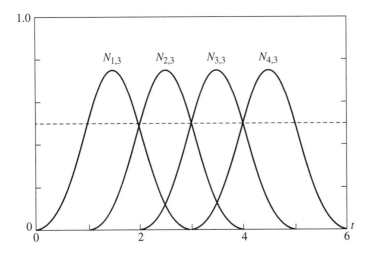

Figure 3.5 Periodic uniform B-spline basis functions, with $[X] = [0 \ 1 \ 2 \ 3 \ 4 \ 5 \ 6]$, $n + 1 = 4$, $k = 3$.

The resulting open uniform basis functions yield curves that behave most nearly like Bézier curves. (The B-spline curve in Fig. 3.4 was generated using an open uniform knot vector.) When the number of control polygon vertices is equal to the order of the B-spline basis and an open uniform knot vector is used, the B-spline basis reduces to the Bernstein basis. Hence, the

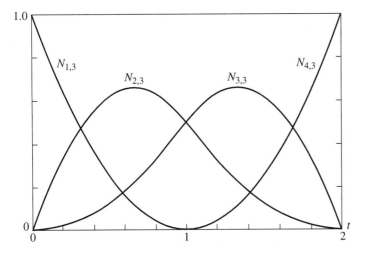

Figure 3.6 Open uniform B-spline basis functions, with $[X] = [0 \ 0 \ 0 \ 1 \ 2 \ 2 \ 2]$, $k = 3$, $n + 1 = 4$.

resulting B-spline curve is a Bézier curve. In that case, the knot vector is just k zeros followed by k ones. For example, for four polygon vertices the fourth order $(k = 4)$ open uniform knot vector is

$$[0 \quad 0 \quad 0 \quad 0 \quad 1 \quad 1 \quad 1 \quad 1]$$

A cubic Bézier/B-spline curve results. The corresponding open uniform basis functions are shown in Fig. 2.4b. Additional open uniform basis functions are shown in Fig. 3.6.

Nonuniform knot vectors may have either unequally spaced and/or multiple internal knot values. They may be periodic or open. Examples are

$$[0 \quad 0 \quad 0 \quad 1 \quad 1 \quad 2 \quad 2 \quad 2] \quad \text{open}$$

$$[0 \quad 1 \quad 2 \quad 2 \quad 3 \quad 4] \quad \text{periodic}$$

$$[0 \quad 0.28 \quad 0.5 \quad 0.72 \quad 1] \quad \text{periodic}$$

Figures 3.7b to 3.7e show several nonuniform B-spline basis functions for order $k = 3$. The knot vectors used to generate the basis functions all have multiplicity of k equal values at the ends. Figure 3.7a gives the basis functions for an open uniform knot vector for comparison. Notice the symmetry of the basis functions in Figs. 3.7a and 3.7b and how that symmetry is lost for the nonuniform basis functions in Figs. 3.7c to 3.7e. Notice also that for multiple knot values within the knot vector a cusp occurs in one of the basis functions. Furthermore, in Figs. 3.7d and 3.7e notice the shift of the location of the cusp corresponding to the change in location of the multiple knot value in the knot vector.

3.4 B-spline Basis Functions

Because the Cox–de Boor formula (see Eqs. (3.2)) used to calculate B-spline basis functions is a recursion relation, a basis function of a given order k depends on lower-order basis functions down to order 1. For a given basis function $N_{i,k}$, this dependence forms a triangular pattern given by

$$
\begin{array}{ccccc}
N_{i,k} & & & & \\
N_{i,k-1} & N_{i+1,k-1} & & & \\
N_{i,k-2} & N_{i+1,k-2} & N_{i+2,k-2} & & \\
\vdots & & & \ddots & \\
N_{i,1} & N_{i+1,1} & N_{i+2,1} & N_{i+3,1} & \cdot & N_{i+k-1,1}
\end{array}
$$

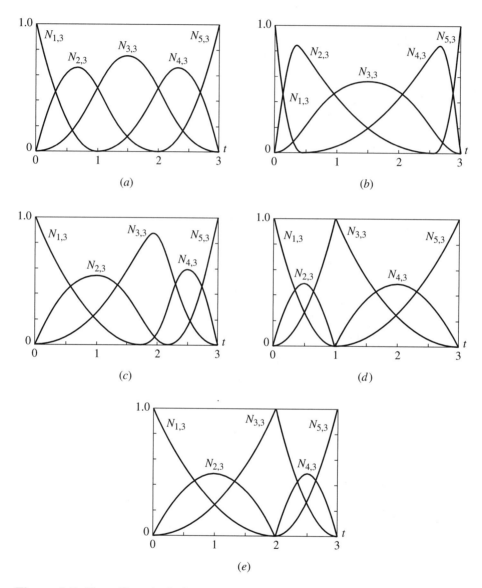

Figure 3.7 Nonuniform basis functions for $n + 1 = 5$, $k = 3$ compared to the open uniform basis function shown in (a). (a) $[X] = [0\ \ 0\ \ 0\ \ 1\ \ 2\ \ 3\ \ 3\ \ 3]$; (b) $[X] = [0\ \ 0\ \ 0\ \ 0.4\ \ 2.6\ \ 3\ \ 3\ \ 3]$; (c) $[X] = [0\ \ 0\ \ 0\ \ 1.8\ \ 2.2\ \ 3\ \ 3\ \ 3]$; (d) $[X] = [0\ \ 0\ \ 0\ \ 1\ \ 1\ \ 3\ \ 3\ \ 3]$; (e) $[X] = [0\ \ 0\ \ 0\ \ 2\ \ 2\ \ 3\ \ 3\ \ 3]$.

The inverse dependence, i.e., the influence of a single first-order basis function $N_{i,1}$ on higher-order basis functions, is given by

$$N_{i-k+1,k} \quad \cdot \quad N_{i+k-1,k} \quad N_{i,k} \quad N_{i+1,k} \quad \cdot \quad N_{i+k-1,k}$$

$$\cdot \qquad \cdot \qquad \cdot \qquad \cdot \qquad \cdot$$

$$N_{i-1,2} \qquad N_{i,2} \qquad N_{i+1,2}$$

$$N_{i,1}$$

Examples more fully illustrate the calculation procedure for basis functions.

Example 3.1 Calculating Periodic Basis Functions

Calculate the four third-order ($k = 3$) basis functions $N_{i,3}(t)$, $i = 1, 2, 3, 4$. Here $n + 1$, the number of basis functions, is 4. The basis function dependencies for $N_{i,3}$ are given by

$$N_{1,3} \quad N_{2,3} \quad N_{3,3} \quad N_{4,3}$$

$$N_{1,2} \quad N_{2,2} \quad N_{3,2} \quad N_{4,2} \quad N_{5,2}$$

$$N_{1,1} \quad N_{2,1} \quad N_{3,1} \quad N_{4,1} \quad N_{5,1} \quad N_{6,1}$$

The inverse dependencies for $i \geq 1$ are given by

$$N_{1,3} \quad N_{2,3} \quad N_{3,3} \quad N_{4,3} \quad N_{5,3} \quad N_{6,3}$$

$$N_{1,2} \quad N_{2,2} \quad N_{3,2} \quad N_{4,2} \quad N_{5,2}$$

$$N_{1,1} \quad N_{2,1} \quad N_{3,1} \quad N_{4,1}$$

Now, what is the knot vector range needed for this calculation? Equations (3.2) show that the calculation of $N_{6,1}$ requires knot values x_6 and x_7, while calculation of $N_{1,1}$ requires knot values x_1 and x_2. Thus, knot values from 0 to $n + k$ are required. The number of knot values is thus $n + k + 1$. Hence, the knot vector for these periodic basis functions is

$$[X] = \begin{bmatrix} 0 & 1 & 2 & 3 & 4 & 5 & 6 \end{bmatrix}$$
$$\quad\quad ① \; ② \; ③ \; ④ \; ⑤ \; ⑥ \; ⑦$$

where $x_1 = 0, \cdots, x_7 = 6$ (numbers in circles show numbering sequence for the knot values). The parameter range is $0 \leq t \leq 6$. Using Eqs. (3.2) and the dependency diagram above, the basis functions for various parameter ranges are

$$0 \leq t < 1$$

$$N_{1,1}(t) = 1; \quad N_{i,1}(t) = 0, \quad i \neq 1$$

$$N_{1,2}(t) = t; \quad N_{i,2}(t) = 0, \quad i \neq 1$$

$$N_{1,3}(t) = \frac{t^2}{2}; \quad N_{i,3}(t) = 0, \quad i \neq 1$$

$1 \leq t < 2$

$N_{2,1}(t) = 1; \qquad N_{i,1}(t) = 0, \quad i \neq 2$

$N_{1,2}(t) = (2 - t); \qquad N_{2,2}(t) = (t - 1); \qquad N_{i,2}(t) = 0, \quad i \neq 1, 2$

$N_{1,3}(t) = \dfrac{t(2 - t)}{2} + \left(\dfrac{3 - t}{2} \right)(t - 1);$

$N_{2,3}(t) = \dfrac{(t - 1)^2}{2}; \qquad N_{i,3}(t) = 0, \quad i \neq 1, 2, 3$

$2 \leq t < 3$

$N_{3,1}(t) = 1; \qquad N_{i,1}(t) = 0, \quad i \neq 3$

$N_{2,2}(t) = (3 - t); \qquad N_{3,2}(t) = (t - 2); \qquad N_{i,2}(t) = 0, \quad i \neq 2, 3$

$N_{1,3}(t) = \dfrac{(3 - t)^2}{2};$

$N_{2,3}(t) = \dfrac{(t - 1)(3 - t)}{2} + \dfrac{(4 - t)(t - 2)}{2};$

$N_{3,3}(t) = \dfrac{(t - 2)^2}{2}; \qquad N_{i,3}(t) = 0, \quad i \neq 1, 2, 3$

$3 \leq t < 4$

$N_{4,1}(t) = 1; \qquad N_{i,1}(t) = 0, \quad i \neq 4$

$N_{3,2}(t) = (4 - t); \qquad N_{4,2}(t) = (t - 3); \qquad N_{i,2}(t) = 0, \quad i \neq 3, 4$

$N_{2,3}(t) = \dfrac{(4 - t)^2}{2}; \qquad N_{3,3}(t) = \dfrac{(t - 2)(4 - t)}{2} + \dfrac{(5 - t)(t - 3)}{2};$

$N_{4,3}(t) = \dfrac{(t - 3)^2}{2}; \qquad N_{i,3}(t) = 0, \quad i \neq 2, 3, 4$

$4 \leq t < 5$

$N_{5,1}(t) = 1; \qquad N_{i,1}(t) = 0, \quad i \neq 5$

$N_{4,2}(t) = (5 - t); \qquad N_{5,2}(t) = (t - 4); \qquad N_{i,2}(t) = 0, \quad i \neq 4, 5$

$N_{3,3}(t) = \dfrac{(5 - t)^2}{2};$

$N_{4,3}(t) = \dfrac{(t - 3)(5 - t)}{2} + \dfrac{(6 - t)(t - 4)}{2};$

$N_{i,3}(t) = 0, \quad i \neq 3, 4$

$5 \leq t < 6$

$N_{6,1}(t) = 1; \qquad N_{i,1}(t) = 0, \quad i \neq 6$

$N_{5,2}(t) = (6 - t); \qquad N_{i,2}(t) = 0, \quad i \neq 5$

$N_{4,3}(t) = \dfrac{(6 - t)^2}{2}; \qquad N_{i,3}(t) = 0, \quad i \neq 4$

Note that because of the $<$ sign in the definition of $N_{i,1}$, all basis functions are precisely zero at $t = 6$.

These results are shown in Fig. 3.5 and Fig. 3.8c. Note that each one of the third-order basis functions is a piecewise parabolic (quadratic) curve. Here, three piecewise parabolic segments on the intervals $x_i \rightarrow x_{i+1}$, $x_{i+1} \rightarrow x_{i+2}$, $x_{i+2} \rightarrow x_{i+3}$ are joined together to form each $N_{i,3}$ basis function. Furthermore, note that each of the basis functions is simply a translate of the other.

Using the results of Ex. 3.1, the buildup of the higher-order basis functions $N_{i,3}$ from lower-order basis functions is easily illustrated. Figure 3.8a shows the first-order basis functions determined in Ex. 3.1, Fig. 3.8b shows the second-order basis functions, and Fig. 3.8c repeats the third-order basis functions of Fig. 3.5 for completeness. Notice how the range of nonzero basis function values spreads with increasing order. The basis function is said to provide support on the interval x_i to x_{i+k}.

Examining Fig. 3.5 closely reveals an important property of uniform basis functions. Recalling from Eq. (3.3) that $\sum N_{i,k}(t) = 1$ at any parameter value t shows that a complete set of periodic basis functions for $k = 3$ is defined only in the range $2 \leq t \leq 4$. Outside of this range the $\sum N_{i,k}(t) \neq 1$. For a uniform knot vector beginning at 0 with integer spacings, the usable parameter range is $k - 1 \leq t \leq (n + k) - (k - 1) = n + 1$. For more general or normalized knot vectors, the reduction in usable parameter range corresponds to the loss of $k - 1$ knot value intervals at each end of the knot vector.

Example 3.2 Calculating Open Uniform Basis Functions

Calculate the four $(n = 3)$ third-order $(k = 3)$ basis functions, $N_{i,3}(t)$, $i = 1, 2, 3, 4$, with an open knot vector. Recall that formally an open knot vector with integer intervals between internal knot values is given by

$$x_i = 0 \qquad 1 \leq i \leq k$$

$$x_i = i - k \qquad k + 1 \leq i \leq n + 1$$

$$x_i = n - k + 2 \qquad n + 2 \leq i \leq n + k + 1$$

The parameter range is $0 \leq t \leq n - k + 2$, i.e., from zero to the maximum knot value. Again, as in Ex. 3.1 the number of knot values is $n + k + 1$. Using integer knot values, the knot vector for the current example is

$$[X] = [0 \quad 0 \quad 0 \quad 1 \quad 2 \quad 2 \quad 2]$$

where $x_1 = 0, \cdots, x_7 = 2$. The parameter range is from $0 \leq t \leq 2$.

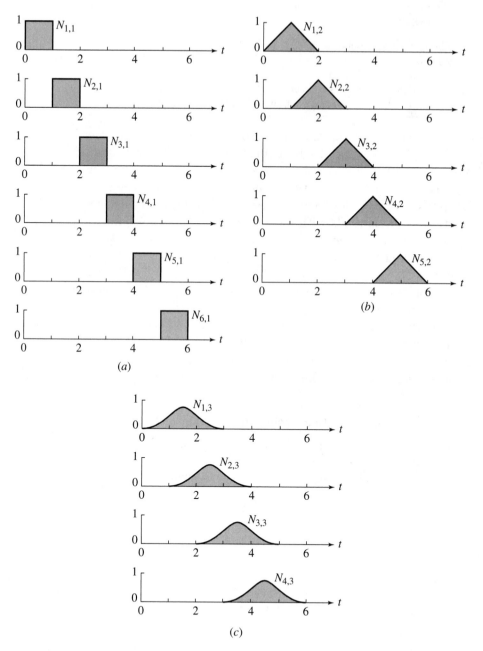

Figure 3.8 Periodic basis function buildup, $n + 1 = 4$. (a) $k = 1$; (b) $k = 2$; (c) $k = 3$.

Using Eqs. (3.2) and the dependency diagrams, the basis functions for various parameter ranges are

$0 \leq t < 1$

$N_{3,1}(t) = 1;$ $\qquad N_{i,1}(t) = 0,$ $\quad i \neq 3$

$N_{2,2}(t) = 1 - t;$ $\qquad N_{3,2}(t) = t;$ $\qquad N_{i,2}(t) = 0,$ $\quad i \neq 2,3$

$N_{1,3}(t) = (1-t)^2;$ $\qquad N_{2,3}(t) = t(1-t) + \dfrac{(2-t)}{2}t;$

$N_{3,3}(t) = \dfrac{t^2}{2};$ $\qquad N_{i,3}(t) = 0,$ $\quad i \neq 1,2,3$

$1 \leq t < 2$

$N_{4,1}(t) = 1;$ $\qquad N_{i,1}(t) = 0,$ $\quad i \neq 4$

$N_{3,2}(t) = (2-t);$ $\qquad N_{4,2}(t) = (t-1);$ $\qquad N_{i,2}(t) = 0,$ $\quad i \neq 3,4$

$N_{2,3}(t) = \dfrac{(2-t)^2}{2};$ $\qquad N_{3,3}(t) = \dfrac{t(2-t)}{2} + (2-t)(t-1);$

$N_{4,3}(t) = (t-1)^2;$ $\qquad N_{i,3}(t) = 0,$ $\quad i \neq 2,3,4$

These results are shown in Fig. 3.9.

Comparing the results from Ex. 3.2 shown in Fig. 3.9 with those from Ex. 3.1 shown in Fig. 3.8 illustrates that significantly different results are obtained when using periodic uniform or open uniform knot vectors. In particular, note that for open uniform knot vectors a complete set of basis functions is defined for the entire parameter range; i.e., $\sum N_{i,k}(t) = 1$ for all $t, 0 \leq t \leq n - k + 2$. Notice also the reduction in parameter range compared to that for a periodic uniform knot vector.

Example 3.3 Calculating Nonuniform Basis Functions

Calculate the five ($n + 1 = 5$) third-order ($k = 3$) basis functions $N_{i,3}(t)$, $i = 1,2,3,4,5$, using the knot vector

$$[X] = [0 \quad 0 \quad 0 \quad 1 \quad 1 \quad 3 \quad 3 \quad 3]$$

which contains an internal multiple (repeated) knot value. Using Eqs. (3.2) and the dependency diagrams, the basis functions are

$0 \leq t < 1$

$N_{3,1}(t) = 1;$ $\qquad N_{i,1}(t) = 0,$ $\quad i \neq 2$

$N_{2,2}(t) = 1 - t;$ $\qquad N_{3,2}(t) = t;$ $\qquad N_{i,2}(t) = 0,$ $\quad i \neq 2,3$

$N_{1,3}(t) = (1-t)^2;$ $\qquad N_{2,3}(t) = t(1-t) + (1-t)t = 2t(1-t);$

$N_{3,3}(t) = t^2;$ $\qquad N_{i,3}(t) = 0,$ $\quad i \neq 1,2,3$

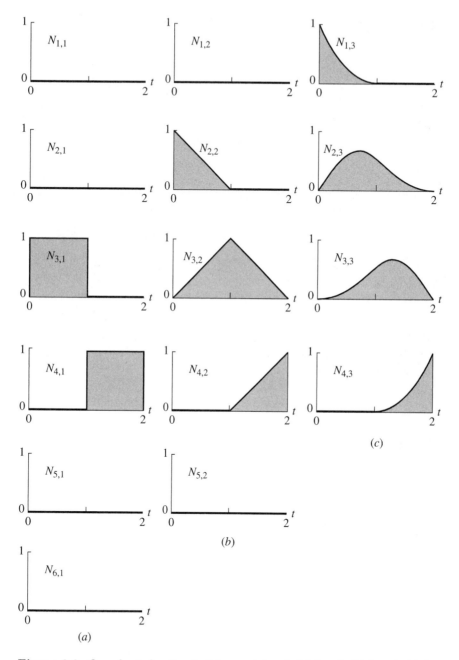

Figure 3.9 Open basis function buildup, $n + 1 = 4$. (a) $k = 1$; (b) $k = 2$; (c) $k = 3$.

$$1 \le t < 1$$
$$N_{i,1}(t) = 0, \quad \text{all } i$$
$$N_{i,2}(t) = 0, \quad \text{all } i$$
$$N_{i,3}(t) = 0, \quad \text{all } i$$

Notice specifically that as a consequence of the multiple knot value, $N_{4,1}(t) = 0$ for all t

$$1 \le t < 3$$
$$N_{5,1}(t) = 1; \qquad N_{i,1}(t) = 0, \quad i \ne 5$$
$$N_{4,2}(t) = \frac{(3-t)}{2}; \qquad N_{5,2}(t) = \frac{(t-1)}{2}; \qquad N_{i,2}(t) = 0, \quad i \ne 4,5$$
$$N_{3,3}(t) = \frac{(3-t)^2}{4};$$
$$N_{4,3}(t) = \frac{(t-1)(3-t)}{4} + \frac{(3-t)(t-1)}{4} = \frac{(3-t)(t-1)}{2};$$
$$N_{5,3}(t) = \frac{(t-1)^2}{4}; \qquad N_{i,3}(t) = 0, \quad i \ne 3,4,5$$

The results are shown in Fig. 3.7d.

Notice also that for each value of t the $\sum N_{i,k}(t) = 1.0$, e.g., with $0 \le t < 1$

$$\sum_{i=1}^{5} N_{i,3}(t) = (1-t)^2 + 2t(1-t) + t^2 = 1 - 2t + t^2 + 2t - 2t^2 + t^2 = 1$$

Similarly, for $1 \le t < 3$

$$\sum_{i=1}^{5} N_{i,3}(t) = \frac{1}{4} \left[(3-t)^2 + 2(3-t)(t-1) + (t-1)^2 \right]$$
$$= \frac{1}{4} \left[9 - 6t + t^2 - 6 + 8t - 2t^2 + 1 - 2t + t^2 \right]$$
$$= \frac{4}{4} = 1$$

This discussion shows the significant influence of the choice of knot vector on the shape of the B-spline basis functions and hence on the shape of any resulting B-spline curve.

B-spline Curve Controls

Because of the flexibility of B-spline basis functions and hence of the resulting B-spline curves, different types of control 'handles' are used to influence the shape of B-spline curves. Control is achieved by

changing the type of knot vector and hence basis function: periodic uniform, open uniform or nonuniform;

changing the order k of the basis function;

changing the number and position of the control polygon vertices;

using multiple polygon vertices;

using multiple knot values in the knot vector.

These effects are illustrated first with open B-spline curves, then with open nonuniform B-spline curves, and finally with periodic B-spline curves.

3.5 Open B-spline Curves

The behavior of an open B-spline curve is in many respects analogous to that of a Bézier curve. In fact, as previously mentioned, when the order of a B-spline curve is equal to the number of control polygon vertices, the B-spline basis reduces to the Bernstein basis. Consequently, the resulting B-spline curve is identical to a Bézier curve. For an open B-spline curve of any order $(k \geq 2)$, the first and last points on the curve are coincident with the first and last polygon vertices. Furthermore, the slope of the B-spline curve at the first and last polygon vertices is equal to the slope of the first and last polygon spans.

Figure 3.10 shows three open B-spline curves of different order, each defined by the same four polygon vertices. The fourth-order curve corresponds to the Bézier curve. This curve is a single cubic polynomial segment. The

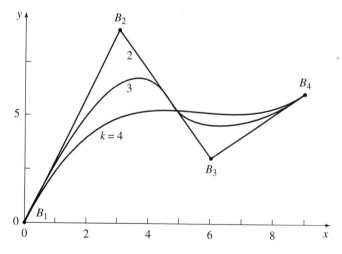

Figure 3.10 Effect of varying order on B-spline curves.

third-order curve is composed of two parabolic curve segments joined at the center of the second span with C^1 continuity. The second-order curve reproduces the control polygon. It consists of three linear 'curve' segments joined at the second and third polygon vertices with C^0 continuity. Notice that all three curves have the same end slopes determined by the slope of the first and last spans of the control polygon. Notice also that as the order of the curve increases, the resulting curve looks less like the control polygon. Thus, increasing the order 'tightens' or 'smooths' the curve.

Figure 3.11 illustrates the effect of multiple or coincident vertices in the control polygon. The B-spline curves are all of order $k = 4$. The lowest curve is defined by four polygon vertices, as shown. Here, the knot vector is given by $[0\ \ 0\ \ 0\ \ 0\ \ 1\ \ 1\ \ 1\ \ 1]$. The intermediate curve is defined by five polygon vertices, with two coincident vertices at the second polygon vertex, i.e., $[3\ \ 9]$. The knot vector for this curve is $[0\ \ 0\ \ 0\ \ 0\ \ 1\ \ 2\ \ 2\ \ 2\ \ 2]$. The highest curve is defined by six polygon vertices with three coincident vertices at $[3\ \ 9]$. The knot vector is $[0\ \ 0\ \ 0\ \ 0\ \ 1\ \ 2\ \ 3\ \ 3\ \ 3\ \ 3]$. Thus, the control polygons for the three curves are B_1, B_2, B_3, B_4; $B_1, B_2, B_2, B_3,$ B_4 and $B_1, B_2, B_2, B_2, B_3, B_4$, respectively.

The lowest curve is composed of a single cubic segment. The intermediate curve is composed of two segments joined midway between B_2 and B_3. The highest curve is composed of three segments. The first is from B_1 to B_2, the second from B_2 to midway between B_2 and B_3. The final segment is

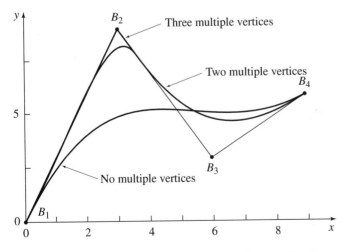

Figure 3.11 Effect of multiple vertices at B_2 on a B-spline curve, $k = 4$.

from midway between B_2 and B_3 to B_4. Notice that as the number of multiple vertices at B_2 increases, the curve is pulled closer to B_2. If the number of multiple vertices is $k-1$, then a sharp corner or cusp is created. This sharp corner is predicted by the convex hull properties of B-spline curves. Close examination of Fig. 3.11 shows that on both sides of the multiple vertex location a linear segment occurs.

Although a cusp exists when $k-1$ multiple vertices occur, the C^{k-2} differentiability of the curve is maintained. At first glance, this might seem contradictory. However, a cusp is defined by a zero tangent vector. But a zero tangent vector does not preclude the tangent vector varying continuously. The ability to include sharp corners or cusps within a continuously C^{k-2} differentiable curve is an important characteristic of B-spline curves. Finally, notice that each of the curves has the same slope at the ends.

Figure 3.12 shows three fourth-order B-spline curves. The control polygons each have eight vertices, as indicated. The three curves shown are obtained by moving the polygon vertex B_5 successively to B_5' and B_5''. Note that moving B_5 influences the curve only over a limited region. Specifically, only the curve segments corresponding to the polygon spans B_3B_4, B_4B_5 and B_5B_6, B_6B_7 are affected by the movement of B_5. In general, the curve

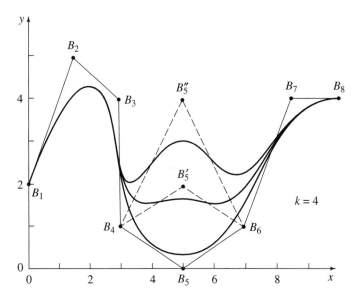

Figure 3.12 Local control of B-spline curves.

is affected only over those curve segments corresponding to $\pm k/2$ polygon spans around the displaced point.

A detailed example more fully illustrates the technique for calculating open B-spline curves.

Example 3.4 Calculating an Open B-spline Curve

Consider the same control polygon used previously in Ex. 2.1 to determine a Bézier curve, i.e.

$$B_1 [1 \quad 1], \ B_2 [2 \quad 3], \ B_3 [4 \quad 3], \ B_4 [3 \quad 1]$$

Calculate both second- and fourth-order B-spline curves.

For $k = 2$, the open knot vector is

$$[0 \quad 0 \quad 1 \quad 2 \quad 3 \quad 3]$$

where $x_1 = 0$, $x_2 = 0, \cdots, x_6 = 3$. The parameter range is $0 \le t \le 3$. The curve is composed of three linear $(k - 1 = 1)$ segments. For $0 \le t < 3$, the basis functions are

$0 \le t < 1$

$\quad N_{2,1}(t) = 1; \qquad N_{i,1}(t) = 0, \quad i \ne 2$

$\quad N_{1,2}(t) = 1 - t; \qquad N_{2,2}(t) = t; \qquad N_{i,2}(t) = 0, \quad i \ne 1, 2$

$1 \le t < 2$

$\quad N_{3,1}(t) = 1; \qquad N_{i,1}(t) = 0, \quad i \ne 3$

$\quad N_{2,2}(t) = 2 - t; \qquad N_{3,2}(t) = (t - 1); \qquad N_{i,2}(t) = 0, \quad i \ne 2, 3$

$2 \le t < 3$

$\quad N_{4,1}(t) = 1; \qquad N_{i,1}(t) = 0, \quad i \ne 4$

$\quad N_{3,2}(t) = (3 - t); \qquad N_{4,2}(t) = (t - 2); \qquad N_{i,2}(t) = 0, \quad i \ne 3, 4$

Using Eq. (3.1), the parametric B-spline curve is

$$P(t) = B_1 N_{1,2}(t) + B_2 N_{2,2}(t) + B_3 N_{3,2}(t) + B_4 N_{4,2}(t)$$

For each of these intervals, the curve is given by

$$P(t) = (1 - t)B_1 + tB_2 = B_1 + (B_2 - B_1)t \qquad 0 \le t < 1$$

$$P(t) = (2 - t)B_2 + (t - 1)B_3 = B_2 + (B_3 - B_2)t \qquad 1 \le t < 2$$

$$P(t) = (3 - t)B_3 + (t - 2)B_4 = B_3 + (B_4 - B_3)t \qquad 2 \le t < 3$$

In each case, the result is the equation of the parametric straight line for the polygon span, i.e., the 'curve' is the control polygon.

The last point on the curve ($t = t_{\max} = 3$) requires special consideration. Because of the open right-hand interval in Eq. (3.2a), all the basis functions $N_{i,k}$ at $t = 3$ are zero. Consequently, the last polygon point does not technically lie on the B-spline curve. However, from a practical viewpoint it does. Consider $t = 3 - \epsilon$, where ϵ is an infinitesimal value. Letting $\epsilon \to 0$ shows that in the limit the last point on the curve and the last polygon vertex are coincident. Practically, this result is incorporated by either artificially adding the last polygon vertex to the curve description or by defining $N(t = t_{\max}) = 1.0$.

For $k = 4$, the order of the curve is equal to the number of control polygon vertices. Thus, the B-spline curve reduces to a Bézier curve. The knot vector with $t_{\max} = n - k + 2 = 3 - 4 + 2 = 1$ is $[0 \ \ 0 \ \ 0 \ \ 0 \ \ 1 \ \ 1 \ \ 1 \ \ 1]$. The basis functions are

$$0 \le t < 1$$
$$N_{4,1}(t) = 1; \qquad N_{i,1}(t) = 0, \quad i \ne 4$$
$$N_{3,2}(t) = (1-t); \qquad N_{4,2}(t) = t; \qquad N_{i,2}(t) = 0, \quad i \ne 3, 4$$
$$N_{2,3}(t) = (1-t)^2; \qquad N_{3,3}(t) = 2t(1-t);$$
$$N_{4,3}(t) = t^2; \qquad N_{i,3}(t) = 0, \quad i \ne 2, 3, 4$$
$$N_{1,4}(t) = (1-t)^3; \qquad N_{2,4}(t) = t(1-t)^2 + 2t(1-t)^2 = 3t(1-t)^2;$$
$$N_{3,4}(t) = 2t^2(1-t) + (1-t)t^2 = 3t^2(1-t); \qquad N_{4,4}(t) = t^3$$

Using Eq. (3.1), the parametric B-spline is

$$P(t) = B_1 N_{1,4}(t) + B_2 N_{2,4}(t) + B_3 N_{3,4}(t) + B_4 N_{4,4}(t)$$
$$P(t) = (1-t)^3 B_1 + 3t(1-t)^2 B_2 + 3t^2(1-t) B_3 + t^3 B_4$$

Thus, at $t = 0$

$$P(0) = B_1$$

and at $t = 1/2$

$$P(1/2) = 1/8 \, B_1 + 3/8 \, B_2 + 3/8 \, B_3 + 1/8 \, B_4$$

and

$$P(1/2) = 1/8 \, [1 \quad 1] + 3/8 \, [2 \quad 3] + 3/8 \, [4 \quad 3] + 1/8 \, [3 \quad 1]$$
$$= [11/4 \quad 5/2]$$

Comparison with Ex. 2.1 shows that the current results are identical. The resulting curve is shown in Fig. 2.5.

3.6 Nonuniform B-spline Curves

Turning now to nonuniform B-spline curves, Fig. 3.13 illustrates the effect of multiple interior knot values on the resulting curve. The upper third-order ($k = 3$) curve in Fig. 3.13 is generated with the open knot vector

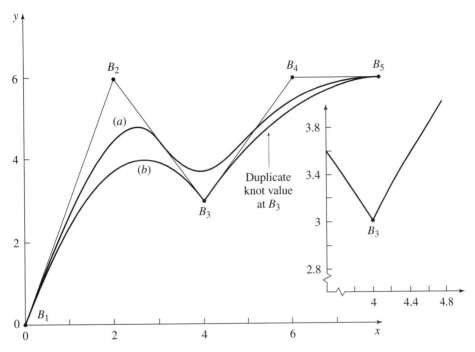

Figure 3.13 Nonuniform B-spline curves, $k = 3$. (a) $[X] = [0 \ 0 \ 0 \ 1 \ 2 \ 3 \ 3 \ 3]$; (b) $[X] = [0 \ 0 \ 0 \ 1 \ 1 \ 3 \ 3 \ 3]$.

$[0 \ 0 \ 0 \ 1 \ 2 \ 3 \ 3 \ 3]$. The basis functions for this curve are shown in Fig. 3.7a. The lower third-order curve in Fig. 3.13 is generated with the nonuniform knot vector $[0 \ 0 \ 0 \ 1 \ 1 \ 3 \ 3 \ 3]$. The basis functions are shown in Fig. 3.7d. An identical curve is obtained with the nonuniform knot vector $[0 \ 0 \ 0 \ 2 \ 2 \ 3 \ 3 \ 3]$ and the basis functions shown in Fig. 3.7e.

Figure 3.13 shows that the multiple interior knot value yields a sharp corner or cusp at B_3. A multiple knot value introduces a span of zero length. Consequently, the width of support of the basis functions is reduced. Furthermore, multiple interior knot values, in contrast to multiple polygon vertices, reduce the differentiability of the basis function at x_i to C'^{k-m-1} where $m \le k - 1$ is the multiplicity of the interior knot value. Locally, the nonuniform curve in Fig. 3.13 is C^0 ($k - m - 1 = 3 - 2 - 1 = 0$) continuous near B_3. Thus, a position discontinuity or 'corner' in the curve occurs.

Figure 3.14 shows third-order ($k = 3$) open nonuniform B-spline curves generated using a knot vector with interior knot values proportional to the

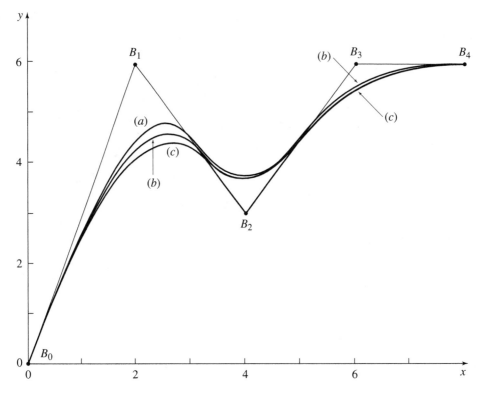

Figure 3.14   Comparison of open nonuniform B-spline curves. (a) Uniform knot vector; (b) nonuniform chord distance proportional knot vector; (c) nonuniform chord distance proportional knot vector with double vertex at B_2.

chord distances between polygon vertices. Specifically, the knot vector is given by

$$x_i = 0 \qquad 1 \le i \le k$$

$$x_{i+k} = \frac{\left(\dfrac{i}{n-k+2}\right)c_{i+1} + \displaystyle\sum_{j=1}^{i} c_j}{\sum_{i=1}^{n} c_i} \ (n-k+2) \qquad 1 \le i \le n-k+1$$

$$x_i = n-k+2 \qquad n+1 \le i \le n+k \tag{3.4}$$

where $c_i = |B_{i+1} - B_i|$. For equally spaced polygon vertices the result reduces to equally spaced integer interior knot values, i.e., an open uniform knot vector. Hartley and Judd [Hart78] suggest a similar scheme that yields distinct interior knot values. The curve generated with an open uniform knot vector is shown for comparison. Also shown is the curve obtained with a pair of coincident vertices at B_2.

From these results it appears that nonuniform B-spline curves do not greatly differ from uniform B-spline curves unless the relative distances between polygon vertices vary radically. An example illustrates these effects.

Example 3.5 Nonuniform B-spline Curve

Using a nonuniform knot vector with knot values proportional to the chord distances between control polygon vertices, determine the third-order open B-spline curve defined by

$$B_1 [0 \quad 0], \; B_2 [2 \quad 6], \; B_3 [4 \quad 3], \; B_4 [6 \quad 6], \; B_5 [8 \quad 6]$$

First, determine the chord lengths

$$c_1 = \sqrt{(2-0)^2 + (6-0)^2} = \sqrt{40} = 6.325$$

$$c_2 = \sqrt{(4-2)^2 + (3-6)^2} = \sqrt{13} = 3.606$$

$$c_3 = \sqrt{(6-4)^2 + (6-3)^2} = \sqrt{13} = 3.606$$

$$c_4 = \sqrt{(8-6)^2 + (6-6)^2} = \sqrt{4} = 2.0$$

The total chord length is

$$\sum_{i=1}^{4} c_i = 15.537$$

Using Eq. (3.4), the interior knot values are

$$x_4 = \left[\frac{c_2/3 + c_1}{15.537} \right] (3) = 1.453$$

$$x_5 = \left[\frac{2c_3/3 + c_1 + c_2}{15.537} \right] (3) = 2.382$$

The knot vector is thus

$$[x] = [0 \quad 0 \quad 0 \quad 1.45 \quad 2.382 \quad 3 \quad 3 \quad 3]$$

where $x_1 = 0$, $x_2 = 0, \cdots, x_8 = 3$. The parameter range is $0 \le t \le 3$. The curve is composed of three parabolic ($k - 1 = 2$) segments.

For $0 \le t < 1.453$, the basis functions are

$$N_{3,1}(t) = 1; \qquad N_{i,1}(t) = 0, \quad i \ne 3$$

$$N_{2,2}(t) = \frac{(1.453 - t)}{1.453}; \quad N_{3,2}(t) = \frac{t}{1.453}; \qquad N_{i,2}(t) = 0, \quad i \ne 2,3$$

$$N_{1,3}(t) = \frac{(1.453 - t)^2}{(1.453)^2}; \quad N_{2,3}(t) = \frac{t}{(1.453)^2}(1.453 - t) + \frac{(2.382 - t)t}{(2.382)(1.453)};$$

$$N_{3,3}(t) = \frac{t^2}{(2.382)(1.453)}; \quad N_{i,3}(t) = 0, \quad i \neq 1,2,3$$

For $1.453 \leq t < 2.382$, the basis functions are

$$N_{4,1}(t) = 1; \quad N_{i,1}(t) = 0, \quad i \neq 4$$

$$N_{3,2}(t) = \frac{(2.382 - t)}{(2.382 - 1.453)};$$

$$N_{4,2}(t) = \frac{(t - 1.453)}{(2.382)(1.453)}; \quad N_{i,2}(t) = 0, \quad i \neq 3,4$$

$$N_{2,3}(t) = \frac{(2.382 - t)^2}{2.382(2.382 - 1.453)};$$

$$N_{3,3}(t) = \frac{t}{2.382}\frac{(2.382 - t)}{(2.382 - 1.453)} + \frac{(3 - t)}{(3 - 1.453)}\frac{(t - 1.453)}{(2.382 - 1.453)};$$

$$N_{4,3}(t) = \frac{(t - 1.453)^2}{(3 - 1.453)(2.382 - 1.453)}; \quad N_{i,3}(t) = 0, \quad i \neq 2,3,4$$

For $2.382 \leq t < 3$

$$N_{5,1}(t) = 1; \quad N_{i,1}(t) = 0, \quad i \neq 5$$

$$N_{4,2}(t) = \frac{(3 - t)}{(3 - 2.382)};$$

$$N_{5,2}(t) = \frac{(t - 2.382)}{(3 - 2.382)}; N_{i,2}(t) = 0, \quad i \neq 4,5$$

$$N_{3,3}(t) = \frac{(3 - t)^2}{(3 - 1.453)(3 - 2.382)};$$

$$N_{4,3}(t) = \frac{(t - 1.453)(3 - t)}{(3 - 1.453)(3 - 2.382)} + \frac{(3 - t)(t - 2.382)}{(3 - 2.382)^2};$$

$$N_{5,3}(t) = \frac{(t - 2.382)^2}{(3 - 2.382)^2}; \quad N_{i,3}(t) = 0, \quad i \neq 3,4,5$$

Recalling that a point on the B-spline curve is given by

$$P(t) = N_{1,3}(t)B_1 + N_{2,3}(t)B_2 + N_{3,3}(t)B_3 + N_{4,3}(t)B_4 + N_{5,3}(t)B_5$$

then for $t = 1/2$

$$P(1/2) = 0.430B_1 + 0.498B_2 + 0.072B_3 + (0)B_4 + (0)B_5$$

$$= 0.430\begin{bmatrix} 0 & 0 \end{bmatrix} + 0.498\begin{bmatrix} 2 & 6 \end{bmatrix} + 0.072\begin{bmatrix} 4 & 3 \end{bmatrix}$$

$$= \begin{bmatrix} 1.284 & 3.202 \end{bmatrix}$$

and for $t = 2$

$$P(2) = (0)B_1 + 0.066B_2 + 0.726B_3 + 0.208B_4 + (0)B_5$$

$$= 0.066\begin{bmatrix} 2 & 6 \end{bmatrix} + 0.726\begin{bmatrix} 4 & 3 \end{bmatrix} + 0.208\begin{bmatrix} 6 & 6 \end{bmatrix}$$

$$= \begin{bmatrix} 4.284 & 3.822 \end{bmatrix}$$

Complete results are shown in Fig. 3.14.

3.7 Periodic B-spline Curves

Turning now to periodic B-spline curves, Fig. 3.15 shows three periodic B-spline curves of different orders. Each of the curves is defined by the same polygon vertices as the open B-spline curves in Fig. 3.10. For $k = 2$, the B-spline curve again coincides with the control polygon. However, notice that for periodic B-spline curves for $k > 2$ the first and last points on the B-spline curve do *not* correspond to the first and last control polygon vertices. Nor, in general, is the slope at the first and last points the same as that of the first and last polygon spans. For $k = 3$, the B-spline curve starts at the midpoint of the first polygon span and ends at the midpoint of the last polygon span, as indicated by the arrows. These effects are a result of the reduced parameter range for periodic B-spline basis functions. For $k = 2$, the periodic knot vector is $\begin{bmatrix} 0 & 1 & 2 & 3 & 4 & 5 \end{bmatrix}$, with a parameter range of

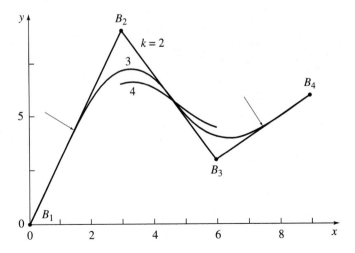

Figure 3.15 Effect of varying order on periodic B-spline curves.

$1 \leq t \leq 4$. For $k = 3$, the periodic knot vector is $[0 \quad 1 \quad 2 \quad 3 \quad 4 \quad 5 \quad 6]$, with parameter range of $2 \leq t \leq 4$. For $k = 4$, the periodic knot vector is $[0 \quad 1 \quad 2 \quad 3 \quad 4 \quad 5 \quad 6 \quad 7]$, with parameter range of $3 \leq t \leq 4$. Comparing these results with those for open knot vectors in Fig. 3.10 shows that the multiple knot values at the ends of the open knot vector permit the curve to be defined over the full range of parameter values. The effect is to 'pull' the curve out to the ends of the control polygon.

Here again, the fourth-order curve consists of a single cubic polynomial segment, the third-order curve of two parabolic segments joined at the center of the second polygon span with C^1 continuity, and the second-order 'curve' of three linear segments joined at the second and third polygon vertices with C^0 continuity. Notice that again increasing order has a 'smoothing' effect on the curve, but here it also decreases the curve length.

Figure 3.16 illustrates that the effect of multiple vertices in the control polygon is similar for periodic and open B-spline curves. The small inset shows the details near B_2.

Example 3.6 Calculating a Periodic B-spline Curve

Again, consider the control polygon shown in Fig. 3.15. The polygon vertices are

$$B_1 [0 \quad 0], \quad B_2 [3 \quad 9], \quad B_3 [6 \quad 3], \quad B_4 [9 \quad 6]$$

Determine the fourth-order ($k = 4$) periodic B-spline curve defined by this polygon. For $k = 4$

$$[0 \quad 1 \quad 2 \quad 3 \quad 4 \quad 5 \quad 6 \quad 7]$$

with parameter range $3 \leq t < 4$ is the knot vector for the periodic basis functions. The first-order basis functions for this parameter range are (see Eq. (3.2a))

$$3 \leq t < 4 \quad N_{4,1}(t) = 1; \quad N_{i,1}(t) = 0, \quad i \neq 4$$

From Eq. (3.2b), the higher-order basis functions are then

$$N_{3,2}(t) = (4 - t) \quad N_{4,2}(t) = (t - 3) \quad N_{i,2}(t) = 0, \quad i \neq 3, 4$$

$$N_{2,3}(t) = \frac{(4 - t)^2}{2} \quad N_{3,3}(t) = \frac{(t - 2)(4 - t)}{2} + \frac{(5 - t)(t - 3)}{2}$$

$$N_{4,3}(t) = \frac{(t - 3)^2}{2} \quad N_{i,3}(t) = 0, \quad i \neq 2, 3, 4$$

$$N_{1,4}(t) = \frac{(4 - t)^3}{6}$$

$$N_{2,4}(t) = \frac{(t - 1)(4 - t)^2}{6} + \frac{(5 - t)(4 - t)(t - 2)}{6} + \frac{(5 - t)^2(t - 3)}{6}$$

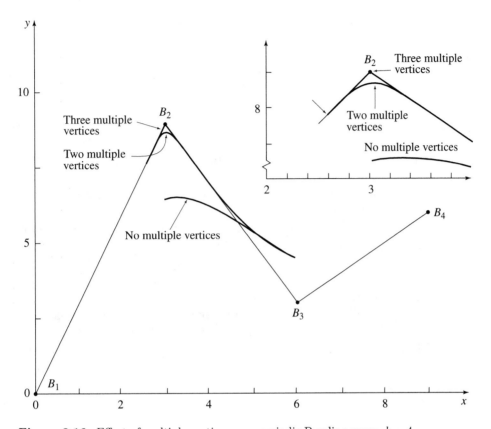

Figure 3.16 Effect of multiple vertices on a periodic B-spline curve, $k = 4$.

$$N_{3,4}(t) = \frac{(t-2)^2(4-t)}{6} + \frac{(t-2)(t-3)(5-t)}{6} + \frac{(6-t)(t-3)^2}{6}$$

$$N_{4,4}(t) = \frac{(t-3)^3}{6}$$

At $t = 3$

$$N_{1,4}(3) = \frac{(4-3)^2}{6} = \text{\textonehalf}_6$$

$$N_{2,4}(3) = \frac{(3-1)(4-3)^2}{6} + \frac{(5-3)(4-3)(3-2)}{6} + \frac{(5-3)^2(3-3)}{6} = \text{\texttwosuperior}_3$$

$$N_{3,4}(3) = \frac{(3-2)^2(4-3)}{6} + \frac{(3-2)(3-3)(5-3)}{6} + \frac{(6-3)(3-3)^2}{6} = \text{\textonehalf}_6$$

$$N_{4,4}(3) = \frac{(3-3)^3}{6} = 0$$

The point on the B-spline curve at $t = 3$ is thus

$$P(3) = \frac{1}{6} B_1 + \frac{2}{3} B_2 + \frac{1}{6} B_3 + 0 B_4$$

$$= \frac{1}{6} \begin{bmatrix} 0 & 0 \end{bmatrix} + \frac{2}{3} \begin{bmatrix} 3 & 9 \end{bmatrix} + \frac{1}{6} \begin{bmatrix} 6 & 3 \end{bmatrix} + 0 \begin{bmatrix} 9 & 6 \end{bmatrix}$$

$$= \begin{bmatrix} 3 & 13/2 \end{bmatrix}$$

The complete curve is shown in Fig. 3.15.

Periodic B-spline curves are also useful for generating closed curves. Figure 3.17a shows a fourth-order ($k = 4$) periodic cubic B-spline curve generated using the closed polygon $B_1 B_2 B_3 B_4 B_5 B_6 B_7 B_8 B_1$. Here, the first vertex is repeated as the last vertex to close the polygon. Because of the restricted parameter range used with periodic basis functions, the resulting B-spline curve is not closed. Here, the periodic uniform knot vector is $\begin{bmatrix} 0 & 1 & 2 & \cdots & 10 & 11 & 12 \end{bmatrix}$, with a usable parameter range of $3 \le t \le 9$.

By repeating a total of $k - 2$ polygon vertices at the beginning and/or end of the closed control polygon, a closed periodic B-spline curve is obtained. (An alternate technique using a matrix formulation is discussed in Sec. 3.8.) Figure 3.17b shows the results. $B_8 B_1 B_2 B_3 B_4 B_5 B_6 B_7 B_8 B_1 B_2$, with the periodic uniform knot vector $\begin{bmatrix} 0 & 1 & 2 & \cdots & 12 & 13 & 14 \end{bmatrix}$ with the usable parameter range of $3 \le t \le 11$, is the control polygon for Fig. 3.17b.

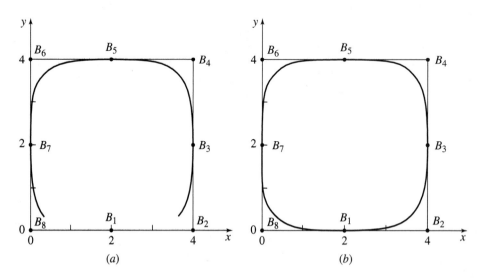

(a)   (b)

Figure 3.17   Closed periodic B-spline curve. (a) $B_1 B_2 B_3 B_4 B_5 B_6 B_7 B_8 B_1$ as the control polygon; (b) $B_8 B_1 B_2 B_3 B_4 B_5 B_6 B_7 B_8 B_1 B_2$ as the control polygon.

The control polygons $B_1B_2B_3B_4B_5B_6B_7B_8B_1B_2B_3$ or $B_7B_8B_1B_2B_3B_4B_5$ $B_6B_7B_8B_1$ yield the same results.

Figure 3.18 shows the effect of moving the single polygon vertex B_4. Again, the effect is confined to those curve segments corresponding to $\pm k/2$ polygon spans on either side of the displaced point.

Figure 3.19 shows the effect of multiple vertices at B_4. The details near B_4 are shown in the inset. Again, notice that the excellent local control properties of B-spline curves confine the effect to those curve segments corresponding to $\pm k/2$ polygon spans on either side of the multiple vertex location.

3.8 Matrix Formulation of B-spline Curves

The equations for B-spline curves can be expressed in a matrix form similar to those for Bézier curves (see Eq. (2.6)). The matrix form is particularly simple for periodic B-spline curves.

Recall that periodic B-spline basis functions are all translates of each other (see Fig. 3.5) and that the 'spread' or influence of a given basis function is limited to k intervals. Thus, for integer knot values all periodic basis functions on the unit interval $0 \le t^* < 1$ have the same form, $N^*_{i,k}(t^*)$.

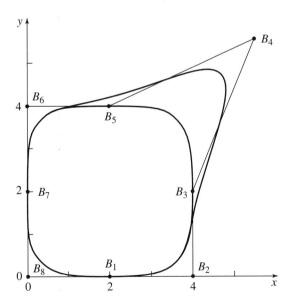

Figure 3.18 Effect of moving a single polygon vertex on a closed periodic B-spline curve.

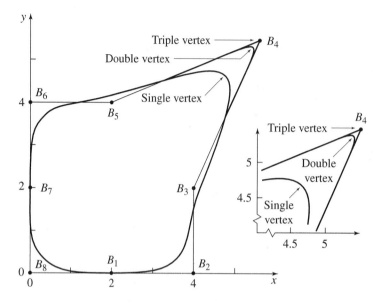

Figure 3.19   Effect of multiple vertices on a closed periodic B-spline curve.

Hence, it is sometimes convenient to reparameterize the basis functions to this interval. A point on a parametric B-spline curve on the reparameterized unit interval is given by

$$P_j(t^*) = \sum_{i=0}^{k-1} N^*_{i+1,k}(t^*)B_{j+i} \qquad 1 \le j \le n-k+1, \ 0 \le t^* < 1 \qquad (3.5)$$

where j counts the curve segments. Again, n is one less than the number of control polygon vertices. Notice that when written out Eq. (3.5) has only k terms, i.e.

$$P_j(t^*) = N^*_{1,k}B_j + N^*_{2,k}B_{j+1} + \cdots + N^*_{k,k}B_{j+k-1}$$

For $k = 3$, the reparameterized basis functions on the interval $0 \le t^* < 1$ are

$$N^*_{1,3}(t^*) = \frac{(1-t^*)^2}{2}$$

$$N^*_{2,3}(t^*) = \frac{-2t^{*2} + 2t^* + 1}{2}$$

$$N^*_{3,3}(t^*) = \frac{t^{*2}}{2}$$

Equation (3.5) then becomes

$$2P_j(t^*) = (1 - 2t^* + t^{*2})B_j + (-2t^{*2} + 2t^* + 1)B_{j+1} + t^{*2}B_{j+2}$$
$$= t^{*2}(B_j - 2B_{j+1} + B_{j+2}) + t^*(-2B_j + 2B_{j+1} + 0B_{j+2})$$
$$+ (B_j + B_{j+1} + 0B_{j+2})$$

Rewriting in matrix form yields

$$P_j(t^*) = [T^*][N^*][G]$$

$$= \tfrac{1}{2} [t^{*2} \quad t^* \quad 1] \begin{bmatrix} 1 & -2 & 1 \\ -2 & 2 & 0 \\ 1 & 1 & 0 \end{bmatrix} \begin{bmatrix} B_j \\ B_{j+1} \\ B_{j+2} \end{bmatrix} \qquad (3.6)$$

Similarly, for $k = 4$ the reparameterized basis functions on the interval $0 \le t^* < 1$ are

$$N_{1,4}^*(t^*) = \frac{-t^{*3} + 3t^{*2} - 3t^* + 1}{6}$$

$$N_{2,4}^*(t^*) = \frac{3t^{*3} + 6t^{*2} + 4}{6}$$

$$N_{3,4}^*(t^*) = \frac{-t^{*3} + 3t^{*2} + 3t^* + 1}{6}$$

$$N_{4,4}^*(t^*) = \frac{t^{*3}}{6}$$

For $k = 4$, the matrix form is

$$P_j(t^*) = [T^*][N^*][G]$$

$$= \frac{1}{6} [t^{*3} \quad t^{*2} \quad t^* \quad 1] \begin{bmatrix} -1 & 3 & -3 & 1 \\ 3 & -6 & 3 & 0 \\ -3 & 0 & 3 & 0 \\ 1 & 4 & 1 & 0 \end{bmatrix} \begin{bmatrix} B_j \\ B_{j+1} \\ B_{j+2} \\ B_{j+3} \end{bmatrix} \qquad (3.7)$$

Notice that Eqs. (3.6) and (3.7) are of the form of a blending function times a geometry matrix (see Eq. 2.6), i.e.

$$P_j(t^*) = [T^*][N^*][G] = [F][G] \qquad 1 \le j \le n - k + 1, \qquad 0 \le t^* < 1$$
$$(3.8)$$

where here

$$[T^*] = [t^{*k-1} \quad t^{*k-2} \quad \cdots \quad t^* \quad 1] \qquad 0 \le t^* < 1$$

$[G]^T = [B_j \; \cdots \; B_{j+k-1}]$ contains the geometry represented by the control vertices, and $[F]$ is composed of appropriate B-spline basis functions.

For periodic B-spline curves, Cohen and Riesenfeld [Cohe82] show that the generalized form of $[N]$ is

$$[N^*] = [N^*_{i+1,j+1}] \tag{3.9}$$

where

$$N^*_{i+1,j+1} = \frac{1}{(k-1)!} \binom{k-1}{i} \sum_{\ell=j}^{k-1} (k - (\ell+1))^i (-1)^{\ell-j} \binom{k}{\ell - j}$$

$$0 \le i, \; j \le k - 1$$

Recall that for closed periodic B-spline curves it is necessary to repeat some of the control polygon vertices to close the curve. A matrix formulation makes this more convenient. A closed periodic B-spline curve is given by

$$P_{j+1}(t^*) = \sum_{i=0}^{k-1} N^*_{i+1,k}(t^*) B_{((j+i) \bmod (n+1))+1} \qquad 0 \le j \le n \tag{3.10}$$

Or in matrix form

$$P_{j+1}(t^*) = [T^*][N^*] \begin{bmatrix} B_{(j \bmod (n+1))+1} \\ B_{((j+1) \bmod (n+1))+1} \\ \vdots \\ B_{((j+1+n-k) \bmod (n+1))+1} \end{bmatrix} \tag{3.11}$$

where $[T^*]$ and $[N^*]$ are as given in Eq. (3.8) and mod is the modulo or remainder function; e.g., 3 mod 2 = 1.

While open B-spline curves can also be represented in matrix form, the existence of multiple knot values at the ends precludes obtaining as compact a result as for periodic B-splines. In general, the matrix representation of an open B-spline curve with integer knot values is given by

$$P(t) = [F][G] = [T][N][G] \tag{3.12}$$

where

$$[G]^T = [B_1 \quad \cdots \quad B_{n+1}]$$

and where the elements of $[F]$ or $[N]$ are obtained using the Cox–de Boor algorithm (see Eqs. (3.2)) for each nonzero interval in the knot vector $[X]$.

For low-order B-spline curves described by control polygons with large numbers of vertices, most of the terms in $[F]$ are zero. Significant computational efficiencies result by taking advantage of this fact.[†] Cohen and Riesenfeld (see [Cohe82]) give a generalized formulation for $[N^*]$ on the reparameterized interval $0 \le t^* < 1$. However, because of the multiplicity of knot values at the ends of the knot vector, the first and last $(k-1)[N^*]$ matrices are special cases. The matrices for the interior intervals are given by Eq. (3.9).

An example illustrates the matrix method.

Example 3.7 Calculating a Closed Periodic B-spline Curve

Determine the fourth-order $(k = 4)$ closed B-spline curve defined by the polygon shown in Fig. 3.17b. Use the matrix formulation. The polygon vertices are

$$B_1 [2 \quad 0], \; B_2 [4 \quad 0], \; B_3 [4 \quad 2], \; B_4 [4 \quad 4], \; B_5 [2 \quad 4],$$

$$B_6 [0 \quad 4], \; B_7 [0 \quad 2], \; B_8 [0 \quad 0], \; B_9 [2 \quad 0]$$

Thus, $n = 8$.

For each unit interval $0 \le t^* < 1$, Eqs. (3.7) and (3.11) yield

$$P_{j+1}(t^*) = \tfrac{1}{6} [t^{*3} \quad t^{*2} \quad t^* \quad 1] \begin{bmatrix} -1 & 3 & -3 & 1 \\ 3 & -6 & 3 & 0 \\ -3 & 0 & 3 & 0 \\ 1 & 4 & 1 & 0 \end{bmatrix} \begin{bmatrix} B_{(j \bmod 8)+1} \\ B_{((j+1) \bmod 8)+1} \\ B_{((j+2) \bmod 8)+1} \\ B_{((j+3) \bmod 8)+1} \end{bmatrix}$$

At $t^* = \tfrac{1}{2}$ on the first segment $(j = 0)$ of the curve, the result is

$$P_1(\tfrac{1}{2}) = \tfrac{1}{6} [\tfrac{1}{8} \quad \tfrac{1}{4} \quad \tfrac{1}{2} \quad 1] \begin{bmatrix} -1 & 3 & -3 & 1 \\ 3 & -6 & 3 & 0 \\ -3 & 0 & 3 & 0 \\ 1 & 4 & 1 & 0 \end{bmatrix} \begin{bmatrix} B_1 \\ B_2 \\ B_3 \\ B_4 \end{bmatrix}$$

$$= \tfrac{1}{48} [1 \quad 23 \quad 23 \quad 1] \begin{bmatrix} 2 & 0 \\ 4 & 0 \\ 4 & 2 \\ 4 & 4 \end{bmatrix}$$

$$= \tfrac{1}{48} [190 \quad 50] = [3.958 \quad 1.042]$$

[†]See the algorithm in Appendix G.

At $t^* = 1/2$ on segment eight ($j = 7$), the result is

$$P_8(1/2) = 1/48 \begin{bmatrix} 1 & 23 & 23 & 1 \end{bmatrix} \begin{bmatrix} B_8 \\ B_1 \\ B_2 \\ B_3 \end{bmatrix} = 1/48 \begin{bmatrix} 1 & 23 & 23 & 1 \end{bmatrix} \begin{bmatrix} 0 & 0 \\ 2 & 0 \\ 4 & 0 \\ 4 & 2 \end{bmatrix}$$

$$= 1/48 \begin{bmatrix} 142 & 2 \end{bmatrix} = \begin{bmatrix} 2.958 & 0.0417 \end{bmatrix}$$

Complete results are shown in Fig. 3.17b.

3.9 End Conditions for Periodic B-spline Curves

As previously shown, periodic B-spline curves do not start and end at the first and last vertices of the control polygon. Two questions thus occur. First, where do they start and end and what are the conditions (derivatives) at these points? Second, how can the starting and ending points and conditions at those points be controlled? Barsky [Bars82] studied these conditions for the specific case of cubic ($k = 4$) B-spline curves. The present discussion is somewhat more general.

Start and End Points

In general, a periodic B-spline curve starts at $P_s = P(t = x_k)$ and ends at $P_e = P(t = x_{n+1})$. For integer knot values beginning at zero, $P_s = P(t = k)$ and $P_e = P(t = n)$. Recalling Eqs. (3.5) and (3.9) and that any point on a B-spline curve is affected by only k control vertices, then, for the reparameterized interval $0 \le t^* < 1$, the starting point occurs for $t^* = 0$. Thus

$$P_s = \frac{1}{(k-1)!} (N^*_{k,1} B_1 + N^*_{k,2} B_2 + \cdots + N^*_{k,k} B_k)$$

Noting that $N^*_{k,k} = 0$ for all k yields

$$P_s = \frac{1}{(k-1)!} (N^*_{k,1} B_1 + N^*_{k,2} B_2 + \cdots + N^*_{k,k-1} B_{k-1}) \qquad n \ge k \qquad (3.13)$$

At the end of the reparameterized interval $t^* = 1$. Noting that $\sum_{i=1}^{k} N^*_{i,1} = 0$, the end point is given by

$$P_e = \frac{1}{(k-1)!} \left(\sum_{i=1}^{k} N^*_{i,2} B_{n-k+3} + \sum_{i=1}^{k} N^*_{i,3} B_{n-k+4} + \cdots + \sum_{i=1}^{k} N^*_{i,k} B_{n+1} \right)$$

$$n \ge k \qquad (3.14)$$

For quadratic ($k = 3$) periodic B-spline curves, Eqs. (3.13) and (3.14) yield

$$P_s = \tfrac{1}{2}(B_1 + B_2)$$
$$P_e = \tfrac{1}{2}(B_n + B_{n+1})$$

Thus, quadratic periodic B-spline curves start and end at the midpoint of the first and last spans of the control polygon, respectively.

For cubic ($k = 4$) periodic B-spline curves, the start and end points are

$$P_s = \tfrac{1}{6}(B_1 + 4B_2 + B_3)$$
$$P_e = \tfrac{1}{6}(B_{n-1} + 4B_n + B_{n+1})$$

Start and End Point Derivatives

Recalling Eq. (3.8), the first derivative at the starting point is

$$P'_s = [T^{*'}]_{t^*=0} [N^*][G]$$
$$= \frac{1}{(k-1)!}(N^*_{k-1,1}B_1 + N^*_{k-1,2}B_2 + \cdots + N^*_{k-1,k-1}B_{k-1}) \qquad (3.15)$$

because $N^*_{k-1,k} = 0$ for all k. The first derivative at the end point is

$$P'_e = [T^{*'}]_{t^*=1} [N^*][G] = \frac{1}{(k-1)!}\left(\sum_{i=1}^{k-1}(k-i)N^*_{i,2}B_{n-k+3}\right.$$
$$\left. + \sum_{i=1}^{k-1}(k-i)N^*_{i,3}B_{n-k+4} + \cdots + \sum_{i=1}^{k-1}(k-i)N^*_{i,k}B_{n+1}\right) \qquad (3.16)$$

where $[T^{*'}] = [(k-1)t^{*(k-2)} \quad (k-2)t^{*(k-3)} \quad \cdots \quad 1 \quad 0]$ is the derivative of the parameter vector.

For quadratic ($k = 3$) periodic B-spline curves, these results reduce to

$$P'_s = \tfrac{1}{2}(-2B_1 + 2B_2) = B_2 - B_1$$
$$P'_e = \tfrac{1}{2}(-2B_n + 2B_{n+1}) = B_{n+1} - B_n$$

the tangent vectors (slopes) of the first and last polygon spans.

For cubic ($k = 4$) curves, the results are

$$P'_s = \tfrac{1}{6}(-3B_1 + 3B_3) = \tfrac{1}{2}(B_3 - B_1)$$
$$P'_e = \tfrac{1}{6}(-3B_{n-2} + 3B_{n+1}) = \tfrac{1}{2}(B_{n+1} - B_{n-1})$$

Here, the tangent vectors (slopes) are given by the tangent vectors of the lines from the first to the third and the third from last to the last control polygon vertices.

The second derivatives at the start and end points are

$$P''_s = \left[T^{*''} \right]_{t^*=0} \left[N^* \right] \left[G \right]$$

$$= \frac{2}{(k-1)!} (N^*_{k-2,1} B_1 + N^*_{k-2,2} B_2 + \cdots + N^*_{k-2,k-1} B_{k-1}) \quad (3.17)$$

and $$P''_e = \left[T^{*''} \right]_{t^*=1} \left[N^* \right] \left[G \right]$$

$$= \frac{1}{(k-1)!} \left(\sum_{i=1}^{k-2} (k-i)(k-i-1) N^*_{i,2} B_{n-k+3} \right.$$

$$+ \sum_{i=1}^{k-2} (k-i)(k-i-1) N^*_{i,3} B_{n-k+4}$$

$$\left. + \cdots + \sum_{i=1}^{k-2} (k-i)(k-i-1) N^*_{i,k} B_{n+1} \right) \quad (3.18)$$

where $\left[T^{*''} \right] = [(k-1)t^{*(k-2)} \quad (k-2)t^{*(k-3)} \quad \cdots \quad 1 \quad 0]$ is the second derivative of the parameter vector.

For cubic $(k = 4)$ curves, Eqs. (3.17) and (3.18) yield

$$P''_s = \tfrac{1}{6}(6B_1 - 12B_2 + 6B_3) = B_1 - 2B_2 + B_3$$

$$P''_e = \tfrac{1}{6}(6B_{n-1} - 12B_n + 6B_{n+1}) = B_{n-1} - 2B_n + B_{n+1}$$

Controlling Start and End Points

Techniques for controlling the position of the start and end points and the conditions at those points fall into two categories: multiple vertices and pseudovertices.

Multiple Coincident Vertices

Defining multiple coincident vertices at an end of a periodic B-spline curve pulls the starting or ending point of the curve closer to the vertex. When $k-1$ multiple coincident vertices are defined, then the end point of the curve is coincident with the vertices; and the tangent vector (slope) of the curve is given by the direction of the adjacent nonzero length polygon span.

For example, for $k = 3$ with double vertices at the ends, i.e., with $B_1 = B_2$ and $B_n = B_{n+1}$, Eqs. (3.13) and (3.14) yield

$$P_s = \frac{1}{2}(B_1 + B_2) = \frac{1}{2}(2B_1) = B_1$$
$$P_e = \frac{1}{2}(B_n + B_{n+1}) = \frac{1}{2}(2B_{n+1}) = B_{n+1}$$

For $k = 4$ with double vertices at the ends, Eqs. (3.13) and (3.14) yield

$$P_s = \frac{1}{6}(5B_1 + B_3)$$
$$P_e = \frac{1}{6}(B_{n-1} + 5B_{n+1})$$

Thus, the starting point is one-sixth of the distance along the span from B_1 to B_3, and the end point is five-sixths of the distance along the span from B_{n-1} to B_{n+1}.

With triple vertices at the ends, i.e., with $B_1 = B_2 = B_3$ and $B_{n-1} = B_n = B_{n+1}$, the results for $k = 4$ are

$$P_s = \frac{1}{6}(B_1 + 4B_1 + B_1) = B_1$$
$$P_e = \frac{1}{6}(B_{n+1} + 4B_{n+1} + B_{n+1}) = B_{n+1}$$

The curve starts and ends at the first and last polygon vertices. Figure 3.20 shows the effect of multiple coincident vertices at the beginning and end of the control polygon.

With triple vertices at the ends, the first and last B-spline curve segments for $k = 4$ are given by (see Eq. (3.7))

$$P_1(t^*) = B_1 + \frac{t^{*3}}{6}[B_4 - B_1] = B_3 + \frac{t^{*3}}{6}[B_4 - B_3] \qquad 0 \le t^* < 1$$

and
$$P_n(t^*) = B_{n+1} + \frac{(1 - t^{*3})}{6}(B_n - B_{n+1})$$

Inspection shows that the first and last segments are linear. The first curve segment is coincident with and extends one-sixth of the distance along the span from $B_1 = B_2 = B_3$ to B_4. The last segment is coincident with and extends from five-sixths of the distance along the span from B_{n-2} to $B_{n-1} = B_n = B_{n+1}$.

Although this short straight curve segment can be made arbitrarily small, it can cause difficulties in certain design applications. Open B-spline

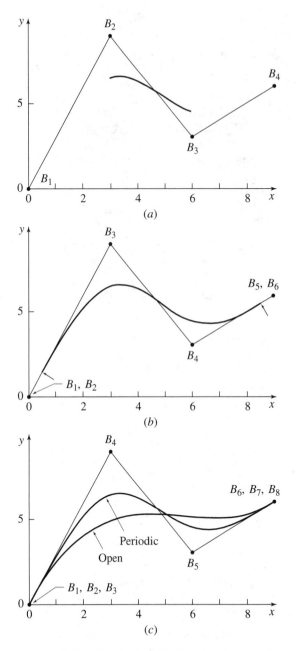

Figure 3.20 Effect of multiple coincident vertices at the ends of the control polygon ($k = 4$). (a) No multiple vertices; (b) two multiple vertices; (c) three multiple vertices and the corresponding open B-spline curves.

curves do not exhibit this characteristic and thus may be more suitable for these design applications.

Pseudovertices

Instead of multiple vertices at the ends of a periodic B-spline curve, pseudovertices can be constructed to control both the location of, and conditions at, the start and end points. Generally, these pseudovertices are neither displayed nor can a user manipulate them. Here, as shown in Fig. 3.21, B_0 and B_{n+2} are used to designate the pseudovertices at the start and end of a B-spline curve. With this notation, Eqs. (3.13) and (3.14) become

$$P_s = \frac{1}{(k-1)!} \left(N_{k,1}^* B_0 + N_{k,2}^* B_1 + \cdots + N_{k,k-1}^* B_{k-2} \right) \qquad n \geq k \qquad (3.19)$$

and

$$P_e = \frac{1}{(k-1)} ! \left(\sum_{i=1}^{k} N_{i,2}^* B_{n-k+4} + \sum_{i=1}^{k} N_{i,3}^* B_{n-k+5} + \cdots + \sum_{i=1}^{k} N_{i,k}^* B_{n+2} \right)$$
$$n \geq k \qquad (3.20)$$

With $P_s = B_1$ and $P_e = B_{n+1}$, these equations yield

$$B_0 = \left((k-1)! - N_{k,2}^* \right) B_1 - \left(N_{k,3}^* B_2 + \cdots + N_{k,k-1}^* B_{k-2} \right)$$
$$n \geq k \qquad (3.21)$$

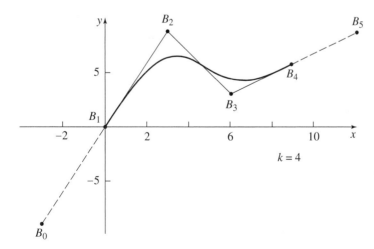

Figure 3.21 Pseudovertices control start and end points of periodic B-spline curves.

and

$$B_{n+2} = \left((k-1)! - \sum_{i=1}^{k} N_{i,k-1}^* \right) B_{n+1}$$

$$- \left(\sum_{i=1}^{k} N_{i,2}^* B_{n-k+4} + \cdots + \sum_{i=1}^{k} N_{i,k-2}^* B_n \right) \qquad n \geq k \quad (3.22)$$

where the fact that $N_{k,1}^* = 1$ and $\sum_{i=1}^{k} N_{i,k}^* = 1$ is used.

For $k = 3$, Eqs. (3.21) and (3.22) yield $B_0 = B_1$ and $B_{n+2} = B_{n+1}$, i.e., duplicate vertices at the ends!

For $k = 4$, the results are

$$B_0 = (6-4)B_1 - B_2 = 2B_1 - B_2$$

and
$$B_{n+2} = (6-4)B_{n+1} - B_n = 2B_{n+1} - B_n$$

Figure 3.21 illustrates these results.

The first and second derivatives at the ends of the curve are given by Eqs. (3.15) and (3.16), appropriately modified to account for the pseudovertices. As an example, after using the above results for B_0, Eqs. (3.15) and (3.16) for $k = 4$ yield

$$P'_s = {}^{1}\!/_{2}(B_2 - B_0) = {}^{1}\!/_{2}\left(B_2 - (2B_1 - B_2) \right) = B_2 - B_1$$

and $P'_e = {}^{1}\!/_{2}(B_{n+2} - B_n) = {}^{1}\!/_{2}(2B_{n+1} - B_n - B_n) = B_{n+1} - B_n$

Thus, the curve is tangent to the first and last control polygon spans.

Similarly, after using the above results for B_0 and B_{n+2}, for $k = 4$ Eqs. (3.17) and (3.18) yield

$$P''_s = B_0 - 2B_1 + B_2 = 2B_1 - B_2 - 2B_1 + B_2 = 0$$

$$P''_e = B_n + 2B_{n+1} + B_{n+2} = B_n - 2B_{n+1} + 2B_{n+1} - B_n = 0$$

Thus, the 'curvature' at the ends is zero.

Rewriting Eqs. (3.15) and (3.16) allows the determination of pseudovertices that yield specified tangent vectors at the ends of the curve. Specifically, Eq. (3.15) yields

$$B_0 = \frac{1}{N_{k-1,1}^*}\left((k-1)! \, P'_s - (N_{k-1,2}^* B_1 + \cdots + N_{k-1,k-1}^* B_{k-2}) \right)$$

$$n \geq k \qquad (3.23)$$

and Eq. (3.16) yields

$$B_{n+2} = \frac{1}{\displaystyle\sum_{i=1}^{k-1}(k-1)N_{i,k}^*} \left\{ (k-1)! \, P'_e \right.$$

$$\left. - \left(\sum_{i=1}^{k-1}(k-1)N_{i,2}^* B_{n-k+4} + \cdots + \sum_{i=1}^{k-1}(k-1)N_{i,k-1}^* B_{n+1} \right) \right\}$$

$$n \geq k \qquad (3.24)$$

For $k = 4$, Eqs. (3.23) and (3.24) reduce to

$$B_0 = B_2 - 2P'_s$$
$$B_{n+2} = 2P'_e + B_n$$

Typical results are shown in Fig. 3.22. The start and end points for the resulting curve are obtained by substituting these values into Eqs. (3.19) and (3.20). Notice from Fig. 3.22 that the start and end points for the curve with specified tangent vectors at the ends, defined by $B_0B_1B_2B_3B_4B_5$, are quite different from those for the curve defined only by $B_1B_2B_3B_4$ (marked by ×s).

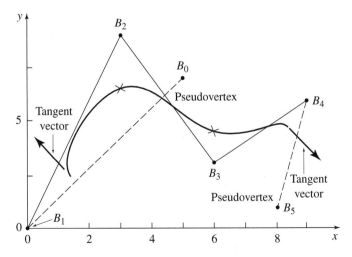

Figure 3.22 Tangent vector control for periodic B-spline curves, $k = 4$.

The second derivative, or approximate curvature at the start and end points of the curve, is controlled by rewriting Eqs. (3.17) and (3.18) to yield

$$B_0 = \frac{1}{N^*_{k-2,1}} \left\{ \frac{(k-1)!}{2} P''_s - (N^*_{k-2,2}B_1 + \cdots + N^*_{k-2,k-1}B_{k-2}) \right\}$$

$$n \geq k \qquad (3.25)$$

and

$$B_{n+2} = \frac{1}{\displaystyle\sum_{i=1}^{k-1}(k-1)(k-i-1)N^*_{i,k}} \left\{ (k-1)! \, P''_e \right.$$

$$- \left(\sum_{i=1}^{k-2}(k-1)(k-i-1)N^*_{i,2}B_{n-k+4} \right.$$

$$\left. \left. + \cdots + \sum_{i=1}^{k-2}(k-1)(k-i-1)N^*_{i,k-1}B_{n+1} \right) \right\} \qquad n \geq k \quad (3.26)$$

For $k = 4$, Eqs. (3.25) and (3.26) yield

$$B_0 = P''_s + 2B_1 - B_2$$

$$B_{n+2} = P''_e + 2B_{n+1} - B_n$$

Again, the start and end points are obtained by substituting these values into Eqs. (3.19) and (3.20). Similarly, the tangent vectors are obtained by using Eqs. (3.15) and (3.16) rewritten in terms of B_0 to B_{n+2}.

3.10 B-spline Curve Derivatives

The derivatives of a B-spline curve at any point on the curve are obtained by formal differentiation. Specifically, recalling Eq. (3.1), i.e.

$$P(t) = \sum_{i=1}^{n+1} B_i N_{i,k}(t) \qquad (3.1)$$

the first derivative is

$$P'(t) = \sum_{i=1}^{n+1} B_i N'_{i,k}(t) \qquad (3.27)$$

while the second derivative is

$$P''(t) = \sum_{i=1}^{n+1} B_i N''_{i,k}(t) \qquad (3.28)$$

Here, the primes denote differentiation with respect to the parameter t.

The derivatives of the basis functions are also obtained by formal differentiation. Differentiating Eq. (3.2b) once yields

$$N'_{i,k}(t) = \frac{N_{i,k-1}(t) + (t - x_i)N'_{i,k-1}(t)}{x_{i+k-1} - x_i}$$
$$+ \frac{(x_{i+k} - t)N'_{i+1,k-1}(t) - N_{i+1,k-1}(t)}{x_{i+k} - x_{i+1}} \qquad (3.29)$$

Note from Eq. (3.2a) that $N'_{i,1}(t) = 0$ for all t. Consequently, for $k = 2$ Eq. (3.29) reduces to

$$N'_{i,2}(t) = \frac{N_{i,1}(t)}{x_{i+1} - x_i} - \frac{N_{i+1,1}(t)}{x_{i+2} - x_{i+1}} \qquad (3.30)$$

Differentiating Eq. (3.29) yields the second derivative of the basis function

$$N''_{i,k}(t) = \frac{2N'_{i,k-1}(t) + (t - x_i)N''_{i,k-1}(t)}{x_{i+k-1} - x_i}$$
$$+ \frac{(x_{i+k} - t)N''_{i+1,k-1}(t) - 2N'_{i+1,k-1}(t)}{x_{i+k} - x_{i+1}} \qquad (3.31)$$

Here, note that both $N''_{i,1}(t) = 0$ and $N''_{i,2}(t) = 0$ for all t. Consequently, for $k = 3$ Eq. (3.29) reduces to

$$N''_{i,3}(t) = 2\left(\frac{N'_{i,2}(t)}{x_{i+2} - x_i} - \frac{N'_{i+1,2}(t)}{x_{i+3} - x_{i+1}} \right) \qquad (3.32)$$

Figure 3.23 shows several B-spline basis functions and their first and second derivatives for $k = 4$. Notice that for $k = 4$ each B-spline basis function is described by piecewise cubic equations—the first derivatives by piecewise parabolic equations and the second derivatives by piecewise linear equations. The third derivative, if shown, would be described by discontinuous constant values.

An example is instructive.

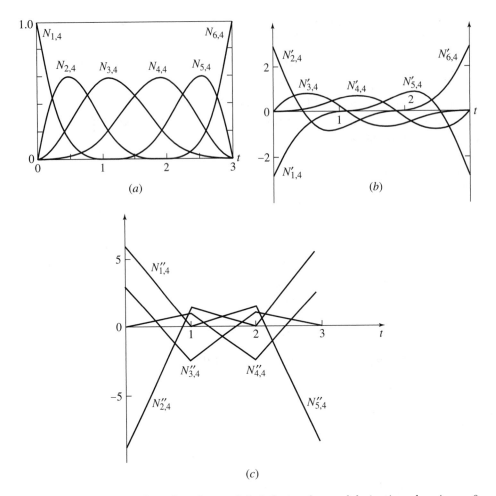

Figure 3.23　B-spline basis functions and their first and second derivatives, $k = 4$, $n = 6$. (a) Basis functions; (b) first derivative; (c) second derivative.

Example 3.8　Calculating B-spline Curve Derivatives

Consider the control polygon previously used in Ex. 3.4 to calculate the open B-spline curve, i.e.

$$B_1 \begin{bmatrix} 1 & 1 \end{bmatrix}, \ B_2 \begin{bmatrix} 2 & 3 \end{bmatrix}, \ B_3 \begin{bmatrix} 4 & 3 \end{bmatrix}, \ B_4 \begin{bmatrix} 3 & 1 \end{bmatrix}$$

Determine the first derivative of the second-order curve ($k = 2$).

For $k = 2$, the open knot vector is

$$\begin{bmatrix} 0 & 0 & 1 & 2 & 3 & 3 \end{bmatrix}$$

where $x_1 = 0$, $x_2 = 0, \cdots, x_6 = 3$. The parameter range is $0 \leq t \leq 3$.

From Eq. (3.27), the first derivative of the curve for $n = 3$, $k = 2$ is

$$P'(t) = B_1 N'_{1,2}(t) + B_2 N'_{2,2}(t) + B_3 N'_{3,2}(t) + B_4 N'_{4,2}(t)$$

From Eq. (3.30)

$$N'_{i,2}(t) = \frac{N_{i,1}(t)}{x_{i+k-1} - x_i} - \frac{N_{i+1,1}(t)}{x_{i+k} - x_{i+1}}$$

Using results from Ex. 3.4 for $0 \leq t < 1$ yields

$$N_{2,1}(t) = 1; \qquad N_{i,1}(t) = 0, \quad i \neq 2$$

and $\qquad N'_{1,2}(t) = -1; \qquad N'_{2,2}(t) = 1; \qquad N'_{i,2}(t) = 0, \quad i \neq 1, 2$

Thus $\qquad\qquad\qquad\qquad P'(t) = B_2 - B_1$

which is the slope (tangent vector) of the first polygon span, as it should be. For $1 \leq t < 2$

$$N_{3,1}(t) = 1; \quad N_{i,1}(t) = 0 \quad i \neq 3$$

and $\qquad N'_{2,2}(t) = -1; \quad N'_{3,2}(t) = 1; \quad N'_{i,2}(t) = 0 \quad i \neq 2, 3$

which, as expected, yields $P'(t) = B_3 - B_2$, the slope (tangent vector) of the second polygon span.

Finally, for $2 \leq t < 3$

$$N_{4,1}(t) = 1; \quad N_{i,1}(t) = 0 \quad i \neq 4$$

and $\qquad N'_{3,2}(t) = -1; \quad N'_{4,2}(t) = 1; \quad N'_{i,2}(t) = 0 \quad i \neq 3, 4$

which yields $P'(t) = B_4 - B_3$, the slope (tangent vector) of the last polygon span.

At $t = 3$, $N_{i,1}(3) = 0$ for all i. Consequently, formally $P'(3) = 0$. However, again considering the limiting result for $t = 3 - \epsilon$, $\epsilon \to 0$ shows that, practically, $P'(3) = (B_4 - B_3)$.

3.11 B-spline Curve Fitting

The previous sections discussed the generation of a B-spline curve from its control polygon. Here, determining a control polygon that generates a B-spline curve for a set of *known* data points is considered. The problem is shown schematically in Fig. 3.24.

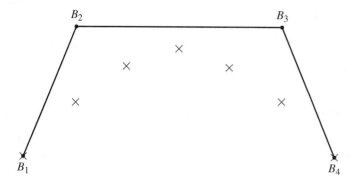

Figure 3.24 Determining a B-spline polygon for a known data set.

If a data point lies on the B-spline curve, then it must satisfy Eq. (3.1). Writing Eq. (3.1) for each of j data points yields

$$D_1(t_1) = N_{1,k}(t_1)B_1 + N_{2,k}(t_1)B_2 + \cdots + N_{n+1,k}(t_1)B_{n+1}$$

$$D_2(t_2) = N_{1,k}(t_2)B_1 + N_{2,k}(t_2)B_2 + \cdots + N_{n+1,k}(t_2)B_{n+1}$$

$$\vdots$$

$$D_j(t_j) = N_{1,k}(t_j)B_1 + N_{2,k}(t_j)B_2 + \cdots + N_{n+1,k}(t_j)B_{n+1}$$

where $2 \leq k \leq n+1 \leq j$. This system of equations is more compactly written in matrix form as

$$[D] = [N][B] \tag{3.33}$$

where
$$[D]^T = [\,D_1(t_1) \quad D_2(t_2) \quad \cdots \quad D_j(t_j)\,]$$

$$[B]^T = [\,B_1 \quad B_2 \quad \cdots \quad B_{n+1}\,]$$

$$[N] = \begin{bmatrix} N_{1,k}(t_1) & \cdots & \cdots & N_{n+1,k}(t_1) \\ \vdots & \ddots & & \vdots \\ \vdots & & \ddots & \vdots \\ N_{1,k}(t_j) & \cdots & \cdots & N_{n+1,k}(t_j) \end{bmatrix}$$

The parameter value t_j for each data point is a measure of the distance of the data point along the B-spline curve. One useful approximation for this parameter value uses the chord length between data points. Specifically, for j data points the parameter value at the ℓth data point is

$$t_1 = 0$$

$$\frac{t_\ell}{t_{\max}} = \frac{\sum_{s=2}^{\ell} |D_s - D_{s-1}|}{\sum_{s=2}^{j} |D_s - D_{s-1}|} \qquad \ell \geq 2$$

The maximum parameter value, $t_{\max}$, is usually taken as the maximum value of the knot vector. Similar schemes are mentioned by de Boor [deBo72] and by Gordon and Riesenfeld [Gord74].

If $2 \leq k \leq n+1 = j$, then the matrix $[N]$ is square and the control polygon is obtained directly by matrix inversion, i.e.

$$[B] = [N]^{-1}[D] \qquad \leq k \leq n+1 = j \qquad (3.34)$$

In this case, the resulting B-spline curve passes through each data point; i.e., a curve fit is obtained. Although the continuity of the resulting curve is everywhere C^{k-2}, it may not be 'smooth', or 'sweet' or 'fair'. The fitted curve may develop unwanted wiggles or undulations.

A fairer or smoother curve is obtained by specifying fewer control polygon points than data points, i.e., $2 \leq k \leq n+1 < j$. Here, $[N]$ is no longer square; the problem is overspecified and can only be solved in a mean sense. Recalling that a matrix times its transpose is always square, the control polygon for a B-spline curve that fairs or smooths the data is given by

$$[D] = [N][B]$$

$$[N]^T[D] = [N]^T[N][B]$$

and

$$[B] = [[N]^T [N]]^{-1}[N]^T[D] \qquad (3.35)$$

Both of these techniques assume that the matrix $[N]$ is known. Provided that the order of the B-spline basis k, the number of control polygon vertices $n+1$, and the parameter values along the curve are known, then the basis functions $N_{i,k}(t_j)$ and hence the matrix $[N]$ can be obtained. Within the restrictions $2 \leq k \leq n+1 \leq j$, the order and number of polygon vertices are arbitrary.

For an open uniform knot vector with multiplicity of the knot values at the ends equal to k, a Bézier curve is obtained when $n = k$. Additional curve-fitting techniques are discussed by Piegl and Tiller [Pieg95]. An example illustrates these techniques.

Example 3.9 B-spline Curve Fit

For the five data points

$$D_1 \begin{bmatrix} 0 & 0 \end{bmatrix},\ D_2 \begin{bmatrix} 3/2 & 2 \end{bmatrix},\ D_3 \begin{bmatrix} 3 & 5/2 \end{bmatrix},\ D_4 \begin{bmatrix} 9/2 & 2 \end{bmatrix},\ D_5 \begin{bmatrix} 6 & 0 \end{bmatrix}$$

determine the third-order $(k = 3)$ control polygon having five and four polygon vertices that generate a B-spline curve 'through' the data points. Use the chord length approximation for the parameter values along the B-spline curve corresponding to the data points.

First, determine the chord lengths

$$D_{21} = |D_2 - D_1| = \sqrt{(x_2 - x_1)^2 + (y_2 - y_1)^2} = \sqrt{(3/2)^2 + (2)^2} = \sqrt{25/4} = 5/2$$

$$D_{32} = |D_3 - D_2| = \sqrt{(3/2)^2 + (1/2)^2} = 1.58$$

$$D_{43} = |D_4 - D_3| = \sqrt{(3/2)^2 + (-1/2)^2} = 1.58$$

$$D_{54} = |D_5 - D_4| = \sqrt{(3/2)^2 + (-2)^2} = 5/2$$

and

$$\sum_{s=2}^{5} (D_s - D_{s-1}) = D_{51} = 8.16$$

Thus

$$t_1 = 0$$

$$\frac{t_2}{t_{max}} = \frac{D_{21}}{D_{51}} = \frac{2.5}{8.16} = 0.31$$

$$\frac{t_3}{t_{max}} = \frac{D_{31}}{D_{51}} = \frac{(2.5 + 1.58)}{8.16} = 0.5$$

$$\frac{t_4}{t_{max}} = \frac{D_{41}}{D_{51}} = \frac{(2.5 + 1.58 + 1.58)}{8.16} = 0.69$$

$$\frac{t_5}{t_{max}} = \frac{D_{51}}{D_{51}} = 1$$

For five polygon vertices, the maximum value of the knot vector for a third-order B-spline curve is $n - k + 2 = 4 - 3 + 2 = 3$. n is one less than the number of polygon vertices. The knot vector with multiplicity k at the ends is

$$\begin{bmatrix} 0 & 0 & 0 & 1 & 2 & 3 & 3 & 3 \end{bmatrix}$$

With these values, Eq. (3.33) becomes

$$[D] = [N][B]$$

$$
\begin{bmatrix}
0 & 0 \\
3/2 & 2 \\
3 & 5/2 \\
9/2 & 2 \\
6 & 0
\end{bmatrix}
=
\begin{bmatrix}
1 & 0 & 0 & 0 & 0 \\
0.007 & 0.571 & 0.422 & 0 & 0 \\
0 & 0.125 & 0.75 & 0.125 & 0 \\
0 & 0 & 0.422 & 0.571 & 0.007 \\
0 & 0 & 0 & 0 & 1
\end{bmatrix}
[B]
$$

Solving for $[B]$ yields

$$[B] = [N]^{-1}[D]$$

$$
=
\begin{bmatrix}
1 & 0 & 0 & 0 & 0 \\
-0.013 & 2.037 & -1.307 & 0.286 & -0.002 \\
0.003 & -0.387 & 1.769 & -0.387 & 0.003 \\
-0.002 & 0.286 & -1.307 & 2.037 & -0.013 \\
0 & 0 & 0 & 0 & 1
\end{bmatrix}
\begin{bmatrix}
0 & 0 \\
3/2 & 2 \\
3 & 5/2 \\
9/2 & 2 \\
6 & 0
\end{bmatrix}
$$

$$
=
\begin{bmatrix}
0 & 0 \\
0.409 & 1.378 \\
3 & 2.874 \\
5.591 & 1.377 \\
6 & 0
\end{bmatrix}
$$

Figure 3.25a shows the original data points, the calculated control polygon and the resulting curve.

For four polygon vertices, the knot vector with multiplicity k at the ends is

$$[0 \; 0 \; 0 \; 1 \; 2 \; 2 \; 2]$$

$[N]$ becomes

$$
[N] =
\begin{bmatrix}
1 & 0 & 0 & 0 \\
0.15 & 0.662 & 0.188 & 0 \\
0 & 0.5 & 0.5 & 0 \\
0 & 0.188 & 0.662 & 0.15 \\
0 & 0 & 0 & 1
\end{bmatrix}
$$

Multiplying by $[N]^T$ and taking the inverse yields

$$
[[N]^T[N]]^{-1} =
\begin{bmatrix}
0.995 & -0.21 & 0.106 & -0.005 \\
-0.21 & 2.684 & -1.855 & 0.106 \\
0.106 & -1.855 & 2.684 & -0.21 \\
-0.005 & 0.106 & -0.21 & 0.995
\end{bmatrix}
$$

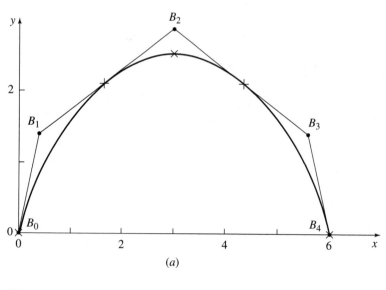

(a)

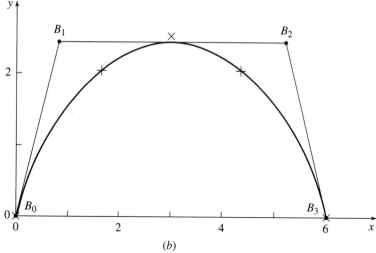

(b)

Figure 3.25 Results for Ex. 3.9. (a) Five polygon vertices; (b) four polygon vertices.

Equation (3.35) then gives

$$[B] = [[N]^T[N]]^{-1}[N]^T[D] = \begin{bmatrix} 0 & 0 \\ 0.788 & 2.414 \\ 5.212 & 2.414 \\ 6 & 0 \end{bmatrix}$$

The original data, the calculated control polygon and the resulting curve are shown in Fig. 3.25b. Notice that except at the ends the curve does not pass through the original data points.

The above fitting technique allows each of the determined control polygon vertices for the B-spline curve to be located anywhere in three space. In some design situations it is more useful to constrain the control polygon vertices to lie at a particular coordinate value, say, $x = $ constant. An example of such a design situation is in fitting B-spline curves to existing ships' lines. Rogers and Fog [Roge89] developed such a technique for both curves and surfaces. Essentially, the technique iterates the parameter value of the fixed coordinate until the value on the B-spline curve at the assumed parameter value, calculated with the control polygon obtained using the above fitting technique, is within some specified amount of the fixed value, i.e., $|x_{\text{fixed}} - x_{\text{calc}}| \leq$ error. The resulting fit is less accurate but more convenient for subsequent modification. Piegl and Tiller [Pieg95] present additional useful discussion of B-spline curve-fitting techniques.

3.12 Degree Elevation

There are two basic techniques for increasing the flexibility of a B-spline curve—degree elevation and knot insertion (subdivision). Degree elevation, or degree raising, is briefly discussed here. One of the advantages of degree elevation is that the B-spline curve remains infinitely differentiable, whereas subdivision reduces the differentiability at the inserted knots (see Sec. 3.14). The loss of differentiability at the new knots depends on the multiplicity of the knot values. For simple knot vectors with no multiple internal knot values, the differentiability reduces to C^{k-2} at the knot values.

Early degree elevation algorithms were developed by Cohen, Lyche and Schumacher [Cohe85] and Prautzsch [Prau84b]. More efficient algorithms are given by Prautzsch and Piper [Prau91] and Piegl and Tiller [Pieg94, 97].

Piegl and Tiller take a software engineering approach. First, the B-spline curve is decomposed into piecewise Bézier curve segments by inserting $k-1$ multiple knot values at each internal knot (see Sec. 3.14). These Bézier curve segments are then degree elevated (see Sec. 2.5). Finally, any unnecessary knot values are removed (see Sec. 3.15). Algorithmically, this reduces to

    for each nonzero knot interval
        extract the Bézier curve segment
        degree elevate the Bézier segment
        remove unnecessary knot values between the Bézier segments

The algorithmic details of this general approach are discussed by Piegl and Tiller (see [Pieg94, 97]).

Cohen, Lyche and Schumacher [Cohe85] present a general solution to B-spline degree elevation. The mathematical details are somewhat complex, and for simplicity they are avoided here. Fundamentally, when elevating the degree of a B-spline curve the new curve must be identical to the original curve, i.e.

$$P(t) = \sum_{i=1}^{n+1} B_i N_{i,k} = \sum_{i=1}^{m+1} B_i^* N_{i,k+1}$$

where B_i^* are the $m+1 > n+1$ control polygon vertices for the new curve. The knot vector for the original NURBS curve in the current notation is

$$[X] = \underbrace{0,\ldots,0}_{k}, \underbrace{a,\ldots,a}_{p_1}, \ldots, \underbrace{b,\ldots,b}_{p_s}, \ldots, \underbrace{n-k+2,\ldots,n-k+2}_{k}$$

where the p_i represent the multiplicity of any internal knot values, and s measures the number of occurrences of multiple internal knot values. For example, in the knot vector $[0\ 0\ 0\ 0\ 1\ 1\ 2\ 2\ 2\ 3\ 3\ 3\ 3]$ $p_1 = 2$, $p_2 = 3$ and $s = 2$. When there are no multiple internal knot values $s = 0$, as in the knot vector $[0\ 0\ 0\ 0\ 1\ 2\ 2\ 2\ 2]$.

Recall from Fig. 3.10 that increasing the order (degree) of a B-spline curve loosens or smooths the curve with respect to the control polygon. Also recall from our discussion that the effect of multiple internal knot values on B-spline basis functions (see Sec. 3.4) is to decrease the continuity at the knot value and to draw the resulting B-spline curve closer to the control polygon. These effects suggest that the new knot vector contain multiple internal knot values.

Because $P(t)$ must have the same continuity at each internal knot, after raising the degree (order) of the curve the new knot vector has multiplicity of $k+1$ at the ends, and $m+1$ for any internal knot values. The new knot vector is now

$$[Y] = \underbrace{0,\ldots,0}_{k+1}, \underbrace{a,\ldots,a}_{p_1+1}, \ldots, \underbrace{b,\ldots,b}_{p_s+1}, \ldots, \underbrace{n-k+2,\ldots,n-k+2}_{k+1}$$

The number of new polygon vertices, B_i^*, is $\hat{n} = n+s+k+1$. As an example, consider the open knot vector $[0\ 0\ 1\ 2\ 3\ 3]$ for $k = 2, n+1 = 4$, with $s = 0$. The new knot vector for the third-order, $k = 3$, NURBS curve is

$$[0\ 0\ 0\ 1\ 1\ 2\ 2\ 3\ 3\ 3]$$

and the number of new control polygon vertices, B_i^*, is $(\hat{n}+1) = (n+1) + s + k + 1 = (3+1) + 0 + 2 + 1 = 7$.

Algorithms

Two specialized algorithms due to Cohen, Lyche and Schumacher [Cohe85] for low-order (degree) B-splines are given here. Each algorithm increases the order by one.

The first algorithm increases a second-order (degree one) B-spline curve to a third-order (degree two) B-spline curve.

raise23(b(),x(),npts; bstar(),mpts)
```
   mpts = 1
   if x(1) < x(2) then
      bstar(1,1) = b(1,1)/2
      bstar(1,2) = b(1,2)/2
      bstar(1,3) = b(1,3)/2
      mpts = mpts + 1
   end if
   bstar(mpts,1) = b(1,1)
   bstar(mpts,2) = b(1,2)
   bstar(mpts,3) = b(1,3)
   for i = 2 to npts
      if x(i) < x(i+1) then
         mpts = mpts + 1
         bstar(mpts,1) = (b(i,1) + b(i−1,1))/2
         bstar(mpts,2) = (b(i,2) + b(i−1,2))/2
         bstar(mpts,3) = (b(i,3) + b(i−1,3))/2
      end if
      mpts = mpts + 1
      bstar(mpts,1) = b(i,1)
      bstar(mpts,2) = b(i,2)
      bstar(mpts,3) = b(i,3)
   next i
   if x(npts + 2) > x(npts + 1) then
      mpts = mpts + 1
      bstar(mpts,1) = b(npts,1)/2
      bstar(mpts,2) = b(npts,2)/2
      bstar(mpts,3) = b(npts,3)/2
   end if
   return
```

An example illustrates the algorithm.

Example 3.10 Degree Elevation—Linear to Quadratic

Consider the second-order (first-degree) B-spline curve defined by the open knot vector

$$[X] = [0 \quad 0 \quad 1 \quad 2 \quad 3 \quad 3]$$

and $B_1[1 \quad 1 \quad 1]$, $B_2[2 \quad 2 \quad 1]$, $B_3[3 \quad 2 \quad 1]$, $B_4[4 \quad 1 \quad 1]$

Raise the order of the curve to three (degree two). Find the new control polygon vertices, B^*, and the new knot vector, $[X^*]$.

There are no multiple internal knot values. Hence $s = 0$, and the number of control polygon vertices is

$$\hat{n} + 1 = n + 1 + s + k + 1 = 3 + 1 + 0 + 2 + 1 = 7$$

The new knot vector is

$$[X^*] = [0 \quad 0 \quad 0 \quad 1 \quad 1 \quad 2 \quad 2 \quad 3 \quad 3 \quad 3]$$

Applying algorithm **raise23** shows that seven new control polygon vertices

$$B_1^*[1 \quad 1 \quad 1], \ B_2^*[{}^3\!/_2 \quad {}^3\!/_2 \quad 1], \ B_3^*[2 \quad 2 \quad 1], \ B_4^*[{}^5\!/_2 \quad 2 \quad 1],$$
$$B_5^*[3 \quad 2 \quad 1], \ B_6^*[{}^7\!/_2 \quad {}^3\!/_2 \quad 1], \ B_7^*[4 \quad 1 \quad 1]$$

are required to represent the curve.

The original four control polygon vertices marked by the dots, and the seven new control polygon vertices marked by the +s, are shown in Fig. 3.26. The curve coincides exactly with the polygon, as expected.

The second algorithm raises the degree from cubic to quartic.

raise45(b(), x(), npts, mpts; bstar())
```
    for j = 1 to 3
        bstar(1,j) = b(1,j)
        bstar(2,j) = (b(1,j) + 3*b(2,j))/4
        bstar(mpts,j) = b(npts,j)
        bstar(mpts−1,j) = (b(npts,j)+ 3*b(npts−1,j))/4
    next j
    if npts = 4 then
        bstar(3,1) = (b(2,1)+ b(3,1))/2
        bstar(3,2) = (b(2,2)+ b(3,2))/2
```

```
        bstar(3,3) = (b(2,3)+ b(3,3))/2
   else
      for j = 1 to 3
         bstar(3,j) = (3*b(2,j) + b(3,j))/4
         bstar(mpts−2,j) = (3*b(npts−1,j) + b(npts−2,j))/4
      next j
      if npts = 5 then
         bstar(4,j) = (b(2,j) + 6*b(3,j) + b(4,j))/8
      else
         for j = 1 to 3
            bstar(4,j) = (3*b(2,j) + 19*b(3,j) + 2*b(4,j))/24
            bstar(mpts−3,j) = (3*b(npts−1,j) + 19*b(npts−2,j) + 2*b(npts−3,j))/24
            bstar(5,j) = (b(3,j) + b(4,j))/2
         next j
         if npts > 6 then
            n4 = npts−4
            for i = 3 to n4
               twoi = i + i
               for j = 1 to 3
                  bstar(twoi,j) = (b(i,j) + 10*b(i+1,j) + b(i+2,j))/12
                  bstar(twoi+1,j) = (b(i+1,j) + b(i+2,j))/2
               next j
            next i
         end if
      end if
   end if
return
```

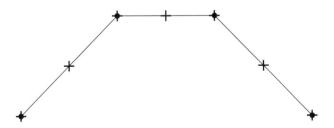

Figure 3.26 Results from raising the degree from one to two. •s indicate original control
polygon; +s indicate degree-elevated control polygon.

Example 3.11 Degree Elevation—Cubic to Quartic

Consider the fourth-order (cubic) B-spline curve defined by the knot vector

$$[X] = [0 \quad 0 \quad 0 \quad 0 \quad 1 \quad 1 \quad 1 \quad 1]$$

and by

$$B_1[1 \quad 1 \quad 1],\ B_2[2 \quad 2 \quad 1],\ B_3[3 \quad 2 \quad 1],\ B_4[4 \quad 1 \quad 1]$$

Find the new control polygon and knot vector.

Because the number of control polygon vertices equals the order of the B-spline basis, the original curve is a Bézier curve. Using algorithm **raise45** yields the new control polygon vertices

$$B_1^*[1 \quad 1 \quad 1],\ B_2^*[7/4 \quad 7/4 \quad 1],\ B_3^*[5/2 \quad 2 \quad 1],$$
$$B_4^*[13/4 \quad 7/4 \quad 1],\ B_5^*[4 \quad 1 \quad 1]$$

The new knot vector is

$$[X^*] = [0 \quad 0 \quad 0 \quad 0 \quad 0 \quad 1 \quad 1 \quad 1 \quad 1 \quad 1]$$

The new curve is also a Bézier curve. Complete results are shown in Fig. 3.27. (See Sec. 2.5 for a discussion of degree elevation for Bézier curves.)

A more complex example further illustrates the algorithm.

Example 3.12 Degree Elevation—Complex Curve, Cubic to Quartic

Consider the fourth-order (cubic) B-spline curve defined by

$$B_1[1 \quad 1 \quad 1],\ B_2[2 \quad 2 \quad 1],\ B_3[3 \quad 2 \quad 1],\ B_4[4 \quad 1 \quad 1],$$

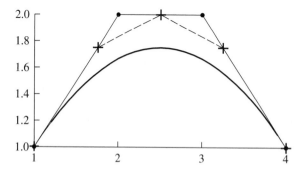

Figure 3.27 Results from raising the degree from three to four. •s indicate original control polygon; +s indicate degree-elevated control polygon.

$$B_5 \begin{bmatrix} 5 & 0 & 1 \end{bmatrix}, \ B_6 \begin{bmatrix} 6 & 0 & 1 \end{bmatrix}, \ B_7 \begin{bmatrix} 7 & 1 & 1 \end{bmatrix}$$

Find the new control polygon and knot vector.

The original knot vector is

$$\begin{bmatrix} 0 & 0 & 0 & 0 & 1 & 2 & 3 & 4 & 4 & 4 & 4 \end{bmatrix}$$

The new knot vector is

$$\begin{bmatrix} 0 & 0 & 0 & 0 & 0 & 1 & 1 & 2 & 2 & 3 & 3 & 4 & 4 & 4 & 4 & 4 \end{bmatrix}$$

Using algorithm **raise45** yields the new control polygon vertices

$$B_1^* \begin{bmatrix} 1 & 1 & 1 \end{bmatrix}, \ B_2^* \begin{bmatrix} 7/4 & 7/4 & 1 \end{bmatrix}, \ B_3^* \begin{bmatrix} 9/4 & 2 & 1 \end{bmatrix}, \ B_4^* \begin{bmatrix} 71/24 & 23/12 & 1 \end{bmatrix},$$

$$B_5^* \begin{bmatrix} 7/2 & 3/2 & 1 \end{bmatrix}, B_6^* \begin{bmatrix} 4 & 1 & 1 \end{bmatrix}, B_7^* \begin{bmatrix} 9/2 & 1/2 & 1 \end{bmatrix}, B_8^* \begin{bmatrix} 121/24 & 5/6 & 1 \end{bmatrix},$$

$$B_9^* \begin{bmatrix} 23/4 & 0 & 1 \end{bmatrix}, B_{10}^* \begin{bmatrix} 25/4 & 1/4 & 1 \end{bmatrix}, B_{11}^* \begin{bmatrix} 7 & 1 & 1 \end{bmatrix}$$

The complete results are shown in Fig. 3.28, where the original polygon is marked by dots and the new polygon by +s.

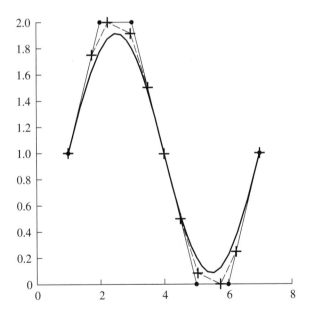

Figure 3.28 Results from raising the degree from three to four for a complex B-spline curve. •s indicate original control polygon; +s indicate degree-elevated control polygon.

3.13 Degree Reduction

In contrast to degree elevation, degree reduction is an approximate process, i.e., the resulting degree-reduced curve is not exactly the same as the original curve. There are a number of mathematical descriptions of degree reduction, especially of Bézier curves, starting with Forrest's seminal paper [Forr72]. (See also [Dann85; Lach88; Watk88; Wein92; Eck93; Fari93].) Not all Bézier or B-spline curves are reducible. For example, a cubic curve containing an inflection point is not reducible to a quartic curve. Hence, degree reduction is considerably less useful than degree elevation.

The degree-reducing problem is formally stated as: For the B-spline curve of order k (degree $k - 1$) described by

$$P(t) = \sum_{i=1}^{n+1} B_i N_{i,k}(t) \qquad (3.36a)$$

on the knot vector

$$[X] = \left[\underbrace{x_1 = x_2, \ldots, = x_k,}_{k} \ldots, \underbrace{x_i, \ldots, = x_{i+p_i-1},}_{p_i} \ldots, \underbrace{x_s, \ldots, = x_{s+p_s-1},}_{p_s} \ldots, \right.$$

$$\left. \underbrace{x_{n+2} = x_{n+3}, \ldots, = x_{n+k+1}}_{k} \right] \qquad (3.36b)$$

find the equivalent B-spline curve of order $k - 1$ (degree $k - 2$)

$$P^*(t) = \sum_{i=1}^{\hat{n}} B_i^* N_{i,k-1}(t) \qquad (3.37a)$$

on the knot vector

$$[X^*] = \left[\underbrace{x_1 = x_2, \ldots, = x_{k-1},}_{k-1} \ldots, \underbrace{x_i, \ldots, = x_{i+p_i-2},}_{p_i-1} \ldots, \underbrace{x_s, \ldots, = x_{s+p_s-2},}_{p_s-1} \right.$$

$$\left. \ldots, \underbrace{x_{\hat{n}+2} = x_{\hat{n}+3}, \ldots, = x_{\hat{n}+k}}_{k-1} \right] \qquad (3.37b)$$

where $\hat{n} = n - s - 1$. Equations (3.36) and (3.37) show that the problem is overspecified, i.e., there is more information than is required to solve the problem. Hence, some information must be discarded. It is for this reason that only an approximate solution is obtained.

Piegl and Tiller [Pieg95, 97] suggest an algorithmic procedure for degree-reducing B-spline curves and surfaces. The procedure is applicable to either rational or nonrational B-spline curves. It is similar to the one they suggest for degree elevation (see Sec. 3.12). Specifically

for each nonzero knot interval
    extract the Bézier curve segment
    degree reduce the Bézier segment
    remove any unnecessary knot values between the $(i-1)$th and the
        ith segment

Bézier Curve Degree Reduction

Degree reduction of Bézier curves is divided into two cases, the order is even or the order is odd. If the order is odd (degree even), then the new control polygon vertices are given by

$$B_1^* = B_1 \tag{3.38a}$$

$$B_i^* = \frac{B_i - \alpha_i B_{i-1}^*}{1 - \alpha_i} \qquad i = 2, \ldots, r+1 \tag{3.38b}$$

$$B_i^* = \frac{B_{i+1} - (1 - \alpha_{i+1}) B_{i+1}^*}{\alpha_{i+1}} \qquad i = k-2, \ldots, r+2 \tag{3.38c}$$

$$B_{k-1}^* = B_k \tag{3.38d}$$

where $r = \text{Integer}((k-2)/2)$ and $\alpha_i = (i-1)/(k-1)$.

Here, Piegl and Tiller give the error as

$$|P(t) - P^*(t)| = \left| J_{k-1,r+1}(t) \left(B_{r+2} - \tfrac{1}{2} \left(B_{r+1}^* + B_{r+2}^* \right) \right) \right| \tag{3.39}$$

where $J_{k-1,r+1}$ is the center Bernstein basis function (see Eq. (2.13)).

When the order is even (degree odd), the new control polygon vertices are

$$B_1^* = B_1 \tag{3.40a}$$

$$B_i^* = \frac{B_i - \alpha_i B_{i-1}^*}{1 - \alpha_i} \qquad i = 2, \ldots, r \tag{3.40b}$$

$$B_i^* = \frac{B_{i+1} - (1 - \alpha_{i+1})B_{i+1}^*}{\alpha_{i+1}} \qquad i = k - 2, \, \ldots, \, r + 2 \qquad (3.40c)$$

$$B_{r+1}^* = \frac{1}{2}\left(\left(\frac{B_{r+1} - \alpha_{r+1}B_r^*}{1 - \alpha_{r+1}}\right) + \left(\frac{B_{r+2} - (1 - \alpha_{r+2})B_{r+2}^*}{\alpha_{r+2}}\right)\right) \qquad (3.40d)$$

$$B_{k-1}^* = B_k \qquad (3.40e)$$

where here the error is

$$|P(t) - P^*(t)| = \frac{1}{2}\left|\left(J_{k-1,r}(t) - J_{k-1,r+1}(t)\right)\right.$$

$$\left.\left(\frac{B_{r+1} - \alpha_{r+1}B_r^*}{1 - \alpha_{r+1}} - \frac{B_{r+2} - (1 - \alpha_{r+2})B_{r+2}^*}{\alpha_{r+2}}\right)\right| \qquad (3.41)$$

Note that the error equations yield the parametric error. The geometric error, i.e., the difference between the curves in geometric (xyz) space, may be different; and the maximum geometric error may occur at a different location along the curve. One important characteristic of these results is that the parametric continuity of the reduced curve at the end points is $C^{(k-3)/2}$. A detailed implementation of the algorithm is given by Piegl and Tiller [Pieg95, 97]. Two simple examples illustrate degree reduction of Bézier curves. First, an odd-order (even-degree) example is considered.

Example 3.13 Bézier Degree Reduction—Odd Order

Find the new control polygon vertices after reduction of a fifth-order (fourth-degree), $k = 5$, Bézier curve to fourth order (third degree), $k = 4$. The original control polygon vertices are B_1, B_2, B_3, B_4, B_5.

From Eq. (3.38a) and (3.38d), the new end point vertices B_1^* and B_4^* are

$$B_1^* = B_1 \qquad \text{and} \qquad B_4^* = B_5$$

Now $\qquad r = \text{Integer}\left(\dfrac{k - 2}{2}\right) = \text{Integer}\left(\dfrac{5 - 2}{2}\right) = 1$

Thus, for $i = 2$ and $\alpha_2 = \frac{1}{4}$, Eq. (3.38b) yields

$$B_2^* = \frac{B_i^* - \alpha_i B_{i-1}^*}{1 - \alpha_i} = \frac{B_2 - \frac{1}{4}B_1^*}{\frac{3}{4}} = \frac{1}{3}(4B_2 - B_1^*) = \frac{1}{3}(4B_2 - B_1)$$

Similarly, for $i = 3$, $\alpha_{i+1} = \frac{3}{4}$ and

$$B_3^* = \frac{B_{i+1} - (1 - \alpha_{i+1})B_{i+1}^*}{\alpha_{i+1}} = \frac{B_4 - \frac{1}{4}B_4^*}{\frac{3}{4}} = \frac{1}{3}(4B_4 - B_4^*) = \frac{1}{3}(4B_4 - B_5)$$

The next degree reduction example concerns even-order (odd-degree) Bézier curves.

Example 3.14 Bézier Degree Reduction—Even Order

Reduce the sixth-order (fifth degree) Bézier curve to fifth-order (fourth degree). The original control polygon vertices are $B_1, \ldots, B_6$.

From Eqs. (3.40a) and (3.40e), we have

$$B_1^* = B_1 \quad\text{and}\quad B_5^* = B_6$$

With $r = 2$, $i = 2, \ldots, 2$, $\alpha_2 = \frac{1}{5}$, Eq. (3.40b) yields

$$B_2^* = \frac{B_2 - \frac{1}{5}B_1^*}{\frac{4}{5}} = \frac{1}{4}(5B_2 - B_1^*) = \frac{1}{4}(5B_2 - B_1)$$

With $i = 4, \ldots, 4$ and $\alpha_5 = \frac{4}{5}$, Eq. (3.40c) yields

$$B_4^* = \frac{B_5 - (1 - \frac{4}{5})B_5^*}{\frac{4}{5}} = \frac{1}{4}(5B_5 - B_5^*)$$

Now Eq. (3.40d), with $\alpha_{r+1} = \frac{2}{5}$, $\alpha_{r+2} = \frac{3}{5}$, yields

$$B_3^* = \frac{1}{2}\left(\frac{B_3 - \frac{2}{5}B_2^*}{\frac{3}{5}} + \frac{B_4 - (1 - \frac{3}{5})B_4^*}{\frac{3}{5}}\right)$$

$$= \frac{1}{2}\left(\frac{1}{3}(5B_3 - 2B_2^*) + \frac{1}{3}(5B_4 - 2B_4^*)\right)$$

$$B_3^* = \frac{1}{6}(5(B_3 + B_4) - 2(B_2^* + B_4^*))$$

$$B_5^* = B_6$$

3.14 Knot Insertion and B-spline Curve Subdivision

The flexibility of a Bézier curve is increased by raising the degree of the polynomial curve by adding an additional vertex to the control polygon (see Sec. 2.5). The flexibility of a B-spline curve is also increased by raising the order of the B-spline basis and hence of the polynomial segments. Cohen et al. [Cohe85] provide both the theory and an algorithm for degree elevation of B-spline curves (see Sec. 3.12).

As an alternative to degree elevation, the flexibility of a B-spline curve is increased by inserting additional knot values into the knot vector. Inserting a single knot value is referred to as knot insertion. Inserting multiple knot values is called knot refinement. The effect is to locally split a piecewise polynomial segment for a given knot value interval (parametric interval) into two piecewise polynomial segments over that interval. There are two basic methods for accomplishing knot value insertion. The first is the so-called Oslo algorithm developed by Cohen et al. [Cohe80] and the one developed by Prautzsch [Prau84a], which simultaneously insert multiple knot values into the knot vector. The second method, by Boehm [Boeh80, 85], sequentially inserts single knot values into the knot vector. Here, only the Oslo algorithm is presented.

The basic idea behind either degree elevation or knot insertion is to increase the flexibility of the curve (or surface) basis, and hence of the curve, *without* changing the shape of the curve (or surface). The success of the idea depends on the fact that there are an infinite number of control polygons with more than the minimum number of vertices that represent identical B-spline curves. Subsequent manipulation of the new control polygon vertices is used to change the curve shape.

Consider the original curve $P(t)$ defined by

$$P(t) = \sum_{i=1}^{n+1} B_i N_{i,k}(t) \tag{3.1}$$

with knot vector

$$[X] = [x_1 \quad x_2 \quad \cdots \quad x_{n+k+1}]$$

After knot insertion, the new curve is $R(s)$ defined by

$$R(s) = \sum_{j=1}^{m+1} C_j M_{j,k}(s) \tag{3.42}$$

with the new knot vector

$$[Y] = [y_1 \quad y_2 \quad \cdots \quad y_{m+k+1}]$$

where $m > n$. The objective is to determine the new control polygon vertices, C_j, such that $P(t) = R(s)$. By the Oslo algorithm (see [Prau84a]), the new C_js are

$$C_j = \sum_{i=1}^{n+1} \alpha_{i,j}^k B_i \qquad 1 \le i \le n, \qquad 1 \le j \le m \tag{3.43}$$

where the $\alpha_{i,j}^k$s are given by the recursion relation

$$\alpha_{i,j}^1 = \begin{cases} 1 & x_i \leq y_j < x_{i+1} \\ 0 & \text{otherwise} \end{cases} \tag{3.44a}$$

$$\alpha_{i,j}^k = \frac{y_{j+k-1} - x_i}{x_{i+k-1} - x_i} \alpha_{i,j}^{k-1} + \frac{x_{i+k} - y_{j+k-1}}{x_{i+k} - x_{i+1}} \alpha_{i+1,j}^{k-1} \tag{3.44b}$$

Note that $\sum_i^{n+1} \alpha_{i,j}^k = 1$.

At first glance it appears that after insertion of a knot value, if the original knot vector was uniform, either periodic or open, then the final knot vector is nonuniform. However, a uniform knot vector is maintained by inserting multiple knot values midway in each existing nonzero interval. An example serves to more fully illustrate this subdivision technique.

Example 3.15   General Subdivision of a B-spline Curve

Consider an open third-order ($k = 3$) B-spline curve initially defined by four ($n + 1 = 4$) polygon vertices

$$B_1 \begin{bmatrix} 0 & 0 \end{bmatrix}, \ B_2 \begin{bmatrix} 1 & 1 \end{bmatrix}, \ B_3 \begin{bmatrix} 2 & 1 \end{bmatrix}, \ B_4 \begin{bmatrix} 3 & 0 \end{bmatrix}$$

Subdivide the curve by inserting additional knot values while maintaining an open uniform knot vector.

Initially, the open uniform knot vector is defined by

$$[X'] = \begin{bmatrix} 0 & 0 & 0 & 1 & 2 & 2 & 2 \end{bmatrix}$$

where the two nonzero knot intervals $0 \rightarrow 1$ and $1 \rightarrow 2$ yield two piecewise parabolic segments comprising the B-spline curve. For convenience, a uniform knot vector with integer intervals is required after subdivision. Thus, the curve is reparameterized (see Sec. 3.16) by multiplying each knot value in $[X']$ by 2 to obtain

$$[X] = \begin{bmatrix} 0 & 0 & 0 & 2 & 4 & 4 & 4 \end{bmatrix}$$

with $x_1 = 0$, $x_2 = 0, \cdots, x_7 = 4$. The resulting curve is exactly the same.

While maintaining a uniform knot vector, the original curve is subdivided by inserting knot values of 1 and 3 in the intervals $0 \rightarrow 2$ and $2 \rightarrow 4$, respectively. The new knot vector is

$$[Y] = \begin{bmatrix} 0 & 0 & 0 & 1 & 2 & 3 & 4 & 4 & 4 \end{bmatrix}$$

with $y_1 = 0$, $y_2 = 0, \cdots, y_9 = 4$. Four piecewise parabolic segments now comprise the B-spline curve.

The six new control polygon vertices, C_j, are given by Eq. (3.43). The $\alpha^3_{i,j}$s are obtained by using the recursion relations given in Eqs. (3.44). Specifically, Eq. (3.44a) shows that the only nonzero first-order ($k = 1$) $\alpha^1_{i,j}$s are

$$\alpha^1_{3,1} = \alpha^1_{3,2} = \alpha^1_{3,3} = \alpha^1_{3,4} = \alpha^1_{4,5} = \alpha^1_{4,6} = 1$$

From Eq. (3.44b), the nonzero second-order ($k = 2$) $\alpha^2_{i,j}$s are

$j = 1$

$$\alpha^2_{3,1} = \frac{y_2 - x_3}{x_4 - x_3} \alpha^1_{3,1} = \frac{0 - 0}{2 - 0}(1) = 0$$

$$\alpha^2_{2,1} = \frac{x_4 - y_2}{x_4 - x_3} \alpha^1_{3,1} = \frac{2 - 0}{2 - 0}(1) = 1$$

$j = 2$

$$\alpha^2_{2,2} = \frac{x_4 - y_3}{x_4 - x_3} \alpha^1_{3,1} = \frac{2 - 0}{2 - 0}(1) = 1$$

$$\alpha^2_{3,2} = \frac{y_3 - x_3}{x_4 - x_3} \alpha^1_{3,2} = \frac{0 - 0}{2 - 0}(1) = 0$$

$j = 3$

$$\alpha^2_{3,3} = \frac{y_4 - x_3}{x_4 - x_3} \alpha^1_{3,3} = \frac{1 - 0}{2 - 0}(1) = 1/2$$

$$\alpha^2_{2,3} = \frac{x_4 - y_4}{x_4 - x_3} \alpha^1_{3,3} = \frac{2 - 1}{2 - 0}(1) = 1/2$$

$j = 4$

$$\alpha^2_{3,4} = \frac{y_5 - x_3}{x_4 - x_3} \alpha^1_{3,4} = \frac{2 - 0}{2 - 0}(1) = 1$$

$$\alpha^2_{2,4} = \frac{x_4 - y_5}{x_4 - x_3} \alpha^1_{3,4} = \frac{2 - 2}{2 - 0}(1) = 0$$

$j = 5$

$$\alpha^2_{4,5} = \frac{y_6 - x_4}{x_5 - x_4} \alpha^1_{4,5} = \frac{3 - 2}{4 - 2}(1) = 1/2$$

$$\alpha^2_{3,5} = \frac{x_5 - y_6}{x_5 - x_4} \alpha^1_{4,5} = \frac{4 - 3}{4 - 2}(1) = 1/2$$

$j = 6$

$$\alpha^2_{4,6} = \frac{y_7 - x_4}{x_5 - x_4} \alpha^1_{4,6} = \frac{4 - 2}{4 - 2}(1) = 1$$

$$\alpha^2_{3,6} = \frac{x_5 - y_7}{x_5 - x_4} \alpha^1_{4,6} = \frac{4 - 4}{4 - 2}(1) = 0$$

The required third-order ($k = 3$) nonzero $\alpha^3_{i,j}$s are

$j = 1$

$$\alpha^3_{2,1} = \frac{y_3 - x_2}{x_4 - x_2} \alpha^2_{2,1} = \frac{0 - 0}{2 - 0}(1) = 0$$

$$\alpha^3_{1,1} = \frac{x_4 - y_3}{x_4 - x_2} \alpha^2_{2,1} = \frac{2 - 0}{2 - 0}(1) = 1$$

$j = 2$

$$\alpha_{1,2}^3 = \frac{x_4 - y_4}{x_4 - x_2}\,\alpha_{2,2}^2 = \frac{2-1}{2-0}\,(1) = {}^1\!/_2$$

$$\alpha_{2,2}^3 = \frac{y_4 - x_2}{x_4 - x_2}\,\alpha_{2,2}^2 = \frac{1-0}{2-0}\,(1) = {}^1\!/_2$$

$j = 3$

$$\alpha_{3,3}^3 = \frac{y_5 - x_3}{x_5 - x_3}\,\alpha_{3,3}^2 = \frac{2-0}{4-0}\,({}^1\!/_2) = {}^1\!/_4$$

$$\alpha_{2,3}^3 = \frac{y_5 - x_2}{x_4 - x_2}\,\alpha_{2,3}^2 + \frac{x_5 - y_5}{x_5 - x_3}\,\alpha_{3,3}^2 = \frac{2-0}{2-0}\,({}^1\!/_2) + \frac{4-2}{4-0}\,({}^1\!/_2) = {}^1\!/_2 + {}^1\!/_4 = {}^3\!/_4$$

$$\alpha_{1,3}^3 = \frac{x_4 - y_5}{x_4 - x_2}\,\alpha_{2,3}^3 = \frac{2-2}{2-0}\,({}^1\!/_2) = 0$$

$j = 4$

$$\alpha_{3,4}^3 = \frac{y_6 - x_3}{x_5 - x_3}\,\alpha_{3,4}^2 = \frac{3-0}{4-0}\,(1) = {}^3\!/_4$$

$$\alpha_{2,4}^3 = \frac{x_5 - y_6}{x_5 - x_3}\,\alpha_{3,4}^2 = \frac{4-3}{4-0}\,(1) = {}^1\!/_4$$

$j = 5$

$$\alpha_{2,5}^3 = \frac{x_5 - y_7}{x_5 - x_3}\,\alpha_{3,5}^2 = \frac{4-4}{4-0}\,({}^1\!/_2) = 0$$

$$\alpha_{3,5}^3 = \frac{y_7 - x_3}{x_5 - x_3}\,\alpha_{3,5}^2 + \frac{x_6 - y_7}{x_6 - x_4}\,\alpha_{4,5}^2 = \frac{4-0}{4-0}\,({}^1\!/_2) + \frac{4-4}{4-2}\,({}^1\!/_2) = {}^1\!/_2$$

$$\alpha_{4,5}^3 = \frac{y_7 - x_4}{x_6 - x_4}\,\alpha_{4,5}^2 = \frac{4-2}{4-2}\,({}^1\!/_2) = {}^1\!/_2$$

$j = 6$

$$\alpha_{4,6}^3 = \frac{y_8 - x_4}{x_6 - x_4}\,\alpha_{4,6}^2 = \frac{4-2}{4-2}\,(1) = 1$$

$$\alpha_{3,6}^3 = \frac{x_6 - y_8}{x_6 - x_4}\,\alpha_{4,6}^2 = \frac{4-4}{4-2}\,(1) = 0$$

The new polygon vertices are given by Eq. (3.43), e.g.

$$C_1 = \sum_{i=1}^{n+1} \alpha_{i,1}^3 B_i = \alpha_{1,1}^3 B_1 + \alpha_{2,1}^3 B_2 + \alpha_{3,1}^3 B_3 + \alpha_{4,1}^3 B_4$$

$$= \alpha_{1,1}^3 B_1 = B_1 = \begin{bmatrix} 0 & 0 \end{bmatrix}$$

Similarly

$$C_2 = {}^1\!/_2(B_1 + B_2) = {}^1\!/_2(\begin{bmatrix} 0 & 0 \end{bmatrix} + \begin{bmatrix} 1 & 1 \end{bmatrix}) = \begin{bmatrix} {}^1\!/_2 & {}^1\!/_2 \end{bmatrix}$$

$$C_3 = {}^3\!/_4 B_2 + {}^1\!/_4 B_3 = {}^3\!/_4\begin{bmatrix} 1 & 1 \end{bmatrix} + {}^1\!/_4\begin{bmatrix} 2 & 1 \end{bmatrix} = \begin{bmatrix} {}^5\!/_4 & 1 \end{bmatrix}$$

$$C_4 = {}^1\!/_4 B_2 + {}^3\!/_4 B_3 = {}^1\!/_4\begin{bmatrix} 1 & 1 \end{bmatrix} + {}^3\!/_4\begin{bmatrix} 2 & 1 \end{bmatrix} = \begin{bmatrix} {}^7\!/_4 & 1 \end{bmatrix}$$

$$C_5 = {}^1\!/_2(B_3 + B_4) = {}^1\!/_2(\begin{bmatrix} 2 & 1 \end{bmatrix} + \begin{bmatrix} 3 & 0 \end{bmatrix}) = \begin{bmatrix} {}^5\!/_2 & {}^1\!/_2 \end{bmatrix}$$

$$C_6 = B_4 = \begin{bmatrix} 3 & 0 \end{bmatrix}$$

The result is increased flexibility of the entire curve.

The next example illustrates the addition of a single knot value to an initially open uniform knot vector. The result is a nonuniform knot vector with a multiple knot value.

Example 3.16   Local Subdivision of a B-spline Curve

Consider the open third-order ($k = 3$) B-spline curve previously considered in Ex. 3.15. Subdivide the curve by inserting the knot value 1 in the interval $0 \rightarrow 1$ of the knot vector

$$[X] = [0 \quad 0 \quad 0 \quad 1 \quad 2 \quad 2 \quad 2]$$

with $x_1 = 0$, $x_2 = 0, \cdots, x_7 = 2$. The new knot vector is

$$[Y] = [0 \quad 0 \quad 0 \quad 1 \quad 1 \quad 2 \quad 2 \quad 2]$$

with $y_1 = 0$, $y_2 = 0, \cdots, y_8 = 2$. There are five new polygon vertices $C_1 \cdots C_5$.

The nonzero $\alpha_{i,j}^k$s required to determine the C_js are

$$k = 1$$
$$\alpha_{3,1}^1 = \alpha_{3,2}^1 = \alpha_{3,3}^1 = \alpha_{3,4}^1 = \alpha_{4,5}^1 = 1$$

$$k = 2$$
$$\alpha_{2,1}^2 = \alpha_{2,2}^2 = \alpha_{3,3}^2 = \alpha_{3,4}^2 = \alpha_{4,5}^2 = 1$$

$$k = 3$$
$$\alpha_{1,1}^3 = \alpha_{2,2}^3 = \alpha_{3,4}^3 = \alpha_{4,5}^3 = 1, \quad \alpha_{3,3}^3 = \alpha_{2,3}^3 = 1/2$$

The new polygon vertices are

$$C_1 = \alpha_{3,1}^3 B_1 = B_1 = [0 \quad 0]$$

$$C_2 = \alpha_{3,2}^3 B_2 = B_2 = [1 \quad 1]$$

$$C_3 = \alpha_{2,3}^3 B_2 + \alpha_{3,3}^3 B_3 = 1/2(B_2 + B_3) = 1/2([1 \quad 1] + [2 \quad 1]) = [3/2 \quad 1]$$

$$C_4 = \alpha_{3,4}^3 B_3 = B_3 = [2 \quad 1]$$

$$C_5 = \alpha_{4,5}^3 B_4 = B_4 = [3 \quad 0]$$

If C_3 is moved to coincide with C_2, i.e., $C_2 = C_3 = [1 \quad 1]$, both a double vertex and a double knot value corresponding to $C_2 = C_3$ exist. The resulting B-spline curve for $k = 3$ has a cusp or sharp corner at $C_2 = C_3$ (see Appendix B, Prob. 3.14).

3.15 Knot Removal

Knot removal is an integral part of effectively using B-spline curves and surfaces for design and modeling. It is also an integral part of algorithms for degree elevation (see Sec. 3.12) and degree reduction (see Sec. 3.13).

Knot removal is the reverse of knot insertion (see Sec. 3.14). Boehm [Boeh80] briefly mentions knot removal but provides few details. Tiller [Till92] gives algorithms for removing a specified number of knot values and as many knot values as possible for both B-spline curves and surfaces. The algorithms are applicable to both rational and nonrational B-spline curves and surfaces. For rational B-spline curves and surfaces the algorithms are applied to the four-dimensional coordinates in homogeneous space (see Chapter 4).

Tiller assumes that a knot is removable if and only if it leaves the original curve or surface unchanged both parametrically and geometrically. However, as Tiller points out, knot removal, like degree reduction, results in an overspecified problem and thus can only be solved within some tolerance.

To illustrate the underlying mathematical concepts, assume all homogeneous weighting factors (see Sec. 4.2), $h_i > 0$, and a knot vector of the form

$$[X] = \left[\underbrace{x_1 = x_2, \ldots, = x_k}_{k}, \ldots, x_i = x_{i+1}, \ldots, = x_{i+p_i-1}, \ldots, x_j, x_s = x_{s+1}, \right.$$

$$\left. \ldots, = x_{s+p_s-1}, \ldots, \underbrace{x_{n+2} = x_{n+3}, \ldots, = x_{n+k+1}}_{k} \right]$$

As a specific example, assume a fourth-order B-spline curve with knot vector

$$[X] = \begin{bmatrix} 0 & 0 & 0 & 0 & 1 & 1 & 1 & 2 & 2 & 2 & 2 \end{bmatrix}$$

and control polygon given by $B_1, \ldots, B_7$, as shown in Fig. 3.29a. This curve is actually composed of two cubic Bézier segments, as indicated by the three multiple knot values equal to 1.

One of the multiple knot values is removable if and only if the first derivative is continuous at $x_i = 1$. Note that, although the B-spline basis functions are only C^0 continuous at $x_i = 1$, the curve itself may or may not be continuous. If

$$\frac{k-1}{x_7 - x_4}(B_4 - B_3) = \frac{k-1}{x_8 - x_5}(B_5 - B_4) \tag{3.45}$$

then the first derivative of the curve is continuous at $x_i = 1$ and a single knot value, say $x_6 = 1$, is removable. Letting $x = x_5 = x_7$, Eq. (3.45) becomes

$$B_4 = \frac{x - x_4}{x_8 - x_4} B_5 + \frac{x_8 - x}{x_8 - x_4} B_3$$

Noting that $B_3^* = B_3$ and $B_4^* = B_5$ (see Figs. 3.29a and 3.29b), where the star indicates a new control polygon vertex, yields

$$B_4 = \alpha_4 B_4^* + (1 - \alpha_4) B_3^* \quad \text{with} \quad \alpha_4 = \frac{x - x_4}{x_8 - x_4} \tag{3.46}$$

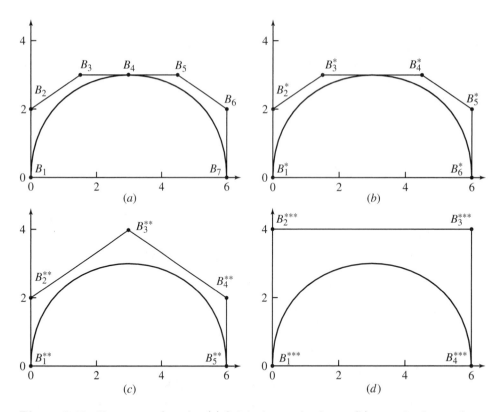

Figure 3.29 Knot removal results. (a) Original control polygon; (b) control polygon after removal of one multiple knot value; (c) control polygon after removal of the second multiple knot value; (d) control polygon after removal of the third multiple knot value.

which is just the equation for inserting a new knot value, $x_6 = 1$, into the new control polygon to yield the original control polygon; i.e., a knot value is removable if knot insertion is reversible. However, note that for rational curves continuity must be maintained using the four-dimensional B_i^h coordinates and not just the three-dimensional B_is.

Furthermore, the second multiple knot value is removable if the second derivative is continuous. The second derivative is continuous if and only if

$$B_3^* = \alpha_3 B_3^{**} + (1 - \alpha_3) B_2^{**} \qquad (3.47a)$$

$$B_4^* = \alpha_4 B_4^{**} + (1 - \alpha_4) B_3^{**} \qquad (3.47b)$$

where $\qquad \alpha_i = \dfrac{x - x_i}{x_{i+k+1} - x_i} \qquad i = 3, 4$

Finally, the third multiple knot value is removable if the third derivative is continuous, i.e.

$$B_2^{**} = \alpha_2 B_2^{***} + (1 - \alpha_2) B_1^{***} \qquad (3.48a)$$

$$B_3^{**} = \alpha_3 B_3^{***} + (1 - \alpha_3) B_2^{***} \qquad (3.48b)$$

$$B_4^{**} = \alpha_4 B_4^{***} + (1 - \alpha_4) B_3^{***} \qquad (3.48c)$$

where $\qquad \alpha_i = \dfrac{x - x_i}{x_{i+k+2} - x_i} \qquad i = 2, 3, 4$

Examining Eq. (3.46) and recalling that $B_3^* = B_3$ and $B_4^* = B_5$ shows that there are no unknown values. Hence, the equation is satisfied, and the knot value is removable, if the left-hand side equals the right-hand side to within a specified tolerance.

For removal of the second knot value, Eqs. (3.48) contain one unknown value, B_3^{**}. Solving the two equations individually for B_3^{**} yields

$$B_3^{**} = \frac{B_3^* - (1 - \alpha_3) B_2^{**}}{\alpha_3} \qquad (3.49a)$$

$$B_3^{**} = \frac{B_4^* - \alpha_4 B_4^{**}}{1 - \alpha_4} \qquad (3.49b)$$

B_3^{**} is separately computed using Eqs. (3.49a) and (3.49b). If the results agree within some tolerance, the second knot value is removable. Hence, B_3^* and B_4^* are replaced by B_3^{**}.

To remove the third multiple knot value, Eqs. (3.48a) and (3.48c) are solved for B_2^{***} and B_3^{***} to yield

$$B_2^{***} = \frac{B_2^{**} - (1 - \alpha_2)B_1^{***}}{\alpha_2} \tag{3.50a}$$

$$B_3^{***} = \frac{B_4^{**} - \alpha_3 B_4^{***}}{1 - \alpha_4} \tag{3.50b}$$

where $B_1^{***} = B_1$ and $B_4^{***} = B_7$ and hence are known.

For more complex B-spline curves, the general solution technique is to solve the first and last equations and work toward the center of the system. Using this technique, if the number of equations is even the final control vertex is computed twice.

Pseudocode

To remove a single knot value where $x = x_s$ is a knot value with multiplicity multi ($0 < $ multi $\leq k - 1$) and $x \neq x_{s+1}$, the pseudocode to determine the new control polygon vertices is

```
i = s - k
j = s- multi
while j - i > 0
    αᵢ = (x - xᵢ)/(xᵢ₊ₖ - xᵢ)
    αⱼ = (x - xⱼ)/(xⱼ₊ₖ - xⱼ)
    Bᵢ* = (Bᵢ - (1 - αᵢ)Bᵢ₋₁*)/αᵢ
    Bⱼ* = (Bⱼ - αⱼBⱼ₊₁*)/(1 - αⱼ)
    i = i + 1
    j = j - 1
end while
```

Similarly, the pseudocode to remove the knot value $x = x_s$, ntimes where $1 \leq$ ntimes $\leq$ multi, and determine the new control vertices is

```
start = s - k
end = s - multi  - 1
for t = 1 to ntimes
    start = start -1
    end = end +1
    i = start
```

$j = $ end
while $j - 1 > t - 1$
$\quad \alpha_i = (x - x_i)/(x_{i+k+t-1} - x_i)$
$\quad \alpha_j = (x - x_{j+1-t})/(x_{j+k} - x_{j+1-t})$
$\quad B_i^t = (B_i^{t-1} - (1 - \alpha_i)B_{i-1}^t)/\alpha_i$
$\quad B_j^t = (B_j^{t-1} - \alpha_j B_{j+1}^t)/(1 - \alpha_j)$
$\quad i = i + 1$
$\quad j = j - 1$
end while
loop

where t indicates the number of knots removed.

In general, knot removal involves three steps:

Compute some (or possibly no) new control vertices.

Using the new control vertices and possibly some of the original control vertices, determine if the new control vertices yield the original curve within some tolerance.

Remove (or do not remove) the knot value.

The more detailed pseudocode given below, which removes a single knot value, uses this general approach. The algorithm is based on those given by Tiller [Till92]. Tiller gives complete algorithms (in C) that remove a specified number of multiple knot values or as many knots as possible. The more general algorithms are rather messy, hence they are not explicitly given here.

remknot(B,npts,k,X,m,x,s,multi,tol)

Although not indicated here, the control polygon vertices are multidimensional

fout = INTEGER$((2*s - multi - (k-1))/2)$
last = s−multi
first = s−(k−1)
$\quad$ off = first − 1
$\quad$ temp(1) = B(off)
$\quad$ temp(last+2−off) = B(last+1)
$\quad$ i = first
$\quad$ j = last
$\quad$ ii = 2

jj = last−off+1
remflag = 0
determine the possibly new control polygon vertices
while (j−i) > 0
    alphai = (x−X(i))/(X(i+k+t)−X(i))
    alphaj = (x−X(j−t))/(X(j+k)−X(j−t))
    temp(ii) = (B(i) − (1−alphai)*temp(ii−1))/alphai
    temp(jj) = (B(j) − alphaj*temp(jj+1))/(1−alphaj)
    i=i+1
    j=j−1
    ii=ii+1
    jj=jj−1
end while
check if the knot value is removable
if (j−i)<0 **then**
    Dist(temp(ii − 1), temp(jj + 1))   *Dist is a distance function*
    if Dist≤tol **then**
        remflag=1
    end if
else
    alphai = (x−X(i))/(X(i+k)−X(i))
    Dist(B(i),alphai*temp(ii+1)+(1-alphai)*temp(ii−1))
    if Dist ≤ tol **then**
        remflag=1
    end if
end if
if remflag = 0 **then**
    Cannot remove knot
    exit while
else   *knot is removable, save new control polygon vertices*
    i=first
    j=last
    while (j−i) > 0
        B(i) = temp(i−off+1)
        B(j) = temp(j−off+1)
        i=i+1
        j=j−1
    end while

end if
first=first−1
last=last+1
end while
shift the knot vector
kk = s+1
while kk ≤ m
   X(kk−1) = X(kk)
   kk = kk+1
end while
continue output of new control polygon vertices by overwriting
   the B(j) through B(i) original control polygon vertices
j = fout
i = j
kk = i+1
while kk ≤ npts
   B(j) = B(kk)
   j=j+1
   kk = kk+1
end while
return

A simple example illustrates the algorithm results.

Example 3.17 Knot Removal

Consider a fourth-order (cubic) B-spline curve originally defined by

$$B_1 \begin{bmatrix} 0 & 0 \end{bmatrix}, B_2 \begin{bmatrix} 0 & 2 \end{bmatrix}, B_3 \begin{bmatrix} 3/2 & 3 \end{bmatrix}, B_4 \begin{bmatrix} 3 & 3 \end{bmatrix}, B_5 \begin{bmatrix} 9/2 & 3 \end{bmatrix}, B_6 \begin{bmatrix} 6 & 2 \end{bmatrix}, B_7 \begin{bmatrix} 6 & 0 \end{bmatrix}$$

as shown in Fig. 3.29a by the solid dots, with knot vector

$$[X] = \begin{bmatrix} 0 & 0 & 0 & 0 & 1 & 1 & 1 & 2 & 2 & 2 & 2 \end{bmatrix}$$

Remove the three multiple internal knot values $x_5 = x_6 = x_7 = 1$, and determine the new control polygon vertices.

First, notice that there are two piecewise cubic curve segments, as indicated by the two nonzero knot intervals $0 - 1$ and $1 - 2$. Furthermore, the existence of the three multiple knot values $x_5 = x_6 = x_7 = 1$, with multiplicity three equal to the degree of the piecewise curve segments, shows that the two piecewise segments are, in fact, Bézier curve segments.

Using the pseudocode algorithm with $k = 4$, $s = 7$, $x = 1$, multi $= 3$ yields the new knot vector

$$[X^*] = [0 \quad 0 \quad 0 \quad 0 \quad 1 \quad 1 \quad 2 \quad 2 \quad 2 \quad 2]$$

and the new control polygon given by

$$B_1^* [0 \quad 0], \; B_2^* [0 \quad 2], \; B_3^* [\sfrac{3}{2} \quad 3], \; B_4^* [\sfrac{9}{2} \quad 3], \; B_5^* [6 \quad 2], \; B_6^* [6 \quad 0]$$

as shown in Fig. 3.29b. Re-entering the algorithm with $k = 4$, $s = 6$, $x = 1$, multi $= 2$ yields the knot vector

$$[X^{**}] = [0 \quad 0 \quad 0 \quad 0 \quad 1 \quad 2 \quad 2 \quad 2 \quad 2]$$

and the new control polygon given by

$$B_1^{**} [0 \quad 0], \; B_2^{**} [0 \quad 2], \; B_3^{**} [3 \quad 4], \; B_4^{**} [6 \quad 2], \; B_5^{**} [6 \quad 0]$$

as shown in Fig. 3.29c.

The final knot at $x = 1$ is removed using $s = 5$, $k = 4$, multi $= 1$ to yield the knot vector

$$[X^{***}] = [0 \quad 0 \quad 0 \quad 0 \quad 2 \quad 2 \quad 2 \quad 2]$$

and the control polygon shown in Fig. 3.29d

$$B_1^{***} [0 \quad 0], \; B_2^{***} [0 \quad 4], \; B_3^{***} [6 \quad 4], \; B_4^{***} [6 \quad 0]$$

The final result is, of course, a cubic Bézier curve. Notice the removal of a single knot value also decreases the number of control polygon vertices by 1.

3.16 Reparameterization

Although B-spline curves and surfaces are typically mathematically continuous when represented in a computer, they are discretized. For example, to display a B-spline curve (or surface) on a monitor, several discrete points on the curve (or surface) are calculated and then connected by short *straight* line segments. A similar technique is used to convert curves (or surfaces) to numerical control codes to drive a machine tool. The results can be strange, wondrous, amusing, befuddling, or in some cases disastrous, depending on your viewpoint. Figure 3.30a illustrates the difficulties.

The knot vector $[X] = [0 \quad 0 \quad 0 \quad 1 \quad 1 \quad 3 \quad 3 \quad 3]$ is used to generate the third-order B-spline curve in Fig. 3.30a. The multiple knot value ensures that the curve passes through B_3. The piecewise B-spline curve is composed of two Bézier curve segments. Notice that the two nonzero intervals in the

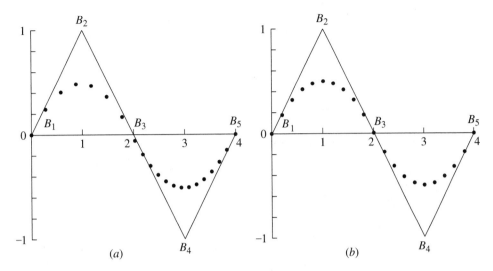

Figure 3.30 Reparameterization of a B-spline curve. (a) Original third-order curve with knot vector $[0 \quad 0 \quad 0 \quad 1 \quad 1 \quad 3 \quad 3 \quad 3]$; (b) reparameterized third-order curve with knot vector $[0 \quad 0 \quad 0 \quad \sfrac{3}{2} \quad \sfrac{3}{2} \quad 3 \quad 3 \quad 3]$.

knot vector, $0-1$ and $1-3$, are of unequal length. Thus, a uniform increment in the parameter range $0-3$ results in a nonuniform distribution of points along the curve, as shown by the solid dots in Fig. 3.30a. As a result, if, for example, the orientation of the chord between the computed points in the range between control polygon vertices B_1 to B_3 is used to determine the local normal to the curve, the results are different from those in the range B_3 to B_5, even though the curve segments have the 'same' shape.

Similarly, if a machine tool is driven along the path defined by connecting the computed points on the curve, the results are different for the segments from B_1 to B_3 and from B_3 to B_5. What is desired is a uniform distribution of points for the range from B_1 to B_3 and for the range from B_3 to B_5. Reparameterizing the B-spline curve, and in particular the knot vector, accomplishes this.

In general, if a kth-order B-spline (or NURBS) curve

$$P(t) = \sum_{i=1}^{n+1} B_i N_{i,k}(t)$$

is defined on a knot vector

$$[X] = [x_1, \ldots, x_k, \ldots, x_{n+2}, \ldots, x_{n+1+k}]$$

and a reparameterized k^*th-order B-spline (or NURBS) curve

$$P(t^*) = \sum_{i=1}^{n+1} B_i^* N_{i,k^*}^*(t^*)$$

is defined on a knot vector

$$[X^*] = [x_1^*, \ldots, x_{k^*}^*, \ldots, x_{n+2}^*, \ldots, x_{n+1+k^*}^*]$$

where $x^* = x(s)$, with $x(s)$ a qth-degree polynomial, then the degree of the resulting B-spline curve is pq, where p is the degree of the original B-spline curve. Except for $q = 1$, reparameterization is another technique for raising the degree of a B-spline curve. Piegl and Tiller [Pieg97] give the details for finding the new control polygon in the general case. Here, we concentrate on the linear case, i.e., $q = 1$.

When $q = 1$, the relationship between the knot values in $[X]$ and $[X^*]$ has the form

$$x^* = \alpha x + \beta$$

where α and β are constants. In this special case, it can be shown that both the control polygon and the derivatives at the ends of the B-spline curve remain unchanged; i.e., $B_i^* = B_i$, $i = 1$ to $n + 1$, and $P'(t) = P'(t^*)$ at $t = t^* = 0$ and $t = t^* = n + k + 1$ (see [Pieg97]). A simple example serves to illustrate the technique.

Example 3.18   Reparameterization

Consider the third-order B-spline curve defined by

$$B_1[0 \quad 0], \ B_2[1 \quad 1], \ B_3[2 \quad 0], \ B_4[3 \quad -1], \ B_5[4 \quad 0]$$

with the knot vector

$$[X] = [0 \quad 0 \quad 0 \quad 1 \quad 1 \quad 3 \quad 3 \quad 3]$$

as shown in Fig. 3.30. The solid dots represent the location of computed points on the curve. As a result of the unequal intervals from $0 - 1$ and $1 - 3$ in the knot vector, the computed points on the curve are unequally spaced in geometric (real) space, although they are equally spaced in parametric space. Find a linear reparameterization that yields equally spaced computed points on the curve in geometric space.

The knot vector is reparameterized to yield equal open intervals, i.e., the desired new knot vector is

$$[X^*] = [0 \quad 0 \quad 0 \quad {}^3\!/_2 \quad {}^3\!/_2 \quad 3 \quad 3 \quad 3]$$

Assuming the new knot vector starts at zero, the conditions on

$$x^* = \alpha x + \beta$$

are
$$x^* = {}^3\!/_2 \quad \text{at} \quad x = 1, \qquad x > 0$$
$$x^* = 3 \quad \text{at} \quad x = 3, \qquad x > 0$$

Substituting yields
$$3 = 3\alpha + \beta$$
$${}^3\!/_2 = \alpha + \beta$$

Solving gives $\alpha = \beta = {}^3\!/_4$. Hence, the linear reparameterization is

$$x^* = {}^3\!/_4 (x + 1), \qquad x > 0$$

The reparameterized curve is shown in Fig. 3.30b.

Reparameterization of curves and surfaces where either multiple coincident vertices or multiplicity of internal knot values (see Fig. 3.30) are used to control the shape of the curve or surface is particularly important if reasonable distribution of computed points is desired. For rational B-spline curves or surfaces where manipulation of the homogeneous weighting factors (see Chapters 4 and 7) occurs, reparameterization is also important in obtaining acceptable computed point distributions. Piegl and Tiller [Pieg97] provide additional insight into the uses and characteristics of reparameterization.

Elaine Cohen
Tom Lyche
Rich Riesenfeld

Pure happenstance so affected our coming together to work on the Oslo Algorithms that you could become a fatalist thinking about it. In the late 1970s, Jeff Lane, Rich's former student who went to Boeing, and Rich had worked on figuring out subdivision schemes for Bézier surfaces and uniform B-spline surfaces. The technique promised to accomplish many central systems functions, from performing Boolean operations on free-form surfaces to rendering them dynamically. As they wrote up the results in a fundamental IEEE paper, Rich felt encouraged over what had been done but frustrated because he realized that the problem needed to be solved for B-splines with nonuniformly spaced knots. The methods that they used would not generalize further. Although they produced a paper that had considerable influence on the direction of the field, they did not know how to solve the general problem, which was necessary to make the technique widely applicable for nonuniform B-splines.

In early 1979 Elaine Cohen and Rich headed for Oslo on the second part of a sabbatical leave from Utah to join the CAD Group at the Central Institute (SI), a research laboratory adjacent to the University of Oslo. Blindly following instincts, they went there on the vaguest of notions. Norway was a leader in CAD in shipbuilding, and its elegant taste in traditional design appealed. Frank Lillehagen, an energetic former student of Rich, was there heading the CAD Group, and so was Even Mehlum, a CAD pioneer. Elaine and Rich thought that Frank's group would provide an interesting and stimulating context, although they had *no* idea what might follow. Because of her background in signal processing and her relevant thesis work in approximation theory, Elaine was affiliated with Even Mehlum's group, which was pursuing Even's novel ideas for extracting energy from ocean waves.

One fateful day at SI, Lillehagen asked Elaine and Rich to do him a favor. He wanted to improve the level of exchange with the University of Oslo. The climate was friendly, but there was little collaboration. Frank felt that he should at least have more communications with Professor Tom Lyche, but Tom was a mathematician and the SI group were engineers. Hence, Frank had the idea that Elaine and Rich make contact with Tom and simply chat. Maybe some ideas on how to involve Tom in SI's agenda would emerge. This brought on an immediate flashback for Rich, who had talked with Larry Schumacher while skiing a few years prior and remembered Larry describing a graduate student from Norway working on discrete splines. This closed the loop in a truly incredible way. It all made immediate sense that Tom's background might be the missing ingredient to solve nonuniform refinement for B-splines.

They met in Tom's office, in a somewhat formal conversation characteristic of two unfamiliar parties who were not completely sure what they had in common. They did the standard professors' protocol of describing their recent activities and exchanging some papers. Tom got the Lane and Riesenfeld paper, and Elaine and Rich got some papers on discrete splines. There was no arrangement for anything to follow. The next day, Tom called at SI to say that he had looked at the Lane and Riesenfeld paper and felt that some of his work on discrete splines could be applied to solving the general case.

Only Tom and Rich met on the second occasion, but it did not go so well. The gap between Tom's facility in approximation theory and splines and Rich's background in CAD bogged down the pace. It was clear that progress was going to be too slow, so Rich asked Elaine to come next time to act as a facilitator, someone with experience in both disciplines. As young married professionals, Elaine and Rich had always maintained an external facade of separate professional identities, although she worked with Rich in private. At this juncture, they quickly decided that this opportunity was greater than any need for professional separation.

Well, the research still was not straightforward; but they did make daily progress working as a threesome. Everything they tried had some subtle problem, but they were gaining understanding. Time was running out on their visit, and the pace became feverish, for they knew that finishing this from afar would be slow and awkward. They struggled to get the details of definitions to work right. At the end of spring 1979, they finished the research and had the results, which they called the 'Oslo Algorithms,' for performing arbitrary, multiple knot insertion, i.e., refinement and subdivision, of B-splines. They named the work to honor the lovely locale that brought them together in such a fruitful way. So he would know immediately, Jeff Lane in Seattle got a call from Rich to tell him of the breakthrough. They all were excited, for they knew they had something good.

Tom was quite inspired by the new directions that appeared. His previous work, which had been aimed at the numerical approximation community, had consequently become part of an important CAD process with widespread applications. Using the Oslo Algorithms, you could now implement general refinement and subdivision of nonuniform B-splines; this meant that you could simply locally refine with extra knots only where they were needed. With uniform refinement, you had been trapped with the restrictive scheme of refining the entire surface to the full extent that any particular region needed. Because of this new tool, nonuniform B-splines finally had a chance of becoming widely adopted. Moreover, the framework of the research included a general theory that revealed an elegant and profound connection between the continuous and discrete (control) points of the B-spline scheme. This inspired much subsequent work.

Lane and Riesenfeld later published a theoretical result, showing that you could use the 'Oslo technique' to produce a straightforward geometric proof of the variation-diminishing property of B-spline approximation, which previously required the formidable theory of total positivity. This paper, together with the Lane and Riesenfeld subdivision paper, generated interest from the approximation community when it was shown that impact could flow from CAD to theory, as well as from theory to CAD. Today there is a worldwide, active community of researchers pursuing results in both directions.

As for SI, Tom's student Tor Dokken immediately implemented the Oslo Algorithm at SI, where it became a central part of their commercial B-spline package SISSEL. Lillehagen's wish for close collaboration between Tom's group at the University and the group at SI was fulfilled. During the ensuing 20 years, this symbiotic relationship has become a point of reference for successful outreach. In short, the 'Oslo work' effected a lasting positive change in Oslo.

All of our careers were stimulated and propelled by the joint 'Oslo work'. We enjoyed each other personally, became close friends, and have collaborated on many productive occasions since. We have made several extended visits to each other's home turf. For Tom, this event launched him as a well-known name in a new field of endeavor. In view of the new possibilities that we could see, Rich was renewed in his commitment to this field. Elaine decided to pursue CAD as her major field of research. She and Rich returned to Utah to launch the Alpha_1 experimental CAD system, in an effort to exploit the important systems implications of this work and to test its viability. Tom continued with more knot manipulation research as he developed data reduction schemes based on what can be properly viewed as an 'Inverse Oslo Algorithm' approach, i.e., eliminating knots and, therefore, degrees of freedom. One of Elaine's follow-up activities concerned solving the degree raising problem for B-splines, which resulted in further collaborations with Larry Schumacher and Tom.

In short, the Oslo Algorithm had major impact on the field and also on the lives of the developers, who have continued to collaborate on many subsequent fundamental results and to enjoy a close friendship.

Elaine Cohen
Tom Lyche
Rich Riesenfeld
Oslo, January 2000

Chapter 4

Rational B-spline Curves 4

Rational curve and surface descriptions were first introduced into the computer graphics literature by Steve Coons [Coon67]. Rational forms of the Bézier curves are well known in the literature (see [Forr68, 80; Boeh82; Faro85; Pieg86]). Rational forms of the conic sections are also well known (see [Ball77]). Both because of space limitations and because they form a unifying foundation, the current discussion is limited to rational B-spline curves. Rational B-splines provide a single precise mathematical form capable of representing the common analytical shapes—lines, planes, conic curves including circles, free-form curves, quadric and sculptured surfaces—that are used in computer graphics and computer aided design. Currently, NURBS (NonUniform Rational B-Spline) curves and surfaces are the standard for curve and surface description in computer graphics.

Versprille [Vers75] was the first to discuss rational B-splines. The seminal papers by Tiller [Till83] and Piegl and Tiller [Pieg87] form the basis of the current discussion. Interestingly enough, nonuniform rational B-splines have been an Initial Graphics Exchange Specification (IGES) standard since

1983 (see [IGES86]). IGES is one of the standards for the interchange of design information between various computer aided design systems and between computer aided design and computer aided manufacturing systems. Furthermore, rational B-splines (NURBS) are incorporated into most of the current geometric modeling systems.

4.1 Rational B-spline Curves (NURBS)

A rational B-spline curve is the projection of a nonrational (polynomial) B-spline curve defined in four-dimensional (4D) homogeneous coordinate space[†] back into three-dimensional (3D) physical space. Specifically

$$P(t) = \sum_{i=1}^{n+1} B_i^h N_{i,k}(t) \tag{4.1}$$

where the B_i^hs are the four-dimensional homogeneous control polygon vertices for the nonrational four-dimensional B-spline curve. $N_{i,k}(t)$ is the nonrational B-spline basis function previously given in Eqs. (3.2).

Projecting back into three-dimensional space by dividing through by the homogeneous coordinate yields the rational B-spline curve

$$P(t) = \frac{\displaystyle\sum_{i=1}^{n+1} B_i h_i N_{i,k}(t)}{\displaystyle\sum_{i=1}^{n+1} h_i N_{i,k}(t)} = \sum_{i=1}^{n+1} B_i R_{i,k}(t) \tag{4.2}$$

where the B_is are the three-dimensional control polygon vertices for the rational B-spline curve and the

$$R_{i,k}(t) = \frac{h_i N_{i,k}(t)}{\displaystyle\sum_{i=1}^{n+1} h_i N_{i,k}(t)} \tag{4.3}$$

are the rational B-spline basis functions. Here, $h_i \geq 0$ for all values of i.[‡]

[†]For a discussion of homogeneous coordinates, see Rogers and Adams [Roge90a].

[‡]Note that rational B-spline basis functions for $h_i < 0$ are valid (see [Vers75] and Sec. 7.2) but are not convenient in terms of the current discussion.

Characteristics of NURBS

Rational B-spline basis functions and curves are a generalization of nonrational B-spline basis functions and curves. Thus, they carry forward nearly all the analytic and geometric characteristics of their nonrational B-spline counterparts. In particular:

Each rational basis function is positive or zero for all parameter values, i.e., $R_{i,k} \geq 0$.

The sum of the rational B-spline basis functions for any parameter value t is one, i.e.

$$\sum_{i=1}^{n+1} R_{i,k}(t) \equiv 1 \qquad (4.4)$$

Except for first-order basis functions, i.e., $k = 1$, each rational basis function has precisely one maximum.

A rational B-spline curve of order k (degree $k-1$) is C^{k-2} continuous everywhere.

The maximum order of the rational B-spline curve is equal to the number of control polygon vertices.

A rational B-spline curve exhibits the variation-diminishing property.

A rational B-spline curve generally follows the shape of the control polygon.

For $h_i > 0$, a rational B-spline curve lies within the union of convex hulls formed by k successive control polygon vertices.

Any *projective* transformation is applied to a rational B-spline curve by applying it to the control polygon vertices; i.e., the curve is invariant with respect to a *projective* transformation. Note that this is a stronger condition than that for a nonrational B-spline, which is only invariant with respect to an *affine* transformation.

From Eqs. (3.3) and (4.3), it is clear that when all $h_i = 1$, $R_{i,k}(t) = N_{i,k}(t)$. Thus, nonrational B-spline basis functions and curves are included as a special case of rational B-spline basis functions and curves. Furthermore, it is easy to show that an open rational B-spline curve with order equal to the number of control polygon vertices is a rational Bézier curve. For the case of all $h_i = 1$, the rational Bézier curve reduces to a nonrational Bézier curve. Thus, both rational and nonrational Bézier curves are included as special cases of rational B-spline curves.

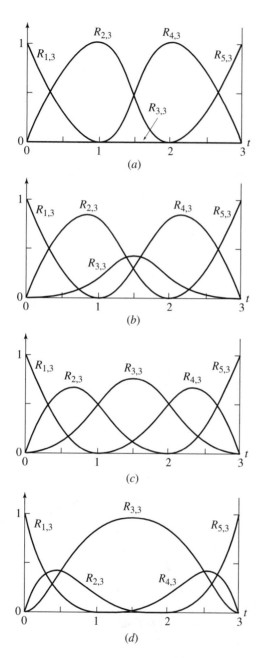

Figure 4.1   Rational B-spline basis functions for $n + 1 = 5$, $k = 3$ with open knot vector
$[X] = [0\ \ 0\ \ 0\ \ 1\ \ 2\ \ 3\ \ 3\ \ 3]$, $[H] = [1\ \ 1\ \ h_3\ \ 1\ \ 1]$. (a) $h_3 = 0$;
(b) $h_3 = 1/4$; (c) $h_3 = 1$; (d) $h_3 = 5$.

Because rational B-splines are a four-dimensional generalization of nonrational B-splines, algorithms for degree elevation (see [Cohe85], Sec. 3.12 and Ex. 7.5), subdivision (see Sec. 3.14 and [Boeh80, 85; Cohe80; Prau84b]) and curve fitting (see Sec. 3.11) of nonrational B-spline curves are valid for rational B-splines by applying them to the four-dimensional control vertices.

4.2 Rational B-spline Basis Functions and Curves

Open uniform, periodic uniform and nonuniform knot vectors are used to generate rational B-spline basis functions and rational B-spline curves.

Open Rational B-spline Basis Functions and Curves

In Eqs. (4.2) and (4.3), the homogeneous coordinates h_i (occasionally called homogeneous weighting factors, or just weights) provide additional blending capability. $h = 1$ is called the affine space. By convention it corresponds to physical space. The effect of the homogeneous coordinates h on the rational B-spline basis functions is shown in Fig. 4.1. Here, an open uniform knot vector $[0 \quad 0 \quad 0 \quad 1 \quad 2 \quad 3 \quad 3 \quad 3]$ $(n + 1 = 5, k = 3)$ is used with a homogeneous coordinate vector $h_i = 1, i \neq 3$. Values of h_3 range from 0 to 5. The rational B-spline basis functions shown in Fig. 4.1c with $h = 1$ are identical to the corresponding nonrational basis functions. Figure 4.2 shows

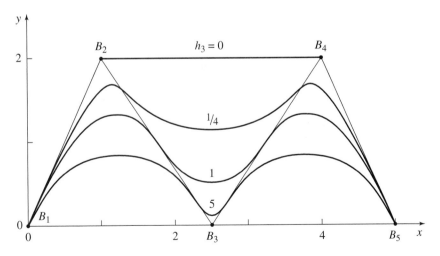

Figure 4.2 Rational B-spline curves for $n + 1 = 5$, $k = 3$ with open knot vector $[X] = [0 \quad 0 \quad 0 \quad 1 \quad 2 \quad 3 \quad 3 \quad 3]$ and $[H] = [1 \quad 1 \quad h_3 \quad 1 \quad 1]$.

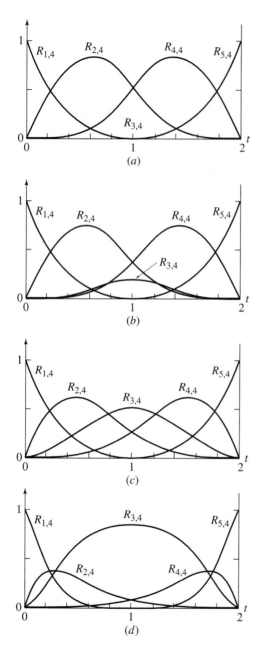

Figure 4.3   Rational B-spline basis functions for $n + 1 = 5$, $k = 4$ with open knot vector $[X] = [0 \; 0 \; 0 \; 0 \; 1 \; 2 \; 2 \; 2 \; 2]$, $[H] = [1 \; 1 \; h_3 \; 1 \; 1]$. (a) $h_3 = 0$; (b) $h_3 = \frac{1}{4}$; (c) $h_3 = 1$; (d) $h_3 = 5$.

the rational B-spline curve for $h_3 = 1$, which is also identical to the corresponding nonrational B-spline curve. Notice that for $h_3 = 0$ (see Fig. 4.1a) $R_{3,3} = 0$ everywhere. Thus, the corresponding polygon vertex, B_3, has no influence on the shape of the corresponding B-spline curve. This effect is shown in Fig. 4.2, where the defining polygon vertices B_2 and B_4 are connected by a straight line. Figure 4.1 also shows that as h_3 increases $R_{3,3}$ also increases; but, as a consequence of Eq. (4.4), $R_{2,3}$ and $R_{4,3}$ decrease. The effects on the corresponding rational B-spline curves are shown in Fig. 4.2. Note, in particular, that as h_3 increases the curve is pulled closer to B_3. Hence, as mentioned previously, the homogeneous coordinates provide additional blending capability. Similar characteristics are exhibited for the fourth-order ($k = 4$) rational B-spline basis functions and curves shown in Figs. 4.3 and 4.4, respectively. However, for the higher-order curve shown in Fig. 4.4, note that for $h_3 = 0$ the curve does not degenerate to a straight line between B_2 and B_4.

Periodic Rational B-spline Basis Functions and Curves

Figure 4.5 shows periodic uniform basis functions for $n + 1 = 5$, $k = 3$ for a knot vector $[X] = [0 \quad 1 \quad 2 \quad 3 \quad 4 \quad 5 \quad 6 \quad 7]$ and homogeneous coordinate vector $[H] = [1 \quad 1 \quad h_3 \quad 1 \quad 1]$, with $0 \le h_3 \le 5$. Here, as for nonrational

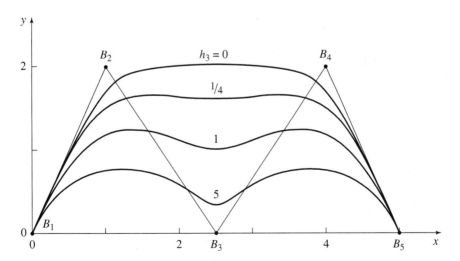

Figure 4.4 Rational B-spline curves for $n + 1 = 5$, $k = 4$ with open knot vector $[X] = [0 \quad 0 \quad 0 \quad 0 \quad 1 \quad 2 \quad 2 \quad 2 \quad 2]$, $[H] = [1 \quad 1 \quad h_3 \quad 1 \quad 1]$.

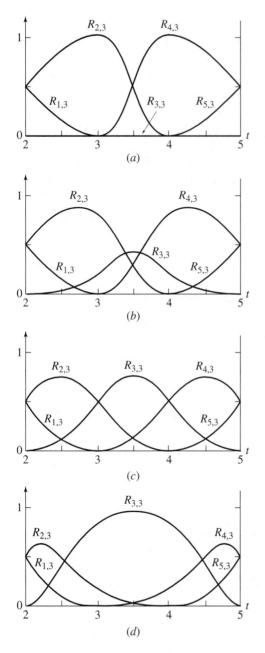

Figure 4.5 Rational B-spline basis functions for $n + 1 = 5$, $k = 3$ with periodic knot
vector $[X] = [0 \; 1 \; 2 \; 3 \; 4 \; 5 \; 6 \; 7]$ and $[H] = [1 \; 1 \; h_3 \; 1 \; 1]$.
(a) $h_3 = 0$; (b) $h_3 = 1/4$; (c) $h_3 = 1$; (d) $h_3 = 5$.

B-spline basis functions, the usable parameter range is $2 \le t \le 5$. Only this parameter range is shown in Fig. 4.5. Again, the rational B-spline basis functions for $h_3 = 1$ are identical to the corresponding nonrational basis functions. However, note that for $h_3 \ne 1$ the basis functions are no longer periodic and hence no longer translates of each other. Figure 4.6 shows the corresponding rational B-spline curves. Notice that, as shown by the arrows, the end points of all the curves are coincident.

Figures 4.7 and 4.8 show the corresponding rational B-spline fourth-order $(k = 4)$ basis functions and curves. Here, notice that the start and end points of the curves lie along a straight line.

Returning now to open rational B-spline curves, recall the $(t_{\max} - \epsilon)_{\epsilon \to 0}$ argument of Ex. 3.4, evaluation of Eqs. (4.2) and (4.3) at the ends of the curve shows that the first and last points are coincident with the first and last control polygon vertices. Specifically

$$P(0) = B_1 \qquad \text{and} \qquad P(t_{\max}) = P(n - k + 2) = B_{n+1}$$

The open rational B-spline curve of Fig. 4.9 shows that the effect of moving a single polygon vertex is similar to the results for nonrational B-splines. Here, $[H] = [1 \quad 1 \quad 1/4 \quad 1 \quad 1]$. If $h_3 = 0$, moving B_3 has no effect on the curve. As the value of h_3 increases, the effect of moving B_3 increases.

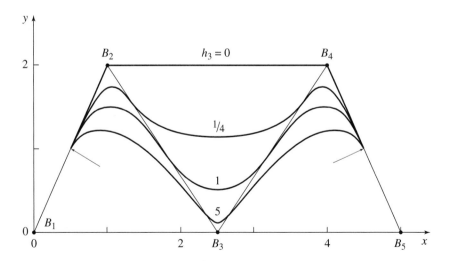

Figure 4.6 Rational B-spline curves for $n + 1 = 5$, $k = 4$ with periodic knot vector $[X] = [0 \quad 1 \quad 2 \quad 3 \quad 4 \quad 5 \quad 6 \quad 7]$ and $[H] = [1 \quad 1 \quad h_3 \quad 1 \quad 1]$.

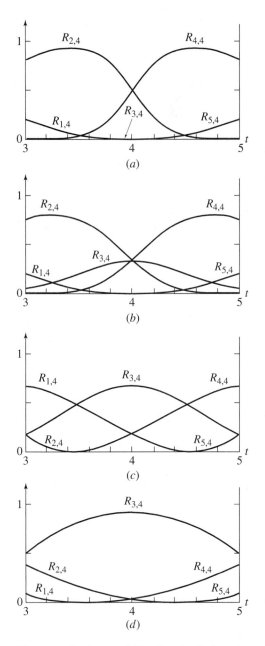

Figure 4.7   Rational B-spline basis functions for $n + 1 = 5$, $k = 4$ with periodic knot vector $[X] = [0 \quad 1 \quad 2 \quad 3 \quad 4 \quad 5 \quad 6 \quad 7 \quad 8]$ and $[H] = [1 \quad 1 \quad h_3 \quad 1 \quad 1]$. (a) $h_3 = 0$; (b) $h_3 = 1/4$; (c) $h_3 = 1$; (d) $h_3 = 5$.

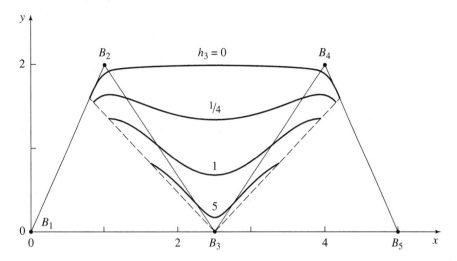

Figure 4.8 Rational B-spline curves for $n + 1 = 5$, $k = 4$ with periodic knot vector $[X] = [0 \quad 1 \quad 2 \quad 3 \quad 4 \quad 5 \quad 6 \quad 7 \quad 8]$, $[H] = [1 \quad 1 \quad h_3 \quad 1 \quad 1]$.

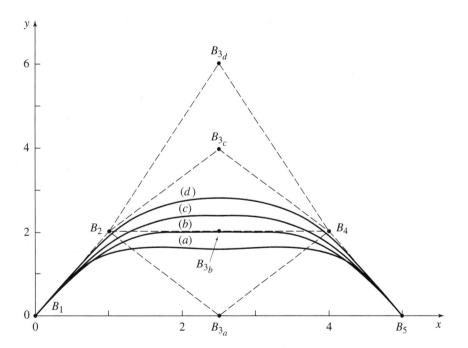

Figure 4.9 The effect of moving a single polygon vertex on a rational B-spline curve, $n + 1 = 5$, $k = 4$, $[H] = [1 \quad 1 \quad 1/4 \quad 1 \quad 1]$.

Figure 4.10 shows the effect of multiple coincident vertices at B_3 on a fourth-order rational B-spline curve. Note that, like their nonrational counterparts, $k-1$ coincident vertices yield a sharp corner, or cusp. Furthermore, because multiple coincident vertices yield spans of zero length, the existence of the sharp corner or cusp is independent of the values of $h_i \geq 0$ corresponding to the multiple vertices (see Appendix B, Prob. 4.3).

4.3 Calculating Rational B-spline Curves

An example more fully illustrates the procedure for calculation of rational B-spline curves.

Example 4.1   Calculation of Open Rational B-spline Curves

Consider the control polygon given by the vertices

$$B_1\,[0 \quad 1],\ B_2\,[1 \quad 2],\ B_3\,[5\!/2 \quad 0],\ B_4\,[4 \quad 2],\ B_5\,[5 \quad 0]$$

Determine the point at $t = 3\!/2$ for the third-order $(k = 3)$ open rational B-spline curve with homogeneous weighting factors given by $[H] = [1 \quad 1 \quad h_3 \quad 1 \quad 1]$, $h_3 = 0, 1\!/4, 1, 5$.

The knot vector is $[0 \quad 0 \quad 0 \quad 1 \quad 2 \quad 3 \quad 3 \quad 3]$. The parameter range is $0 \leq t \leq 3$. The curves are composed of three piecewise rational quadratics, one for each of the interior intervals in the knot vector.

Using Eqs. (3.2) on the interval $1 \leq t < 2$, the nonrational B-spline basis functions are

$$1 \leq t < 2$$

$$N_{4,1}(t) = 1; \qquad N_{i,1}(t) = 0, \quad i \neq 4$$

$$N_{3,2}(t) = (2 - t); \qquad N_{4,2}(t) = (t - 1); \qquad N_{i,2}(t) = 0, \quad i \neq 3, 4$$

$$N_{2,3}(t) = \frac{(2 - t)^2}{2}; \qquad N_{3,3}(t) = \frac{t(2 - t)}{2} + \frac{(3 - t)(t - 1)}{2};$$

$$N_{4,3}(t) = \frac{(t - 1)^2}{2}; \qquad N_{i,3}(t) = 0, \quad i \neq 2, 3, 4$$

From Eq. (4.3) and these results, after first determining the denominator

$$S = \sum_{i=1}^{n+1} h_i N_{i,k}(t) = h_1 N_{1,3}(t) + h_2 N_{2,3}(t) + h_3 N_{3,3}(t)$$

$$+ h_4 N_{4,3}(t) + h_5 N_{5,3}(t)$$

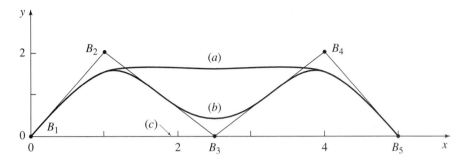

Figure 4.10 The effect of multiple vertices at B_3 on a rational B-spline curve with $n + 1 = 5$, $k = 4$. (a) Single vertex, $[H] = [1 \quad 1 \quad 1/4 \quad 1 \quad 1]$; (b) double vertex, $[H] = [1 \quad 1 \quad 1/4 \quad 1/4 \quad 1 \quad 1]$; (c) triple vertex, $[H] = [1 \quad 1 \quad 1/4 \quad 1/4 \quad 1/4 \quad 1 \quad 1]$.

the rational B-spline basis functions are

$$1 \le t < 2$$

$$h_3 = 0$$

$$S = h_2 N_{2,3}(t) + h_4 N_{4,3}(t)$$

$$= \frac{(2 - t)^2}{2} + \frac{(t - 1)^2}{2} = \frac{2t^2 - 6t + 5}{2}$$

$$R_{1,3}(t) = 0$$

$$R_{2,3}(t) = \frac{h_2 N_{2,3}(t)}{S} = \frac{(2 - t)^2}{2t^2 - 6t + 5}$$

$$R_{3,3}(t) = 0$$

$$R_{4,3}(t) = \frac{h_4 N_{4,3}(t)}{S} = \frac{(t - 1)^2}{2t^2 - 6t + 5}$$

$$R_{5,3}(t) = 0$$

$$h_3 = 1/4$$

$$S = h_2 N_{2,3}(t) + h_3 N_{3,3}(t) + h_4 N_{4,3}(t)$$

$$= \frac{(2 - t)^2}{2} + \frac{t(2 - t)}{8} + \frac{(3 - t)(t - 1)}{8} + \frac{(t - 1)^2}{2}$$

$$= \frac{6t^2 - 18t + 17}{8}$$

$$R_{1,3}(t) = 0$$

$$R_{2,3}(t) = \frac{4(2 - t)^2}{6t^2 - 18t + 17}$$

$$R_{3,3}(t) = \frac{t(2-t) + (3-t)(t-1)}{6t^2 - 18t + 17} = \frac{-2t^2 + 6t - 3}{6t^2 - 18t + 17}$$

$$R_{4,3}(t) = \frac{4(t-1)^2}{6t^2 - 18t + 17}$$

$$R_{5,3}(t) = 0$$

$h_3 = 1$

$S = 1$

$$R_{1,3}(t) = 0$$

$$R_{2,3}(t) = N_{2,3}(t) = \frac{(2-t)^2}{2}$$

$$R_{3,3}(t) = N_{3,3}(t) = \frac{t(2-t)}{2} + \frac{(3-t)(t-1)}{2}$$

$$R_{4,3}(t) = N_{4,3}(t) = \frac{(t-1)^2}{2}$$

$$R_{5,3}(t) = 0$$

$h_3 = 5$

$$S = \frac{(2-t)^2}{2} + \frac{5t(2-t)}{2} + \frac{5(3-t)(t-1)}{2} + \frac{(t-1)^2}{2}$$

$$= -4t^2 + 12t - 5$$

$$R_{1,3}(t) = 0$$

$$R_{2,3}(t) = \frac{(2-t)^2}{2(-4t^2 + 12t - 5)}$$

$$R_{3,3}(t) = \frac{5t(2-t) + 5(3-t)(t-1)}{2(-4t^2 + 12t - 5)} = \frac{5(-2t^2 + 6t - 3)}{2(-4t^2 + 12t - 5)}$$

$$R_{4,3}(t) = \frac{(t-1)^2}{2(-4t^2 + 12t - 5)}$$

$$R_{5,3}(t) = 0$$

Complete results are shown in Fig. 4.1. Evaluating these results at $t = 3/2$ yields

$h_3 = 0$: $R_{1,3}(3/2) = 0$; $R_{2,3}(3/2) = 1/2$; $R_{3,3}(3/2) = 0$;
$\qquad\qquad$ $R_{4,3}(3/2) = 1/2$; $R_{5,3}(3/2) = 0$

$h_3 = 1/4$: $R_{1,3}(3/2) = 0$; $R_{2,3}(3/2) = 2/7$; $R_{3,3}(3/2) = 3/7$;
$\qquad\qquad$ $R_{4,3}(3/2) = 2/7$; $R_{5,3}(3/2) = 0$

$h_3 = 1$: $R_{1,3}(3/2) = 0$; $R_{2,3}(3/2) = 1/8$; $R_{3,3}(3/2) = 3/4$;
$\qquad\qquad$ $R_{4,3}(3/2) = 1/8$; $R_{5,3}(3/2) = 0$

$h_3 = 5$: $R_{1,3}(3/2) = 0$; $R_{2,3}(3/2) = 1/32$; $R_{3,3}(3/2) = 15/16$;
$\qquad\qquad$ $R_{4,3}(3/2) = 1/32$; $R_{5,3}(3/2) = 0$

The corresponding points on the rational B-spline curves are

$$h_3 = 0: \qquad P(\tfrac{3}{2}) = \tfrac{1}{2}\,[1 \quad 2] + \tfrac{1}{2}\,[4 \quad 2] = [\tfrac{5}{2} \quad 2]$$

$$h_3 = \tfrac{1}{4}: \qquad P(\tfrac{3}{2}) = \tfrac{2}{7}\,[1 \quad 2] + \tfrac{3}{7}\,[\tfrac{5}{2} \quad 0] + \tfrac{2}{7}\,[4 \quad 2] = [\tfrac{5}{2} \quad \tfrac{8}{7}]$$

$$h_3 = 1: \qquad P(\tfrac{3}{2}) = \tfrac{1}{8}\,[1 \quad 2] + \tfrac{3}{4}\,[\tfrac{5}{2} \quad 0] + \tfrac{1}{8}\,[4 \quad 2] = [\tfrac{5}{2} \quad \tfrac{1}{2}]$$

$$h_3 = 5: \qquad P(\tfrac{3}{2}) = \tfrac{1}{32}\,[1 \quad 2] + \tfrac{15}{16}\,[\tfrac{5}{2} \quad 0] + \tfrac{1}{32}\,[4 \quad 2] = [\tfrac{5}{2} \quad \tfrac{1}{8}]$$

Complete results are shown in Fig. 4.2.

4.4 Derivatives of NURBS Curves

The derivatives of rational B-spline curves are obtained by formal differentiation of Eqs. (4.2) and (4.3). Specifically

$$P'(t) = \sum_{i=1}^{n+1} B_i R'_{i,k}(t) \tag{4.5}$$

with

$$R'_{i,k}(t) = \frac{h_i N'_{i,k}(t)}{\displaystyle\sum_{i=1}^{n+1} h_i N_{i,k}} - \frac{h_i N_{i,k} \displaystyle\sum_{i=1}^{n+1} h_i N'_{i,k}}{\left(\displaystyle\sum_{i=1}^{n+1} h_i N_{i,k}\right)^2} \tag{4.6}$$

Evaluating these results at $t = 0$ and $t = n - k + 2$ yields

$$P'(0) = (k-1)\frac{h_2}{h_1}(B_2 - B_1) \tag{4.7}$$

$$P'(n - k + 2) = (k-1)\frac{h_n}{h_{n+1}}(B_{n+1} - B_n) \tag{4.8}$$

which shows that the direction of the slope is along the first and last polygon spans, respectively. Higher-order derivatives are obtained in a similar manner (see Appendix B, Probs. 4.4 and 4.5).

A simple example illustrates these results.

Example 4.2 Derivatives of Open Rational B-spline Curves

Consider the control polygon previously used in Exs. 3.4 and 3.8. The polygon vertices are

$$B_1\,[1 \quad 1],\; B_2\,[2 \quad 3],\; B_3\,[4 \quad 3],\; B_4\,[3 \quad 1]$$

Determine the first derivative of the second-order rational B-spline curve $(k = 2)$ with $[H] = [1 \quad 1/2 \quad 1 \quad 1]$.

The knot vector is

$$[X] = [0 \quad 0 \quad 1 \quad 2 \quad 3 \quad 3]$$

The parameter range is $0 \le t \le 3$. From Eq. (4.5), the first derivative is

$$P'(t) = B_1 R'_{1,2}(t) + B_2 R'_{2,2}(t) + B_3 R'_{3,2}(t) + B_4 R'_{4,3}(t)$$

From Eqs. (3.2) and (3.29), the nonrational basis functions and their derivatives are

$0 \le t < 1$

$$N_{1,2}(t) = 1 - t; \qquad N_{2,2}(t) = t; \qquad N_{i,2}(t) = 0, \quad i \ne 1, 2$$
$$N'_{1,2}(t) = -1; \qquad N'_{2,2}(t) = 1; \qquad N'_{i,2}(t) = 0, \quad i \ne 1, 2$$

Using Eq. (4.6), the rational basis functions and their derivatives are

$$\sum_{i=1}^{n+1} h_i N_{i,2} = \frac{2 - t}{2}; \qquad \sum_{i=1}^{n+1} h_i N'_{i,2} = -1/2;$$

$$R'_{1,2}(t) = \frac{2}{2 - t}\left((-1) - (1 - t)\frac{(-1)}{(2 - t)}\right) = \frac{-2}{(2 - t)^2}$$

$$R'_{2,2}(t) = 1/2\left(\frac{2}{2 - t}\right)\left(1 - t\frac{(-1)}{(2 - t)}\right) = \frac{2}{(2 - t)^2}$$

$$R'_{i,2}(t) = 0, \quad i \ne 1, 2$$

Thus

$$P'(t) = \frac{2}{(2 - t)^2}(B_2 - B_1)$$

In contrast to the nonrational B-spline curve of Ex. 3.8, note here that although the direction is that of the first polygon span, the magnitude now varies along the curve length. At $t = 0$ (the beginning of the curve)

$$P'(t) = 1/2\,(B_2 - B_1)$$

which shows that the magnitude is half that found for the nonrational B-spline curve in Ex. 3.8.

For the interval

$1 \le t < 2$

$$N_{2,2}(t) = 2 - t; \qquad N_{3,2}(t) = t - 1; \qquad N_{i,2}(t) = 0, \quad i \ne 2, 3$$
$$N'_{2,2}(t) = -1; \qquad N'_{3,2}(t) = 1; \qquad N'_{i,2}(t) = 0, \quad i \ne 2, 3$$

Here

$$\sum_{i=1}^{n+1} h_i N_{i,2} = \frac{t}{2}; \qquad \sum_{i=1}^{n+1} h_i N'_{i,2} = \frac{1}{2};$$

$$R'_{2,2}(t) = \frac{1}{2} \frac{2}{t} \left((-1) - (2-t) \left(\frac{1}{t} \right) \right) = -\frac{2}{t^2}$$

$$R'_{3,2}(t) = \frac{2}{t} \left((1) - (t-1) \left(\frac{1}{t} \right) \right) = \frac{2}{t^2}$$

$$R'_{i,2}(t) = 0, \quad i \neq 2,3$$

Thus

$$P'(t) = \frac{2}{t^2}(B_3 - B_2)$$

For the interval

$$2 \leq t < 3$$

$$N_{3,2}(t) = 3 - t; \qquad N_{4,2}(t) = t - 2; \qquad N_{i,2}(t) = 0, \quad i \neq 3,4$$

$$N'_{3,2}(t) = -1; \qquad N'_{4,2}(t) = 1; \qquad N'_{i,2}(t) = 0, \quad i \neq 3,4$$

With

$$\sum_{i=1}^{n+1} h_i N_{i,2} = 1; \qquad \sum_{i=1}^{n+1} h_i N'_{i,2} = 0;$$

$$R'_{3,2}(t) = N'_{3,2}(t) = -1; \qquad R'_{4,2}(t) = N'_{4,2}(t) = 1;$$

$$R'_{i,2}(t) = 0, \quad i \neq 3,4$$

Hence

$$P'(t) = B_4 - B_3$$

Using the $t = (3 - \epsilon)$, $\epsilon \to 0$ argument yields the same result at $t = 3$.

4.5 Conic Sections

As mentioned previously, rational B-spline curves are used to represent all the conic sections. Furthermore, they provide a single mathematical description capable of blending the conic sections into free-form curves. Because the conic sections are described by quadratic equations, it is convenient to first consider a quadratic rational B-spline ($k = 3$) defined by three polygon vertices ($n + 1 = 3$), with knot vector $[X] = [0 \ \ 0 \ \ 0 \ \ 1 \ \ 1 \ \ 1]$. Writing this out yields

$$P(t) = \frac{h_1 N_{1,3}(t)B_1 + h_2 N_{2,3}(t)B_2 + h_3 N_{3,3}(t)B_3}{h_1 N_{1,3}(t) + h_2 N_{2,3}(t) + h_3 N_{3,3}(t)} \tag{4.9}$$

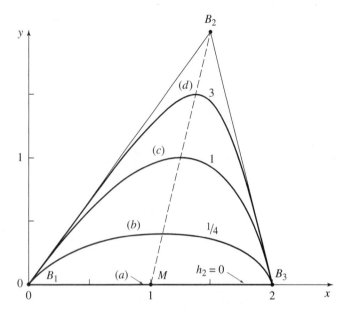

Figure 4.11   Conic sections defined by rational B-spline (Bézier) curves. (a) Straight line, $h_2 = 0$; (b) elliptic, $h_2 = 1/4$; (c) parabolic, $h_2 = 1$; (d) hyperbolic, $h_2 = 3$.

which, in fact, is a third-order rational Bézier curve (see Fig. 4.11). It is convenient to assume $h_1 = h_3 = 1$. Equation (4.9) then reduces to

$$P(t) = \frac{N_{1,3}(t)B_1 + h_2 N_{2,3}(t)B_2 + N_{3,3}(t)B_3}{N_{1,3}(t) + h_2 N_{2,3}(t) + N_{3,3}(t)} \qquad (4.10)$$

Now, if $h_2 = 0$, a straight line between B_1 and B_3 results. If $h_2 \to \infty$, the control polygon is reproduced. When $h_2 = 0$ and $t = 1/2$, the midpoint of the line $B_1 B_3$, labeled M in Fig. 4.11, is obtained. Similarly, when $h_2 \to \infty$, $t = 1/2$ yields the polygon point at B_2. For $0 < h_2 < \infty$, the point S corresponding to the point at $t = 1/2$ on the curve $P(t)$ moves along the straight line connecting M and B_2. S is called the shoulder point. The value of h_2 determines the type of conic section. Lee [Lee86] showed that if

$h_2 = 0$ a straight line results;

$0 < h_2 < 1$ an elliptic curve segment results;

$h_2 = 1$ a parabolic curve segment results;

$h_2 > 1$ a hyperbolic curve segment results.

Using Eqs. (3.2) and substituting $t = 1/2$ into Eq. (4.10) yields

$$P(t) = \frac{(1-t)^2 B_1 + 2h_2 t (1-t) B_2 + t^2 B_3}{(1-t)^2 + 2h_2 t (1-t) + t^2}$$

For $t = 1/2$, $P(t) = S$, which yields

$$S = \frac{1}{1+h_2} \frac{B_1 + B_3}{2} + \frac{h_2}{1+h_2} B_2 = \frac{M}{1+h_2} + \frac{h_2}{1+h_2} B_2 \qquad (4.11)$$

Writing the parametric equation of the straight line between M and B_2 gives

$$S = (1-s)M + sB_2 \qquad (4.12)$$

where s is the parameter. Equating coefficients of Eqs. (4.11) and (4.12) shows that

$$s = \frac{h_2}{1+h_2} \qquad \text{and} \qquad h_2 = \frac{s}{1-s} = \frac{M-S}{S-B_2} \qquad (4.13)$$

The parameter s controls the shape of the curve and its conic form. Hence, it is a good design tool.

Because a circle is a special case of an ellipse, for a particular value of h_2 Eq. (4.10) yields a circular arc. Because of symmetry, B_1, B_2 and B_3 for a circular arc form an isosceles triangle, as shown in Fig. 4.12. The required value of h_2 is determined from the geometry shown in Fig. 4.12.

Because the triangle $B_1 B_2 B_3$ is isosceles, S is the maximum point on the curve. Hence, the tangent at S is parallel to the line $B_1 B_3$. The triangle $B_1 q S$ is also isosceles, with equal base angles $\angle SB_1 q$ and $\angle B_1 Sq$, labeled $\theta/2$ in Fig. 4.12. Because the tangent at S is parallel to the line $B_1 B_3$, the angles $\angle qSB_1$ and $\angle SB_1 M$ are equal. Thus, the angle $\angle SB_1 M = \theta/2$ is half the base angle of the isosceles triangle formed by B_1, B_2 and B_3.

From Eq. (4.13) and these results, h_2 is

$$h_2 = \frac{M-S}{S-B_2} = \frac{e \tan(\theta/2)}{f \sin\theta - e \tan(\theta/2)}$$

Recalling that $\tan(\theta/2) = \sin\theta/(1 + \cos\theta)$ yields

$$h_2 = \frac{\dfrac{e \sin\theta}{1 + \cos\theta}}{f \sin\theta - \dfrac{e \sin\theta}{1 + \cos\theta}} = \frac{e}{f(1 + \cos\theta) - e} = \frac{e}{f} = \cos\theta \qquad (4.14)$$

The portion of the circle subtended by the arc is twice the angle θ. For an arc of $120°$, $\theta = 60°$ and $h_2 = 1/2$. For this particular case, the radius of the circle is $2(S - M)$.

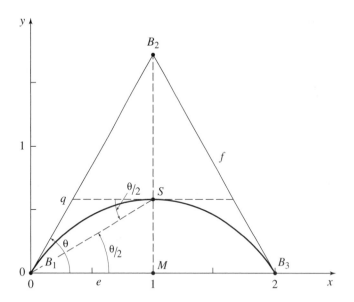

Figure 4.12 Circular arc formed as a rational B-spline curve.

A full circle is formed by piecing together multiple segments. Specifically, a full circle is given by the three rational quadratic B-spline curve segments, each subtending an arc of 120°. The control polygon vertices form an equilateral triangle, as shown in Fig. 4.13a. The nonuniform knot and homogeneous coordinate vectors are

$$[X] = [0 \quad 0 \quad 0 \quad 1 \quad 1 \quad 2 \quad 2 \quad 3 \quad 3 \quad 3]$$

$$[H] = [1 \quad \tfrac{1}{2} \quad 1 \quad \tfrac{1}{2} \quad 1 \quad \tfrac{1}{2} \quad 1]$$

Similarly, a full circle is also given by the four rational quadratic B-spline curve segments, each subtending an arc of 90° with the control polygon forming a square, as shown in Fig. 4.13b. Here, the nonuniform knot and homogeneous coordinate vectors are

$$[X] = [0 \quad 0 \quad 0 \quad 1 \quad 1 \quad 2 \quad 2 \quad 3 \quad 3 \quad 4 \quad 4 \quad 4]$$

$$[H] = [1 \quad \sqrt{2}/2 \quad 1 \quad \sqrt{2}/2 \quad 1 \quad \sqrt{2}/2 \quad 1 \quad \sqrt{2}/2 \quad 1]$$

An example illustrates the techniques for generating conic sections using rational B-splines and smoothly blending them into free-form curves.

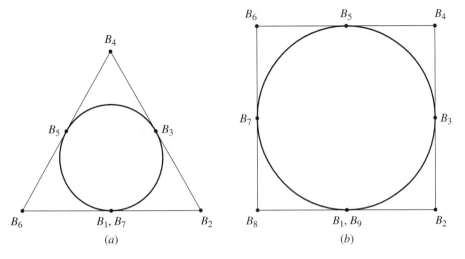

Figure 4.13 Rational B-spline circles. (a) Three 120° segments; (b) four 90° segments.

Example 4.3 Conic Sections Using Rational B-splines

Construct a single third-order rational B-spline curve that smoothly blends a 90° circular arc defined by a quadratic rational B-spline curve with polygon vertices

$$B_1\begin{bmatrix}0 & 0\end{bmatrix},\ B_2\begin{bmatrix}0 & 2\end{bmatrix},\ B_3\begin{bmatrix}2 & 2\end{bmatrix}$$

into the third-order quadratic rational B-spline curve defined by

$$B_3\begin{bmatrix}2 & 2\end{bmatrix},\ B_4\begin{bmatrix}4 & 2\end{bmatrix},\ B_5\begin{bmatrix}6 & 3\end{bmatrix},\ B_6\begin{bmatrix}7 & 5\end{bmatrix}$$

with $h_i = 1$, $4 \leq i \leq 6$.

The 90° circular arc has knot vector

$$\begin{bmatrix}0 & 0 & 0 & 1 & 1 & 1\end{bmatrix}$$

and homogeneous coordinate vector $\begin{bmatrix}1 & \sqrt{2}/2 & 1\end{bmatrix}$. The rational B-spline curve that is defined by B_3, B_4, B_5, B_6 has knot vector

$$\begin{bmatrix}0 & 0 & 0 & 1 & 2 & 2 & 2\end{bmatrix}$$

with homogeneous coordinate vector $\begin{bmatrix}1 & 1 & 1 & 1\end{bmatrix}$.

$$[X] = \begin{bmatrix}0 & 0 & 0 & 1 & 1 & 2 & 3 & 3 & 3\end{bmatrix}$$

is the nonuniform knot vector for the combined curve, with

$$\begin{bmatrix}1 & \sqrt{2}/2 & 1 & 1 & 1 & 1\end{bmatrix}$$

the homogeneous coordinate vector. The result is shown in Fig. 4.14.

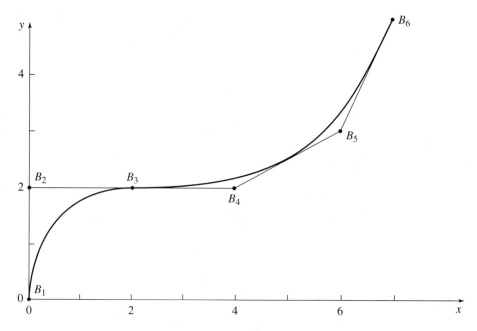

Figure 4.14   Blended quadratic rational B-spline curve.

Lewis Knapp

The way I usually tell the story, it starts like this. There I was on the Syracuse campus in the middle of winter, starting graduate school. I had just left the military, where I had spent the better part of four years in the bowels of the nuclear deterrent missile system. It was in the middle of the Vietnam War, and I was aware that I was now among civilians again. My first class (IBM assembler language) was taught by a long curly-headed graduate student from New Jersey. I did think it a bit strange that he was dressed in bright blue stretch ski pants because he was headed directly to the slopes after class, but I later became familiar with that concept firsthand.

The computer graphics community at Syracuse centered around Steve Coons. Coons had consulted with Ford and McDonnell Douglas in addition to his MIT experience, in what must have been the early days of computer aided design. He carried in his head a profound understanding of the 'surface description problem,' and a methodology of structuring ways to define surfaces in a highly distilled matrix form that hid the necessity of having to fully understand the 'magic matrices,' which formed its mathematical basis.

Steve frequently hosted visiting professors, and a broad mix of research opportunities prevailed. Working with Robin Forrest, Bill Gordon and Professor Bézier was stimulating. Being seated with people who knew the mathematics and understood how graphics could help in design provided a fertile context for exploring techniques in graphics and in surface modeling.

While at Syracuse, I had the good fortune to participate in an informal student exchange program with the University of Cambridge, England, which originated as a result of connections made while Charles Lang was a member of D.T. Ross's research team at MIT. Robin Forrest subsequently visited Coons at MIT, Rich Riesenfeld as graduate student went to Cambridge, Robin as visiting professor came to Syracuse, and I spent several months in summer 1972 at Cambridge as Robin's visitor. When I visited, the lab was just bringing up a three-dimensional foam cutter, a lightweight alternative to heavy-duty N.C. machines for the visualization of shapes. I implemented a tensor product B-spline surface package and cut some test shapes to see what the surfaces really looked like when you made them into physical objects.

The research area I eventually became interested in was at the juncture of B-splines, user interaction, and surfaces that had nice continuity properties. There was a lot of emphasis placed on surface curvature continuity by the user communities with which we had contact—the auto stylists, the aircraft engineers and the shipbuilders.

The simplicity of Bézier's interactive design system, UNISURF, with its large drawing board interface for the stylists at Renault, was a very profound coupling of user interface to deep mathematical underpinnings.

The uniform basis B-spline was exciting from several viewpoints: second-order parametric continuity at the knots, the possibility of local shape deformation, all at the cost of calculating cubic polynomials. The discovery that the B-spline was an appropriate spline generalization of the Bézier curve and its Bernstein polynomial pedigree gave an academic assurance that the B-spline was not just a hack. It led to uncovering what the parametric 'knot vector' had to do with the curve shape. The nonuniform basis B-spline allowed many nonobvious ways to control continuity and to implement interactive user interface methods. The instructor in the blue ski pants was, of course, Rich Riesenfeld; and I learned much about the B-spline from him.

It took a bit of study to find that MIT MAC TR-41 (Steve Coons's 'red book') wasn't so much about cryptic matrix notation and the bicubic Coons patch as about the very general form of blending surfaces he had invented.

The vision that the nonengineering user, or 'creative type' like the automobile stylist, could use B-spline curve and surface forms directly had a lot of appeal. My studies focused on using nonuniform basis B-splines in the framework of Coons's Boolean sum surfaces to address both user interaction and control of surface shape continuity.

After I left Syracuse, I had the good fortune to spend a year at Pratt & Whitney Aircraft as an Evans & Sutherland employee. My task was to support an interactive graphics device (The Picture System, SN 6) that was used for visualization of many aspects of jet engine design. I got to see firsthand how a large CAM/CAD investment in the manufacturing process committed the company to the tools and methods of the day. It was pretty hard to stir up much interest in new curve and surface math in an environment that had many existing solutions to the surface representation problem.

I went on to Utah, spent quite a while working on graphics hardware and software at E&S, and worked with Rich Riesenfeld and Elaine Cohen on the Alpha_1 project for several years before going off to California to seek my fortune.

I currently live and work in Santa Cruz, CA, where I design and fabricate motion-controlled camera and object positioners for QuickTimeVR object photography.

Lewis Knapp
Santa Cruz, January 2000

Lewie Knapp and Robin Forrest at the Cambridge University CAD laboratory examine some of the B-spline surfaces generated on the foam-cutting machine (circa 1973). (Courtesy of Robin Forrest.)

Chapter 5

Bézier Surfaces 5

Surfaces and their description play a critical role in design and manufacturing. The design and manufacture of automobile bodies, ship hulls, aircraft fuselages and wings; propeller, turbine, compressor and fan blades; glassware and bottles; and furniture and shoes are obvious examples. Surface shape or geometry is the essence of design for either functional or aesthetic reasons. Surface description also plays an important role in the representation of data obtained from medical, geological, physical and other natural phenomena.

In design and engineering, the traditional way of representing a surface is to use multiple orthogonal projections. In effect, the surface is defined by a net or mesh of orthogonal plane curves lying in plane sections, plus multiple orthogonal projections of certain three-dimensional 'feature' lines (see Fig. 5.1). The curves can originally be designed on paper, or they can be taken (digitized) from a three-dimensional model, e.g., the clay stylist's model traditionally used in the automotive industry.

In computer graphics and computer aided design, it is advantageous to develop a 'true' three-dimensional mathematical model of a surface. Such a model allows early and relatively easy analysis of surface characteristics, e.g., curvature, or of physical quantities that depend on the surface, e.g.,

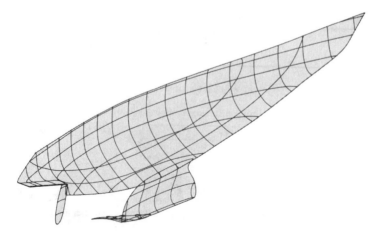

Figure 5.1   A surface described as a net of orthogonal planar curves. (Courtesy of George Hazen.)

volume, surface area, moment of inertia. Visual rendering of the surface for design or design verification is simplified. Furthermore, generation of the necessary information required to fabricate the surface, e.g., numerical control codes, is also considerably simplified as compared to the traditional 'net of lines' approach. Early work by Bézier [Bezi71,72], Sabin [Sabi71]) and Peters [Pete73], among others, demonstrated the feasibility of this approach.

There are two basic philosophies embedded in surface description techniques. The first philosophy seeks to create a mathematical surface from known data. The second, mostly associated with the name of Bézier, seeks to create a mathematical surface ab initio. Initially, disciplines that depended upon numerical parameters, e.g., engineering, were attracted to the first approach, while disciplines that depended upon visual, tactile or aesthetic factors, e.g., stylists and graphic artists, were attracted to the ab initio techniques. Original work by Rogers [Roge77, 79, 80, 82] with real-time interactive systems for design of ship hulls, and by Cohen [Cohe83] for general surface design, show that the two approaches are compatible. Today the use of B-spline surfaces, in particular nonuniform rational B-spline surfaces (NURBS), is the standard in the computer graphics industry, in computer aided design and in the entertainment industry, to name only a few.

Analytical descriptions exist for many surfaces, e.g., quadric surfaces, i.e., spheres, ellipsoids, paraboloids, as well as for general implicit surfaces (see [Bloo97]). There are, however, many surfaces for which analytical descriptions do not exist. Typical examples of this are automobile bodies, ship hulls, aircraft fuselages and wings, sculptures, bottles, shoes, to name a few. These surfaces are represented in a *piecewise* fashion, i.e., similar to a patchwork quilt. A vector-valued parametric representation is used because it is axis independent, avoids infinite slope values with respect to some arbitrary axis system, allows the unambiguous representation of multivalued surfaces or space functions, facilitates the representation of surfaces in homogeneous coordinates and is compatible with the use of the three-dimensional homogeneous coordinate transformations (see Chapter 1 and [Roge90a]).

The remainder of this book is concerned with a discussion of the techniques and methods of mathematically describing surface patches. The intention is to join individual patches together along their edges to create a complete surface.

5.1 Mapping Parametric Surfaces

The methods of parametric surface description are most conveniently described in terms of the mapping of a two-parameter planar surface in uw parametric space into three-dimensional xyz object space. Here, the discussion is restricted to mapping the rectangular planar surface in parametric space shown in Fig. 5.2 and given by

$$C_1 \leq u \leq C_2$$

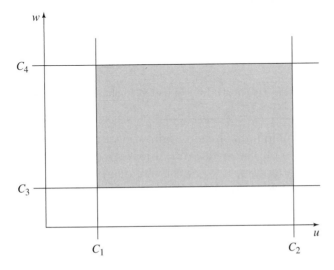

Figure 5.2 Rectangular parametric planar surface.

$$C_3 \leq w \leq C_4 \qquad (5.1)$$

where C_1, C_2, C_3, C_4 define the boundaries (edges) of the rectangular planar surface. A surface in object space is represented by the functions that map this parametric surface into xyz object space, i.e.

$$x = x(u, w)$$

$$y = y(u, w)$$

$$z = z(u, w) \qquad (5.2)$$

A simple two-dimensional example serves to illustrate the technique.

Example 5.1 Two-dimensional Surface Mapping

Map the surface described by

$$x = 3u + w \qquad 0 \leq u \leq 1$$

$$y = 2u + 3w + uw \qquad 0 \leq w \leq 1$$

$$z = 0$$

in parametric space into object space. First, note that because $z = \text{constant} = 0$, the surface in object space is also two-dimensional lying in the $z = 0$ plane.

The boundaries of the surface in object space are defined by mapping the boundaries of the rectangle in parametric space to object space. Thus, for

$u = 0 \qquad x = w, \; y = 3w \quad \text{and} \quad y = 3x$

$u = 1 \qquad x = w + 3, \; y = 2(2w + 1) \quad \text{and} \quad y = 2(2x - 5)$

$w = 0 \qquad x = 3u, \; y = 2u \quad \text{and} \quad y = \frac{2}{3}x$

$w = 1 \qquad x = 3u + 1, \; y = 3u + 3 \quad \text{and} \quad y = x + 2$

In each case, the value of the parameter (u or w) is eliminated to obtain $y = y(x)$. The results are shown in Fig. 5.3.

As shown in this example, holding a single parametric value constant in parametric space yields a curve on the surface in object space. The curve is called an isoparametric or parametric line. Specifying one parameter as a function of the other in parametric space, i.e., $u = u(w)$, also yields a curve on the surface in object space. For example, the functions

$$u = w \qquad 0 \leq w \leq 1$$

$$u = 1 - w$$

represent the diagonals of the unit square in parametric space.

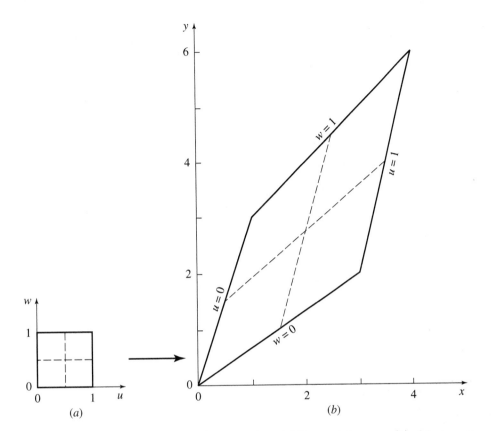

Figure 5.3 Two-dimensional surface mapping. (a) Parametric space; (b) object space.

Specifying both parametric values yields a point on the surface in object space. Alternatively, a point (or points) is specified by the intersection of two curves in parametric space, e.g., $f(u, w) = 0$ and $g(u, w) = 0$. The intersection in parametric space transforms (or maps) into the intersection in object space (see also Chapter 1). A more complex three-dimensional example further illustrates the mapping concept.

Example 5.2 Three-dimensional Surface Mapping

Map the surface described by

$$x(u, w) = (u - w)^2 \qquad 0 \le u \le 1$$
$$y(u, w) = u - w^2 \qquad 0 \le w \le 1$$
$$z(u, w) = uw$$

in parametric space into object space. Determine the boundary curves, and calculate the coordinates of the point at $u = w = 1/2$ on the surface in object space.

First, determine the boundary curves

$$u = 0 \qquad x = w^2, y = -w^2, z = 0 \quad \text{and} \quad x = -y, z = 0$$

$$u = 1 \qquad x = (1 - w)^2, y = 1 - w^2, z = w \quad \text{and} \quad x = (1 - z)^2, y = 1 - z^2$$

$$w = 0 \qquad x = u^2, y = u, z = 0 \quad \text{and} \quad x = y^2, z = 0$$

$$w = 1 \qquad x = (u - 1)^2, y = u - 1, z = u \quad \text{and} \quad x = y^2, z = 1 + y$$

The boundary curves are shown by heavy lines in Fig. 5.4d.

Now writing the parametric surface as the vector-valued function

$$Q(u, w) = [\, x(u, w) \quad y(u, w) \quad z(u, w) \,] = [\, (u - w)^2 \quad u - w^2 \quad uw \,]$$

yields
$$Q(1/2, 1/2) = [\, 0 \quad 1/4 \quad 1/4 \,]$$

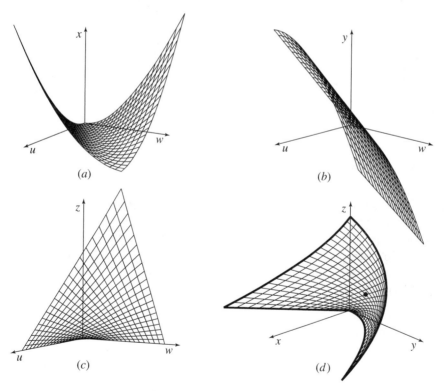

(a)

(b)

(c)

(d)

Figure 5.4 Three-dimensional surface mapping. (a) x component; (b) y component; (c) z component; (d) complete.

as the coordinates of the point at $u = w = 1/2$, shown as the dot in Fig. 5.4*d*. Notice that each of the components of the surface in object space is also a function of the parameters u, w. Each of these individual components is shown in Figs. 5.4*a*, 5.4*b* and 5.4*c*. The total surface shown in Fig. 5.4*d* is a composite of each of the individual mapped components.

Finally, the mappings for the degenerate patches corresponding to a point and a line are of interest. For a point, the mapping is

$$x = \text{constant}, \quad y = \text{constant}, \quad z = \text{constant}$$

For a line, the mapping is of the form $x = u$, $y = \text{constant}$, $z = \text{constant}$.

5.2 Bézier Surface Definition and Characteristics

A Cartesian or tensor product Bézier surface is given by

$$Q(u, w) = \sum_{i=0}^{n} \sum_{j=0}^{m} B_{i,j} J_{n,i}(u) K_{m,j}(w) \tag{5.3}$$

where $J_{n,i}(u)$ and $K_{m,j}(w)$ are the Bernstein basis functions in the u and w parametric directions (see Eqs. (2.2) and (2.3)). Repeating the definition previously given in Sec. 2.1 for convenience yields

$$J_{n,i}(u) = \binom{n}{i} u^i (1 - u)^{n-i} \quad (0)^0 \equiv 1 \tag{2.2}$$

$$K_{m,j}(w) = \binom{m}{j} w^j (1 - w)^{m-j}$$

with

$$\binom{n}{i} = \frac{n!}{i!(n - i)!} \quad 0! \equiv 1 \tag{2.3}$$

$$\binom{m}{j} = \frac{m!}{j!(m - j)!}$$

The $B_{i,j}$s are the vertices of a polygonal control net, as shown in Fig. 5.5. The indices n and m are one less than the number of polygon vertices in the u and w directions, respectively. For quadrilateral surface patches, the control net must be topologically rectangular, i.e., the net must have the same number of vertices in each 'row'.

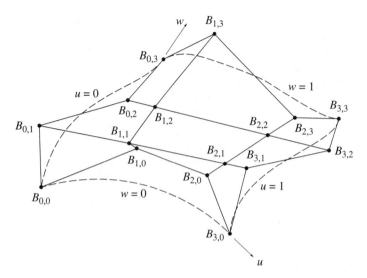

Figure 5.5 Bézier surface nomenclature.

Again, as when defining Bézier curves, because the Bernstein basis is used for the surface-blending functions, many properties of the Bézier surface are known. For example:

The degree of the surface in each parametric direction is one less than the number of control net vertices in that direction.

The continuity of the surface in each parametric direction is two less than the number of control net vertices in that direction.

The surface generally follows the shape of the control net.

Only the corner points of the control net and the resulting Bézier surface are coincident.

The surface is contained within the convex hull of the control net.

The surface does not exhibit the variation-diminishing property. The variation-diminishing property for bivariant surfaces is both undefined and unknown.

The surface is invariant under an affine transformation.

Each of the boundary curves of a Bézier surface is a Bézier curve. Keeping this fact in mind and considering the control net for a 4×4 bicubic Bézier surface shown schematically in Fig. 5.6, it is easy to see that the tangent vectors for each of the boundary curves at the patch corners are controlled, both in direction and magnitude, by the position of adjacent points along the edges of the net. Specifically, the tangent vectors in the u, w directions at A are controlled by the control net vertices $B_{0,1}$ and $B_{1,0}$, respectively. Similarly, the control net vertices $B_{2,0}$, $B_{3,1}$, $B_{3,2}$, $B_{2,3}$ and $B_{1,3}$, $B_{0,2}$ control the tangent vectors in the u, w directions at the corners B, C, D, respectively. The four interior control net vertices, $B_{1,1}$, $B_{2,1}$, $B_{2,2}$ and $B_{1,2}$, *influence* the direction and magnitude of the twist vectors at the corners A, B, C, D, respectively, of the patch. Twist vectors, mathematically defined by the cross derivative at the patch corners, $Q_{uw}(u,w)$ (see Eq. 5.9), influence the shape of the surface interior near the patch corners. Note that by manipulating the control net the user can shape the surface patch without an intimate knowledge of tangent or twist vectors.

Figure 5.7 shows several bicubic Bézier surfaces and their control nets. The base control net is 4×4, centered at the origin with corners at ± 15 in x, z. The y component of the corner vertices is zero. All other vertices have a y component of five. The base control net and the resulting Bézier surface are shown in Fig. 5.7a. In Fig. 5.7, $B_{0,0}$ is the leftmost corner vertex, and $B_{3,3}$ is the rightmost corner vertex. Notice that the center vertices of the base control net form a planar cross (shown shaded). Consequently, the center of the resulting surface, although not flat, is minimally curved.

Figure 5.7b illustrates the effect of increasing the tangent vector magnitudes at $B_{0,0}$ in both the u and w parametric directions by a factor of 2, by

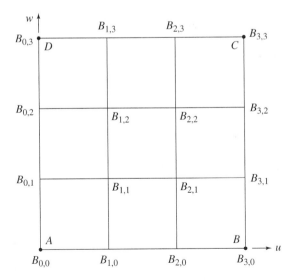

Figure 5.6 Schematic of the control net for a 4×4 Bézier surface.

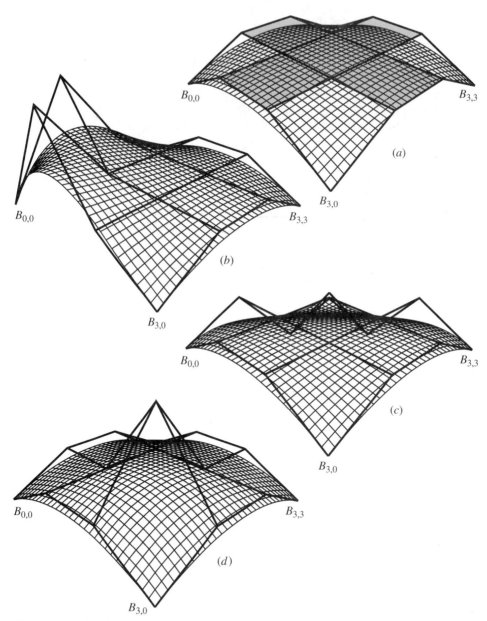

Figure 5.7 Bicubic Bézier surfaces. (a) Base surface; (b) effect of a change in both tangent vector magnitudes at $B_{0,0}$; (c) effect of a change in tangent vector direction at $B_{0,3}$; (d) effect of a change in twist vector magnitude at $B_{0,0}$.

moving $B_{1,0}$ and $B_{0,1}$. The twist vector is not changed. Notice the increased curvature of the boundary curves corresponding to $u = 0$ and $w = 0$, and the resulting change in the interior of the surface.

Figure 5.7c shows the effect of reversing the directions of the tangent vectors at $B_{0,3}$ in both the u and w parameter directions, by moving $B_{2,3}$ and $B_{3,2}$. Notice the resulting reverse curvature of the boundary curves near $B_{0,3}$ and of the interior of the surface compared with that of the base surface.

Figure 5.7d illustrates the effect of doubling the magnitude of the twist vector at $B_{0,0}$ without changing its direction. Here, only $B_{1,1}$ is moved. The effects are subtle but nonetheless important for design. Careful comparison with the base surface in Fig. 5.7a shows that the parametric lines near $B_{0,0}$ have more curvature. The effect extends nearly to the center of the surface.

Matrix Representation

In matrix form, a Cartesian product Bézier surface is given by

$$Q(u, w) = [U][N][B][M]^T[W] \tag{5.4}$$

where

$$[U] = [u^n \quad u^{n-1} \quad \cdots \quad 1]$$

$$[W] = [w^m \quad w^{m-1} \quad \cdots \quad 1]^T$$

$$[B] = \begin{bmatrix} B_{0,0} & \cdots & B_{0,m} \\ \vdots & \ddots & \vdots \\ B_{n,0} & \cdots & B_{n,m} \end{bmatrix}$$

$[N]$ and $[M]$ are given by Eq. (2.9).

For the specific case of a 4×4 bicubic Bézier surface, Eq. (5.4) reduces to

$$Q(u, w) = [u^3 \quad u^2 \quad u \quad 1] \begin{bmatrix} -1 & 3 & -3 & 1 \\ 3 & -6 & 3 & 0 \\ -3 & 3 & 0 & 0 \\ 1 & 0 & 0 & 0 \end{bmatrix} \times$$

$$\begin{bmatrix} B_{0,0} & B_{0,1} & B_{0,2} & B_{0,3} \\ B_{1,0} & B_{1,1} & B_{1,2} & B_{1,3} \\ B_{2,0} & B_{2,1} & B_{2,2} & B_{2,3} \\ B_{3,0} & B_{3,1} & B_{3,2} & B_{3,3} \end{bmatrix} \begin{bmatrix} -1 & 3 & -3 & 1 \\ 3 & -6 & 3 & 0 \\ -3 & 3 & 0 & 0 \\ 1 & 0 & 0 & 0 \end{bmatrix} \begin{bmatrix} w^3 \\ w^2 \\ w \\ 1 \end{bmatrix} \tag{5.5}$$

A Bézier surface need not be square. For a 5×3 net, Eq. (5.4) yields

$$Q(u, w) = \begin{bmatrix} u^4 & u^3 & u^2 & u & 1 \end{bmatrix} \begin{bmatrix} 1 & -4 & 6 & -4 & 1 \\ -4 & -12 & -12 & 4 & 0 \\ 6 & -12 & 6 & 0 & 0 \\ -4 & 4 & 0 & 0 & 0 \\ 1 & 0 & 0 & 0 & 0 \end{bmatrix} \times$$

$$\begin{bmatrix} B_{0,0} & B_{0,1} & B_{0,2} \\ B_{1,0} & B_{1,1} & B_{1,2} \\ B_{2,0} & B_{2,1} & B_{2,2} \\ B_{3,0} & B_{3,1} & B_{3,2} \\ B_{4,0} & B_{4,1} & B_{4,2} \end{bmatrix} \begin{bmatrix} 1 & -2 & 1 \\ -2 & 2 & 0 \\ 1 & 0 & 0 \end{bmatrix} \begin{bmatrix} w^2 \\ w \\ 1 \end{bmatrix} \qquad (5.6)$$

The 5×3 Bézier surface is composed of quartic polynomial curves in the u parametric direction and quadratic polynomial curves in the w parametric direction. An example of a 5×3 Bézier surface is shown in Fig. 5.8. Here, as shown by Fig. 5.8b, changing the central polygon vertex on the control net side with five control vertices does not affect the tangent vectors at the corners.

An example more fully illustrates the Bézier surface concept.

Example 5.3 Bézier Surface

For the Bézier surface shown in Fig. 5.7a, determine the surface point for the parameter values $u = w = 1/2$. Also determine the surface point for the modified surface shown in Fig. 5.7d. The 4×4 Bézier control net vertices are

$$[B] = \begin{bmatrix} \begin{bmatrix} -15 & 0 & 15 \end{bmatrix} & \begin{bmatrix} -15 & 5 & 5 \end{bmatrix} & \begin{bmatrix} -15 & 5 & -5 \end{bmatrix} & \begin{bmatrix} -15 & 0 & -15 \end{bmatrix} \\ \begin{bmatrix} -5 & 5 & 15 \end{bmatrix} & \begin{bmatrix} -5 & 5 & 5 \end{bmatrix} & \begin{bmatrix} -5 & 5 & -5 \end{bmatrix} & \begin{bmatrix} -5 & 5 & -15 \end{bmatrix} \\ \begin{bmatrix} 5 & 5 & 15 \end{bmatrix} & \begin{bmatrix} 5 & 5 & 5 \end{bmatrix} & \begin{bmatrix} 5 & 5 & -5 \end{bmatrix} & \begin{bmatrix} 5 & 5 & -15 \end{bmatrix} \\ \begin{bmatrix} 15 & 0 & 15 \end{bmatrix} & \begin{bmatrix} 15 & 5 & 5 \end{bmatrix} & \begin{bmatrix} 15 & 5 & -5 \end{bmatrix} & \begin{bmatrix} 15 & 0 & -15 \end{bmatrix} \end{bmatrix}$$

For the modified surface shown in Fig. 5.7d, only the $B_{1,1} \begin{bmatrix} 0 & 10 & 0 \end{bmatrix}$ vertex changes, i.e., only the twist vector at the $B_{0,0}$ corner is influenced.

Recall the matrix formulation given in Eqs. (5.4) and (5.5), i.e.

$$Q(u, w) = [U][N][B][N]^T[W]$$

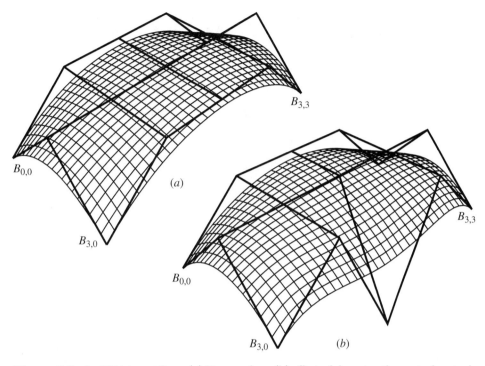

Figure 5.8 5×3 Bézier surface. (a) Base surface; (b) effect of changing the central control vertex on the side with five vertices.

Here

$$[N][B][N]^T = \begin{bmatrix} -1 & 3 & -3 & 1 \\ 3 & -6 & 3 & 0 \\ -3 & 3 & 0 & 0 \\ 1 & 0 & 0 & 0 \end{bmatrix} [B] \begin{bmatrix} -1 & 3 & -3 & 1 \\ 3 & -6 & 3 & 0 \\ -3 & 3 & 0 & 0 \\ 1 & 0 & 0 & 0 \end{bmatrix}$$

$$= \begin{bmatrix} [0 \; 0 \; 0] & [0 \; 0 \; 0] & [0 \; 0 \; 0] & [0 \; 0 \; 0] \\ [0 \; 0 \; 0] & [0 \; -45 \; 0] & [0 \; 45 \; 0] & [0 \; -15 \; 0] \\ [0 \; 0 \; 0] & [0 \; 45 \; 0] & [0 \; -45 \; 0] & [30 \; 15 \; 0] \\ [0 \; 0 \; 0] & [0 \; -15 \; 0] & [0 \; 15 \; -30] & [-15 \; 0 \; 15] \end{bmatrix}$$

The surface point is thus

$$Q(^1/_2, ^1/_2) = [^1/_8 \quad ^1/_4 \quad ^1/_2 \quad 1][N][B][N]^T \begin{bmatrix} ^1/_8 \\ ^1/_4 \\ ^1/_2 \\ 1 \end{bmatrix}$$

$$= [0 \quad 4.6875 \quad 0]$$

The modified surface of Fig. 5.7d changes only the value $B_{1,1}$ of the standard surface. The new value is $B_{1,1}\,[0 \quad 10 \quad 0]$. The new value of

$$[N]\,[B]\,[N]^{T} =$$

$$
\begin{bmatrix}
[45 \quad 45 \;-45] & [-90 \;-90 \quad 90] & [45 \quad 45 \;-45] & [0 \quad 0 \quad 0] \\
[-90 \;-90 \quad 90] & [180 \quad 135 \;-180] & [-90 \;-45 \quad 90] & [0 \;-15 \quad 0] \\
[45 \quad 45 \;-45] & [-90 \;-45 \quad 90] & [45 \quad 0 \;-45] & [30 \quad 15 \quad 0] \\
[0 \quad 0 \quad 0] & [0 \;-15 \quad 0] & [0 \quad 15 \;-30] & [-15 \quad 0 \quad 15]
\end{bmatrix}
$$

The new surface point at $u = w = 1/2$ is

$$Q(1/2, 1/2) = [0.703 \quad 5.391 \quad -0.703]$$

Here, notice that because the polygonal control net is no longer symmetrical about the y-axis, the surface is no longer symmetrical about the y-axis. This result shows that the twist vector at a single corner has a subtle, but significant, influence on the shape of the entire surface.

The above discussion of Bézier surfaces concentrates on the definition and characteristics of a single surface patch. For more complex surfaces, multiple Bézier surface patches are joined together in a piecewise fashion (see Sec. 1.4). A complete discussion of the details is beyond the scope of this text. The interested reader is referred to the books by Faux and Pratt [Faux79], Bézier [Bezi86] or the recent book by Piegl and Tiller [Pieg95]. The difficulties of joining Bézier surface patches while maintaining continuity across the edges is illustrated by considering joining two bicubic Bézier surface patches along a single edge, as shown in Fig. 5.9.

For positional or C^0 continuity along the edge, it is necessary for the two boundary curves and hence the two boundary polygons along the edge to be coincident.[†] To maintain slope or tangent vector, that is C^1 parametric continuity, across the boundary of the adjacent surface patches, the surface normal direction along the adjacent surface patch boundary edges must be the same for both patches. This condition may be achieved using either of two techniques. The first technique requires that the four polygon net lines that meet at and cross the boundary edge be colinear, as shown by the heavy lines in Fig. 5.9a. The second less restrictive technique requires only that the three polygon net edges meeting at the ends of the boundary curve be coplanar, as shown by the heavy lines in Fig. 5.9b.

[†] Recall the discussion in Sec. 2.4 on the continuity of Bézier curve segments.

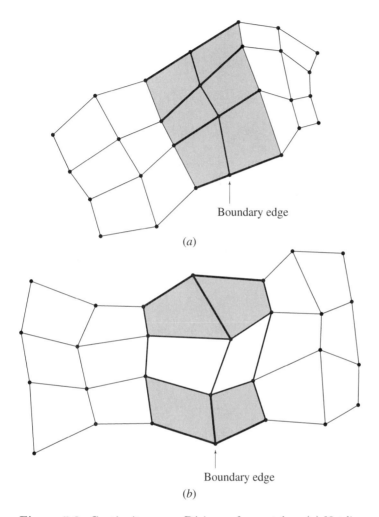

Boundary edge

(a)

Boundary edge

(b)

Figure 5.9   Continuity across Bézier surface patches. (a) Net lines colinear; (b) polygon edges coplanar.

5.3   Bézier Surface Derivatives

The derivatives of a Bézier surface are obtained by formal differentiation of Eq. (5.3) or (5.4). Specifically, using Eq. (5.3), the first and second parametric partial derivatives are

$$Q_u(u, w) = \sum_{i=0}^{n} \sum_{j=0}^{m} B_{i,j} J'_{n,i}(u) K_{m,j}(w) \tag{5.7}$$

$$Q_w(u,w) = \sum_{i=0}^{n} \sum_{j=0}^{m} B_{i,j} J_{n,i}(u) K'_{m,j}(w) \tag{5.8}$$

$$Q_{uw}(u,w) = \sum_{i=0}^{n} \sum_{j=0}^{m} B_{i,j} J'_{n,i}(u) K'_{m,j}(w) \tag{5.9}$$

$$Q_{uu}(u,w) = \sum_{i=0}^{n} \sum_{j=0}^{m} B_{i,j} J''_{n,i}(u) K_{m,j}(w) \tag{5.10}$$

$$Q_{ww}(u,w) = \sum_{i=0}^{n} \sum_{j=0}^{m} B_{i,j} J_{n,i}(u) K''_{m,j}(w) \tag{5.11}$$

where the prime denotes differentiation with respect to the parametric variable and Q_u represents $\partial Q/\partial u$, etc. The derivatives of the Bernstein basis functions $J'_{n,i}$, $J''_{n,i}$, $K'_{m,j}$ and $K''_{m,j}$ are given by Eqs. (2.13) and (2.14).

Recalling Eq. 5.4 in matrix notation, the derivatives at a point on a Bézier surface are given by

$$Q_u(u,w) = [U'][N][B][N]^T[W]$$
$$Q_w(u,w) = [U][N][B][N]^T[W']$$
$$Q_{uw}(u,w) = [U'][N][B][N]^T[W']$$
$$Q_{u,u}(u,w) = [U''][N][B][N]^T[W]$$
$$Q_{ww}(u,w) = [U][N][B][N]^T[W''] \tag{5.12}$$

where
$$[U'] = [\, nu^{n-1} \quad (n-1)u^{n-2} \quad \cdots \quad 0\,]$$
$$[U''] = [\, n(n-1)u^{n-2} \quad (n-1)(n-2)u^{n-3} \quad \cdots \quad 0\,]$$
$$[W'] = [\, mw^{m-1} \quad (m-1)w^{m-2} \quad \cdots \quad 0\,]$$
$$[W''] = [\, m(m-1)w^{m-2} \quad (m-1)(m-2)w^{m-3} \quad \cdots \quad 0\,]$$

An example more fully illustrates the concept.

Example 5.4 Bézier Surface Derivatives

For the Bézier surface shown in Fig. 5.7a, determine the first derivatives in both the u and w parametric directions for the parameter values $u = w = 1/2$. Also determine the derivatives for the modified surface shown in Fig. 5.7d.

In matrix notation (see Eq. (5.12)), the derivatives in the parametric directions are given by

$$Q_u(1/2, 1/2) = \begin{bmatrix} 3u^2 & 2u & 1 & 0 \end{bmatrix} [N][B][N]^T \begin{bmatrix} w^3 \\ w^2 \\ w \\ 1 \end{bmatrix}$$

$$= \begin{bmatrix} 3/4 & 1 & 1 & 0 \end{bmatrix} [N][B][N]^T \begin{bmatrix} 1/8 \\ 1/4 \\ 1/2 \\ 1 \end{bmatrix}$$

and using $[N][B][N]^T$ from Ex. 5.3, we have

$$Q_u(1/2, 1/2) = \begin{bmatrix} 30 & 0 & 0 \end{bmatrix}$$

Similarly

$$Q_w(1/2, 1/2) = \begin{bmatrix} u^3 & u^2 & u & 1 \end{bmatrix} [N][B][N]^T \begin{bmatrix} 3w^2 \\ 2w \\ 1 \\ 0 \end{bmatrix}$$

$$= \begin{bmatrix} 1/8 & 1/4 & 1/2 & 1 \end{bmatrix} [N][B][N]^T \begin{bmatrix} 3/4 \\ 1 \\ 1 \\ 0 \end{bmatrix}$$

Again using $[N][B][N]^T$ from Ex. 5.3, we have

$$Q_w(1/2, 1/2) = \begin{bmatrix} 0 & 0 & -30 \end{bmatrix}$$

Notice that Q_u and Q_w are orthogonal.

Recall Ex. 5.3 and turn now to the modified surface of Fig. 5.7d, where the twist vector at the corner is modified by moving only the control point at $B_{1,1}$. Here, the new parametric derivatives at $u = w = 1/2$ are

$$Q_u(1/2, 1/2) = \begin{bmatrix} 28.594 & -1.406 & 1.406 \end{bmatrix}$$
$$Q_w(1/2, 1/2) = \begin{bmatrix} -1.406 & -1.406 & -28.594 \end{bmatrix}$$

Here, notice that although Q_u and Q_w are still orthogonal, both their magnitudes and directions are different. Again, as in Ex. 5.3, these results show that the twist vector at a single corner has a subtle, but significant, influence on the shape of the entire surface.

5.4 Transforming Between Surface Descriptions

Occasionally it is necessary to transform a Bézier surface into an alternate surface description, e.g., a Coons surface (see [Roge90a] for the details of Coons surfaces). As an example, the relationship between a bicubic Bézier and a bicubic Coons surface is easily found. A Coons surface is written in matrix form as

$$Q_{\text{Coons}}(u, w) = [U][N_C][P][N_C]^T[W]$$

where $[N_C]$ is given by

$$[N_C] = \begin{bmatrix} 2 & -2 & 1 & 1 \\ -3 & 3 & -2 & -1 \\ 0 & 0 & 1 & 0 \\ 1 & 0 & 0 & 0 \end{bmatrix}$$

and the surface geometry matrix $[P]$ contains the position, tangent and twist vectors at the corner points of the quadrilateral surface patch. Recalling the matrix form of a Bézier surface (Eq. (5.4)) and equating yields

$$Q_{\text{Coons}}(u, w) = Q_{\text{Bézier}}(u, w)$$

$$[U][N_C][P][N_C]^T[W] = [U][N_B][B][N_B]^T[W]$$

Hence, the bicubic Coons surface geometric matrix $[P]$ is given in terms of the Bézier surface control net as

$$[P] = [N_C]^{-1}[N_B][B][N_B]^T\left[[N_C]^T\right]^{-1}$$

or

$$\begin{bmatrix} P(0,0) & P(0,1) & P_w(0,0) & P_w(0,1) \\ P(1,0) & P(1,1) & P_w(1,0) & P_w(1,1) \\ P_u(0,0) & P_u(0,1) & P_{uw}(0,0) & P_{uw}(0,1) \\ P_u(1,0) & P_u(1,1) & P_{uw}(1,0) & P_{uw}(1,1) \end{bmatrix} = \begin{bmatrix} B_{0,0} & & B_{0,3} \\ B_{3,0} & & B_{3,3} \\ 3(B_{1,0} - B_{0,0}) & & 3(B_{1,3} - B_{0,3}) \\ 3(B_{3,0} - B_{2,0}) & & 3(B_{3,3} - B_{2,3}) \end{bmatrix}$$

$$\left.\begin{array}{ll} 3(B_{0,1} - B_{0,0}) & 3(B_{0,3} - B_{0,2}) \\ 3(B_{3,1} - B_{3,0}) & 3(B_{3,3} - B_{3,2}) \\ 9(B_{0,0} - B_{1,0} - B_{0,1} + B_{1,1}) & 9(B_{0,2} - B_{1,2} - B_{0,3} + B_{1,3}) \\ 9(B_{2,0} - B_{3,0} - B_{2,1} + B_{3,1}) & 9(B_{2,2} - B_{3,2} - B_{2,3} + B_{3,3}) \end{array}\right] \qquad (5.13)$$

Examining the lower right 2×2 submatrix in Eq. (5.13) confirms that the center four control net vertices *influence* the twist vector at the bicubic Bézier patch corners. However, the twist vector at a corner is *controlled* by not only the center control net vertices but also by the adjacent tangent vectors. In fact, the twist vector at the corner is controlled by the shape of the nonplanar quadrilateral formed by the corner, the two adjacent boundary points and the adjacent center point.

Using Eqs. (5.7) to (5.9) shows that

$$
\begin{bmatrix}
P(0,0) & P(0,1) & P_w(0,0) & P_w(0,1) \\
P(1,0) & P(1,1) & P_w(1,0) & P_w(1,1) \\
P_u(0,0) & P_u(0,1) & P_{uw}(0,0) & P_{uw}(0,1) \\
P_u(1,0) & P_u(1,1) & P_{uw}(1,0) & P_{uw}(1,1)
\end{bmatrix} =
$$

$$
\begin{bmatrix}
Q(0,0) & Q(0,1) & Q_w(0,0) & Q_w(0,1) \\
Q(1,0) & Q(1,1) & Q_w(1,0) & Q_w(1,1) \\
Q_u(0,0) & Q_u(0,1) & Q_{uw}(0,0) & Q_{uw}(0,1) \\
Q_u(1,0) & Q_u(1,1) & Q_{uw}(1,0) & Q_{uw}(1,1)
\end{bmatrix}
\tag{5.14}
$$

Similarly, the inverse relationship between $[P]$ and $[B]$, which gives Bézier control net vertices in terms of Coons bicubic surface parameters, is

$$
\begin{bmatrix}
B_{0,0} & B_{0,1} & B_{0,2} & B_{0,3} \\
B_{1,0} & B_{1,1} & B_{1,2} & B_{1,3} \\
B_{2,0} & B_{2,1} & B_{2,2} & B_{2,3} \\
B_{3,0} & B_{3,1} & B_{3,2} & B_{3,3}
\end{bmatrix} =
$$

$$
\tfrac{1}{3}
\begin{bmatrix}
3P(0,0) & 3P(0,0) + P_w(0,0) \\
3P(0,0) + P_u(0,0) & \tfrac{1}{3}\Big(P_{uw}(0,0) + 9P(0,0) - 3(P_w(0,0) + P_u(0,0))\Big) \\
3P(1,0) - P_u(1,0) & \tfrac{1}{3}\Big(P_{uw}(1,0) + 9P(1,0) + 3(P_w(1,0) - P_u(1,0))\Big) \\
3P(1,0) & 3P(1,0) + P_w(1,0)
\end{bmatrix}
$$

$$
\begin{bmatrix}
3P(0,1) - P_w(0,1) & 3P(0,1) \\
\tfrac{1}{3}\Big(P_{uw}(0,1) + 9P(0,1) + 3(P_u(0,1) - P_w(0,1))\Big) & 3P(0,1) + P_u(0,1) \\
\tfrac{1}{3}\Big(P_{uw}(1,1) + 9P(1,1) - 3(P_u(1,1) + P_w(1,1))\Big) & 3P(1,1) - P_u(1,1) \\
3P(1,1) - P_w(1,1) & 3P(1,1)
\end{bmatrix}
$$

$$
\tag{5.15}
$$

Ken Versprille

Twenty-five years. Looking back, the memories—or now more flashes of memories—stay with me. The most vivid of Steve Coons, which I have used myself during a short teaching stint at Boston University, remembers him writing a matrix equation on the whiteboard. Then leaping into our midst and sitting in a student chair, he holds his hands up, thumbs together— the 'movie director' scanning his shot—and announces, "It just doesn't look pretty!" The man saw beauty in math, often uncovering a flaw gone undiscovered by the 'experts' with a simple balancing of the equation shape. He beamed and flashed us all that smile I will remember forever.

I yield my discovery of Steve to fate. A bored mathematics undergraduate major, tired of theory, I found myself at Syracuse University with an NSF scholarship in hand. Computers promised real application for years of mathematical formulas drilled into my head. Proving that a theorem could be proved had been the final straw. I needed reality. Student savvy, I quickly signed up first semester to take the course taught by my randomly assigned student advisor, someone called Steve Coons—no fool here. That first class—that first day—it's difficult to describe now or then how I felt— finally a match to all my likes and skills! Then things got interesting as Steve became our friend as well as teacher.

We all spent time at Steve's house, 'Mama', his wife, cooking us huge stomach-groaning meals of the best Hungarian food this side of the Atlantic. We were 'the children'. During the days he prodded us, taught us, advised us. Evenings and weekends at his home gained us a true respect for the man as a man, warm and excited by life. I wonder how many of his 'children' still remember that New Year's Eve party at Steve and Mama's. After hours of good food and drink, suddenly the music comes on loud and they both reappear in the living room, Steve in a gold lamé sport coat and Mama, as my wife still talks of today, wearing "every piece of jewelry" the woman owned. They danced and danced until we all faded into the background, quietly leaving them together.

I call it the 'golden age.' Still twenty-five years later, nowhere at no time were the same minds and energy together working on free-form surface design. Steve was the draw. We saw Bill Gordon arrive, then Robin Forrest. Visits by Bézier and even a then young—as we all were—Nick Negraponte from the MIT Media Lab—scandal in Central New York as he lectured about "true user interfaces" to an auditorium crowd wearing a silk see-through shirt! We loved the energy.

Bézier taught of a new approach—will we ever get it right? Is it 'poles' or 'control points?' Suddenly, however, the interface to free-form blew past the dreaded understanding of 'twist vectors' on a Coons patch. My first reaction was that this was French marionettes, but it grew and prospered.

My most intense memory of Bill Gordon focuses on a class he taught one day. I only remember four or five of us as graduate students in the room—Rich, Elaine, myself—I'm not sure of the others. Bill covered the whiteboard in a flurry of rapid equations, triple integrals everywhere. He was like a football coach sketching plays. That man knew and was comfortable with more mathematics than anyone I have ever met then or since. I heard a groan, everyone around me complaining they couldn't follow him. This lowly graduate student 'grew up' that day. I realized I not only understood him, I was already anticipating what came next. It surprised even me, but I kept my mouth shut because I knew no way could I ever reproduce what Bill had written.

My guide through research, however, was Robin. I don't remember if I ever thanked him to his face for his insights, his suggestions, his perseverance with me—and a cheerful Scottish accent I could actually understand. If not, I do so now. His systematic approach to research led me to my own. Building atop the groundbreaking efforts put forth by Rich working with Bill, I in many ways only took their work forward in a classical expansion of the mathematical approach—go rational, and go nonuniform. It wasn't until twelve years later, after I had run off into industry at Computervision Corporation, that what Robin had helped me discover was worth big money. A check arrived from the University of Michigan extension for royalties on copies of my dissertation—the outlandish sum of $26! Someone had named it NURBS.

I still smile at the comment buried deep in my paper that nonuniform is 'overkill.' While in 1975 that may have been true, I now run into numerous CAD programmers who would like to 'overkill' the one who started all this. I point to Boeing, who discovered NURBS, hoping to thwart the arrows in my direction.

I of course remember the days spent in frustration poring over my page-long equations while sitting with coffee in one of the university cafeterias. I always hid in the back corner so as not to scare the poor undergraduates too much. The laughs with Lewie Knapp while we pulled our hair—Lewie will love that comment—trying to get the refresh screen in the basement of Machinery Hall to display wild looking curves and surfaces.

Now I am that dreaded 'industry analyst' of CAD software. My task is to critique and push the CAD software vendors forward. Many years have passed, but now I finally see a new push in free-form design and anticipate with excitement new things to come. But in everything I do, somewhere in the back of my mind I hope Steve is still smiling.

Ken Versprille
Merrimack, New Hampshire, January 2000

Steven Anson (Steve) Coons at home in Syracuse (circa 1972). (Courtesy of Robin Forrest.)

Chapter 6

B-spline Surfaces 6

We now turn our attention to nonrational B-spline surfaces. Nonrational B-spline surfaces are useful for describing sculptured surfaces, e.g., automobile bodies, aircraft, ships, or any surface where the fairness or smoothness of the surface is a design requirement (see [Roge80]). Nonrational B-spline surfaces are not quite as flexible as nonuniform rational B-spline surfaces (NURBS), which have additional degrees of freedom. Furthermore, nonrational B-spline surfaces can only approximate the conic surfaces, whereas NURBS can exactly reproduce them (see Chapter 7). A nonrational Bézier surface is a special case of the nonrational B-spline surface.

6.1 B-spline Surfaces

The natural extension of the Bézier surface is the Cartesian product B-spline surface defined by

$$Q(u,w) = \sum_{i=1}^{n+1} \sum_{j=1}^{m+1} B_{i,j} N_{i,k}(u) M_{j,\ell}(w) \qquad (6.1)$$

where $N_{i,k}(u)$ and $M_{j,\ell}(w)$ are the B-spline basis functions in the biparametric u and w directions, respectively (see Eqs. (3.2)). The definition for the basis functions given previously in Sec. 3.1 is repeated here for convenience.

$$N_{i,1}(u) = \begin{cases} 1 & \text{if } x_i \le u < x_{i+1} \\ 0 & \text{otherwise} \end{cases} \tag{3.2a}$$

$$N_{i,k}(u) = \frac{(u - x_i)N_{i,k-1}(u)}{x_{i+k-1} - x_i} + \frac{(x_{i+k} - u)N_{i+1,k-1}(u)}{x_{i+k} - x_{i+1}} \tag{3.2b}$$

and

$$M_{j,1}(w) = \begin{cases} 1 & \text{if } y_j \le w < y_{j+1} \\ 0 & \text{otherwise} \end{cases} \tag{3.2a}$$

$$M_{j,\ell}(w) = \frac{(w - y_j)M_{j,\ell-1}(w)}{y_{j+l-1} - y_j} + \frac{(y_{j+\ell} - w)M_{j+1,\ell-1}(w)}{y_{j+\ell} - y_{j+1}} \tag{3.2b}$$

where the x_i and y_j are elements of knot vectors, as discussed in Sec. 3.3. Again, the $B_{i,j}$s are the vertices of a polygonal control net. For quadrilateral surface 'patches', the polygonal control net must be topologically rectangular. The indices n and m are one less than the number of control polygon vertices in the u and w parametric directions, respectively.

As with B-spline curves, the shape and character of a B-spline surface is significantly influenced by the knot vectors $[X]$ and $[Y]$. Open, periodic and nonuniform knot vectors are used. Although it is common to use the same type of knot vector in both parametric directions, it is not required. For example, it is possible to use an open knot vector and its associated B-spline basis functions for one parametric direction, and a periodic knot vector and its associated B-spline basis functions for the other. A practical example is a cylindrical surface of varying cross-sectional area.

Because the B-spline basis is used both to describe the boundary curves and to blend the interior of the surface, several properties of the B-spline surface are immediately known:

The maximum possible order of the surface in each parametric direction is equal to the number of control polygon vertices in that direction.

The continuity of the surface in each parametric direction is two less than the order in each direction, i.e., C^{k-2} and $C^{\ell-2}$ in the u and w directions, respectively.

The surface is invariant with respect to an affine transformation; i.e., the surface is transformed by transforming the control net.

The variation-diminishing property for B-spline surfaces is currently not known.

The influence of a single control net vertex is limited to $\pm k/2$, $\pm \ell/2$ spans in each parametric direction.

If the number of control polygon net vertices is equal to the order in each parametric direction and there are no interior knot values, then the B-spline surface reduces to a Bézier surface.

If triangulated, the control net forms a planar approximation to the B-spline surface.

The surface lies within the convex hull of the control net formed by taking the union of all of the convex hulls of k, ℓ neighboring control net vertices.

6.2 Convex Hull Properties

Recalling the previous discussion of the convex hull properties of B-spline curves (see Sec. 3.2) immediately shows that, as a consequence of these strong convex hull properties, a B-spline surface can contain embedded flat regions and lines of sharp discontinuity. This is a particularly desirable characteristic for many design situations. Figures 6.1a to 6.1d show a series of open B-spline surfaces and their control nets that are third order in each parametric direction. Notice that each of the control net lines in the w direction is a straight line with four vertices. The resulting surface is ruled in the w direction (see Sec. 7.7). The B-spline surface shown in Fig. 6.1a, defined by four control vertices in the u direction, is smoothly curved in that direction.

The B-spline surface shown in Fig. 6.1b is defined by five control net vertices in the u direction. The three central vertices are colinear. Notice that the center of the resulting surface is flat. Similarly, five of the seven control net vertices in the u direction for the surface shown in Fig. 6.1c are colinear. Again, the surface is flat in the central region. The flat area is larger than in Fig. 6.1b.

Figure 6.1d shows that these very strong convex hull properties extend to both parametric directions. Thus, a flat region can be embedded in the interior of a sculptured surface. The flat region becomes smaller as the order of the surface increases.

Figure 6.2 illustrates the effect of coincident net lines. In Fig. 6.2a three coincident net lines are used to generate a hard line or knuckle in the center of a fourth-order B-spline surface. Figure 6.2b shows the result when three

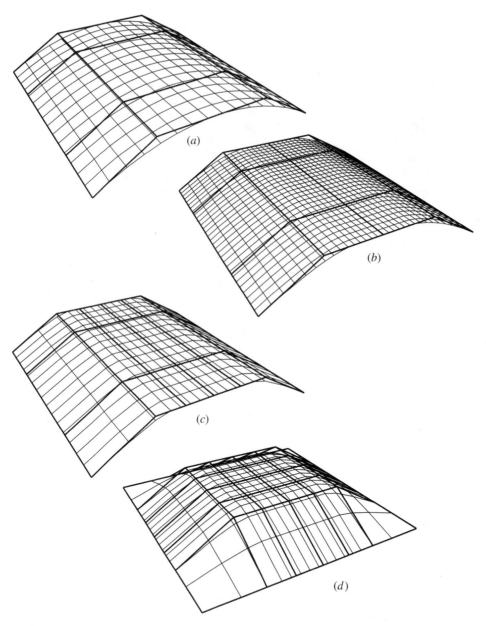

Figure 6.1 Third-order B-spline surfaces. (a) Smooth ruled surface; (b) small interior flat region caused by three colinear net vertices in u; (c) larger interior flat region caused by five colinear net vertices in u; (d) flat region embedded within a sculptured surface.

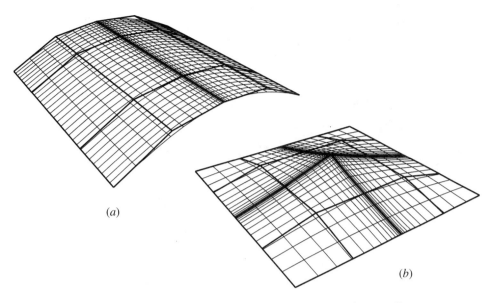

Figure 6.2   Fourth-order B-spline surfaces with multiple coincident net lines.

coincident net lines are used in *both* parametric directions. Here, the fourth-order B-spline surface contains two ridges that rise to a point in the center of the surface. As with B-spline curves, a hard line or knuckle is formed if $k-1$ or $\ell-1$ net lines are coincident. Furthermore, because a B-spline surface is everywhere $C^{k-2}/C^{\ell-2}$ continuous, it has parametric continuity at the hard line or knuckle. In addition, this property ensures that the transition from curved surface to flat surface is also $C^{k-2}/C^{\ell-2}$ continuous.

6.3 Local Control

The excellent local control properties of B-spline curves (see Chapter 3) carry over to B-spline surfaces. An example is shown in Fig. 6.3. Here, an open bicubic ($k = \ell = 4$) B-spline surface is defined by a 9×9 ($m = n = 8$) control net. The control net, shown as the upper surface in Fig. 6.3, is flat except for the center point. The open knot vector in both parametric directions is

$$[0 \quad 0 \quad 0 \quad 0 \quad 1 \quad 2 \quad 3 \quad 4 \quad 5 \quad 6 \quad 6 \quad 6 \quad 6]$$

Thus, there are six parametric spans in each direction, i.e., $0-1, \cdots, 5-6$. Each parametric quadrilateral, for example, $0 \le u \le 1$, $0 \le w \le 1$, forms

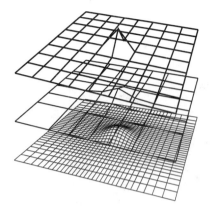

Figure 6.3 Local control in B-spline surfaces.

a B-spline surface subpatch.[†] The middle surface shown in Fig. 6.3 is composed of parametric lines at the ends of each parametric interval, i.e., at $u, w = 0, 1, 2, 3, 4, 5, 6$. Each quadrilateral represents a subpatch. Notice the influence of the displaced point is confined to $\pm k/2, \ell/2$ spans or subpatches.

6.4 Calculating Open B-spline Surfaces

Calculating a B-spline surface by hand is not difficult, it is just a bit tedious. As shown previously in Ex. 3.2, calculating the basis functions required care, especially at the ends of each interval. An example illustrates the method for calculating a B-spline surface.

Example 6.1   Calculating an Open B-spline Surface

Consider the B-spline surface defined by the 4×4 control net

$B_{1,1} \begin{bmatrix} -15 & 0 & 15 \end{bmatrix}$ $B_{2,1} \begin{bmatrix} -5 & 5 & 15 \end{bmatrix}$ $B_{3,1} \begin{bmatrix} 5 & 5 & 15 \end{bmatrix}$ $B_{4,1} \begin{bmatrix} 15 & 0 & 15 \end{bmatrix}$

$B_{1,2} \begin{bmatrix} -15 & 5 & 5 \end{bmatrix}$ $B_{2,2} \begin{bmatrix} -5 & 10 & 5 \end{bmatrix}$ $B_{3,2} \begin{bmatrix} 5 & 10 & 5 \end{bmatrix}$ $B_{4,2} \begin{bmatrix} 15 & 5 & 5 \end{bmatrix}$

$B_{1,3} \begin{bmatrix} -15 & 5 & -5 \end{bmatrix}$ $B_{2,3} \begin{bmatrix} -5 & 10 & -5 \end{bmatrix}$ $B_{3,3} \begin{bmatrix} 5 & 10 & -5 \end{bmatrix}$ $B_{4,3} \begin{bmatrix} 15 & 5 & -5 \end{bmatrix}$

$B_{1,4} \begin{bmatrix} -15 & 0 & -15 \end{bmatrix}$ $B_{2,4} \begin{bmatrix} -5 & 5 & -15 \end{bmatrix}$ $B_{3,4} \begin{bmatrix} 5 & 5 & -15 \end{bmatrix}$ $B_{4,4} \begin{bmatrix} 15 & 0 & -15 \end{bmatrix}$

The surface is fourth order in the u direction ($k = 4$) and third order in the w

---

[†]Some authors designate each subpatch as a B-spline surface. Here, the surface is considered the entity, defined by the complete control net taken as an entity.

direction ($\ell = 3$). Thus, the surface is composed of two subpatches, one defined by $0 \leq u \leq 1$, $0 \leq w \leq 1$ and the other by $0 \leq u \leq 1$, $1 \leq w \leq 2$. Determine the surface point at the center of the surface, i.e., at $u = 1/2$, $w = 1$.

Writing out Eq. (6.1) yields

$$Q(u, w) = \sum_{i=1}^{4} \sum_{j=1}^{4} B_{i,j} N_{i,4}(u) M_{j,3}(w)$$

$$= N_{1,4}(u)(B_{1,1} M_{1,3}(w) + B_{1,2} M_{2,3}(w) + B_{1,3} M_{3,3}(w) + B_{1,4} M_{4,3}(w))$$

$$+ N_{2,4}(u)(B_{2,1} M_{1,3}(w) + B_{2,2} M_{2,3}(w) + B_{2,3} M_{3,3}(w) + B_{2,4} M_{4,3}(w))$$

$$+ N_{3,4}(u)(B_{3,1} M_{1,3}(w) + B_{3,2} M_{2,3}(w) + B_{3,3} M_{3,3}(w) + B_{3,4} M_{4,3}(w))$$

$$+ N_{4,4}(u)(B_{4,1} M_{1,3}(w) + B_{4,2} M_{2,3}(w) + B_{4,3} M_{3,3}(w) + B_{4,4} M_{4,3}(w))$$

Here, the knot vector in the u direction is

$$[X] = [0 \quad 0 \quad 0 \quad 0 \quad 1 \quad 1 \quad 1 \quad 1]$$

Recalling Ex. (3.4) yields the basis functions, i.e.

$$N_{1,4}(u)(1/2) = (1 - u)^3 = (1/2)^3 = 1/8$$

$$N_{2,4}(u)(1/2) = 3u(1 - u)^2 = (3)(1/2)(1/2)^2 = 3/8$$

$$N_{3,4}(u)(1/2) = 3u^2(1 - u) = (3)(1/2)^2(1/2) = 3/8$$

$$N_{4,4}(u)(1/2) = u^3 = (1/2)^3 = 1/8$$

Similarly, the knot vector in the w direction is

$$[Y] = [0 \quad 0 \quad 0 \quad 1 \quad 2 \quad 2 \quad 2]$$

Recalling Ex. (3.2) yields the basis functions, i.e.

$$M_{1,3}(w)(1) = 0$$

$$M_{2,3}(w)(1) = \frac{(2 - w)^2}{2} = \frac{(2 - 1)^2}{2} = 1/2$$

$$M_{3,3}(w)(1) = \frac{(2 - w)(3w - 2)}{2} = \frac{(2 - 1)(3 - 2)}{2} = 1/2$$

$$M_{4,3}(w)(1) = (w - 1)^2 = (1 - 1) = 0$$

Thus
$$Q(^1\!/_2, 1) = ^1\!/_8\,(0\,B_{1,1} + ^1\!/_2 B_{1,2} + ^1\!/_2 B_{1,3} + 0\,B_{1,4})$$
$$+ ^3\!/_8\,(0\,B_{2,1} + ^1\!/_2 B_{2,2} + ^1\!/_2 B_{2,3} + 0\,B_{2,4})$$
$$+ ^3\!/_8\,(0\,B_{3,1} + ^1\!/_2 B_{3,2} + ^1\!/_2 B_{3,3} + 0\,B_{3,4})$$
$$+ ^1\!/_8\,(0\,B_{4,1} + ^1\!/_2 B_{4,2} + ^1\!/_2 B_{4,3} + 0\,B_{4,4})$$
$$Q(^1\!/_2, 1) = ^1\!/_{16}\,(B_{1,2} + B_{1,3}) + ^3\!/_{16}\,(B_{2,2} + B_{2,3})$$
$$+ ^3\!/_{16}\,(B_{3,2} + B_{3,3}) + ^1\!/_{16}\,(B_{4,2} + B_{4,3})$$
$$= ^1\!/_{16}([-15\quad 5\quad 5] + [-15\quad 5\quad -5])$$
$$+ ^3\!/_{16}([-5\quad 10\quad 5] + [-5\quad 10\quad -5])$$
$$+ ^3\!/_{16}([5\quad 10\quad 5] + [5\quad 10\quad -5])$$
$$+ ^1\!/_{16}\,[15\quad 5\quad 5] + [15\quad 5\quad -5])$$
$$= [0\quad ^{35}\!/_4\quad 0]$$

6.5 Periodic B-spline Surfaces

Periodic B-spline surfaces are easily generated using periodic knot vectors to obtain periodic basis functions for use in Eq. (6.1). Figure 6.4 shows several examples of periodic B-spline surfaces formed by open control nets. The control nets for Figs. 6.4a and 6.4b correspond to that of Figs. 6.1a and 6.1c and that of Fig. 6.4c to Fig. 6.2b. Recalling our discussion of periodic B-spline curves (see Chapter 3), notice that for each case, because of the reduced parameter range used for periodic B-spline basis functions, the edge of the surface and the polygon edge do not coincide.

Closed periodic B-spline surfaces exhibit properties analogous to closed periodic B-spline curves. Figure 6.5 shows examples of three third-order surfaces. The control net for Fig. 6.5a is formed by equally spacing the control polygon for the closed B-spline curve of Fig. 3.17b along the z-axis from $z = -8$ to $z = 8$. The result is a cylindrical surface. Notice that the surface does not touch the planes of the first and last control polygon. The control polygon for Fig. 6.5b is obtained by increasing the x and y dimensions of the second and fourth control polygons of Fig. 6.5a by one. The result is a wavy cylinder. Figure 6.5c shows the local effect of perturbing a single control net vertex.

It is possible to combine open and periodic B-spline basis functions in Eq. (6.1). Two examples of the results are shown in Fig. 6.6. Here, an open knot vector and the resulting open basis function are used in one parametric direction and a periodic knot vector and the resulting periodic basis function in the other parametric direction. Figure 6.6a shows a combined B-spline surface defined by the open control net of Fig. 6.1a. Figure 6.6b shows a combined B-spline surface defined by the closed control net of Fig. 6.5b. Notice that the surface is coincident with the end control net lines in the u direction. This characteristic is useful in some design situations.

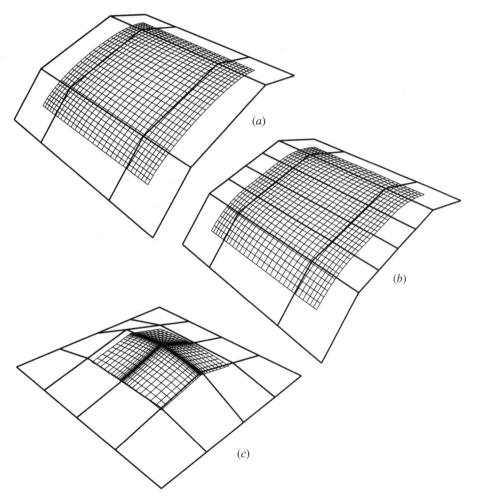

Figure 6.4 Periodic B-spline surfaces for open control nets. (a) Third-order smooth ruled surface; (b) third-order large interior flat region caused by five colinear net vertices in u; (c) point in a fourth-order surface caused by multiple intersecting net lines.

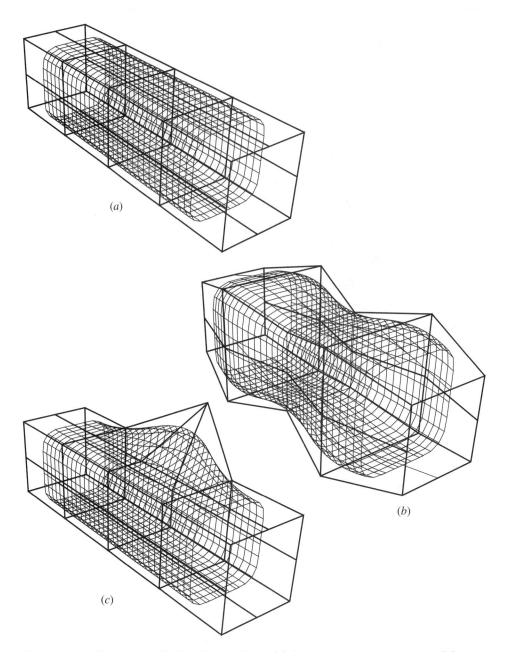

Figure 6.5   Closed periodic B-spline surfaces. (a) Straight cylindrical surface; (b) perturbed wavy cylindrical surface; (c) effect of perturbing a single net vertex.

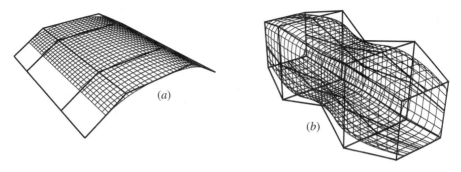

Figure 6.6 Third-order combined open and periodic B-spline surfaces. (a) Open control
net; (b) closed control net.

6.6 Matrix Formulation of B-spline Surfaces

A matrix formulation for periodic B-spline surfaces is of the form

$$Q_{s,t} = [U^*][N^*][B^*_{s,t}][M^*]^T[W^*]^T \tag{6.2}$$

where $[U^*]$ and $[W^*]$ are the reparameterized parametric variables on the
intervals $0 \le u^* \le 1$ and $0 \le w^* \le 1$ given in Eq. (3.8). $[N^*]$ and $[M^*]$
are given by Eq. (3.9). The matrix $[B^*_{s,t}]$ represents a $k \times \ell$ sliding net
of control vertices, which define a subpatch on the surface. For periodic
B-spline surfaces defined by open polygonal control nets

$$[B^*_{s,t}] = [B_{i,j}] \tag{6.3}$$

where
$$1 \le s \le n - k + 2 \quad s \le i \le s + k - 1$$

$$1 \le t \le m - \ell + 2 \quad t \le j \le t + \ell - 1 \tag{6.4}$$

and $B_{i,j}$ represents individual elements of the control net.

For control nets closed along $u = 0$, i.e., with the first and last net lines
in the u direction coincident, the sliding net is given by[†]

$$1 \le s \le n - k + 2$$

$$1 \le t \le m + \ell$$

$$s \le i \le s + k - 1$$

$$j \in [(t-1) \bmod (m+1) + 1 : (t+\ell-2) \bmod (m+1) + 1] \tag{6.5}$$

[†]$j \in [a : b]$ means in the set $a \ldots b$. Here, the control vertex lists must be considered as
circular. For example, if $m + 1 = 4$, then $j \in [3 : 2]$ means in the set $3, 4, 1, 2$ in that
order. Also, mod is the modulo function.

Similarly, for control nets closed along $w = 0$, the sliding net is given by

$$1 \leq s \leq n + 1$$

$$1 \leq t \leq m - \ell + 2$$

$$i \in [(s - 1) \bmod (n + 1) + 1 : (s + k - 2) \bmod (n + 1) + 1]$$

$$t \leq j \leq t + \ell - 1 \tag{6.6}$$

Finally, for control nets closed along both $u = 0$ and $w = 0$, the sliding net is given by

$$1 \leq s \leq n - k + 2$$

$$1 \leq t \leq m - \ell + 2$$

$$i \in [(s - 1) \bmod (n + 1) + 1 : (s + k - 2) \bmod (n + 1) + 1]$$

$$j \in [(t - 1) \bmod (m + 1) + 1 : (t + \ell - 2) \bmod (m + 1) + 1] \tag{6.7}$$

Here, a completely closed surface is formed. An example is shown in Fig. 6.7. The control net shown in Fig. 6.7a is formed by translating the control vertices for the periodic B-spline curve of Fig. 3.18 -2 units in x and $+4$ units in y, and then rotating 360° about the x-axis in increments of 45°. The closed periodic bicubic ($k = \ell = 4$) B-spline surface shown in Fig. 6.7b is toroidal in shape.

The matrix formulation for open B-spline surfaces is of the same form as Eq. (6.2). However, as with the matrix formulation for open B-spline curves, the existence of multiple knot values at the ends of the knot vector makes the result both less compact and less useful than for periodic B-spline surfaces. Consequently, the details are not given here.

6.7 B-spline Surface Derivatives

The parametric derivatives of a B-spline surface are obtained by formally differentiating Eq. (6.1) to yield

$$Q_u(u, w) = \sum_{i=1}^{n+1} \sum_{j=1}^{m+1} B_{i,j} N'_{i,k}(u) M_{j,\ell}(w) \tag{6.8}$$

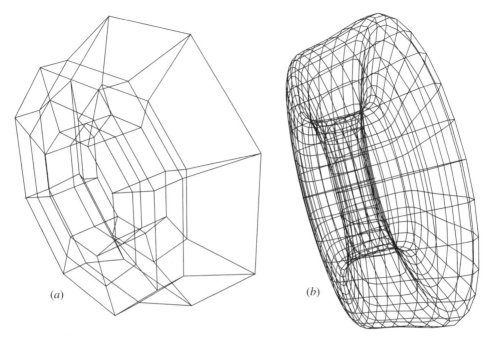

Figure 6.7 Closed toroidal bicubic ($k = \ell = 4$) B-spline surface of revolution. (a) Control net; (b) surface.

$$Q_w(u, w) = \sum_{i=1}^{n+1} \sum_{j=1}^{m+1} B_{i,j} N_{i,k}(u) M'_{j,\ell}(w) \tag{6.9}$$

$$Q_{uw}(u, w) = \sum_{i=1}^{n+1} \sum_{j=1}^{m+1} B_{i,j} N'_{i,k}(u) M'_{j,\ell}(w) \tag{6.10}$$

$$Q_{uu}(u, w) = \sum_{i=1}^{n+1} \sum_{j=1}^{m+1} B_{i,j} N''_{i,k}(u) M_{j,\ell}(w) \tag{6.11}$$

$$Q_{ww}(u, w) = \sum_{i=1}^{n+1} \sum_{j=1}^{m+1} B_{i,j} N_{i,k}(u) M''_{j,\ell}(w) \tag{6.12}$$

where the prime denotes differentiation with respect to the appropriate parameter, and $Q_u = \partial Q / \partial u$, etc. The derivatives of the B-spline basis functions are given by Eqs. (3.29)–(3.32).

6.8 B-spline Surface Fitting

Previous sections discussed the characteristics and generation of B-spline surfaces from a known control net. The inverse problem is also of interest; i.e., given a known set of data on a surface, determine the control net for a B-spline surface that best interpolates that data. Because the edges of the surface represented by the data are generally known, only open B-spline surfaces are considered here. Development of an analogous method for closed surfaces using periodic B-spline surfaces is obvious. Here, the discussion is confined to topologically rectangular nets; i.e., the data is *conceptually* arranged to occupy the intersections of a rectangular grid. The problem is shown schematically in Fig. 6.8, where a 4×4 control net for an 8×8 data matrix is illustrated. This problem was studied by Rogers and Satterfield [Roge82] and by Barsky and Greenberg [Bars80]. Barsky and Greenberg exploited the known characteristics of bicubic B-spline surfaces to obtain additional computational efficiencies. Piegl and Tiller also have a useful discussion (see [Pieg95]). The approach taken here is more straightforward but less computationally efficient (see Sec. 3.11).

Recall Eq. (6.1), and note that here the $Q(u, w)$s are the known surface data points. The $N_{i,k}(u)$ and $M_{j,\ell}(w)$ basis functions are determined for a known order and a known number of control net vertices in each parametric direction, provided that the parametric values u, w are known at the surface data points. Hence, for each known surface data point, Eq. (6.1) provides a linear equation in the unknown control net vertices $B_{i,j}$. Writing Eq. (6.1) out for a single surface data point yields

$$D_{1,1}(u_1, w_1) =$$

$$N_{1,k}(u_1)[M_{1,\ell}(w_1)B_{1,1} + M_{2,\ell}(w_1)B_{1,2} + \cdots + M_{m+1,\ell}(w_1)B_{1,m+1}] +$$

$$\vdots$$

$$N_{n+1,k}(u_1)[M_{1,\ell}(w_1)B_{n+1,1} + M_{2,\ell}(w_1)B_{n+1,2} + \cdots + M_{m+1,\ell}(w_1)B_{n+1,m+1}]$$

where for an $r \times s$ topologically rectangular set of data, $2 \le k \le n + 1 \le r$ and $2 \le \ell \le m + 1 \le s$. Here, u_i and w_i are the parametric values for the surface data point. Writing an equation of this form for each data point yields a system of simultaneous equations. In matrix form, the result is

$$[D] = [C][B] \tag{6.13}$$

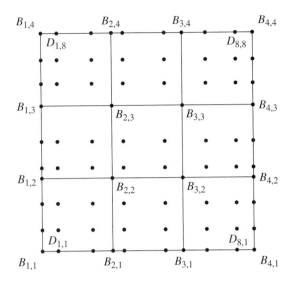

Figure 6.8 Determining a B-spline surface from a known data set.

where $C_{i,j} = N_{i,k}M_{j,\ell}$. For $r \times s$ topologically rectangular surface point data, $[D]$ is an $r*s \times 3$ matrix containing the three-dimensional coordinates of the surface point data, $[C]$ is an $r*s \times n*m$ matrix of the products of the B-spline basis functions, and $[B]$ is an $n*m \times 3$ matrix of the three-dimensional coordinates of the required polygon net points.

If $[C]$ is square, the control net is obtained directly by matrix inversion, that is

$$[B] = [C]^{-1}[D] \tag{6.14}$$

In this case, the resulting surface passes through each data point. Although the resulting surface is everywhere C^{k-2}, $C^{\ell-2}$ continuous, it may not be fair. Experience shows that, in general, the fewer the control net points the fairer the surface.

If $[C]$ is not square, the problem is overspecified and a solution is only obtained in some mean sense. In particular, the solution is given by

$$[B] = [[C]^T[C]]^{-1}[C]^T[D] \tag{6.15}$$

The u_1 and w_1 parametric values for each surface data point are obtained using a chord length approximation (see Sec. 3.11). Specifically, for r data points, the parameter value at the ℓth data point in the u parametric direction is

$$u_1 = 0 \qquad \frac{u_q}{u_{\max}} = \frac{\displaystyle\sum_{g=2}^{q} |D_{g,p} - D_{g-1,p}|}{\displaystyle\sum_{g=2}^{r} |D_{g,p} - D_{g-1,p}|} \qquad 1 \le p \le s \quad 1 \le q \le r \quad (6.16)$$

Similarly, for s data points in the w parametric direction

$$w_1 = 0 \qquad \frac{w_q}{w_{\max}} = \frac{\displaystyle\sum_{g=2}^{q} |D_{p,g} - D_{p,g-1}|}{\displaystyle\sum_{g=2}^{s} |D_{p,g} - D_{p,g-1}|} \qquad 1 \le p \le r \quad 1 \le q \le s \quad (6.17)$$

where $u_{\max}$ and $w_{\max}$ are the maximum values of the appropriate knot vectors. Figure 6.9a shows surface data and the control net generated using this technique. Figure 6.9b shows the B-spline surface generated from this net.

As previously pointed out for B-spline curve fitting (see Sec. 3.11), neither this technique nor that due to Rogers and Satterfield [Roge82] yields hard points or hard lines (discontinuities in the first or second derivatives) in the resulting surface.

From Fig. 6.9 note that the control net vertices obtained using Eq. (6.15) lie anywhere in the three-dimensional plane. If the surface is subsequently

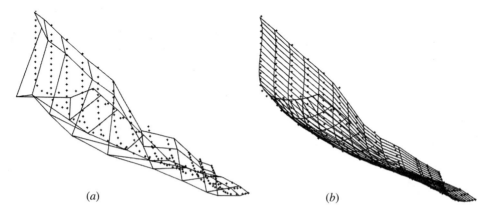

(a)   (b)

Figure 6.9 B-spline surface fit. (a) Data points and fit control net; (b) data points and generated surface.

to be modified, this is inconvenient. Rogers and Fog [Roge89] developed a technique for iterating on the parametric values u, w that constrain the control net vertices to lie in planes or along lines in three space. Piegl and Tiller also present a useful discussion of the constrained B-spline fitting problem [Pieg95].

6.9 B-spline Surface Subdivision

A B-spline surface is subdivided by separately subdividing each control net line in one or both parametric directions. Any of the B-spline curve subdivision techniques can be used (see Sec. 3.14). The technique is best illustrated by an example.

Example 6.2 Subdivision of an Open B-spline Surface

Consider the open B-spline surface defined by the 4×4 control net

$B_{1,1}\,[-15\ \ 0\ \ 15]$	$B_{2,1}\,[-5\ \ 5\ \ 15]$	$B_{3,1}\,[5\ \ 5\ \ 15]$	$B_{4,1}\,[15\ \ 0\ \ 15]$
$B_{1,2}\,[-15\ \ 5\ \ 5]$	$B_{2,2}\,[-5\ \ 10\ \ 5]$	$B_{3,2}\,[5\ \ 10\ \ 5]$	$B_{4,2}\,[15\ \ 5\ \ 5]$
$B_{1,3}\,[-15\ \ 5\ \ -5]$	$B_{2,3}\,[-5\ \ 10\ \ -5]$	$B_{3,3}\,[5\ \ 10\ \ -5]$	$B_{4,3}\,[15\ \ 5\ \ -5]$
$B_{1,4}\,[-15\ \ 0\ \ -15]$	$B_{2,4}\,[-5\ \ 5\ \ -15]$	$B_{3,4}\,[5\ \ 5\ \ -15]$	$B_{4,4}\,[15\ \ 0\ \ -15]$

The surface is fourth order in both parametric directions ($k = \ell = 4$), composed of a single patch with parameter ranges $0 \le u \le 1$, $0 \le w \le 1$. Subdivide the surface into four subpatches. Maintain a uniform open knot vector.

Recalling $[0\ \ 0\ \ 0\ \ 0\ \ 1\ \ 1\ \ 1\ \ 1]$, the knot vector in both parametric directions given in Sec. 3.14 and Ex. 3.15, and reparameterizing this knot vector to $[0\ \ 0\ \ 0\ \ 0\ \ 2\ \ 2\ \ 2\ \ 2]$, the surface is subdivided by inserting a knot value of 1 in the interval $0 \rightarrow 2$. Thus, the new knot vector is given by $[0\ \ 0\ \ 0\ \ 0\ \ 1\ \ 2\ \ 2\ \ 2\ \ 2]$. Applying Eqs. (3.43) and (3.44) to each of the control net lines in both directions yields the control net for the subdivided surface. For example, consider the subdivision of the net line in the w direction defined by $B_{1,j}$, $1 \le j \le 4$. Here, only

$$\alpha'_{4,1} = \alpha'_{4,2} = \alpha'_{4,3} = \alpha'_{4,4} = \alpha'_{4,5} = 1$$

are nonzero.

Using Eqs. (3.44) then yields

$$\alpha^2_{3,1} = \alpha^2_{3,2} = \alpha^2_{3,3} = \alpha^2_{3,5} = 1; \qquad \alpha^2_{3,4} = \alpha^2_{4,4} = {}^1\!/_2$$

$$\alpha^3_{2,1} = \alpha^3_{2,2} = \alpha^3_{3,5} = 1; \qquad \alpha^3_{2,3} = \alpha^3_{3,3} = \alpha^3_{3,4} = \alpha^3_{4,4} = {}^1\!/_2$$

$$\alpha^4_{1,1} = \alpha^4_{3,5} = 1; \qquad \alpha^4_{1,2} = \alpha^4_{2,2} = \alpha^4_{2,3} = \alpha^4_{3,3} = \alpha^4_{3,4} = \alpha^4_{4,4} = {}^1\!/_2$$

Equation (3.43) then yields the new control net vertices. In particular

$$C_{1,1} = \alpha_{1,1}^4 B_{1,1} + \alpha_{2,1}^4 B_{1,2} + \alpha_{3,1}^4 B_{1,3} + \alpha_{4,1}^4 B_{1,4}$$

$$= B_{1,1} = \begin{bmatrix} -15 & 0 & 15 \end{bmatrix}$$

$$C_{1,2} = \alpha_{1,2}^4 B_{1,1} + \alpha_{2,2}^4 B_{1,2} + \alpha_{3,2}^4 B_{1,3} + \alpha_{4,2}^4 B_{1,4}$$

$$= \tfrac{1}{2}(B_{1,1} + B_{1,2}) = \begin{bmatrix} -15 & \tfrac{5}{2} & 10 \end{bmatrix}$$

$$C_{1,3} = \alpha_{1,3}^4 B_{1,1} + \alpha_{2,3}^4 B_{1,2} + \alpha_{3,3}^4 B_{1,3} + \alpha_{4,3}^4 B_{1,4}$$

$$= \tfrac{1}{2}(B_{1,2} + B_{1,3}) = \begin{bmatrix} -15 & 5 & 0 \end{bmatrix}$$

$$C_{1,4} = \alpha_{1,4}^4 B_{1,1} + \alpha_{2,4}^4 B_{1,2} + \alpha_{3,4}^4 B_{1,3} + \alpha_{4,4}^4 B_{1,4}$$

$$= \tfrac{1}{2}(B_{1,3} + B_{1,4}) = \begin{bmatrix} -15 & \tfrac{5}{2} & -10 \end{bmatrix}$$

$$C_{1,5} = \alpha_{1,5}^4 B_{1,1} + \alpha_{2,5}^4 B_{1,2} + \alpha_{3,5}^4 B_{1,3} + \alpha_{4,5}^4 B_{1,4}$$

$$= B_{1,4} = \begin{bmatrix} -15 & 0 & -15 \end{bmatrix}$$

After performing the same operation on each of the net lines in the w direction, the 4×5 control net for the surface, which consists of two subpatches in the w direction and one in the u direction, is

$C_{1,1} \begin{bmatrix} -15 & 0 & 15 \end{bmatrix}$ $C_{2,1} \begin{bmatrix} -5 & 5 & 15 \end{bmatrix}$ $C_{3,1} \begin{bmatrix} 5 & 5 & 15 \end{bmatrix}$ $C_{4,1} \begin{bmatrix} 15 & 0 & 15 \end{bmatrix}$

$C_{1,2} \begin{bmatrix} -15 & \tfrac{5}{2} & 10 \end{bmatrix}$ $C_{2,2} \begin{bmatrix} -5 & \tfrac{15}{2} & 10 \end{bmatrix}$ $C_{3,2} \begin{bmatrix} 5 & \tfrac{15}{2} & 10 \end{bmatrix}$ $C_{4,2} \begin{bmatrix} 15 & \tfrac{5}{2} & 10 \end{bmatrix}$

$C_{1,3} \begin{bmatrix} -15 & 5 & 0 \end{bmatrix}$ $C_{2,3} \begin{bmatrix} -5 & 10 & 0 \end{bmatrix}$ $C_{3,3} \begin{bmatrix} 5 & 10 & 0 \end{bmatrix}$ $C_{4,3} \begin{bmatrix} 15 & 5 & 0 \end{bmatrix}$

$C_{1,4} \begin{bmatrix} -15 & \tfrac{5}{2} & -10 \end{bmatrix}$ $C_{2,4} \begin{bmatrix} -5 & \tfrac{15}{2} & -10 \end{bmatrix}$ $C_{3,4} \begin{bmatrix} 5 & \tfrac{15}{2} & -10 \end{bmatrix}$ $C_{4,4} \begin{bmatrix} 15 & \tfrac{5}{2} & -10 \end{bmatrix}$

$C_{1,5} \begin{bmatrix} -15 & 0 & -15 \end{bmatrix}$ $C_{2,5} \begin{bmatrix} -5 & 5 & -15 \end{bmatrix}$ $C_{3,5} \begin{bmatrix} 5 & 5 & -15 \end{bmatrix}$ $C_{4,5} \begin{bmatrix} 15 & 0 & -15 \end{bmatrix}$

The $\alpha_{i,j}^k$s given above also apply when subdividing the surface in the u direction. The 5×4 control net is then

$C_{1,1} \begin{bmatrix} -15 & 0 & 15 \end{bmatrix}$ $C_{2,1} \begin{bmatrix} -10 & \tfrac{5}{2} & 15 \end{bmatrix}$

$C_{1,2} \begin{bmatrix} -15 & 5 & 5 \end{bmatrix}$ $C_{2,2} \begin{bmatrix} -10 & \tfrac{15}{2} & 5 \end{bmatrix}$

$C_{1,3} \begin{bmatrix} -15 & 5 & -5 \end{bmatrix}$ $C_{2,3} \begin{bmatrix} -10 & \tfrac{15}{2} & -5 \end{bmatrix}$

$C_{1,4} \begin{bmatrix} -15 & 0 & -15 \end{bmatrix}$ $C_{2,4} \begin{bmatrix} -10 & \tfrac{5}{2} & -15 \end{bmatrix}$

$\qquad\qquad\qquad$ $C_{3,1} \begin{bmatrix} 0 & 5 & 15 \end{bmatrix}$ $C_{4,1} \begin{bmatrix} 10 & \tfrac{5}{2} & 15 \end{bmatrix}$ $C_{5,1} \begin{bmatrix} 15 & 0 & 15 \end{bmatrix}$

$\qquad\qquad\qquad$ $C_{3,2} \begin{bmatrix} 0 & 10 & 5 \end{bmatrix}$ $C_{4,2} \begin{bmatrix} 10 & \tfrac{15}{2} & 5 \end{bmatrix}$ $C_{5,2} \begin{bmatrix} 15 & 5 & 5 \end{bmatrix}$

$\qquad\qquad\qquad$ $C_{3,3} \begin{bmatrix} 0 & 10 & -5 \end{bmatrix}$ $C_{4,3} \begin{bmatrix} 10 & \tfrac{15}{2} & -5 \end{bmatrix}$ $C_{5,3} \begin{bmatrix} 15 & 5 & -5 \end{bmatrix}$

$\qquad\qquad\qquad$ $C_{3,4} \begin{bmatrix} 0 & 5 & -15 \end{bmatrix}$ $C_{4,4} \begin{bmatrix} 10 & \tfrac{5}{2} & -15 \end{bmatrix}$ $C_{5,4} \begin{bmatrix} 15 & 0 & -15 \end{bmatrix}$

Here, the surface consists of two subpatches in the u direction and one in the w direction.

Subdividing the surface in both the u and w directions yields a 5×5 control net given by

$C_{1,1} \, [-15 \ 0 \ 15]$ $C_{2,1} \, [-10 \ ^5\!/_2 \ 15]$

$C_{1,2} \, [-15 \ ^5\!/_2 \ 10]$ $C_{2,2} \, [-10 \ 5 \ 10]$

$C_{1,3} \, [-15 \ 5 \ 0]$ $C_{2,3} \, [-10 \ ^{15}\!/_2 \ 0]$

$C_{1,4} \, [-15 \ ^5\!/_2 \ -10]$ $C_{2,4} \, [-10 \ 5 \ -10]$

$C_{1,5} \, [-15 \ 0 \ -15]$ $C_{2,5} \, [-10 \ ^5\!/_2 \ -15]$

$\phantom{C_{1,1}}$ $C_{3,1} \, [0 \ 5 \ 15]$ $C_{4,1} \, [10 \ ^5\!/_2 \ 15]$ $C_{5,1} \, [15 \ 0 \ 15]$

$\phantom{C_{1,1}}$ $C_{3,2} \, [0 \ ^{15}\!/_2 \ 10]$ $C_{4,2} \, [10 \ 5 \ 10]$ $C_{5,2} \, [15 \ ^5\!/_2 \ 10]$

$\phantom{C_{1,1}}$ $C_{3,3} \, [0 \ 10 \ 0]$ $C_{4,3} \, [10 \ ^{15}\!/_2 \ 0]$ $C_{5,3} \, [15 \ 5 \ 0]$

$\phantom{C_{1,1}}$ $C_{3,4} \, [0 \ ^{15}\!/_2 \ -10]$ $C_{4,4} \, [10 \ 5 \ -10]$ $C_{5,4} \, [15 \ ^5\!/_2 \ -10]$

$\phantom{C_{1,1}}$ $C_{3,5} \, [0 \ 5 \ -15]$ $C_{4,5} \, [10 \ ^5\!/_2 \ -15]$ $C_{5,5} \, [15 \ 0 \ -15]$

Note that this net is derivable from either of the two previous nets by using Eqs. (3.43) and (3.44). The original surface and all three of the subdivided control nets are shown in Fig. 6.10. Each of the surfaces is identical to the original surface.

Clearly, as the surface is further subdivided the control net converges to the surface.

6.10 Gaussian Curvature and Surface Fairness

Of fundamental concern in computer aided design is development of appropriate techniques for determining and/or visualizing the fairness or smoothness of surfaces. It is well known that the bicubic surfaces (Coons (see [Roge90a]), Bézier or B-spline) commonly used, although C^2 continuous everywhere, can exhibit unfair bumps, flat spots or undulations. One of the best mathematical techniques for determining surface fairness uses Eulerian (orthogonal) nets of minimum and maximum curvature (see [Munc79, 80]) and of Gaussian curvature (see [Forr79; Munc79, 80; Dill81, 82]).

At any point P on a surface, the curve of intersection of a plane containing the normal to the surface at P and the surface has a curvature κ (see Fig. 6.11). As the plane is rotated about the normal, the curvature changes. Euler, the great Swiss mathematician, showed that unique directions for which the curvature is a minimum and a maximum exist. The curvatures in these directions are called the principal curvatures, $\kappa_{\min}$ and $\kappa_{\max}$. Furthermore, the principal curvature directions are orthogonal. Two combinations

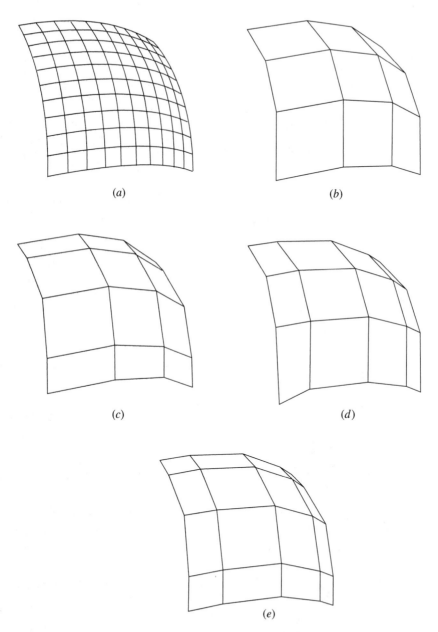

Figure 6.10 B-spline surface subdivision. (a) Surface; (b) original control net; (c) net subdivided in w; (d) net subdivided in u; (e) net subdivided in u and w.

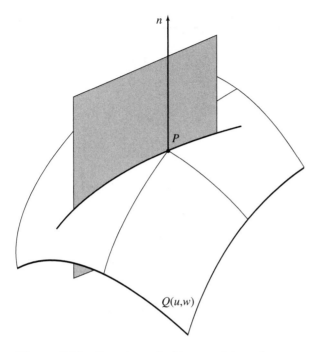

Figure 6.11 Curvature of a biparametric surface.

of the principal curvatures are of particular interest, the average and the Gaussian curvatures. The average curvature is

$$\kappa_a = \frac{\kappa_{\min} + \kappa_{\max}}{2} \tag{6.18}$$

The Gaussian curvature is

$$\kappa_g = \kappa_{\min}\kappa_{\max} \tag{6.19}$$

Dill ([Dill81]) showed that for biparametric surfaces the average and Gaussian curvatures are given by

$$\kappa_a = \frac{A|Q_w|^2 - 2BQ_u \cdot Q_w + C|Q_u|^2}{2|Q_u \times Q_w|^3} \tag{6.20}$$

and

$$\kappa_g = \frac{AC - B^2}{|Q_u \times Q_w|^4} \tag{6.21}$$

where

$$(A\,B\,C) = [Q_u \times Q_w] \cdot [Q_{uu} \quad Q_{uw} \quad Q_{ww}]$$

Table 6.1 Surface Types

$\kappa_{\min}\kappa_{\max}$	K	Shape
Same sign	> 0	Elliptic (bump or hollow)
Opposite sign	< 0	Hyperbolic (saddle point)
One or both zero	0	Cylindrical/conical (ridge, hollow, plane)

Table 6.1 shows that the sign of the Gaussian curvature serves to characterize the local shape of the surface: elliptic, hyperbolic, cylindrical or conical. Thus, the Gaussian curvature at a point on the surface indicates whether the surface is locally elliptic, hyperbolic or parabolic (Gaussian curvature positive, negative or zero).

The average and Gaussian curvature for a surface can be presented using a number of techniques. If display capabilities are limited to line drawings, then contour plots or surface maps are most useful (see [Munc79, 80] and Fig. 7.7c). Dill [Dill81]) and Dill and Rogers [Dill82] show that color or gray scale encoded Gaussian curvature raster displays are an effective technique for determining surface fairness.

Figure 6.12 shows Gaussian curvature surface maps[†] of several test surfaces, along with corresponding control polygon and wire frame parametric representations of the surfaces. The surfaces are all bicubic ($k = \ell = 4$) B-spline surfaces. The three surfaces shown in Fig. 6.12 represent increasing degrees of discontinuity in the smoothness or fairness of the surface. Figure 6.12a is completely smooth and fair. In Fig. 6.12b, the two pronounced ridges of decreased smoothness are caused by the three coincident control net lines at each end. In Fig. 6.12c, the extended 'hard' line in the middle of the surface results from the three coincident control net lines extending across several of the interior polygon lines shown in the control net. Color images are shown in Color Plates 1 and 2 on the back cover. These color images also show the effect of increasing degrees of discontinuity. Color Plate 1 has two ridges formed by three coincident net lines (see Fig. 6.12b), whereas

---

[†]In color encoding the Gaussian curvature images shown in the color plates (see also [Dill82]), curvature values at the four vertices of a dense quadrilateral approximation of the surface were averaged. The average value was assigned to each polygon. The curvature range was divided into a number of equal intervals (except at the ends) corresponding to the available intensity range. A legend giving this range is shown to the right of the image. The aliasing (staircase-like boundaries between different intensities) is due to the limited number of available intensities and *not* to the polygonal approximation.

Color Plate 2 has a single ridge formed by three coincident net lines. Color Plate 2 is the color-encoded image of the Gaussian curvature of the surface in Fig. 6.12c.

In general, the color-encoded Gaussian curvature images make the character of the surfaces more obvious; e.g., Figs. 6.12b and 6.12c and Color Plates 1 and 2 show large negative values at the corners. This negative curvature is a result of constraining the boundaries of the surface to be straight and flat while the interior is full and positively curved. The encoded Gaussian curvature image in Fig. 6.12b and Color Plate 1 emphasizes the flatness of the area between the ridges. Note that because the Gaussian curvature is zero in this region, this portion of the surface is developable (see Sec. 7.7).

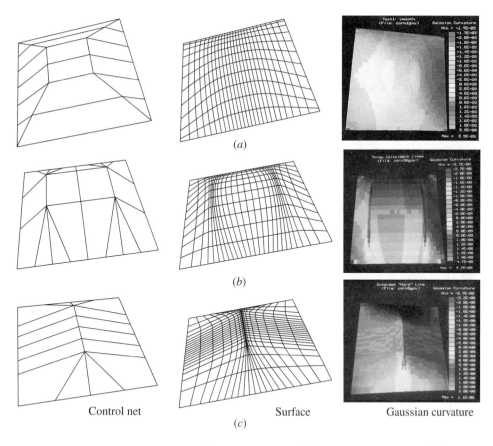

Control net   Surface   Gaussian curvature

Figure 6.12 Gaussian curvature. (a) Smooth surface; (b) two short 'hard' lines; (c) single longer 'hard' line. (Courtesy J.C. Dill and D.F. Rogers.)

Note also that the control net in this region is developable. Finally, the band across the middle of the Gaussian encoded image in Fig. 6.12c and Color Plate 2 shows that in this region the surface is a plane folded in the middle. The fact that the fold is a straight line explains the vanishing of the Gaussian curvature along the line. An example illustrates the technique for calculating the Gaussian curvature.

Example 6.3 Gaussian Curvature

Determine the Gaussian curvature at $u = 1/2$, $w = 1$ for the open B-spline surface previously defined in Ex. 6.1.

First recall the basis functions $N_{i,4}$ and $M_{j,\ell}$ from Ex. 6.1. From these results, the equations needed to determine the required first and second derivatives Q_u, Q_w, Q_{uw}, Q_{uu} and Q_{ww}, and subsequently to calculate the Gaussian curvature are given by

$$N_{1,4} = (1-u)^3 \qquad N'_{1,4} = -3(1-u)^2 \qquad N''_{1,4} = 6(1-u)$$

$$N_{2,4} = 3u(1-u)^2 \qquad N'_{2,4} = 3(1-u)(1-3u) \qquad N''_{2,4} = 6(3u-2)$$

$$N_{3,4} = 3u^2(1-u) \qquad N'_{3,4} = 3u(2-3u) \qquad N''_{3,4} = 6(1-3u)$$

$$N_{4,4} = u^3 \qquad N'_{4,4} = 3u^2 \qquad N''_{4,4} = 6u$$

and

$$M_{1,3} = 0 \qquad\qquad M'_{1,3} = 0 \qquad\qquad M''_{1,3} = 0$$

$$M_{2,3} = \frac{(2-w)^2}{2} \qquad M'_{2,3} = w-2 \qquad M''_{2,3} = 1$$

$$M_{3,3} = \frac{(2-w)(3w-2)}{2} \qquad M'_{3,3} = 4-3w \qquad M''_{3,3} = -3$$

$$M_{4,3} = (w-1)^2 \qquad M'_{4,3} = 2(w-1) \qquad M''_{4,3} = 2$$

Evaluating the derivatives at $u = 1/2$, $w = 1$, and substituting into Eq. (6.1) and Eqs. (6.8)–(6.12), yields

$$Q(1/2, 1) = [\,0 \quad 35/4 \quad 0\,]$$

$$Q_u(1/2, 1) = [\,30 \quad 0 \quad 0\,]$$

$$Q_w(1/2, 1) = [\,0 \quad 0 \quad 10\,]$$

$$Q_{uw}(1/2, 1) = [\,0 \quad 0 \quad 0\,]$$

$$Q_{uu}(1/2, 1) = [\,0 \quad -30 \quad 0\,]$$

$$Q_{ww}(1/2, 1) = [\,0 \quad -10 \quad 10\,]$$

The components of Eq. (6.21) for the Gaussian curvature are

$$Q_u \times Q_w = [30 \quad 0 \quad 0] \times [0 \quad 0 \quad 10] = [0 \quad -300 \quad 0]$$

$$|Q_u \times Q_w|^4 = (300)^4$$

$$A = [Q_u \times Q_w] \cdot Q_{uu} = [0 \quad -300 \quad 0] \cdot [0 \quad -30 \quad 0] = 9000$$

$$B = [Q_u \times Q_w] \cdot Q_{uw} = [0 \quad -300 \quad 0] \cdot [0 \quad 0 \quad 0] = 0$$

$$C = [Q_u \times Q_w] \cdot Q_{ww} = [0 \quad -300 \quad 0] \cdot [0 \quad -10 \quad 10] = 3000$$

Using Eq. (6.21), the Gaussian curvature is

$$\kappa_g = \frac{AC - B^2}{|Q_u \times Q_w|^4} = \frac{(9000)(3000) - (0)}{(300)^4} = 3.33 \times 10^{-3}$$

Because $\kappa_g > 0$, the surface is locally elliptical.

Al Adams
Dave Rogers

My very early work in computer graphics grew out of teaching and research activities centered around using a teletype to plot solutions of the viscous laminar boundary layer equations interactively in the classroom. However, after my longtime office mate, J. Alan Adams (seated), took a sabbatical at Cambridge University during the 1971–1972 academic year, my attention turned to techniques for computer aided curve and surface design. As you can imagine, this early work was particularly inspired by that of Pierre Bézier at Renault and Robin Forrest at Cambridge.

In the fall of 1971, Al Adams had no more than settled in at Cambridge when I appeared for a visit. We visited the Computer Aided Design Group and talked to its head, Charles Lang, who previously was at MIT with project MAC, and to Robin Forrest as well as a number of others. Perhaps most important during that short visit was my introduction to the CAD Group's library of reports and papers, copies of which were generously shared.

During the spring of 1972, I revisited Cambridge. During discussions with Charles Lang at the CAD Laboratory, he indicated that he was getting a Vector General refresh line-drawing graphics display as a peripheral to a PDP 11/45. We also attended a lecture by Robin Forrest on the use of curves in computer aided design. Robin mentioned a student of his at Syracuse University, Rich Riesenfeld, who was developing B-spline curves. We also visited with Malcolm Sabin at British Aerospace Corporation; we discussed his Numerical Master Geometry (NMG) CAD system, which was actively being used to design fuselage sections for the Concorde, the BAC 311 and the BAC 111.

During a visit to Oslo, Norway, and the Kongsberg Vapenfabrikk, we examined the large (up to 2m × 10m long) Kongsberg Kingmatic computer aided drafting machines, which were a staple of the Autokon Ship Design package. While visiting the Central Institute for Industrial Research the next day, we discussed the underlying mathematics of the Autokon system with their primary author, Even Mehlum. These discussions would have far-reaching effects on the development of computer graphics at the United States Naval Academy.

While on sabbatical, Al wrote a comprehensive report called *Geometric Concepts for Computer Graphics*, which included detailed discussions of Bézier and B-spline curves and surfaces. Over the next two years, using Al's report and the Cambridge CAD Group reports as source material, we wrote the first edition of *Mathematical Elements for Computer Graphics* (MECG), which Steve Coons informally reviewed. MECG contained detailed mathematical descriptions, along with detailed computer code, for Bézier and B-spline curves and surfaces. One of the keys to our understanding of Bézier and B-spline curves and surfaces was a listing of a FORTRAN computer program from Lewie Knapp. We promptly rewrote that program in BASIC on an early timesharing system and spent many hours experimenting with it.

From Al's sabbatical, our visits and attempts at teaching computer aided design, we concluded that we needed not only many low-cost machines for student work but also a highly interactive system for serious research and design, as well as an effort in computer aided manufacturing.

Fortunately, at this time the engineering division was designing a new building. Part of the design of a government building is a 'collateral' equipment list. Using the collateral equipment list, I was able to wire every single office, classroom, laboratory and shop for computer access, design in several thousand square feet for a Computer Aided Design/Interactive Graphics (CADIG) laboratory, and acquire funding for significant graphics equipment. However, of more importance was the creation of several positions for CADIG staff.

When the building opened in the spring of 1975, an Evans & Sutherland Picture System I (SN 9), a supporting PDP 11/45, a large Xynetics flatbed plotter, fifty Tektronix 4051 stand-alone graphics workstations, and a large computer-controlled machining center had been purchased. Fortunately, I hired Steve Satterfield as a member of the CADIG staff. Steve did the programming for the graphical user interfaces for the Picture System, while I programmed the underlying mathematics.

In July of 1975, I was fortunate to visit Pierre Bézier at his laboratory outside Paris; Pierre was most cordial. One thing that made a lasting impression on me was his interactive real-time design system. The interface consisted of a standard teletype and a large 2m × 10m Kingmatic flatbed plotter. Interaction was achieved by typing control polygon coordinates on a teletype. With an audible whoosh, the plotter pen drew the new curve. Walking to the plotter, you examined the result by sighting along the curve and decided what changes to make. In this way, a car body was designed at full or nearly full size, with confidence that the lines were fair. No 10×10 inch square on a CRT here. Fairness is in the eye of the beholder, and size helps.

With the CADIG Group well under way, I found that rare research sponsor, Howard Chatterton at United States Coast Guard Headquarters, who understood what I was attempting to do, believed in it, and provided adequate funding on the basis of "Dave, you do your thing and occasionally let me know what's happening." Howard had faith and provided support for nearly fifteen years. I don't think he was disappointed.

Although I felt that surface design should be done with a surface program, the traditional naval architects were not ready to accept a surface approach. Thus, we first developed a lines-fairing program, which Steve Satterfield named CAMILL (Computer Aided Milling). I specified the user interface and wrote the code for four different lines-fairing techniques—cubic splines, parabolically blended curves, Bézier curves and B-spline curves—while Steve wrote and rewrote and rewrote the graphical interface until I could make up my mind about what I wanted. Francisco (Paco) Rodriquez implemented the interface that drove the milling machine from a Tektronix 4051 using CAMILL data, which gave us a working CAD/CAM system.

Using CAMILL, we examined the ease of use and compactness of the data representation for typical ship hull body lines digitized from actual lines plans. Both automatic and interactive fits to the data were investigated. The results were published at SCAHD77 [Roge77]. My conclusion was that interactive B-spline curves were the most advantageous technique.

Using CAMILL, we faired a number of ship hulls. In addition, we began work on a B-spline surface design program called BSSD (B-Spline Surface Design) [Roge80]. Work on this program and its successor, RBSSD (Rational B-Spline Surface Design) [Roge90b], led to the development of the fast B-spline and rational B-spline incremental algorithms given in Sec. 7.10. The rest, as the saying goes, is history.

Dave Rogers
Annapolis, April 2000

Chapter 7

Rational B-spline Surfaces 7

Rational B-spline surfaces, or NURBS, are the standard for surface modeling in much of computer graphics and computer aided design. Many of the typical surface forms used in computer graphics and computer aided design, such as flat planes and quadric surfaces, e.g., cylinders, spheres, ellipsoids of revolution, as well as more complex fully sculptured surfaces, are easily and accurately represented by rational B-spline surfaces. Thus, a single surface description, with excellent local and global control, can be used in a modeler or computer aided design system rather than having to deal with multiple types of surface descriptions.

Here we treat rational B-spline surfaces in general. Technically, a NURBS surface is a special case of a general rational B-spline surface that uses a particular form of knot vector. For a NURBS surface, the knot vector has multiplicity of duplicate knot values equal to the order of the basis function at the ends; i.e., a NURBS surface uses an open knot vector in the terminology of the current text. The knot vector may or may not have nonuniform internal knot values.

7.1   Rational B-spline Surfaces (NURBS)

As with rational curves, rational forms of Bézier surfaces are possible. However, both because of space limitations and because they represent a generalization of rational Bézier surfaces, only rational B-spline surfaces are considered here.

A Cartesian product rational B-spline surface in four-dimensional homogeneous coordinate space is given by

$$Q(u,w) = \sum_{i=1}^{n+1} \sum_{j=1}^{m+1} B_{i,j}^{h} N_{i,k}(u) M_{j,\ell}(w) \tag{7.1}$$

where the $B_{i,j}^{h}$s are the four-dimensional homogeneous polygonal control vertices, and $N_{i,k}(u)$ and $M_{j,\ell}(w)$ are the nonrational B-spline basis functions previously given in Eqs. (3.2).

Projecting back into three-dimensional space by dividing through by the homogeneous coordinate gives the rational B-spline surface

$$Q(u,w) = \frac{\displaystyle\sum_{i=1}^{n+1} \sum_{j=1}^{m+1} h_{i,j} B_{i,j} N_{i,k}(u) M_{j,\ell}(w)}{\displaystyle\sum_{i=1}^{n+1} \sum_{j=1}^{m+1} h_{i,j} N_{i,k}(u) M_{j,\ell}(w)} = \sum_{i=1}^{n+1} \sum_{j=1}^{m+1} B_{i,j} S_{i,j}(u,w) \tag{7.2}$$

where the $B_{i,j}$s are the three-dimensional control net vertices, and the $S_{i,j}(u,w)$ are the bivariate rational B-spline surface basis functions

$$S_{i,j}(u,w) = \frac{h_{i,j} N_{i,k}(u) M_{j,\ell}(w)}{\displaystyle\sum_{i1=1}^{n+1} \sum_{j1=1}^{m+1} h_{i1,j1} N_{i1,k}(u) M_{j1,\ell}(w)} = \frac{h_{i,j} N_{i,k}(u) M_{j,\ell}(w)}{\text{Sum}(u,w)} \tag{7.3}$$

where
$$\text{Sum}(u,w) = \sum_{i1=1}^{n+1} \sum_{j1=1}^{m+1} h_{i1,j1} N_{i1,k}(u) M_{j1,\ell}(w)$$

It is convenient, although not necessary, to assume $h_{i,j} \geq 0$ for all i, j.

Here, it is important to note that $S_{i,j}(u,w)$ is *not* the product of $R_{i,k}(w)$ and $R_{j,\ell}(w)$ (see Eq. 4.3). However, the $S_{i,j}(u,w)$ have similar shapes and analytic properties to the product function $N_{i,k}(u) M_{j,\ell}(w)$. Hence, rational

B-spline surfaces have similar analytic and geometric properties to their nonrational counterparts. Specifically:

The sum of the rational surface basis functions for any u, w values is

$$\sum_{i=1}^{n+1}\sum_{j=1}^{m+1} S_{i,j}(u,w) \equiv 1 \qquad (7.4)$$

Each rational surface basis function is positive or zero for all parameter values u, w, i.e., $S_{i,j} \geq 0$.

Except for $k = 1$ or $\ell = 1$, each rational surface basis function has precisely one maximum.

The maximum possible order of a rational B-spline surface in each parametric direction is equal to the number of control net vertices in that direction.

A rational B-spline surface of order k, ℓ (degree $k - 1$, $\ell - 1$) is C^{k-2}, $C^{\ell-2}$ continuous everywhere.

A rational B-spline surface is invariant with respect to a *projective* transformation; i.e., any *projective* transformation can be applied to the surface by applying it to the control net. Note this is a stronger condition than that for a nonrational B-spline surface.

For $h_{i,j} \geq 0$ for all i, j, the surface lies within the convex hull of the control net formed by taking the union of all convex hulls of k, ℓ neighboring polygon net vertices.

The variation-diminishing property is currently not known for rational B-spline surfaces.

The influence of a single control net vertex is limited to $\pm^k/_2$, $\pm^\ell/_2$ spans in each parametric direction.

If triangulated, the control net forms a planar approximation to the rational B-spline surface.

If the number of control net vertices is equal to the order in each parametric direction and there are no duplicate interior knot values, the rational B-spline surface is a rational Bézier surface.

From Eqs. (7.2) and (7.3) it is clear that when all $h_{i,j} = 1$, $S_{i,j}(u,w) = N_{i,k}(u)M_{j,\ell}(w)$. Thus, rational B-spline surface basis functions and surfaces reduce to their nonrational counterparts. Consequently, rational B-spline surfaces represent a proper generalization of nonrational B-spline surfaces and of rational and nonrational Bézier surfaces.

Again, as is the case for rational B-spline curves, algorithms for degree raising, subdivision and surface fitting of nonrational B-spline surfaces are applicable by simply applying them to the four-dimensional control vertices.

Open and periodic, uniform and nonuniform knot vectors are used to generate rational B-spline basis functions and rational B-spline surfaces. Knot vector types can be mixed. For example, an open uniform knot vector can be used in the u parametric direction and a nonuniform knot vector in the w direction. Here, we initially concentrate on open uniform knot vectors.

7.2   Characteristics of Rational B-spline Surfaces

Figure 7.1 shows a bicubic ($k = \ell = 4$) rational B-spline surface and its control net for $h_{1,3} = h_{2,3} = 0, 1, 5$. All other homogeneous weighting factors are one. Figure 7.1c, with $h_{1,3} = h_{2,3} = 1$, is identical to the nonrational B-spline surface. The effects of varying the homogeneous coordinate values are seen by comparing Fig. 7.1c to Figs. 7.1b and 7.1d. The effects are analogous to, but not as striking as, those for rational B-spline curves (see Chapter 4). Here, the effects are reduced by the fact that $S_{i,j}(u, w)$ is a bivariate blending function.

Comparing the edge defined by $B_{1,1}$, $B_{1,2}$, $B_{1,3}$, $B_{1,4}$ in Figs. 7.1b and 7.1c, notice that with $h_{1,3} = h_{2,3} = 0$ it is as if the control vertex, $B_{1,3}$, did not exist. Furthermore, notice that in Fig. 7.1c the shape of the surface near the control vertex, $B_{2,3}$, is subtly more 'rounded' than in Fig. 7.1b and the parameterization is changed. Turning now to Figs. 7.1d and 7.1c, and again looking at the edge defined by $B_{1,1}$, $B_{1,2}$, $B_{1,3}$, $B_{1,4}$, notice that with $h_{1,3} = h_{2,3} = 5$ the edge is pulled close to the edge control polygon; however, in the interior near the control vertex, $B_{2,3}$, the surface is 'flatter' than in Fig. 7.1c. Figure 7.1 illustrates that using the homogeneous weighting factors allows very fine local control of the characteristics of a rational B-spline surface.

Figures 7.2a and 7.2b illustrate the effect obtained by setting all interior $h_{i,j}$s = 0 and 500, respectively; i.e., $h_{2,2} = h_{2,3} = h_{3,2} = h_{3,3} = h_{4,2} = h_{4,3} = 0, 500$. All other $h_{i,j}$s = 1. The control net is shown in Fig. 7.1a. Setting all the interior $h_{i,j}$s = 0 effectively ignores the interior control net vertices. Only the edge vertices are interpolated. In contrast, setting all the interior $h_{i,j}$s = 500 reduces the influence of the edge vertices to a minimum. Note that changing the $h_{i,j}$s significantly affects the parameterization of the surface. This effect is illustrated by the clustering of the parametric lines near the edges of the surface when the interior $h_{i,j}$s = 0 (see Fig. 7.2a) and in the interior of the surface when the interior $h_{i,j}$s = 500 (see Fig. 7.2b). Hence,

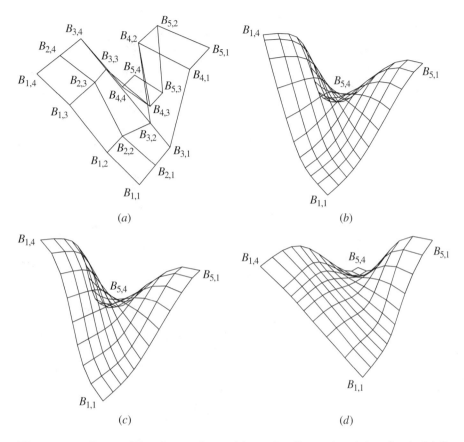

Figure 7.1 Rational B-spline surfaces with $n+1 = 5$, $m+1 = 4$, $k = \ell = 4$. (a) Control net; (b) $h_{1,3} = h_{2,3} = 0$; (c) $h_{1,3} = h_{2,3} = 1$; (d) $h_{1,3} = h_{2,3} = 5$.

reparameterization may be in order (see Sec. 3.16). Figure 7.2 illustrates that using the homogeneous weighting factors allows extreme modification of a rational B-spline surface without changing the control net vertices.

Positive Homogeneous Weighting Factors—Single Vertex

The effects of multiple vertices or net lines are analogous to those for non-rational B-spline surfaces (see Chapter 6) and for rational B-spline curves (see Chapter 4). The results of moving a single vertex on the surface are also analogous, as shown by Fig. 7.3. Figure 7.3a shows the 5×5 control net for a rational B-spline surface. An open knot vector is used. The height of the vertex at $B_{4,3}$ is increased to three times that of the center vertex.

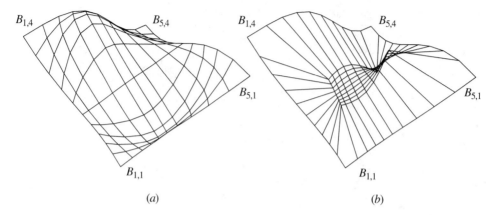

Figure 7.2   Rational B-spline surfaces with $n + 1 = 5$, $m + 1 = 4$, $k = \ell = 4$. (a) All interior $h_{i,j}$s $= 0$; (b) all interior $h_{i,j}$s $= 500$.

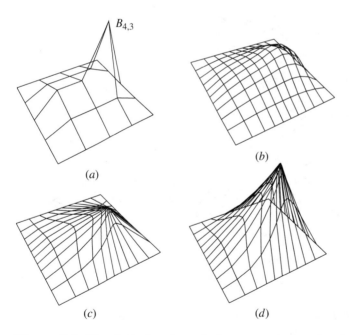

Figure 7.3   The effect of moving a single vertex and of varying the homogeneous weighting factor on a rational B-spline surface. (a) Control net; (b) surface with $h = 1$ at the displaced vertex; (c) surface with $h = 5$ at the displaced vertex; (d) surface with $h = 50$ at the displaced vertex.

Figure 7.3b, with a homogeneous weighting factor $h = 1$, shows the effect of moving the vertex. Figures 7.3c and 7.3d show the effect of increasing the homogeneous weighting factor, from $h = 1$ to $h = 5$ and $h = 50$, respectively, at $B_{4,3}$. The effect is to draw the surface toward the vertex $B_{4,3}$ (see Fig. 7.3b for comparison). Here, notice that the surface still lies within the convex hull of the control net. However, also notice that, although the isoparametric lines were calculated at uniform intervals in parametric space, the spacing of the isoparametric lines on the surface in Cartesian space is no longer uniform. This effect is indicative of a poor or marginal parameterization of the surface. Hence, either the surface must be reparameterized or a very dense isoparametric net must be used in parametric space to adequately describe the surface. An example is illustrative.

Example 7.1 Calculating a Rational B-spline Surface

Consider the open fourth-order piecewise cubic rational B-spline surface defined by the 5×5 control net

$$B_{1,1}\,[-100 \;\; -100 \;\; 0] \quad B_{1,2}\,[-100 \;\; -50 \;\; 0] \quad B_{1,3}\,[-100 \;\; 0 \;\; 0]$$
$$B_{1,4}\,[-100 \;\; 50 \;\; 0] \quad B_{1,5}\,[-100 \;\; 100 \;\; 0]$$
$$B_{2,1}\,[-50 \;\; -100 \;\; 0] \quad B_{2,2}\,[-50 \;\; -50 \;\; 25] \quad B_{2,3}\,[-50 \;\; 0 \;\; 50]$$
$$B_{2,4}\,[-50 \;\; 50 \;\; 25] \quad B_{2,5}\,[-50 \;\; 100 \;\; 0]$$
$$B_{3,1}\,[0 \;\; -100 \;\; 0] \quad B_{3,2}\,[0 \;\; -50 \;\; 25] \quad B_{3,3}\,[0 \;\; 0 \;\; 50]$$
$$B_{3,4}\,[0 \;\; 50 \;\; 25] \quad B_{3,5}\,[0 \;\; 100 \;\; 0]$$
$$B_{4,1}\,[50 \;\; -100 \;\; 0] \quad B_{4,2}\,[50 \;\; -50 \;\; 25] \quad B_{4,3}\,[50 \;\; 0 \;\; 150]$$
$$B_{4,4}\,[50 \;\; 50 \;\; 25] \quad B_{4,5}\,[50 \;\; 100 \;\; 0]$$
$$B_{5,1}\,[100 \;\; -100 \;\; 0] \quad B_{5,2}\,[100 \;\; -50 \;\; 0] \quad B_{5,3}\,[100 \;\; 0 \;\; 0]$$
$$B_{5,4}\,[100 \;\; 50 \;\; 0] \quad B_{5,5}\,[100 \;\; 100 \;\; 0]$$

For all $h_{i,j} = 1$, determine the point on the surface for $u = {}^3\!/_2$, $w = 1$; and compare the result to the point on the surface when $h_{4,3} = 5$ and 50.

For all $h_{i,j} = 1$, the denominator of Eq. (7.3) is exactly 1.0. Hence, $S_{i,j}(u, w) = N_{i,k}(u)M_{j,\ell}(w)$ for all u, w; and Eq. (7.2) with $n = m = 4$ and $k = \ell = 4$ then reduces to

$$Q(u, w) = \sum_{i=1}^{5} \sum_{j=1}^{5} B_{i,j} N_{i,4}(u) M_{j,4}(w)$$

where the knot vectors for $k = \ell = 4$ are

$$[X] = [Y] = [0 \;\; 0 \;\; 0 \;\; 0 \;\; 1 \;\; 2 \;\; 2 \;\; 2 \;\; 2]$$

Thus, the surface is really a nonrational B-spline surface composed of four subpatches: one for $0 \le u \le 1$, $0 \le w \le 1$; one for $0 \le u \le 1$, $1 \le w \le 2$; one for $1 \le u \le 2$, $0 \le w \le 1$; and one for $1 \le u \le 2$, $1 \le w \le 2$.

Writing out Eq. (7.2) yields

$$Q(u, w) = N_{1,4}(B_{1,1}M_{1,4} + B_{1,2}M_{2,4} + B_{1,3}M_{3,4} + B_{1,4}M_{4,4} + B_{1,5}M_{5,4})$$
$$+ N_{2,4}(B_{2,1}M_{1,4} + B_{2,2}M_{2,4} + B_{2,3}M_{3,4} + B_{2,4}M_{4,4} + B_{2,5}M_{5,4})$$
$$+ N_{3,4}(B_{3,1}M_{1,4} + B_{3,2}M_{2,4} + B_{3,3}M_{3,4} + B_{3,4}M_{4,4} + B_{3,5}M_{5,4})$$
$$+ N_{4,4}(B_{4,1}M_{1,4} + B_{4,2}M_{2,4} + B_{4,3}M_{3,4} + B_{4,4}M_{4,4} + B_{4,5}M_{5,4})$$
$$+ N_{5,4}(B_{5,1}M_{1,4} + B_{5,2}M_{2,4} + B_{5,3}M_{3,4} + B_{5,4}M_{4,4} + B_{5,5}M_{5,4})$$

where here $N_{i,k}$ implies $N_{i,k}(u)$ and $M_{j,\ell}$ implies $M_{j,\ell}(w)$ for compactness. Here, the basis functions in the u direction at $u = 3/2$ are (see Eqs. (3.2))

$$N_{1,4}(3/2) = 0; \quad N_{2,4}(3/2) = 1/32; \quad N_{3,4}(3/2) = 1/4;$$
$$N_{4,4}(3/2) = 19/32; \quad N_{5,4}(3/2) = 1/8$$

and in the w direction at $w = 1$ are

$$M_{1,4}(1) = 0; \quad M_{2,4}(1) = 1/4; \quad M_{3,4}(1) = 1/2; \quad M_{4,4}(1) = 1/4; \quad M_{5,4}(1) = 0$$

Thus, the point on the surface at $u = 3/2$, $w = 1$ is

$$Q(3/2, 1) = 0(0\,B_{1,1} + 1/4\,B_{1,2} + 1/2\,B_{1,3} + 1/4\,B_{1,4} + 0B_{1,5})$$
$$+ 1/32\,(0B_{2,1} + 1/4\,B_{2,2} + 1/2\,B_{2,3} + 1/4\,B_{2,4} + 0B_{2,5})$$
$$+ 1/4\,(0B_{3,1} + 1/4\,B_{3,2} + 1/2\,B_{3,3} + 1/4\,B_{3,4} + 0B_{3,5})$$
$$+ 19/32\,(0B_{4,1} + 1/4\,B_{4,2} + 1/2\,B_{4,3} + 1/4\,B_{4,4} + 0B_{4,5})$$
$$+ 1/8\,(0B_{5,1} + 1/4\,B_{5,2} + 1/2\,B_{5,3} + 1/4\,B_{5,4} + 0B_{5,5})$$

$$= 1/128\,(B_{2,2} + B_{2,4} + 19B_{4,2} + 19B_{4,4})$$
$$+ 1/64\,(B_{2,3} + 19B_{4,3})$$
$$+ 1/32\,(B_{5,2} + B_{5,4})$$
$$+ 1/16\,(B_{3,2} + B_{5,3} + B_{3,4})$$
$$+ 1/8\,B_{3,3}$$

$$= 1/128\,([-50 \quad -50 \quad 25] + [-50 \quad 50 \quad 25]$$
$$+ 19[50 \quad -50 \quad 25] + 19[50 \quad 50 \quad 25])$$
$$+ 1/64\,([-50 \quad 0 \quad 50] + 19[50 \quad 0 \quad 150])$$
$$+ 1/32\,([100 \quad -50 \quad 0] + [100 \quad 50 \quad 0])$$
$$+ 1/16\,([0 \quad -50 \quad 25] + [100 \quad 0 \quad 0] + [0 \quad 50 \quad 25])$$
$$+ 1/8\,([0 \quad 0 \quad 50])$$

$$= [40.625 \quad 0 \quad 62.5]$$

Complete results are shown in Fig. 7.3b.

Turning now to the surface with $h_{4,4} = 5$, note that both the knot vectors and the nonrational basis functions remain unchanged. However, the denominator of Eq. (7.3) is no longer 1.0. Hence

$$\text{Sum}(u, w) = \sum_{i1=1}^{n+1} \sum_{j1=1}^{m+1} h_{i1,j1} N_{i1,k}(u) M_{j1,\ell}(w)$$

$$= \sum_{i1=1}^{5} \sum_{j1=1}^{5} h_{i1,j1} N_{i1,4}(3/2) M_{j1,4}(1)$$

$$= N_{1,4}(h_{1,1} M_{1,4} + h_{1,2} M_{2,4} + h_{1,3} M_{3,4} + h_{1,4} M_{4,4} + h_{1,5} M_{5,4})$$

$$+ N_{2,4}(h_{2,1} M_{1,4} + h_{2,2} M_{2,4} + h_{2,3} M_{3,4} + h_{2,4} M_{4,4} + h_{2,5} M_{5,4})$$

$$+ N_{3,4}(h_{3,1} M_{1,4} + h_{3,2} M_{2,4} + h_{3,3} M_{3,4} + h_{3,4} M_{4,4} + h_{3,5} M_{5,4})$$

$$+ N_{4,4}(h_{4,1} M_{1,4} + h_{4,2} M_{2,4} + h_{4,3} M_{3,4} + h_{4,4} M_{4,4} + h_{4,5} M_{5,4})$$

$$+ N_{5,4}(h_{5,1} M_{1,4} + h_{5,2} M_{2,4} + h_{5,3} M_{3,4} + h_{5,4} M_{4,4} + h_{5,5} M_{5,4})$$

Here, note that this expression is similar in form to that for the surface calculation for the nonrational B-spline surface.

Because only one value of $h_{i1,j1} \neq 1$, we have

$$\text{Sum}(3/2, 1) = 1 + (h_{4,3} - 1) N_{4,4}(3/2) M_{3,4}(1)$$

$$= 1 + (5 - 1)(19/32)(1/2)$$

$$= 35/16$$

The surface at $u = 3/2$, $w = 1$ is then given by

$$\text{Sum}(3/2, 1) Q(3/2, 1) = \sum_{i1=1}^{5} \sum_{j1=1}^{5} h_{i1,j1}(3/2, 1) B_{i,j} N_{i1,4}(3/2) M_{j1,4}(1)$$

$$= N_{1,4}(h_{1,1} B_{1,1} M_{1,4} + h_{1,2} B_{1,2} M_{2,4} + h_{1,3} B_{1,3} M_{3,4}$$

$$+ h_{1,4} B_{1,4} M_{4,4} + h_{1,5} B_{1,5} M_{5,4})$$

$$+ N_{2,4}(h_{2,1} B_{2,1} M_{1,4} + h_{2,2} B_{2,2} M_{2,4} + h_{2,3} B_{2,3} M_{3,4}$$

$$+ h_{2,4} B_{2,4} M_{4,4} + h_{2,5} B_{2,5} M_{5,4})$$

$$+ N_{3,4}(h_{3,1} B_{3,1} M_{1,4} + h_{3,2} B_{3,2} M_{2,4} + h_{3,3} B_{3,3} M_{3,4}$$

$$+ h_{3,4} B_{3,4} M_{4,4} + h_{3,5} B_{3,5} M_{5,4})$$

$$+ N_{4,4}(h_{4,1} B_{4,1} M_{1,4} + h_{4,2} B_{4,2} M_{2,4} + h_{4,3} B_{4,3} M_{3,4}$$

$$+ h_{4,4} B_{4,4} M_{4,4} + h_{4,5} B_{4,5} M_{5,4})$$

$$+ N_{5,4}(h_{5,1} B_{5,1} M_{1,4} + h_{5,2} B_{5,2} M_{2,4} + h_{5,3} B_{5,3} M_{3,4}$$

$$+ h_{5,4} B_{5,4} M_{4,4} + h_{5,5} B_{5,5} M_{5,4})$$

Again, because only one value of $h_{i,j} \neq 1$, the new surface is given in terms of the surface with $h_{4,3} = 1$ by

$$\text{Sum}(\tfrac{3}{2}, 1)\, Q(\tfrac{3}{2}, 1) = Q(\tfrac{3}{2}, 1)\big|_{h_{4,3}=1} + (h_{4,3} - 1)N_{4,4}(\tfrac{3}{2})M_{3,4}(1)B_{4,3}$$

$$= [\, 40.625 \quad 0 \quad 62.5\,] + (5 - 1)(\tfrac{19}{32})(\tfrac{1}{2})\,[\, 50 \quad 0 \quad 150\,]$$

and $Q(\tfrac{3}{2}, 1) = (\tfrac{16}{35})\,[\, 40.625 \quad 0 \quad 62.5\,] + (4)(\tfrac{19}{35})(\tfrac{1}{2})\,[\, 50 \quad 0 \quad 150\,]$

$$= [\, 45.714 \quad 0 \quad 110\,]$$

Notice that the surface is pulled toward the vertex at $B_{4,3}$, as shown in Fig. 7.3c.

Turning now to the surface with $h_{4,3} = 50$, from the equation above we have

$$\text{Sum}(\tfrac{3}{2}, 1) = 1 + (50 - 1)(\tfrac{19}{32})(\tfrac{1}{2}) = 15.648$$

$$\text{Sum}(\tfrac{3}{2}, 1)\, Q(\tfrac{3}{2}, 1) = [\, 40.625 \quad 0 \quad 62.5\,] + (50 - 1)(\tfrac{19}{35})(\tfrac{1}{2})\,[\, 50 \quad 0 \quad 150\,]$$

and the point on the surface with $h_{4,3} = 50$ is

$$Q(\tfrac{3}{2}, 1) = [\, 49.397 \quad 0 \quad 144.37\,]$$

Here, the surface point is pulled nearly to the vertex at $B_{4,3}$ $[\, 50 \quad 0 \quad 150\,]$, as shown in Fig. 7.3d.

Negative Homogeneous Weighting Factors

Relaxing the restriction that all $h_{i,j} \geq 0$, Figure 7.4 illustrates the effects of negative homogeneous weighting factors. Figure 7.4a shows the 5×5 control net for the rational B-spline surface. Here, the vertex at $B_{4,3}$ magnifies the effect of the negative homogeneous weighting factor $h_{4,3}$. Figure 7.4b shows the resulting rational B-spline surface with the homogeneous weighting factor, $h_{4,3} = 1$. As expected, the surface is smooth and well parameterized. Figures 7.4c to 7.4e illustrate that the effect of negative values of $h_{4,3} = -1, -\tfrac{3}{2}, -2$, respectively, is to locally depress the surface. In order to more adequately illustrate the surface, the uniformly spaced (in parameter space) isoparametric net is quite dense for Figs. 7.4c to 7.4e as it is for Fig. 7.4b. Again notice that as the homogeneous weighting factor becomes more negative, even for these relatively small negative values of h, the parameterization is significantly affected. However, the most important observation is that for a sufficiently negative homogeneous weighting factor the rational B-spline surface is *not* contained within the convex hull of the control net (see Fig. 7.4e).

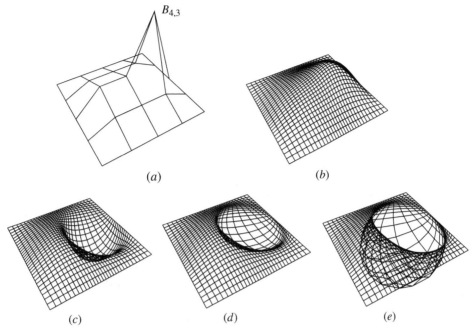

Figure 7.4 The effect of negative homogeneous weighting factors on a rational B-spline surface. (a) Control net; (b) surface with all $h_{i,j} = 1$; (c) surface with $h = -1$ at $B_{4,3}$; (d) surface with $h = -1.5$ at $B_{4,3}$; (e) surface with $h = -2$ at $B_{4,3}$.

Example 7.2 Negative Homogeneous Weights

Recall the open fourth-order piecewise cubic rational B-spline surface defined by the 5×5 control net of Ex. 7.1 (see Fig. 7.4a). Relax the restriction that all $h_{i,j} \geq 0$. Determine the effect of negative homogeneous weighting factors on the surface point $u = 3/2$, $w = 1$ for $h_{4,3} = -1$, $-3/2$, -2. Compare the results to those for $h_{4,3} = 1$ (see Fig. 7.4b and Ex. 7.1).

From Ex. 7.1, for $h_{4,3} = 1$, recall that the surface point is

$$Q(3/2, 1) = [\,40.625 \quad 0 \quad 62.5\,]$$

Recalling the results in Ex. 7.1, the calculation of the denominator of Eq. (7.3) reduces to

$$\text{Sum}(3/2, 1) = 1 + (h_{4,3} - 1)N_{4,4}(3/2)M_{3,4}(1)$$

For $h_{4,3} = -1$, this becomes

$$\text{Sum}(3/2, 1) = 1 + (-1 - 1)(19/32)(1/2)$$
$$= 13/32$$

Similarly, the surface point at $u = 3/2$, $w = 1$ is

$$\text{Sum}(3/2, 1)\, Q(3/2, 1) = Q(3/2, 1)\big|_{h_{4,3}=1} + (h_{4,3} - 1)N_{4,4}(3/2)M_{3,4}(1)B_{4,3}$$

$$= [40.625 \quad 0 \quad 62.5] + (-1 - 1)(19/32)(1/2)[50 \quad 0 \quad 150]$$

and $\qquad Q(3/2, 1) = (32/13)[40.625 \quad 0 \quad 62.5] - (19/13)[50 \quad 0 \quad 150]$

$$= [26.923 \quad 0 \quad -65.385]$$

Notice that the rational B-spline surface is depressed *below* the base plane of the surface, i.e., it lies below and outside the convex hull of the control net. Furthermore, the point on the surface is pushed laterally away from the location of the control vertex, i.e., to the 'left' and 'down', as shown in Fig. 7.4c.

For $h_{4,3} = -3/2$, we have

$$\text{Sum}(3/2, 1) = 1 + (-3/2 - 1)(19/32)(1/2)$$

$$= 33/128$$

and the corresponding surface point at $u = 3/2$, $w = 1$ is

$$Q(3/2, 1) = (128/33)[40.625 \quad 0 \quad 62.5] - (95/33)[50 \quad 0 \quad 150]$$

$$= [13.636 \quad 0 \quad -189.39]$$

The complete results are shown in Fig. 7.4d.

Finally, for $h_{4,3} = -2$, the results are

$$\text{Sum}(3/2, 1) = 1 + (-2 - 1)(19/32)(1/2)$$

$$= 7/64$$

with the corresponding surface point at $u = 3/2$, $w = 1$ given by

$$Q(3/2, 1) = (64/7)[40.625 \quad 0 \quad 62.5] - (57/7)[50 \quad 0 \quad 150]$$

$$= [-35.714 \quad 0 \quad -650.0]$$

Here, the surface is pushed significantly below the convex hull and significantly to the 'left' of the vertex at $B_{4,3}$, as shown in Fig. 7.4e.

Internally Nonuniform Knot Vector

Internally nonuniform knot vectors significantly influence the character of the resulting rational (or nonrational) B-spline surface, as shown in Fig. 7.5. Figure 7.5a shows the 5×5 control net with the vertex at $B_{4,3}$ displaced. The

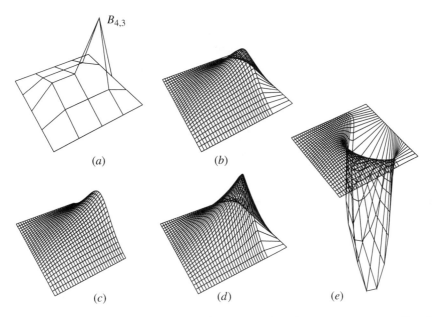

Figure 7.5 The effect of an internally nonuniform knot vector on a rational B-spline surface. Here, the knot vector is $[X] = [0 \quad 0 \quad 0 \quad 0 \quad x_5 \quad 2 \quad 2 \quad 2 \quad 2]$; (a) Control net; (b) surface with all $h_{i,j} = 1$ and $x_5 = 1.9$; (c) surface with all $h_{i,j} = 1$ and $x_5 = 2$; (d) surface with $h_{4,3} = 5$ at $B_{4,3}$ and $x_5 = 1.9$; (e) surface with $h_{4,3} = -1$ at $B_{4,3}$ and $x_5 = 1.9$.

open knot vector in the u parametric direction is now

$$[X] = [0 \quad 0 \quad 0 \quad 0 \quad x_5 = 1.9 \quad 2 \quad 2 \quad 2 \quad 2]$$

in contrast to

$$[X] = [0 \quad 0 \quad 0 \quad 0 \quad x_5 = 1 \quad 2 \quad 2 \quad 2 \quad 2]$$

in Figs. 7.3 and 7.4. Comparing Fig. 7.5b with Fig. 7.3b shows that, as expected from our discussion of internally nonuniform open knot vectors in Sec. 3.4, the effect of the nonuniform knot vector is to concentrate the surface. Here, because of the small interval between $x_5 = 1.9$ and $x_6 = 2$, the effect is to create a ridge in the surface. The right side of the ridge appears to be a 'flat' twisted sweep surface (see Sec. 7.6). Because only the knot vector in the u parametric direction is internally nonuniform, the ridge occurs perpendicular (in parametric space) to the u parametric direction.

If the interval goes to zero, i.e., $x_5 = 2$ and $x_6 = 2$, the effect is to raise the surface off the base plane of the control net, as shown in Fig. 7.5c. In effect, the right side of the ridge disappears. As the interval between the nonuniform values increases, the effect is to move the ridge to the left and decrease the sharpness. An example is illustrative.

Example 7.3 Internally Nonuniform Knot Vectors

Recall the 5×5 open fourth-order piecewise cubic rational B-spline surface defined by the control net in Ex. 7.1 (see Fig. 7.5a). Using an internally nonuniform knot vector in the u parametric direction given by

$$[X] = [0 \quad 0 \quad 0 \quad 0 \quad 1.9 \quad 2 \quad 2 \quad 2 \quad 2]$$

determine the surface point at $u = 3/2$, $w = 1$ for $h_{4,3} = 5$. Compare the results to the surface generated with an internally uniform knot vector (see Ex. 7.1).

First, from Ex. 7.1 for $h_{4,3} = 5$, recall that the surface point is

$$Q(3/2, 1) = [45.71 \quad 0 \quad 110.0]$$

For the nonuniform internal knot vector, the $N_{i,4}$ basis functions at $u = 3/2$ are

$$N_{1,4} = 0.00931; \quad N_{2,4} = 0.1259; \quad N_{3,4} = 0.4207; \quad N_{4,4} = 0.4441; \quad N_{5,4} = 0$$

The uniform internal knot vector in the w parametric direction yields basis functions at $w = 1$ given by

$$M_{1,4} = 0; \quad M_{2,4} = 1/4; \quad M_{3,4} = 1/2; \quad M_{4,4} = 1/4; \quad M_{5,4} = 0$$

The sum function at $u = 3/2$, $w = 1$ is thus

$$\text{Sum}(u, w) = \sum_{i1=1}^{n+1} \sum_{j1=1}^{m+1} h_{i1,j1} N_{i1,k}(u) M_{j1,\ell}(w) = \sum_{i1=1}^{5} \sum_{j1=1}^{5} h_{i1,j1} N_{i1,4}(3/2) M_{j1,4}(1)$$

$$= N_{1,4}(h_{1,1}M_{1,4} + h_{1,2}M_{2,4} + h_{1,3}M_{3,4} + h_{1,4}M_{4,4} + h_{1,5}M_{5,4})$$

$$+ N_{2,4}(h_{2,1}M_{1,4} + h_{2,2}M_{2,4} + h_{2,3}M_{3,4} + h_{2,4}M_{4,4} + h_{2,5}M_{5,4})$$

$$+ N_{3,4}(h_{3,1}M_{1,4} + h_{3,2}M_{2,4} + h_{3,3}M_{3,4} + h_{3,4}M_{4,4} + h_{3,5}M_{5,4})$$

$$+ N_{4,4}(h_{4,1}M_{1,4} + h_{4,2}M_{2,4} + h_{4,3}M_{3,4} + h_{4,4}M_{4,4} + h_{4,5}M_{5,4})$$

$$+ N_{5,4}(h_{5,1}M_{1,4} + h_{5,2}M_{2,4} + h_{5,3}M_{3,4} + h_{5,4}M_{4,4} + h_{5,5}M_{5,4})$$

$$= 0.00931((1)(0) + (1)(1/4) + (1)(1/2) + (1)(1/4) + (1)(0))$$

$$+ 0.1259((1)(0) + (1)(1/4) + (1)(1/2) + (1)(1/4) + (1)(0))$$

$$+ 0.4207((1)(0) + (1)(1/4) + (1)(1/2) + (1)(1/4) + (1)(0))$$

$$+ 0.4441((1)(0) + (1)(1/4) + (5)(1/2) + (1)(1/4) + (1)(0))$$

$$+ 0((1)(0) + (1)(1/4) + (1)(1/2) + (1)(1/4) + (1)(0))$$

$$= 1.8882$$

Recalling Ex. 7.1, the surface point at $u = 3/2$, $w = 1$ is

$$\text{Sum}(3/2, 1)\, Q(3/2, 1) = \sum_{i1=1}^{5} \sum_{j1=1}^{5} h_{i1,j1}(3/2, 1) B_{i,j} N_{i1,4}(3/2) M_{j1,4}(1)$$

$$= 0.00931(0\, B_{1,1} + 1/4\, B_{1,2} + 1/2\, B_{1,3} + 1/4\, B_{1,4} + 0\, B_{1,5})$$

$$+ 0.1259(0\, B_{2,1} + 1/4\, B_{2,2} + 1/2\, B_{2,3} + 1/4\, B_{2,4} + 0\, B_{2,5})$$

$$+ 0.4207(0\, B_{3,1} + 1/4\, B_{3,2} + 1/2\, B_{3,3} + 1/4\, B_{3,4} + 0\, B_{3,5})$$

$$+ 0.4441(0\, B_{4,1} + 1/4\, B_{4,2} + 5/2\, B_{4,3} + 1/4\, B_{4,4} + 0\, B_{4,5})$$

$$+ 0\, (0\, B_{5,1} + 1/4\, B_{5,2} + 1/2\, B_{5,3} + 1/4\, B_{5,4} + 0\, B_{5,5})$$

$$= 0.00931(1/4\,[-100 \quad -50 \quad 0] + 1/2\,[-100 \quad 0 \quad 0]$$
$$+ 1/4\,[-100 \quad 50 \quad 0])$$

$$+ 0.1259(1/4\,[-50 \quad -50 \quad 25] + 1/2\,[-50 \quad 0 \quad 50]$$
$$+ 1/4\,[-50 \quad 50 \quad 25])$$

$$+ 0.4207(1/4\,[0 \quad -50 \quad 25] + 1/2\,[0 \quad 0 \quad 50]$$
$$+ 1/4\,[0 \quad 50 \quad 25])$$

$$+ 0.4441(1/4\,[50 \quad -50 \quad 25] + 5/2\,[50 \quad 0 \quad 150]$$
$$+ 1/4\,[50 \quad 50 \quad 25])$$

$$= [59.389 \quad 0 \quad 192.586]$$

and the surface point is

$$Q(3/2, 1) = [31.45 \quad 0 \quad 101.99]$$

The effect of the nonuniform internal knot vector is to move the surface point to the 'left' and slightly decrease the height. Complete results are shown in Fig. 7.5d.

It is possible to have internally nonuniform knot vectors in both parametric directions, e.g., $x_5 = 1.9$ and $x_6 = 2$, and $y_5 = 1.9$ and $y_6 = 2$. The result is a surface with two intersecting ridges, as shown in Fig. 7.6.

Reparameterization

When using rational B-spline surfaces with large positive or negative values of the homogeneous weighting factors and/or nonuniform internal knot vectors, the parameterization of the resulting surface should be carefully examined. As shown by Figs. 7.3 to 7.6, these factors significantly and nonlinearly affect the parameterization of the surface. If smooth (or fair) surfaces are desired, then reparameterization is in order. However, reparameterization can change the character of the surface. Having said that, the

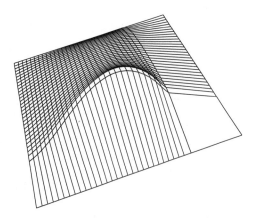

Figure 7.6 Effect of an internally nonuniform knot vector in both parametric directions on a rational B-spline surface. Here, the knot vectors are $[X] = [Y] = [0\ \ 0\ \ 0\ \ 0\ \ 1.9\ \ 2\ \ 2\ \ 2\ \ 2]$ and all $h_{i,j} = 1$.

surface as initally parameterized may be exactly what is desired. For example, the ridge in Fig. 7.5*b* might represent the hard chine of a planing boat, or the faceted surface in Fig. 7.5*e*, appropriately rendered, might represent a faceted jewel.

Unfortunately, many current commercial NURBS-based modeling systems do not allow the designer the flexibility of directly manipulating either the homogeneous weighting factor or the internal knot values.

7.3 A Simple Rational B-spline Surface Algorithm

Equation (7.2) and especially Exs. 7.1 and 7.2 provide the basis for developing a simple algorithm for generating rational B-spline surfaces. Fundamentally, we first specify the control net and the homogeneous weighting factors at each polygon vertex, specify the order of the surface, and specify the number of isoparametric lines in each parametric direction. With this information, the knot vectors are calculated outside the inner loop (see Sec. 3.3) and stored in arrays because they do not change. Knot vectors can also be acquired externally (see the B-spline surface file format in Appendix A).

Equation (7.2) might suggest precalculating the rational basis functions $S(u, w)$ and storing their values in an array. A lookup table is then used to access the required values of the rational basis functions within the inner loop. However, for even modest surfaces represented by modest isoparametric nets, large arrays are required; e.g., a surface represented by a 100×100

isoparametric net requires 10,000 array elements. Furthermore, the data structures and the calculations required to extract an entry from the lookup table may require more work than calculating the Basis and Sum functions on the fly.

Example 7.1 provides guidance on when to calculate the nonrational basis functions, $N_{i,k}$ and $M_{j,\ell}$, as well as the Sum function represented by the denominator of Eq. (7.2), on the fly. Notice from Ex. 7.2 that for a given value of the parameter, u, the basis functions $N_{i,k}$ do not change as the inner summation is evaluated. Furthermore, $M_{j,\ell}$ and the Sum function need only be calculated once for each pass through the inner summation. The resulting algorithm is

Algorithm 7.1 A Simple Rational B-spline Surface

    Specify number of control vertices in the u, w directions.
    Specify order in each of the u, w directions.
    Specify number of isoparametric lines in each of the u, w directions.
    Specify (or acquire) the control net
        and store in an array.
    Calculate (or acquire) the knot vector in the u direction
        and store in an array.
    Calculate (or acquire) the knot vector in the w direction
        and store in an array.
    For each parametric value, u
        Calculate the basis functions, $N_{i,k}(u)$
            and store in an array.
        For each parametric value, w
            Calculate the basis functions, $M_{j,\ell}(w)$
                and store in an array.
            Calculate the Sum function.
                For each control vertex in the u direction
                    For each control vertex in the w direction
                        Calculate the surface point, $Q(u,w)$
                            and store in an array.
                  end loop
              end loop
        end loop
      end loop

A pseudocode implementation of the algorithm called **rbspsurf** is given in Appendix C.

In the context of the algorithm above, the Sum function is simple to evaluate because both $N_{i,k}$ and $M_{j,\ell}$ are available. Hence, it reduces to little more than

Algorithm 7.2 Evaluating the Sum Function

Assume that the $N_{i,k}$ and $M_{j,\ell}$ basis functions are both available.
Assume the homogeneous weighting functions, $h_{i,j}$, are available.
For each control vertex in the u direction
    For each control vertex in the w direction
        Calculate the Sum function.
    end loop
end loop

A pseudocode implementation of the algorithm called **sumrbas** is given in Appendix C.

Looking at the mathematics in Ex. 7.1 suggests an even more efficient rational B-spline surface algorithm, provided only one control vertex or homogeneous weighting factor changes. A detailed discussion of this algorithm is delayed until Sec. 7.10.

7.4 Derivatives of Rational B-spline Surfaces

The derivatives of a rational B-spline surface are obtained by formal differentiation of Eq. (7.2). The results are

$$Q_u = \frac{\bar{N}}{\bar{D}}\left(\frac{\bar{N}_u}{\bar{N}} - \frac{\bar{D}_u}{\bar{D}} \right) \tag{7.5a}$$

$$Q_w = \frac{\bar{N}}{\bar{D}}\left(\frac{\bar{N}_w}{\bar{N}} - \frac{\bar{D}_w}{\bar{D}} \right) \tag{7.5b}$$

$$Q_{uw} = \frac{\bar{N}}{\bar{D}}\left(\frac{\bar{N}_{uw}}{\bar{N}} - \frac{\bar{N}_u}{\bar{N}}\frac{\bar{D}_w}{\bar{D}} - \frac{\bar{N}_w}{\bar{N}}\frac{\bar{D}_u}{\bar{D}} + 2\frac{\bar{D}_u}{\bar{D}}\frac{\bar{D}_w}{\bar{D}} - \frac{\bar{D}_{uw}}{\bar{D}} \right) \tag{7.5c}$$

$$Q_{uu} = \frac{\bar{N}}{\bar{D}}\left(\frac{\bar{N}_{uu}}{\bar{N}} - 2\frac{\bar{N}_u}{\bar{N}}\frac{\bar{D}_u}{\bar{D}} + 2\frac{\bar{D}_u^2}{\bar{D}^2} - \frac{\bar{D}_{uu}}{\bar{D}} \right) \tag{7.5d}$$

$$Q_{ww} = \frac{\bar{N}}{\bar{D}}\left(\frac{\bar{N}_{ww}}{\bar{N}} - 2\frac{\bar{N}_w}{\bar{N}}\frac{\bar{D}_w}{\bar{D}} + 2\frac{\bar{D}_w^2}{\bar{D}^2} - \frac{\bar{D}_{ww}}{\bar{D}} \right) \tag{7.5e}$$

where $\bar{N}$ and $\bar{D}$ are the numerator and denominator, respectively, of Eq. (7.2) with derivatives

$$\bar{N}_u = \sum_{i=1}^{n+1} \sum_{j=1}^{m+1} h_{i,j} B_{i,j} N'_{i,k}(u) M_{j,\ell}(w) \tag{7.6a}$$

$$\bar{N}_w = \sum_{i=1}^{n+1} \sum_{j=1}^{m+1} h_{i,j} B_{i,j} N_{i,k}(u) M'_{j,\ell}(w) \tag{7.6b}$$

$$\bar{N}_{uw} = \sum_{i=1}^{n+1} \sum_{j=1}^{m+1} h_{i,j} B_{i,j} N'_{i,k}(u) M'_{j,\ell}(w) \tag{7.6c}$$

$$\bar{N}_{uu} = \sum_{i=1}^{n+1} \sum_{j=1}^{m+1} h_{i,j} B_{i,j} N''_{i,k}(u) M_{j,\ell}(w) \tag{7.6d}$$

$$\bar{N}_{ww} = \sum_{i=1}^{n+1} \sum_{j=1}^{m+1} h_{i,j} B_{i,j} N_{i,k}(u) M''_{j,\ell}(w) \tag{7.6e}$$

$$\bar{D}_u = \sum_{i=1}^{n+1} \sum_{j=1}^{m+1} h_{i,j} N'_{i,k}(u) M_{j,\ell}(w) \tag{7.6f}$$

$$\bar{D}_w = \sum_{i=1}^{n+1} \sum_{j=1}^{m+1} h_{i,j} N_{i,k}(u) M'_{j,\ell}(w) \tag{7.6g}$$

$$\bar{D}_{uw} = \sum_{i=1}^{n+1} \sum_{j=1}^{m+1} h_{i,j} N'_{i,k}(u) M'_{j,\ell}(w) \tag{7.6h}$$

$$\bar{D}_{uu} = \sum_{i=1}^{n+1} \sum_{j=1}^{m+1} h_{i,j} N''_{i,k}(u) M_{j,\ell}(w) \tag{7.6i}$$

$$\bar{D}_{ww} = \sum_{i=1}^{n+1} \sum_{j=1}^{m+1} h_{i,j} N_{i,k}(u) M''_{j,\ell}(w) \tag{7.6j}$$

The prime denotes a derivative with respect to the appropriate parametric variable. The $N'_{i,k}(u)$, $M'_{j,\ell}(w)$, $N''_{i,k}(u)$, $M''_{j,\ell}(w)$s are given by Eqs. (3.29) to (3.32).

These derivatives are useful in determining the Gaussian curvature of the surface (see Sec. 6.10), as well as other characteristics. An example is illustrative.

Example 7.4   Gaussian Curvature

Determine the Gaussian curvature of the 5×5 open fourth-order piecewise cubic rational B-spline surface of Ex. 7.1, with $h_{4,3} = 5$ at the surface point where $u = 3/2$, $w = 1$.

The nonrational basis functions in the u and w parametric directions in the interval 1 to 2 are given by

$$M_{1,4}(t) = N_{1,4}(t) = 0$$

$$M_{2,4}(t) = N_{2,4}(t) = 1/4 (2 - t)^3$$

$$M_{3,4}(t) = N_{3,4}(t) = 1/4 (2 - t)^2 (4t - 2)$$

$$M_{4,4}(t) = N_{4,4}(t) = 1/4 (2 - t)(3t - 2)t + (2 - t)(t - 1)^2$$

$$M_{5,4}(t) = N_{5,4}(t) = (t - 1)^3$$

where t is u or w as appropriate. Notice that each of the basis functions is a piecewise cubic as expected (see Sec. 3.4). Upon evaluation at $u = 3/2$, the $N_{i,4}$s become

$$N_{1,4}(3/2) = 0; \quad N_{2,4}(3/2) = 1/32; \quad N_{3,4}(3/2) = 1/4;$$

$$N_{4,4}(3/2) = 19/32; \quad N_{5,4}(3/2) = 1/8$$

and in the w direction at $w = 1$ the $M_{j,4}$s are

$$M_{1,4}(1) = 0; \quad M_{2,4}(1) = 1/4; \quad M_{3,4}(1) = 1/2; \quad M_{4,4}(1) = 1/4; \quad M_{5,4}(1) = 0$$

Recalling Eqs. (7.5) and (7.6), calculate the first and second derivatives of the nonrational basis functions. Differentiating the expressions above yields

$$M'_{1,4}(t) = N'_{1,4}(t) = 0$$

$$M'_{2,4}(t) = N'_{2,4}(t) = -3/4 (2 - t)^2$$

$$M'_{3,4}(t) = N'_{3,4}(t) = -1/2 (2 - t)(4t - 2) + (2 - t)^2$$

$$M'_{4,4}(t) = N'_{4,4}(t) = -1/2 (3t - 2)(t - 1) + 1/4 (2 - t)(11t - 8) - (t - 1)^2$$

$$M'_{5,4}(t) = N'_{5,4}(t) = 3(t - 1)^2$$

Notice that each of the first derivatives is a piecewise parabolic function.

Evaluating the $N'_{i,4}$ derivatives at $u = 3/2$ yields

$$N'_{1,4}(1) = 0; \quad N'_{2,4}(1) = -3/16; \quad N'_{3,4}(1) = -3/4; \quad N'_{4,4}(1) = 3/16; \quad N'_{5,4}(1) = 3/4$$

Evaluating the $M'_{i,4}$ derivatives at $w = 1$ yields

$$M'_{1,4}(1) = 0; \quad M'_{2,4}(1) = -3/4; \quad M'_{3,4}(1) = 0; \quad M'_{4,4}(1) = 3/4; \quad M'_{5,4}(1) = 0$$

Differentiating the first derivatives yields the second derivatives

$$M''_{1,4}(t) = N''_{1,4}(t) = 0$$

$$M''_{2,4}(t) = N''_{2,4}(t) = 3/2\,(2-t)$$

$$M''_{3,4}(t) = N''_{3,4}(t) = 1/2\,(4t-2) - 4(2-t)$$

$$M''_{4,4}(t) = N''_{4,4}(t) = -1/2\,(3t-2) + 7/2\,(2-t) - 4(t-1) - 3/2\,t$$

$$M''_{5,4}(t) = N''_{5,4}(t) = 6(t-1)$$

Notice that each second derivative is a piecewise linear function, as expected. Evaluating the $N''_{i,4}$ derivatives at $u = 3/2$ gives

$$N''_{1,4}(3/2) = 0; \quad N''_{2,4}(3/2) = 3/4; \quad N''_{3,4}(3/2) = 0;$$

$$N''_{4,4}(3/2) = -15/4; \quad N''_{5,4}(3/2) = 0$$

Evaluating the $M''_{i,4}$ derivatives at $w = 1$ yields

$$M''_{1,4}(1) = 0; \quad M''_{2,4}(1) = 3/2; \quad M''_{3,4}(1) = -3; \quad M''_{4,4}(1) = 3/2; \quad M''_{5,4}(1) = 0$$

Turning now to the evaluation of the numerator and denominator functions of Eqs. (7.6), from Eq. (7.6a) we have

$$
\bar{N}_u(u,w) = \sum_{i=1}^{n+1}\sum_{j=1}^{m+1} h_{i,j1} N'_i\,k(u) M_{j,\ell}(w) = \sum_{i=1}^{5}\sum_{j=1}^{5} h_{i,j} N'_{i,4}(3/2) M_{j,4}(1)
$$

$$
= N'_{1,4}(h_{1,1}B_{1,1}M_{1,4} + h_{1,2}B_{1,2}M_{2,4} + h_{1,3}B_{1,3}M_{3,4}
$$
$$
+ h_{1,4}B_{1,4}M_{4,4} + h_{1,5}B_{1,5}M_{5,4})
$$

$$
+ N'_{2,4}(h_{2,1}B_{2,1}M_{1,4} + h_{2,2}B_{2,2}M_{2,4} + h_{2,3}B_{2,3}M_{3,4}
$$
$$
+ h_{2,4}B_{2,4}M_{4,4} + h_{2,5}B_{2,5}M_{5,4})
$$

$$
+ N'_{3,4}(h_{3,1}B_{3,1}M_{1,4} + h_{3,2}B_{3,2}M_{2,4} + h_{3,3}B_{3,3}M_{3,4}
$$
$$
+ h_{3,4}B_{3,4}M_{4,4} + h_{3,5}B_{3,5}M_{5,4})
$$

$$
+ N'_{4,4}(h_{4,1}B_{4,1}M_{1,4} + h_{4,2}B_{4,2}M_{2,4} + h_{4,3}B_{4,3}M_{3,4}
$$
$$
+ h_{4,4}B_{4,4}M_{4,4} + h_{4,5}B_{4,5}M_{5,4})
$$

$$
+ N'_{5,4}(h_{5,1}B_{5,1}M_{1,4} + h_{5,2}B_{5,2}M_{2,4} + h_{5,3}B_{5,3}M_{3,4}
$$
$$
+ h_{5,4}B_{5,4}M_{4,4} + h_{5,5}B_{5,5}M_{5,4})
$$

$$
= -3/16\,(1/4\,B_{2,2} + 1/2\,B_{2,3} + 1/4\,B_{2,4})
$$
$$
- 3/4\,(1/4\,B_{3,2} + 1/2\,B_{3,3} + 1/4\,B_{3,4})
$$
$$
+ 3/16\,(1/4\,B_{4,2} + 5/2\,B_{4,3} + 1/4\,B_{4,4})
$$
$$
+ 3/4\,(1/4\,B_{5,2} + 1/2\,B_{5,3} + 1/4\,B_{5,4})
$$

$$
\begin{aligned}
&= -\,{}^{3}\!/\!{}_{64}\,([-50 \quad -50 \quad 25] + 2\,[-50 \quad 0 \quad 50] + [-50 \quad 50 \quad 25]) \\
&\quad - {}^{3}\!/\!{}_{16}\,([0 \quad -50 \quad 25] + 2\,[0 \quad 0 \quad 50] + [0 \quad 50 \quad 25]) \\
&\quad + {}^{3}\!/\!{}_{64}\,([50 \quad -50 \quad 25] + 10\,[50 \quad 0 \quad 150] + [50 \quad 50 \quad 25]) \\
&\quad + {}^{3}\!/\!{}_{16}\,([100 \quad -50 \quad 0] + 2\,[100 \quad 0 \quad 0] + [100 \quad 50 \quad 0]) \\
&= [112.5 \quad 0 \quad 37.5]
\end{aligned}
$$

Similarly, Eqs. (7.6b)–(7.6j) yield

$$
\bar{N}_w = [0 \quad 75 \quad 0]; \quad \bar{N}_{uw} = [0 \quad 0 \quad 0];
$$
$$
\bar{N}_{uu} = [-300 \quad 0 \quad -1425]; \quad \bar{N}_{ww} = [-356.25 \quad 0 \quad -1312.5]
$$
$$
\bar{D}_u = {}^{3}\!/\!{}_{8}; \quad \bar{D}_w = 0; \quad \bar{D}_{uw} = 0; \quad \bar{D}_{uu} = -{}^{15}\!/\!{}_{2}; \quad \bar{D}_{ww} = -{}^{57}\!/\!{}_{8}
$$

In addition, the numerator of Eq. (7.2) is

$$
\bar{N} = [100 \quad 0 \quad 240.625]
$$

and from Ex. 7.1 the denominator is

$$
\bar{D} = {}^{35}\!/\!{}_{16}
$$

With this data to hand, the surface derivatives are obtained from Eqs. (7.5). After first multiplying the ratios out, the results are

$$
Q_u = \frac{\bar{N}}{\bar{D}}\left(\frac{\bar{N}_u}{\bar{N}} - \frac{\bar{D}_u}{\bar{D}}\right) = \frac{\bar{N}_u}{\bar{D}} - \frac{\bar{D}_u}{\bar{D}^2}\bar{N}
$$
$$
= {}^{35}\!/\!{}_{16}\,[112.5 \quad 0 \quad 37.5] - {}^{3}\!/\!{}_{8}\,({}^{35}\!/\!{}_{16})^2\,[100 \quad 0 \quad 240.625]
$$
$$
= [66.651 \quad 0 \quad -349.754]
$$

Similarly

$$
Q_w = \frac{\bar{N}}{\bar{D}}\left(\frac{\bar{N}_w}{\bar{N}} - \frac{\bar{D}_w}{\bar{D}}\right) = \frac{\bar{N}_w}{\bar{D}} - \frac{\bar{D}_w}{\bar{D}^2}\bar{N}
$$
$$
= [0 \quad 34.285 \quad 0]
$$
$$
Q_{uw} = \frac{\bar{N}}{\bar{D}}\left(\frac{\bar{N}_{uw}}{\bar{N}} - \frac{\bar{N}_u}{\bar{N}}\frac{\bar{D}_w}{\bar{D}} - \frac{\bar{N}_w}{\bar{N}}\frac{\bar{D}_u}{\bar{D}} + 2\frac{\bar{D}_u}{\bar{D}}\frac{\bar{D}_w}{\bar{D}} - \frac{\bar{D}_{uw}}{\bar{D}}\right)
$$
$$
= \frac{\bar{N}_{uw}}{\bar{D}} - \bar{N}_u\frac{\bar{D}_w}{\bar{D}^2} - \bar{N}_w\frac{\bar{D}_u}{\bar{D}^2} + 2\frac{\bar{D}_u\bar{D}_w}{\bar{D}^3}\bar{N} - \frac{\bar{D}_{uw}}{\bar{D}^2}\bar{N}
$$
$$
= [0 \quad -5.878 \quad 0]
$$

$$Q_{uu} = \frac{\bar{N}}{\bar{D}}\left(\frac{\bar{N}_{uu}}{\bar{N}} - 2\frac{\bar{N}_u}{\bar{N}}\frac{\bar{D}_u}{\bar{D}} + 2\frac{\bar{D}_u^2}{\bar{D}^2} - \frac{\bar{D}_{uu}}{\bar{D}}\right)$$

$$= \frac{\bar{N}_{uu}}{\bar{D}} - 2\bar{N}_u\frac{\bar{D}_u}{\bar{D}^2} + 2\frac{\bar{D}_u^2}{\bar{D}^3}\bar{N} - \frac{\bar{D}_{uu}}{\bar{D}^2}\bar{N}$$

$$= [\,4.646 \quad 0 \quad -273.698\,]$$

$$Q_{ww} = \frac{\bar{N}}{\bar{D}}\left(\frac{\bar{N}_{ww}}{\bar{N}} - 2\frac{\bar{N}_w}{\bar{N}}\frac{\bar{D}_w}{\bar{D}} + 2\frac{\bar{D}_w^2}{\bar{D}^2} - \frac{\bar{D}_{ww}}{\bar{D}}\right)$$

$$= \frac{\bar{N}_{ww}}{\bar{D}} - 2\bar{N}_w\frac{\bar{D}_w}{\bar{D}^2} + 2\frac{\bar{D}_w^2}{\bar{D}^3}\bar{N} - \frac{\bar{D}_{ww}}{\bar{D}^2}\bar{N}$$

$$= [\,-13.959 \quad 0 \quad -241.714\,]$$

Recall that the Gaussian curvature is given by Eq. (6.21), i.e.

$$\kappa_g = \frac{AC - B^2}{|Q_u \times Q_w|^4}$$

where

$$A = [\,Q_u \times Q_w\,]\cdot Q_{uu}$$

$$B = [\,Q_u \times Q_w\,]\cdot Q_{uw}$$

$$C = [\,Q_u \times Q_w\,]\cdot Q_{ww}$$

Substituting yields

$$[\,Q_u \times Q_w\,] = [\,43.592 \quad 0 \quad -1.714\,] \times [\,0 \quad 34.285 \quad 0\,]$$

$$= [\,58.776 \quad 0 \quad 1494.577\,]$$

$$|Q_u \times Q_w|^4 = 5.005 \times 10^{12}$$

Determining A, B and C, we have

$$A = [\,Q_u \times Q_w\,]\cdot Q_{uu} = [\,58.776 \quad 0 \quad 1494.577\,]\cdot[\,4.646 \quad 0 \quad -273.698\,]$$

$$= -408789.67$$

$$B = [\,Q_u \times Q_w\,]\cdot Q_{uw} = [\,58.776 \quad 0 \quad 1494.577\,]\cdot[\,0 \quad -5.878 \quad 0\,] = 0$$

$$C = [\,Q_u \times Q_w\,]\cdot Q_{ww} = [\,58.776 \quad 0 \quad 1494.577\,]\cdot[\,-13.959 \quad 0 \quad -241.714\,]$$

$$= -362081.13$$

Thus, the Gaussian curvature is

$$\kappa_g = \frac{(-408789.67)(-362081.13) - (0)^2}{5.005 \times 10^{12}} = 2.956 \times 10^{-2}$$

The complete results are shown in Fig. 7.7, where 5000 times the Gaussian curvature is shown as the height (z component) on the base of the 5×5 surface.

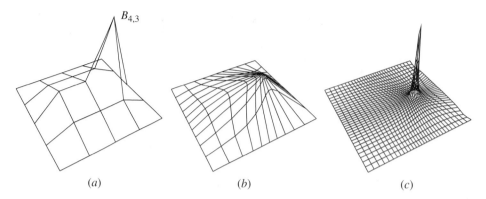

$B_{4,3}$

(a)   (b)   (c)

Figure 7.7   Gaussian curvature of a rational B-spline surface. (a) Control net; (b) surface; (c) 5000 × the Gaussian curvature.

Notice that the surface has both positive, i.e., locally elliptic (see Table 6.1), and negative, i.e., locally hyperbolic, surface curvatures. Notice also the extreme curvature of the surface where the $h = 5$ homogeneous weighting factor is used to draw the surface toward the vertex at $B_{4,3}$.

7.5   Bilinear Surfaces

The classical bilinear surface uses linear blending functions in both parametric directions. It is frequently used for data interpolation in two independent variables. A bilinear surface is easily obtained using rational or nonrational B-spline surfaces. The linear blending functions require that the B-spline surfaces be second order (first degree) in both parametric directions. Specifically, the Cartesian product rational B-spline surface given by Eq. (7.2) reduces to

$$Q(u,w) = \frac{\displaystyle\sum_{i=1}^{2}\sum_{j=1}^{2} h_{i,j} B_{i,j} N_{i,k}(u) M_{j,\ell}(w)}{\displaystyle\sum_{i=1}^{2}\sum_{j=1}^{2} h_{i,j} N_{i,k}(u) M_{j,\ell}(w)} = \sum_{i=1}^{2}\sum_{j=1}^{2} B_{i,j} S_{i,j}(u,w) \qquad (7.7)$$

For a nonrational B-spline surface, Eq. (7.7) reduces to

$$Q(u,w) = \sum_{i=1}^{2}\sum_{j=1}^{2} B_{i,j} N_{i,k}(u) M_{j,\ell}(w) \qquad (7.8)$$

Figure 7.8 shows a bilinear surface defined by a control net whose vertices are the diagonally opposite corners on opposite faces of a cube. Notice in Fig. 7.8c that, although every parametric line on the surface is a straight line, the surface itself is highly curved. In fact, it is a hyperbolic paraboloid. Furthermore, the surface is doubly ruled (see Sec. 7.7).

Figures 7.8a and 7.8b illustrate another interesting point about B-spline bilinear surfaces. Figure 7.8a is defined by just four control vertices, whereas Fig. 7.8b is defined by 25 control vertices. However, also notice that in Fig. 7.8b the control vertices in each direction form straight lines. Hence, each set of control vertices gives the same B-spline surface shown in Fig. 7.8c.

Figure 7.8 suggests that a bilinear surface can be used to create a square tube, as shown in Figs. 7.9a and 7.9b. Here, nine control vertices are used to define the ends of the square tube because the first vertex is repeated. Three control vertices define the length of the tube. Using these extra vertices allows distortion of the tube, as shown in Figs. 7.9c and 7.9d. Here, it is important to realize that along the edges where the tube is closed two isoparametric lines exist, as shown by the darker lines in Figs. 7.9b and 7.9d.

Recall from our previous discussion (see Sec. 7.2) that the effect of positive homogeneous weighting factors is to 'pull' the surface closer to the control net vertex. With that in mind, it is easy to see that positive homogeneous weights have little effect on the shape of a bilinear surface, because a second-order B-spline surface already passes through each of the control vertices. Positive homogeneous weights, however, do change the parameterization of the surface. Negative homogeneous weights definitely have an effect on the surface, as shown in Fig. 7.9e. Figure 7.9e was generated by using a negative homogeneous weighting factor, $h = -0.05$, at the control

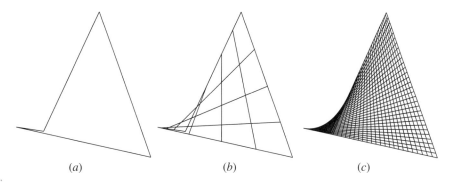

(a)   (b)   (c)

Figure 7.8 Bilinear surface. (a) Simple control net with four vertices; (b) complex control net with 25 vertices; (c) resulting rational B-spline surface from *either* net.

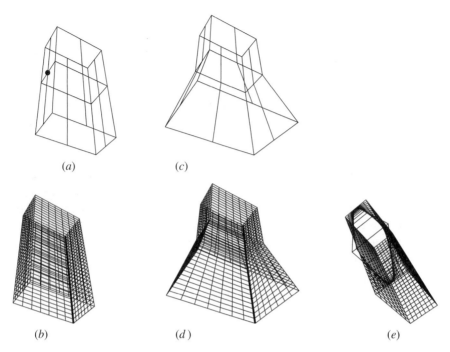

(a) (c)

(b) $(d\,)$ (e)

Figure 7.9   Bilinear surface for a square tube. (a) Control net; (b) surface; (c) control net for distorted tube; (d) distorted surface; (e) effect of a single negative homogeneous weight on the surface.

vertex marked by the dot in Fig. 7.9a. Again, notice that the surface no longer lies within the convex hull of the control net; and also notice the significant effect on the parameterization of the surface.

7.6   Sweep Surfaces

One technique for generating a three-dimensional surface is by traversing an entity, e.g., a line, a polygon or a curve, along a path in space. The resulting surfaces are called sweep surfaces. Sweep surface generation is frequently used in geometric modeling. The simplest sweep entity that generates a surface is a line segment. Recall that the parametric equation of a line segment (see Sec. 1.2) is

$$P(t) = P_1 + (P_2 - P_1)t \qquad 0 \le t \le 1 \tag{7.9}$$

The corresponding sweep surface is given by

$$Q(t,s) = P(t)\,[\,T(s)\,] \qquad 0 \le t \le 1, \quad s_1 \le s \le s_2 \tag{7.10}$$

where $[T(s)]$ is the sweep transformation. If the sweep transformation contains only translations and/or local or overall scalings, the resulting surface is planar. If the sweep transformation contains rotations, the resulting surface is nonplanar. Figure 7.10 shows the helical sweep surface obtained by simultaneously translating along and rotating about the x-axis a line originally coincident with the y-axis, with one end at the origin.

Rational B-spline curves, e.g., open curves, closed polygons or closed curves, can easily be used to generate sweep surfaces. If the end surfaces are included, then the sweep surface encloses a finite volume. Many geometric modeling systems create primitive volumes in this way. A square or rectangle swept along a straight path yields a rectangular parallelepiped. A circle swept along a straight path yields a cylinder. A circle of decreasing radius swept along a straight path yields a cone. Rotation about the sweep axis is also possible. Rational B-splines can be used to define any of these sweep entities.

In sweeping a polygon or closed curve along an arbitrary path, there are two important considerations. The first is, what point in the polygon continuously lies on the path? In general, any point in a polygon or on a closed curve can continuously lie on the path. For different points, the resulting surfaces are different.

The second consideration is, what is the direction of the normal to the polygon or closed curve as the path is swept out? Here, two approaches

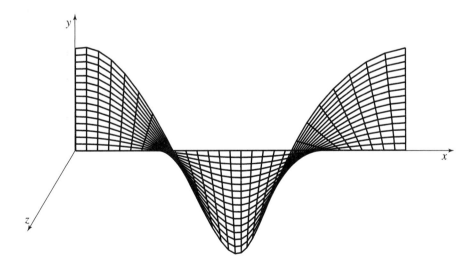

Figure 7.10 A helical sweep surface.

are typically taken. The normal to the polygon or closed curve is in the direction of the instantaneous tangent to the path. Alternatively, the normal direction is specified independent of the path. This latter alternative is extremely flexible.

When generating sweep surfaces, care must be taken to avoid degenerate surfaces or parts of surfaces. An example of a degenerate surface is shown in Fig. 7.11. Here, an s-shaped curve lying in the xy plane is swept parallel to the x-axis. Notice that the 'tails' at the left and right sides are degenerate, i.e., lines of zero area. Such degenerate surface parts cause difficulties in geometric modeling systems.

One of the strong attractions of rational B-spline surfaces is their ability to represent quadric surfaces *and* to blend them smoothly into higher-degree sculptured surfaces. As a simple example of a quadric surface, consider a general cylinder formed by sweeping a rational B-spline curve. It is clear that the surface must be second order, i.e., a straight line, in the sweep direction. Consequently, with the surface swept out in the u parametric direction, the rational B-spline surface representation (see [Pieg87, 95]) is

$$Q(u, w) = \sum_{i=1}^{2} \sum_{j=1}^{m+1} B_{i,j} S_{i,j}(u, w) \qquad (7.11)$$

where $S_{i,j}(u, w)$ is of the order of the curve in the w parametric direction and of order 2 in the u parametric direction. Furthermore, the control net vertices in the u direction are $B_{1,j} = B_j$ and $B_{2,j} = B_j + sD$, where D gives the direction and distance swept. The parameter s is in the range $0 \leq s \leq 1$. The B_js are the control vertices for the swept curve. The

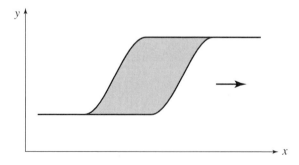

Figure 7.11 A sweep surface with degenerate parts.

homogeneous coordinates are maintained constant in the sweep direction; i.e., $h_{1,j} = h_{2,j} = h_j$, where h_j is the homogeneous coordinate for the swept curve. Figure 7.12 shows an elliptic cylinder generated using the elliptic curve given in Fig. 4.11. The swept curve is shown offset at each end.

7.7   Ruled Rational B-spline Surfaces

Ruled surfaces are frequently used in both the aircraft and the shipbuilding industries, as well as others. For example, most aircraft wings are cylindrical ruled surfaces. Technically, a ruled surface is generated by a straight line moving along a path with one degree of freedom. Alternatively, a ruled surface is identified using the following technique. At any point on the surface, rotate a plane containing the normal to the surface at that point about the normal (see Fig. 7.13). If in at least one orientation every point on the edge of the plane contacts the surface, the surface is ruled in that direction. If the edge of the rotating plane completely touches the surface in more than one orientation, the surface is multiply ruled at that point.

In the context of a mapping from u, w parametric space to object space, a ruled surface is obtained by linearly interpolating between two known boundary curves associated with the opposite sides of the unit square in parametric space, say $P(u, 0)$ and $P(u, 1)$ (see Fig. 5.3). The surface is given by

$$Q(u, w) = P(u, 0)(1 - w) + P(u, 1)w \tag{7.12}$$

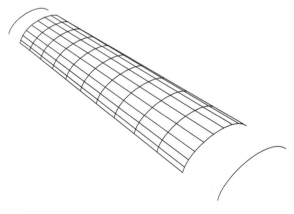

Figure 7.12   Rational B-spline elliptic cylinder generated by sweeping the rational elliptic curve of Fig. 4.11.

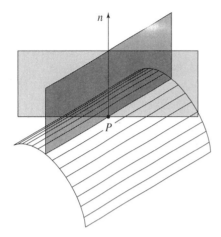

Figure 7.13   Characteristics of a ruled surface.

or $[Q] = [\,x(u,w) \quad y(u,w) \quad z(u,w)\,] = [\,1-w \quad w\,] \begin{bmatrix} P(u,0) \\ P(u,1) \end{bmatrix}$

Note that $Q(0,0) = P(0,0)$, etc., i.e., the ends of the specified curves and the corners of the surface are coincident. Furthermore, note that two of the edges of the blended or interpolated surface are coincident with the given curves, i.e., $Q(u,0) = P(u,0)$ and $Q(u,1) = P(u,1)$.

Alternatively, the curves corresponding to $P(0,w)$ and $P(1,w)$ are assumed known. The ruled surface is then given by

$$Q(u,w) = P(0,w)(1-u) + P(1,w)u$$

or $[Q] = [\,x(u,w) \quad y(u,w) \quad z(u,w)\,] = [\,1-u \quad u\,] \begin{bmatrix} P(0,w) \\ P(1,w) \end{bmatrix}$

Again, the corners of the surface are coincident with the ends of the given curve; and the appropriate edges of the blended surface are coincident with the given boundary curves. An example of a ruled surface is shown in Fig. 7.14. Here, the edge curves shown offset from the surface are third-order nonrational B-spline curves (see Chapter 3).

Rational B-spline surfaces are easily used to generate ruled surfaces. The elliptic cylinder shown in Fig. 7.12 is, of course, a ruled surface. The conditions required to generate a more general ruled surface, using rational B-splines, require that both curves be of the same order (degree), have the same knot vector and have the same number of control vertices. If the

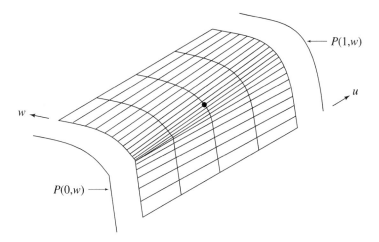

Figure 7.14 Example of a ruled surface.

curves are not of the same order (degree), the degree of the lower order curve is raised (see Sec. 3.12 and Ex. 7.5). The required knot vector is the union of the knot vectors of the two curves. Any multiplicity of knot values for either curve is included in the final knot vector. Knot insertion (see Sec. 3.14) is used to ensure that both knot vectors are identical. Degree elevation (raising) and knot insertion ensure that the number of control vertices is identical for both curves. The resulting rational B-spline ruled surface is described by Eq. (7.11) with

$$P_1(w) = Q(0, w) = \sum_{j=1}^{m+1} B_{1,j} R_{j,\ell}(w) \quad \text{and} \quad P_2(w) = \sum_{j=1}^{m+1} B_{2,j} R_{j,\ell}(w) = Q(1, w)$$

Figure 7.15 shows an example of a ruled surface blending a quarter circle into a fourth-order rational B-spline curve. The curves and their control polygons are shown offset at each end. An example better illustrates the technique.

Example 7.5 Rational B-spline Ruled Surface

Determine the point at $u = w = 1/2$ on a ruled surface formed by blending a $120°$ circular arc represented by a third-order rational B-spline curve defined by

$$B_{1,1} \begin{bmatrix} 0 & 0 & 0 \end{bmatrix}, \; B_{1,2} \begin{bmatrix} 1 & \sqrt{3} & 0 \end{bmatrix}, \; B_{1,3} \begin{bmatrix} 2 & 0 & 0 \end{bmatrix}$$

and

$$[H] = \begin{bmatrix} 1 & 1/2 & 1 \end{bmatrix}$$

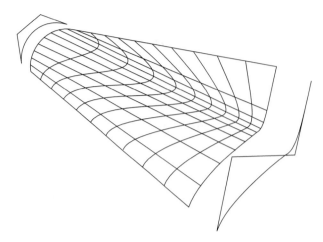

Figure 7.15   Rational B-spline ruled surface.

with a fourth-order rational curve defined by

$$B_{2,1}\begin{bmatrix} 0 & 0 & 10 \end{bmatrix},\ B_{2,2}\begin{bmatrix} 1 & 1 & 10 \end{bmatrix},\ B_{3,2}\begin{bmatrix} 2 & 0 & 10 \end{bmatrix},\ B_{4,2}\begin{bmatrix} 3 & 1 & 10 \end{bmatrix}$$

with
$$[H] = \begin{bmatrix} 1 & 3/4 & 5 & 1 \end{bmatrix}$$

First it is necessary to raise the degree of the circular arc. The circular arc is, in fact, a rational Bézier curve. For the rational case, the degree-elevating technique discussed in Sec. 3.12 is applied to the four-dimensional homogeneous coordinates. The results are

$$B_1^{h*} = B_1^h$$
$$B_i^{h*} = \alpha_i B_{i-1}^h + (1 - \alpha_i) B_i^h \qquad \alpha_i = \frac{i}{n+1} \qquad i = 2, \cdots, n$$
$$B_{n+1}^{h*} = B_n^h$$

Projecting back into three-dimensional space yields

$$B_1^* = B_1$$
$$B_i^* = \frac{\alpha_i h_{i-1} B_{i-1} + (1 - \alpha_i) h_i B_i}{\alpha_i h_{i-1} + (1 - \alpha_i) h_i} \qquad i = 2, \cdots, n$$
$$h_i^* = \alpha_i h_{i-1} + (1 - \alpha_i) h_i$$

Using these results to raise the degree of the 120° arc yields

$$h_{1,1}^* = h_{1,1} = 1$$
$$B_{1,1}^* = B_{1,1} = \begin{bmatrix} 0 & 0 & 0 \end{bmatrix}$$
$$h_{1,2}^* = (1/3)(1) + (2/3)(1/2) = 2/3$$

$$B_{1,2}^* = (1/3 (1) [0 \quad 0 \quad 0] + 2/3 (1/2) [1 \quad \sqrt{3} \quad 0]) / (2/3) = [1/2 \quad \sqrt{3}/2 \quad 0]$$

$$h_{1,3}^* = (2/3)(1/2) + (1/3)(1) = 2/3$$

$$B_{1,3}^* = ((2/3)(1/2) [1 \quad \sqrt{3} \quad 0] + 1/3 (1) [2 \quad 0 \quad 0]) / (2/3) = [3/2 \quad \sqrt{3}/2 \quad 0]$$

$$h_{1,4}^* = h_{1,3}^* = 1$$

$$B_{1,4}^* = B_{1,3} = [2 \quad 0 \quad 0]$$

Each curve now has four control vertices. The knot vector for each curve is

$$[X] = [Y] = [0 \quad 0 \quad 0 \quad 0 \quad 1 \quad 1 \quad 1 \quad 1]$$

Hence, knot insertion is unnecessary.

For $u = w = 1/2$, Eqs. (3.2) yield

$$N_{1,2} = 1/2; \qquad N_{2,2} = 1/2$$

$$M_{1,4} = 1/8; \qquad M_{2,4} = 3/8; \qquad M_{3,4} = 3/8; \qquad M_{4,4} = 1/8$$

Equations (3.2) then yield

$$S_{1,1} = 0.0396 \qquad S_{1,2} = 0.0792 \qquad S_{1,3} = 0.0792 \qquad S_{1,4} = 0.0396$$

$$S_{2,1} = 0.0396 \qquad S_{2,2} = 0.0891 \qquad S_{2,3} = 0.594 \qquad S_{2,4} = 0.0396$$

The surface point is

$$Q(1/2, 1/2) = [1.634 \quad 0.266 \quad 7.624]$$

Complete results are shown in Fig. 7.15.

Developable Surfaces

Of particular practical interest is whether a ruled surface is developable. Not all ruled surfaces are developable. However, all developable surfaces are ruled surfaces. If a surface is developable, then, by a succession of small rotations of the surface about the generating line, the surface can be unfolded or developed onto a plane without stretching or tearing. Developable surfaces are of considerable importance to sheet metal- or plate metal-based industries, and to a lesser extent to fabric-based industries.

To determine if a surface or a portion of a surface is developable, it is necessary to consider the curvature of a parametric surface. For a developable surface, the Gaussian curvature κ_g is everywhere zero (see Sec. 6.10). An example is illustrative.

Example 7.6 Developable Surface

Show that an elliptic cone is a developable surface. The equation for a parametric elliptic cone in terms of u and w is

$$Q(u, w) = [\, au \cos w \quad bu \sin w \quad cu \,]$$

The partial derivatives are

$$Q_u = [\, a \cos w \quad b \sin w \quad c \,]$$

$$Q_w = [\, -au \sin w \quad bu \cos w \quad 0 \,]$$

$$Q_{uw} = [\, -a \sin w \quad b \cos w \quad 0 \,]$$

$$Q_{uu} = [\, 0 \quad 0 \quad 0 \,]$$

$$Q_{ww} = [\, -au \cos w \quad -bu \sin w \quad 0 \,]$$

$$Q_u \times Q_w = [\, -bcu \cos w \quad -acu \sin w \quad abu \,]$$

$$|Q_u \times Q_w|^2 = (abu)^2 \{ (c/a \cos w)^2 + (c/b \sin w)^2 + 1 \} \neq 0 \qquad u > 0$$

and

$$A = [\, -bcu \cos w \quad -acu \sin w \quad abu \,] \cdot [\, 0 \quad 0 \quad 0 \,] = 0$$

$$B = [\, -bcu \cos w \quad -acu \sin w \quad abu \,] \cdot [\, -a \sin w \quad b \cos w \quad 0 \,]$$

$$= abcu \sin w \cos w - abcu \sin w \cos w = 0$$

$$C = [\, -bcu \cos w \quad -acu \sin w \quad abu \,] \cdot [\, -au \cos w \quad -bu \sin w \quad 0 \,]$$

$$= abcu^2 \cos^2 w + abcu^2 \sin^2 w = abcu^2$$

Hence, using Eq. (6.21)

$$\kappa_g = \frac{AC - B^2}{|Q_u \times Q_w|^4} = \frac{(0)(abcu^2) - (0)}{|Q_u \times Q_w|^4} = 0$$

everywhere on the surface, and the surface is developable. Incidentally, note that although for $u = 0$, $|Q_u \times Q_w|^2 = 0$, use of L'Hôpital's rule shows that $\kappa_g = 0/0 = 0$ at $u = 0$.

7.8 Surfaces of Revolution

Perhaps the simplest method for generating a three-dimensional surface is to revolve a two-dimensional entity, e.g., a circle or an open or closed curve, about an axis in space. Such surfaces are called surfaces of revolution and are easily represented by rational B-splines. Assuming that

$$P(w) = \sum_{j=1}^{m+1} B_j R_{j,\ell}(w)$$

with knot vector $[Y]$ is a rational B-spline curve, and recalling that a full circle is obtained by combining four quarter circles defined by nine control vertices (see Sec. 4.5), leads to a rational B-spline surface of revolution defined by (see [Pieg87, 95])

$$Q(u,w) = \sum_{i=1}^{9} \sum_{j=1}^{m+1} B_{i,j} S_{i,j}(u,w) \tag{7.13}$$

where the knot vector

$$[X] = [0 \quad 0 \quad 0 \quad 1 \quad 1 \quad 2 \quad 2 \quad 3 \quad 3 \quad 4 \quad 4 \quad 4]$$

Assuming that rotation occurs about the z-axis, and that the curve $P(w)$ is defined in the xz plane, the $B_{i,j}$s are given by $B_{1,j} = B_j$ for fixed j with $1 \leq i \leq 9$. The control vertices form the corners and midpoints of a square lying in a plane perpendicular to the z-axis with, side dimension twice the radius of the circle of revolution. The homogeneous weighting factors are the product of those for the defining rational B-spline curve and those required to define the circle of revolution. Specifically, for fixed j, $h_{1,j} = h_j$, $h_{2,j} = h_j \sqrt{2}/2$, $h_{3,j} = h_j$, $h_{4,j} = h_j \sqrt{2}/2$, $\cdots$, $h_{9,j} = h_j$. Figure 7.16 shows the control net and curve for the rational B-spline curve to be rotated and the circle of revolution. Also shown in Fig. 7.16 is the composite surface control net and the surface itself.

The common quadric surfaces of revolution, e.g., the torus and the sphere along with their control nets, are shown in Figs. 7.17 and 7.18. The torus is generated by revolving an offset circle about one of the axes. The sphere is generated by revolving a semicircle composed of two 90° arcs about an axis that is a diameter of the semicircle. An example more fully illustrates the technique.

Example 7.7 Torus

Using a rational B-spline surface, find the point on the surface at $u = 3/2$, $w = 3/2$ for the torus shown in Fig. 7.17.

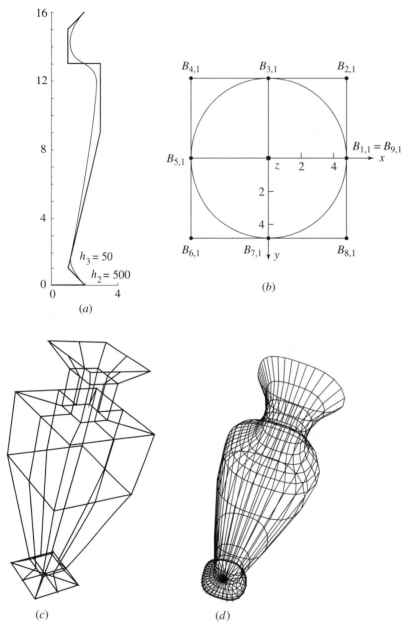

Figure 7.16   Rational B-spline surface of revolution. (a) Generating curve and control polygon; (b) circle of revolution; (c) defining surface control net; (d) surface of revolution.

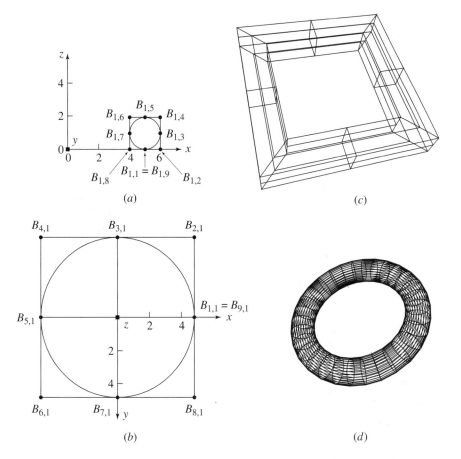

Figure 7.17 Torus generated as a rational B-spline surface. (a) Offset circle and control; (b) circle of revolution and control; (c) control net for torus; (d) torus.

Looking at Fig. 7.17a, the offset circle is defined by

$$B_{1,1}\begin{bmatrix} 5 & 0 & 0 \end{bmatrix} \quad B_{1,2}\begin{bmatrix} 6 & 0 & 0 \end{bmatrix} \quad B_{1,3}\begin{bmatrix} 6 & 0 & 1 \end{bmatrix}$$
$$B_{1,4}\begin{bmatrix} 6 & 0 & 2 \end{bmatrix} \quad B_{1,5}\begin{bmatrix} 5 & 0 & 2 \end{bmatrix} \quad B_{1,6}\begin{bmatrix} 4 & 0 & 2 \end{bmatrix}$$
$$B_{1,7}\begin{bmatrix} 4 & 0 & 1 \end{bmatrix} \quad B_{1,8}\begin{bmatrix} 4 & 0 & 0 \end{bmatrix} \quad B_{1,9}\begin{bmatrix} 5 & 0 & 0 \end{bmatrix}$$

while from Fig. 7.17b the circle of revolution is given by

$$B_{1,1}\begin{bmatrix} 5 & 0 & 0 \end{bmatrix} \quad B_{2,1}\begin{bmatrix} 5 & 5 & 0 \end{bmatrix} \quad B_{3,1}\begin{bmatrix} 0 & 5 & 0 \end{bmatrix}$$
$$B_{4,1}\begin{bmatrix} -5 & 5 & 0 \end{bmatrix} \quad B_{5,1}\begin{bmatrix} -5 & 0 & 0 \end{bmatrix} \quad B_{6,1}\begin{bmatrix} -5 & -5 & 0 \end{bmatrix}$$
$$B_{7,1}\begin{bmatrix} 0 & -5 & 0 \end{bmatrix} \quad B_{8,1}\begin{bmatrix} 5 & -5 & 0 \end{bmatrix} \quad B_{9,1}\begin{bmatrix} 5 & 0 & 0 \end{bmatrix}$$

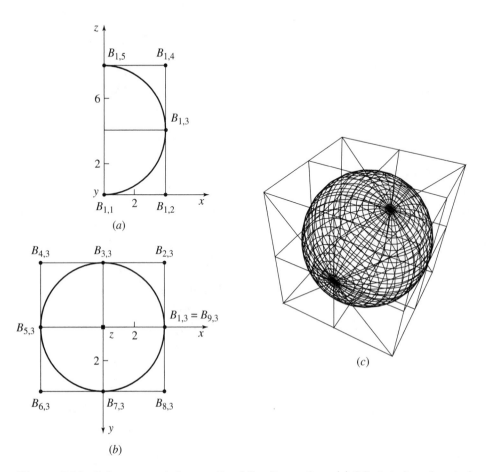

Figure 7.18 Sphere generated as a rational B-spline surface. (a) Offset circle and control
net; (b) circle of revolution and control; (c) control net and sphere.

The circles are both third order, i.e., $k = \ell = 3$, with homogeneous weighting
factors given by

$$h_{i,j} = 1, \qquad i = 1, 3, 5, 7, 9$$

$$h_{i,j} = \sqrt{2}/2, \qquad i = 2, 4, 6, 8$$

The knot vectors are

$$[X] = [Y] = [0 \quad 0 \quad 0 \quad 1 \quad 1 \quad 2 \quad 2 \quad 3 \quad 3 \quad 4 \quad 4 \quad 4]$$

From Eq. (7.13)

$$Q(u, w) = \sum_{i=1}^{9} \sum_{j=1}^{9} B_{i,j} S_{i,j}(u, w)$$

and Eq. (7.3) reduces to

$$S_{i,j}(u,w) = \frac{h_{i,j}\,N_{i,k}(u)\,M_{j,\ell}(w)}{\displaystyle\sum_{i1=1}^{9}\sum_{j1=1}^{9}h_{i1,j1}\,N_{i1,k}(u)\,M_{j1,\ell}(w)} = \frac{h_{i,j}\,N_{i,k}(u)\,M_{j,\ell}(w)}{\mathrm{Sum}(u,w)}$$

At $u = w = 3/2$, the only nonzero basis functions are

$$N_{3,3} = M_{3,3} = 1/4; \qquad N_{4,3} = M_{4,3} = 1/2; \qquad N_{5,3} = M_{5,3} = 1/4$$

The sum function is thus

$$\begin{aligned}
\mathrm{Sum} = {} & N_{3,3}(h_{3,3}M_{3,3} + h_{3,4}M_{4,3} + h_{3,5}M_{5,3}) \\
& + N_{4,3}(h_{4,3}M_{3,3} + h_{4,4}M_{4,3} + h_{4,5}M_{5,3}) \\
& + N_{5,3}(h_{5,3}M_{3,3} + h_{5,4}M_{4,3} + h_{5,5}M_{5,3}) \\
= {} & 1/4\,((1)(1/4) + (1)(1/2) + (1)(1/4)) \\
& + 1/2\,((\sqrt{2}/2)(1/4) + (\sqrt{2}/2)(1/2) + (\sqrt{2}/2)(1/4)) \\
& + 1/4\,((1)(1/4) + (1)(1/2) + (1)(1/4)) \\
= {} & \frac{2 + \sqrt{2}}{4} = 0.8536
\end{aligned}$$

The nonzero bivariant rational B-spline surface basis functions

$$\mathrm{Sum}(u,w)\,S_{i,j}(u,w) = h_{i,j}N_{i,k}(u)M_{j,\ell}(w)$$

at $u = 3/2$, $w = 3/2$ are

$$\begin{aligned}
\mathrm{Sum}\,S_{3,3} &= h_{3,3}N_{3,3}(3/2)M_{3,3}(3/2) = (1)(1/4)(1/4) = 1/16 \\
\mathrm{Sum}\,S_{3,4} &= h_{3,4}N_{3,3}(3/2)M_{4,3}(3/2) = (1)(1/4)(1/2) = 1/8 \\
\mathrm{Sum}\,S_{3,5} &= h_{3,5}N_{3,3}(3/2)M_{5,3}(3/2) = (1)(1/4)(1/4) = 1/16 \\[4pt]
\mathrm{Sum}\,S_{4,3} &= h_{4,3}N_{4,3}(3/2)M_{3,3}(3/2) = (\sqrt{2}/2)(1/2)(1/4) = \sqrt{2}/16 \\
\mathrm{Sum}\,S_{4,4} &= h_{4,4}N_{4,3}(3/2)M_{4,3}(3/2) = (\sqrt{2}/2)(1/2)(1/2) = \sqrt{2}/8 \\
\mathrm{Sum}\,S_{4,5} &= h_{4,5}N_{4,3}(3/2)M_{5,3}(3/2) = (\sqrt{2}/2)(1/2)(1/4) = \sqrt{2}/16 \\[4pt]
\mathrm{Sum}\,S_{5,3} &= h_{5,3}N_{5,3}(3/2)M_{3,3}(3/2) = (1)(1/4)(1/4) = 1/16 \\
\mathrm{Sum}\,S_{5,4} &= h_{5,4}N_{5,3}(3/2)M_{4,3}(3/2) = (1)(1/4)(1/2) = 1/8 \\
\mathrm{Sum}\,S_{5,5} &= h_{5,5}N_{5,3}(3/2)M_{5,3}(3/2) = (1)(1/4)(1/4) = 1/16
\end{aligned}$$

Turning now to the surface point, we have

$$\begin{aligned}
\mathrm{Sum}(3/2, 3/2)\,Q(3/2, 3/2) = {} & S_{3,3}B_{3,3} + S_{4,4}B_{4,4} + S_{5,5}B_{5,5} \\
& + S_{3,4}B_{3,4} + S_{4,3}B_{4,3} \\
& + S_{4,5}B_{4,5} + S_{5,4}B_{5,4} \\
& + S_{5,3}B_{5,3} + S_{3,5}B_{3,5}
\end{aligned}$$

Substituting, we have

$$\text{Sum}(\tfrac{3}{2},\tfrac{3}{2})\,Q(\tfrac{3}{2},\tfrac{3}{2}) = \tfrac{1}{16}\begin{bmatrix} 0 & 6 & 1 \end{bmatrix} + \tfrac{\sqrt{2}}{8}\begin{bmatrix} -6 & 6 & 2 \end{bmatrix} + \tfrac{1}{16}\begin{bmatrix} -5 & 0 & 2 \end{bmatrix}$$

$$+ \tfrac{1}{8}\begin{bmatrix} -6 & 6 & 1 \end{bmatrix} + \tfrac{\sqrt{2}}{16}\begin{bmatrix} 0 & 6 & 2 \end{bmatrix}$$

$$+ \tfrac{\sqrt{2}}{16}\begin{bmatrix} -6 & 0 & 2 \end{bmatrix} + \tfrac{1}{8}\begin{bmatrix} -5 & 5 & 2 \end{bmatrix}$$

$$+ \tfrac{1}{16}\begin{bmatrix} 0 & 5 & 2 \end{bmatrix} + \tfrac{1}{16}\begin{bmatrix} -6 & 0 & 1 \end{bmatrix}$$

$$= \begin{bmatrix} -3.653 & 3.653 & 1.457 \end{bmatrix}$$

Dividing through by Sum yields the point on the surface at $u = \tfrac{3}{2}$, $w = \tfrac{3}{2}$ as

$$Q(\tfrac{3}{2},\tfrac{3}{2}) = \begin{bmatrix} -4.28 & 4.28 & 1.707 \end{bmatrix}$$

Complete results are shown in Fig. 7.17d.

7.9 Blending Surfaces

As mentioned previously, one of the most powerful characteristics of rational versus nonrational B-spline surfaces is their ability to 'bury', include or blend quadric surface elements within a general sculptured surface. For example, a cylindrical surface element can be included as part of a more general surface. Figure 7.19 shows three examples of this. The central portion of each fourth-order surface is a section of a circular cylinder. Figures 7.19a and 7.19b might represent the leading edge[†] of a wing or turbine blade. Figures 7.19c and 7.19d might represent the cylindrical bow (stem) of a ship. Both surfaces are generated by first defining a third-order circular arc (see Sec. 4.5), raising the degree of the arc (see Ex. 7.5), making a ruled surface from the arc and including it between the two fourth-order side surface elements. Incidentally, both of the surfaces shown in Figs. 7.19a and 7.19b are ruled developable surfaces. Figures 7.19e and 7.19f show the cylindrical element buried in a more general surface.

7.10 A Fast Rational B-spline Surface Algorithm

B-spline surfaces, and in particular rational B-spline surfaces, require considerable computation. A number of approaches to achieving dynamic real-time

---

[†]NACA (National Advisory Committee for Aeronautics) airfoil sections use a circular arc to define the leading edge.

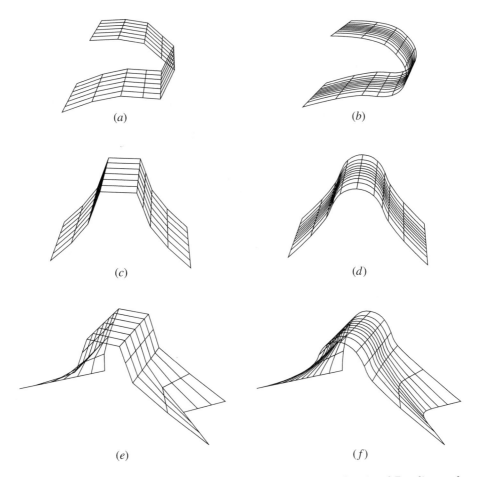

(a)

(b)

(c)

(d)

(e)

(f)

Figure 7.19   A quadric surface element within a more general rational B-spline surface: airfoil leading edge. (a) Control net; (b) surface: a cylinder as the leading edge of a wing; (c) control net; (d) surface: a cylinder as part of a more general surface; (e) control net; (f) surface.

modification, including hardware implementation and forward differences [Shan88], have been used. Interestingly enough, as shown by Clark [Clar74] and by Rogers and Satterfield [Roge82], achieving dynamic real-time modification of nonrational B-spline surfaces in software using a modest general-purpose computer is relatively easy. A fast software algorithm for dynamic modification of rational B-spline surfaces, including direct manipulation of the homogeneous weighting factor, is discussed below (see [Roge90b]).

Five increasingly more efficient algorithms for generating B-spline surfaces are discussed. First, a completely naive algorithm is presented. The efficiency of this algorithm is improved using mathematical knowledge of B-spline basis functions. Assuming that the surface is modified by directly manipulating the control net, and provided only a single control net vertex or a single homogeneous weighting factor is changed, efficient algorithms for incremental calculation of B-spline surfaces are presented.

Naive Algorithms

First consider naive algorithms for generating B-spline surfaces. Recalling Eq. (6.1) and given the control net vertices, the number of net vertices in each parametric direction, $npts = n+1$, $mpts = m+1$, the order of the surface in each parametric direction k, ℓ, and the number of desired parametric lines on the surface, p_1, p_2, in the u, w parametric directions, respectively, a naive pseudocode algorithm for a nonrational B-spline surface consisting of four nested loops is

```
bsurfnaive(b(),k,l,npts,mpts,p1,p2; Q())
    nplusc = npts + k
    mplusc = mpts + l
    calculate the open knot vector [X] in the u parametric direction
    call knot(npts,k; x)
    calculate the open knot vector [Y] in the w parametric direction
    call knot(mpts,l; y)
    calculate the surface
    icnt = 1
    for u = 0 to x(nplusc) step x(nplusc)/(p1−1)
        call basis(k,u,npts,x; nbasis)        u direction
        for w = 0 to y(mplusc) step y(mplusc)/(p2−1)
            call basis(l,w,mpts,y; mbasis)        w direction
            for i = 1 to npts
                jbas = 4*mpts*(i−1)
                for j = 1 to mpts
                    j1 = jbas + 4*(j−1)+1
                    Q(icnt) = Q(icnt) + b(j1+3)*b(j1)*nbasis(i)*mbasis(j)
                    Q(icnt+1) = Q(icnt+1) + b(j1+3)*b(j1+1)*nbasis(i)*mbasis(j)
                    Q(icnt+2) = Q(icnt+2) + b(j1+3)*b(j1+2)*nbasis(i)*mbasis(j)
                next j
```

```
        next i
        icnt = icnt + 3
      next w
    next u
return
```

where **knot** calculates the open uniform knot vector and **basis** calculates the B-spline basis function for a given parameter value. Here, no attempt is made to eliminate the calculation and storage of zero B-spline basis functions. After all, this *is* a naive algorithm. Furthermore, in the context of later discussions, it turns out to be more efficient to calculate and store these zero basis function values. Notice also that only linear arrays are used for storage and that all indexing into the arrays is done locally. Using only locally indexed linear arrays allows easy and consistent implementation in most major computer languages.

Open uniform knot vectors starting at zero are assumed in the above and subsequent algorithms. For uniform periodic knot vectors starting at zero, the limits in the u and w **for** loops are

```
for u = k−1 to npts step (npts−k+1)/(p1−1)
for w = l−1 to mpts step (mpts−l+1)/(p2−1)
```

Nonuniform knot vectors are accommodated by similarly changing the parameter limits.

Recalling Eq. (7.1) and comparing it to Eq. (6.1) shows that two simple additions to the inner loops of the nonrational algorithm yield a naive algorithm for rational B-spline surfaces, i.e.

```
icnt = 1
for u = 0 to x(nplusc) step x(nplusc)/(p1−1)
  call basis(k,u,npts,x; nbasis)
  for w = 0 to y(mplusc) step y(mplusc)/(p2−1)
    call basis(l,w,mpts,y; mbasis)
    call sumrbas(b,nbasis,mbasis,npts,mpts; sum)
    for i = 1 to npts
      jbas = 4*mpts*(i−1)
      for j = 1 to mpts
        j1 = jbas + 4*(j−1) + 1
        q(icnt) = q(icnt) + b(j1+3)*b(j1)*nbasis(i)*mbasis(j)/sum
        q(icnt+1) = q(icnt+1)
```

$$+ \text{ b(j1+3)*b(j1+1)*nbasis(i)*mbasis(j)/sum}$$
$$\text{q(icnt+2)} = \text{q(icnt+2)}$$
$$+ \text{ b(j1+3)*b(j1+2)*nbasis(i)*mbasis(j)/sum}$$
next j
next i
icnt = icnt + 3
next w
next u

Notice that the subroutine **sumrbas**, which calculates the $\text{Sum}(u, w)$ function (see Eq. (7.3)), is now called for each value of u, w, and that division by $\text{Sum}(u, w)$ occurs each time a term in the surface summation is evaluated. Thus, the rational B-spline surface algorithm requires approximately one-third more computational effort than the nonrational algorithm.

These naive algorithms are easy to implement and very *memory* efficient. In the naive algorithms, the most significant computational load occurs in the calculation of the surface points, q. Here, three floating point multiplies, a floating point divide and a floating point add are required for each component. One obvious technique for increasing the efficiency of the algorithm is to avoid these calculations whenever possible.

From our previous discussions of basis functions (see Sec. 3.4) and a number of examples, such as Exs. 3.1–3.5, 4.1, 6.1 and 6.3 in previous chapters and Exs. 7.1 and 7.3 in this chapter, individual B-spline basis functions are frequently zero over much of the parameter range. Examining Eqs. (6.1), (7.2) and (7.3) suggests that significant parts of the surface calculation can be avoided when this occurs. Writing out Eq. (7.3) for the simple case of $k = \ell = n + 1 = m + 1 = 3$ illustrates this, e.g.

$$Q(u, w) = \frac{N_{1,3}(u)}{\text{Sum}(u, w)} \left\{ h_{1,1}B_{1,1}M_{1,3}(w) + h_{1,2}B_{1,2}M_{2,3}(w) + h_{1,3}B_{1,3}M_{3,3}(w) \right\}$$

$$+ \frac{N_{2,3}(u)}{\text{Sum}(u, w)} \left\{ h_{2,1}B_{2,1}M_{1,3}(w) + h_{2,2}B_{2,2}M_{2,3}(w) + h_{2,3}B_{2,3}M_{3,3}(w) \right\}$$

$$+ \frac{N_{3,3}(u)}{\text{Sum}(u, w)} \left\{ h_{3,1}B_{3,1}M_{1,3}(w) + h_{3,2}B_{3,2}M_{2,3}(w) + h_{3,3}B_{3,3}M_{3,3}(w) \right\}$$

$$(7.14)$$

Notice that whenever $N_{i,k}(u) = 0$ the entire calculation in brackets is avoided! Similarly, whenever $M_{j,\ell}(w) = 0$, the calculation of an individual term in brackets is avoided. Furthermore, examination of the $\text{Sum}(u, w)$

function shows that exactly the same techniques apply to its calculation. The addition of two **if** tests to the i and j inner loops of the naive algorithm are all that is required. The inner loops are now

```
for i = 1 to npts
  if nbasis(i) ≠ 0 then
    jbas = 4*mpts*(i−1)
    for j = 1 to mpts
      if mbasis(j) ≠ 0 then
        j1 = jbas + 4*(j−1) + 1
        Q(icnt) = Q(icnt) + b(j1+3)*b(j1)*nbasis(i)*mbasis(j)/sum
        Q(icnt+1) = Q(icnt+1)
            + b(j1+3)*b(j1+1)*nbasis(i)*mbasis(j)/sum
        Q(icnt+2) = Q(icnt+2)
            + b(j1+3)*b(j1+2)*nbasis(i)*mbasis(j)/sum
      end if
    next j
  end if
next i
```

Using this technique, the efficiency of the naive rational B-spline surface algorithm is typically increased by approximately 25%. Note that a similar effect is obtained by calculating only the nonzero basis functions for each u, w value and appropriately modifying the limits of the i and j **for** loops.

A More Efficient Algorithm

In modifying a Bézier or B-spline surface, a designer normally works with a control net of constant size, of constant order in each parametric direction (usually fourth) and with a constant number of isoparametric lines used to display the surface, i.e., $n+1$, $m+1$, k, ℓ, p_1, p_2 are constant. If the designer modifies the surface by manipulating the control net, only occasionally does one of these parameters change during a design session. Typically, the designer increases $n + 1$ or $m + 1$ to achieve additional detail in a specific area or changes p_1 and p_2 to better visualize the surface. If the parameters $n + 1$, $m + 1$, k, ℓ, p_1, p_2 do not change, then neither the basis functions, $N_{i,k}(u)$ or $M_{j,\ell}(w)$, nor the sum function, $\text{Sum}(u, w)$, change while the net is being manipulated. Consequently, the efficiency of the algorithm is increased by precalculating the basis and sum functions and storing them in arrays. Examination of Eq. (7.14) shows that precalculating the basis and sum functions, forming the coefficient $N_{i,k}(u)M_{j,\ell}(w)/\text{Sum}(u,w)$ for each u, w and i, j pair and storing this value in an array yields the most efficient algorithm. For consistency, this is *not* done in the algorithms below.

The algorithm now becomes

bsurfeff(b(),bold(),ibnum,k,l,npts,mpts,p1,p2,itest,niku(),mjlw(),
   rsumuw(); Q())

   if itest $\neq$ (npts + mpts + k + l + p1 + p2) **then**

     calculate the complete surface

     generate the knot vectors—open uniform knot vectors are assumed
     call knot(npts,k,x)   *calculate the u knot vector*
     call knot(mpts,l,y)   *calculate the w knot vector*
     icnt = 1

     calculate and store the basis functions
     stepu = x(npts + k)/(p1−1)
     stepw = y(mpts + l)/(p2−1)
     i1 = 1
     i2 = 1
     i3 = 1

     calculate and store the $N_{i,k}s$ at each u parametric value
     u = 0   *change the initial value as appropriate*
     for uinc = 1 **to** p1
       call basis(k,u,npts,x,nbasis)   *basis function for this value of u*
       for i = 1 **to** npts
         niku(i1) = nbasis(i)
         i1 = i1 + 1
       next i
       u = u + stepu
     next uinc

     calculate and store the $M_{j,\ell}s$ at each w parametric value
     w = 0   *change the initial value as appropriate*
     for winc = 1 **to** p2
       call basis(l,w,mpts,y,mbasis)   *basis function for this value of w*
       for j = 1 **to** mpts
         mjlw(i2) = mbasis(j)
         i2 = i2 + 1
       next j

```
        w = w + stepw
    next winc
    calculate the sum function at each parametric value of u,w
    for uinc = 1 to p1
        for i = 1 to npts        extract basis function for this value of u
            ibas = (uinc − 1)∗npts + i
            nbasis(i) = niku(ibas)
        next i
        for winc = 1 to p2
            for j = 1 to mpts        extract basis function for this value of w
                jbas = (winc−1)∗mpts + j
                mbasis(j) = mjlw(jbas)
            next j
            call sumrbas(b,nbasis,mbasis,npts,mpts; sum)
            rsumuw(i3) = 1/sum        store the reciprocal
            i3 = i3 + 1                to avoid divide in inner loop
        next winc
    next uinc
    itest = 0
end if
generate the complete rational B-spline surface
if itest = 0 then
    icnt = 1
    for uinc = 1 to p1
        for winc = 1 to p2
            scnt = (uinc−1)∗p2 + winc
            for i = 1 to npts
                jbas = 4∗mpts∗(i−1)
                ninc = (uinc−1)∗npts + i
                if (niku(ninc) ≠ 0)        avoid the calculation
                    for j = 1 to mpts
                        j1 = jbas + 4∗(j−1) + 1
                        minc = (winc−1)∗mpts + j
                        if (mjlw(minc) ≠ 0)        avoid the calculation
                            pbasis = b(j1+3)∗niku(ninc)∗mjlw(minc)∗rsumuw(scnt)
                            Q(icnt) = Q(icnt) + b(j1)∗pbasis        calculate surf. pt.
                            Q(icnt+1) = Q(icnt+1) + b(j1+1)∗pbasis
                            Q(icnt+2) = Q(icnt+2) + b(j1+2)∗pbasis
```

$$\textbf{end if}$$
$$\textbf{next } j$$
$$\textbf{end if}$$
$$\textbf{next } i$$
$$\text{icnt} = \text{icnt} + 3$$
$$\textbf{next } \text{winc}$$
$$\textbf{next } \text{uinc}$$
$$\text{itest} = \text{npts} + k + \text{mpts} + l + p1 + p2$$
$$\textbf{end if}$$
$$\textbf{return}$$

Note that here, if the control net, the order and the isoparametric surface net do not change, i.e., **itest** does not change, then the basis and sum functions are not recalculated.

This algorithm improves the performance of the naive rational B-spline surface algorithm by a factor of approximately three. Here, note that if only the nonzero basis functions are calculated and stored, because linear arrays are used the indexing task is computationally more expensive than the compare in the **if** $\neq 0$ statement.

Incremental Surface Calculation

The algorithms above calculate each point on the isoparametric surface net. If only a single control net vertex is manipulated, an incremental algorithm that calculates only those portions of the isoparametric surface net that change is easily developed. This is most easily seen by returning to Eq. (7.14), writing the equation out for the new surface and for the old surface and subtracting. Generalizing this result yields the incremental equation for the new surface, i.e.

$$\text{Sum}_{\text{new}}(u, w) Q_{\text{new}}(u, w) = \text{Sum}_{\text{old}}(u, w) Q_{\text{old}}(u, w)$$

$$+ (h_{i,j_{\text{new}}} B_{i,j_{\text{new}}} - h_{i,j_{\text{old}}} B_{i,j_{\text{old}}}) N_{i,k}(u) M_{j,\ell}(w) \qquad (7.15)$$

If the homogeneous weighting factor does not change, then $\text{Sum}(u, w)$ does not change (see Eq. (7.3)) and Eq. (7.15) becomes

$$Q_{\text{new}}(u, w) = Q_{\text{old}}(u, w) + (B_{i,j_{\text{new}}} - B_{i,j_{\text{old}}}) \frac{h_{i,j}(u) N_{i,k}(u) M_{j,\ell}(w)}{\text{Sum}(u, w)}$$

$$(7.16)$$

If only the homogeneous weighting factor changes, i.e., the spatial position of the control vertex is fixed, then Eq. (7.15) becomes

$$Q_{\text{new}}(u, w) = \frac{\text{Sum}_{\text{old}}(u, w)}{\text{Sum}_{\text{new}}(u, w)} \, Q_{\text{old}}(u, w)$$

$$+ \left(h_{i, j_{\text{new}}} - h_{i, j_{\text{old}}} \right) \frac{B_{i, j} N_{i, k}(u) M_{j, \ell}(w)}{\text{Sum}_{\text{new}}(u, w)} \qquad (7.17)$$

Here, the new $\text{Sum}(u, w)$ function must also be calculated. Referring back to Eq. (7.3) and using our experience in deriving the incremental surface equations yields an incremental equation for the new $\text{Sum}(u, w)$ function (see [Roge90b]) given by

$$\text{Sum}_{\text{new}}(u, w) = \text{Sum}_{\text{old}}(u, w) + \left(h_{i, j_{\text{new}}} - h_{i, j_{\text{old}}} \right) N_{i, k}(u) M_{j, \ell}(w) \qquad (7.18)$$

Notice that if either $N_{i, k}(u)$ or $M_{j, \ell}(w)$ are zero, the calculation is considerably simplified.

   If a nonrational surface is generated, then $\text{Sum}(u, w) = 1$ and all $h_{i, j} = 1$, and Eq. (7.16) becomes (see [Roge82])

$$Q_{\text{new}}(u, w) = Q_{\text{old}}(u, w) + \left(B_{i, j_{\text{new}}} - B_{i, j_{\text{old}}} \right) N_{i, k}(u) M_{j, \ell}(w) \qquad (7.19)$$

   These equations allow dynamic modification of the surface by manipulating either the spatial position of a control net vertex or its homogeneous weighting factor. If multiple vertices are manipulated as an entity, then the incremental algorithm is applied successively to each vertex. An algorithm for incremental calculation of a rational B-spline surface is given by (see [Roge90b])

rbsurf(b(),bold(),ibnum,k,l,npts,mpts,p1,p2,itest,niku(),mjlw(),
      rsumuw(); Q())

   if itest $\neq$ (npts + mpts + k + l + p1 + p2) **then**
      *calculate the complete surface (see **bsurfeff** above)*
      itest = npts + mpts + k + l + p1 + p2
      return
   end if
   calculate the incremental change to the surface
   bx = b(ibnum) − bold(1)
   by = b(ibnum+1) − bold(2)
   bz = b(ibnum+2) − bold(3)
   bh = b(ibnum+3) − bold(4)

if $((\text{bx} \neq 0)$ **or** $(\text{by} \neq 0)$ **or** $(\text{bz} \neq 0)$ **or** $(\text{bh} \neq 0))$ **then**

calculate the i,j index for $B_{i,j}$ *from ibnum, where ibnum is*
assumed to be the index of the x component of $B_{i,j}$

iindex = (ibnum/4/mpts) + 1   *needs integer arithmetic to work*

jindex=(ibnum−4∗mpts∗(iindex−1))/4 + 1

for the special case of the homogeneous weighting factor changing,
the sum function must be recalculated for each value of u,w

if $\text{bh} \neq 0$ **then**

  save the old sum function

  for i1 = 1 **to** p1∗p2

    savrsumuw(i1) = rsumuw(i1)

  next i1

  calculate the new sum function

  scnt = 1

  for uinc = 1 **to** p1

    ninc = (uinc −1)∗npts + iindex

    for winc = 1 **to** p2

      minc = (winc−1)∗mpts + jindex

      if niku(ninc) $\neq 0$ **and** mjlw(minc) $\neq 0$ **then**

        sumold = 1/(rsumuw(scnt))

        sumnew = sumold

          + niku(ninc)∗mjlw(minc)∗(b(ibnum+3)−bold(4))

        rsumuw(scnt) = 1/sumnew

      end if

      scnt = scnt + 1

    next winc

  next uinc

end if

calculate the change in the surface for each u,w

icnt = 1

for uinc = 1 **to** p1

  ninc = (uinc−1)∗npts + iindex

  if niku(ninc) $\neq 0$ **then**

    for winc = 1 **to** p2

      minc = (winc−1)∗mpts + jindex

      if mjlw(minc) $\neq 0$ **then**

        scnt = (uinc−1)∗p2 + winc

if bh = 0 **then**

control net vertex changed

pbasis = b(ibnum+3)∗niku(ninc)∗mjlw(minc)∗rsumuw(scnt)
Q(icnt) = Q(icnt) + bx∗pbasis   *calculate surface point*
Q(icnt+1) = Q(icnt+1) + by∗pbasis
Q(icnt+2) = Q(icnt+2) + bz∗pbasis

else

homogeneous coordinate changed

pbasis = niku(ninc)∗mjlw(minc)∗rsumuw(scnt)
sumratio = rsumuw(scnt)/savrsumuw(scnt)

calculate surface point

Q(icnt) = Q(icnt)∗sumratio + bh∗b(ibnum)∗pbasis
Q(icnt+1) = Q(icnt+1)∗sumratio + bh∗b(ibnum+1)∗pbasis
Q(icnt+2) = Q(icnt+2)∗sumratio + bh∗b(ibnum+2)∗pbasis

end if

end if

icnt = icnt + 3

next winc

else

icnt = icnt + 3∗p2

end if

next uinc

end if

save the current vertex location

bold(1) = b(ibnum)
bold(2) = b(ibnum+1)
bold(3) = b(ibnum+2)
bold(4) = b(ibnum+3)

return

Using this algorithm and changing *only* the spatial coordinates of a single control net vertex (see Eq. (7.16)) improves the efficiency of the naive rational B-spline surface algorithm by a factor of approximately 38. Changing only the homogeneous weighting factor of a single control net vertex (see Eq. (7.17)) reduces the improvement over the naive rational B-spline surface algorithm to a factor of approximately 15. These algorithms are capable of dynamic real-time generation of rational B-spline surfaces using moderately capable general-purpose computers, including personal computers.

Measure of Computational Effort

The computational effort required to calculate a rational B-spline surface logically depends on the number of control net vertices, the order of the rational B-spline basis and the number of isoparametric lines used to display the surface in each parametric direction. For the naive algorithms, a measure of this computational effort is written as

$$ce \propto 4(npts\,mpts) \times (p_1\,p_2) \times (kl) \qquad (7.20)$$

For the incremental algorithm the situation is a bit different. Interestingly enough, small control nets tend to minimize the efficiency of the algorithm, because for small control nets few calculations take advantage of the **if** $N_{i,k} \neq 0$ or **if** $M_{j,\ell} \neq 0$ branches used to avoid the calculations in the inner loop of the algorithm. As the size of the control net, i.e., $n + 1$ and $m + 1$, increases with constant order of the basis functions, k, ℓ, the efficiency of the algorithm increases because zero values of the basis functions are encountered more frequently. Figure 7.20 shows the results of a computational experiment confirming this behavior. Here, the order of the basis functions, k, ℓ, and the number of the isoparametric lines used to display the surface, p_1, p_2, are maintained constant and the number of control net

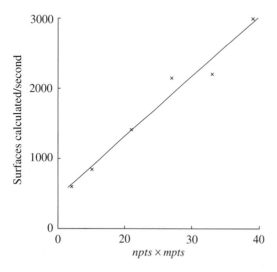

Figure 7.20   Variation of the computational effort for the incremental algorithm, with the size of the control net represented by $npts \times mpts$ (circa 1989).

lines are varied. Figure 7.20 shows that the number of surface calculations per second *increases* with the size of the control net, as represented by the product $npts \times mpts$. Furthermore, this increase is *linear* and nearly directly proportional to $npts \times mpts$.

Figure 7.21 shows the results of an experiment confirming that the computational effort for the incremental algorithm increases with the number of isoparametric lines used to display the surface. Here, the order of the basis functions, k, ℓ, is maintained constant; and the size of the control net, $npts \times mpts$, is also maintained constant. Figure 7.21 shows that the computational effort is *linear* and *inversely* proportional to the product of $p_1 \times p_2$.

With these results in hand, it is reasonable to postulate that for the efficient incremental algorithm the computational effort is

$$ce \propto npts \, mpts \, \frac{1}{p_1 p_2} \, k\ell$$

Consequently, for constant order of the basis functions, k, ℓ, the incremental algorithm is a *constant performance* algorithm, i.e., the number of surface calculations per second is constant as the control net and the number of isoparametric lines used to display the surface increase. Figure 7.22 shows the results of two experiments that confirm this postulate. The results

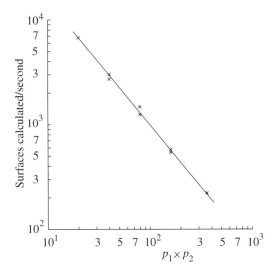

Figure 7.21   Variation of the computational effort for the incremental algorithm, with the size of the isoparametric display net represented by $p_1 \times p_2$ (circa 1989).

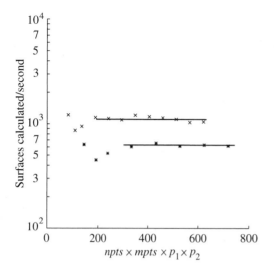

Figure 7.22   Variation of the computational effort for the incremental algorithm, with the size of the control net and the isoparametric display net represented by $npts \times mpts \times p_1 \times p_2$.

marked with a $\times$ were obtained with $p_1 = 3npts$ and $p_2 = 3mpts$, and those marked with a $*$ were obtained with $p_1 = 4npts$ and $p_2 = 4mpts$. The initial dip in both curves is caused by the computational effort associated with the increase in the number of isoparametric lines overwhelming the slight increase in efficiency for small control nets, due to the **if** $\neq 0$ branches in the inner loop of the algorithm. For larger control nets, representative of those typically used by designers, the number of surface calculations per second is constant within $\pm 10\%$ of the average value.

This algorithm provides sufficient performance that dynamic real-time modification of rational B-spline surfaces for design applications using moderately capable general-purpose computers is easily possible. As with almost any algorithm, additional efficiencies are possible. Some of these have been suggested. Others are certainly possible.

B-spline Surface File Format A

A B-spline surface file format for the interchange of surface descriptions is given in Table A.1. Four-dimensional homogeneous coordinates are used to specify the control polygon net. This allows incorporating both the three-dimensional physical control polygon net and the homogeneous coordinate (weighting) factor into a single specification. The proposed format is general enough to handle rational uniform and nonuniform, periodic and open B-spline surfaces. Nonrational B-spline surfaces are specified by setting all the homogeneous coordinate factors (weights) to unity. Rational Bézier surfaces are specified by using uniform open knot vectors of the form [*k zeros k ones*] with appropriate homogeneous coordinate factors. Nonrational Bézier surfaces are specified by using the appropriate knot vectors and again setting all the homogeneous coordinate factors to unity. Multiple surfaces are specified by simply repeating the complete description for each separate surface. Note that this allows specifying different types of B-spline and Bézier surfaces in the same file. The commas must be present as shown. Spaces and blank lines are allowed. The descriptive comments set in italic that appear in the right hand column in Table A.1 are *not* included in an actual file.

Table A.1 Formal B-spline Surface File Format Description

Surface identification string	*For example, hull number*
nonrational, rational	*Rational or nonrational in u, w, respectively*
open, periodic	*Open, periodic, nonuniform in u, w, respectively*
order of basis, order of basis	*Order in u, order in w*
no. net pts., no. net pts.	*No. net pts. in u dir., no. net pts. in w dir*
knot vector in u	*Sequence of numbers 1, 2, 3, …*
knot vector in w	*Sequence of numbers 1, 2, 3, …*
4D net points list	*B(i,j) a ((no. net pts. in u) × (no. net pts. in w),4) array. For B(i,j), j varies fastest with fixed i Each row contains x,y,z,h components of B(i,j), where h is the homogeneous (weighting) factor for each net point Note: For nonrational B-splines, all h = 1*

Example File

Example surface (see Fig. 6.9)

nonrational, nonrational	*The surface is nonrational in both directions*
open, open	*Open basis functions are used in both directions*
4, 4	*Fourth order in both directions*
8, 8	*An 8 × 8 defining polygon net is used*
0, 0, 0, 0, 1, 2, 3, 4, 5, 5, 5, 5	*Open uniform knot vector for u direction*
0, 0, 0, 0, 1, 2, 3, 4, 5, 5, 5, 5	*Open uniform knot vector for w direction*

0	,	62.7896	,	−14.2345	, 1	*Net points B(i,j), j varies fastest*
0	,	58.3546	,	−11.7746	, 1	*with fixed i*
0	,	50.7321	,	−7.7246	, 1
0	,	37.2752	,	−0.7445	, 1
0	,	24.6114	,	0.2266	, 1
0	,	12.2841	,	−.7321	, 1
0	,	0.9638	,	−4.2096	, 1
0	,	−0.02351	,	−0.06207	, 1
13.2994	,	57.2518	,	0	, 1
8.6079	,	50.7918	,	0	, 1
7.2922	,	52.4931	,	0	, 1
−0.6518	,	33.3121	,	0	, 1
1.5411	,	14.3331	,	0	, 1
3.7183	,	13.4063	,	0	, 1
7.87419	,	1.8224	,	0	, 1
0.9025	,	−0.4589	,	0	, 1
17.0482	,	57.6166	,	13.5	, 1
14.0925	,	55.5365	,	13.5	, 1
11.067	,	48.282	,	13.5	, 1
3.0433	,	40.1302	,	13.5	, 1
0.2289	,	21.5281	,	13.5	, 1
3.5539	,	7.0775	,	13.5	, 1

3.0443	, 0.7293	, 13.5	, 1
−0.2092	, 0.08977	, 13.5	, 1
29.2903	, 53.3467	, 54	, 1
30.7639	, 54.1187	, 54	, 1
21.1234	, 48.1403	, 54	, 1
12.0645	, 35.461	, 54	, 1
9.0546	, 17.3787	, 54	, 1
8.6407	, 6.64932	, 54	, 1
5.1127	, −0.7182	, 54	, 1
0.1572	, −0.03143	, 54	, 1
37.8884	, 50.5464	, 108	, 1
33.861	, 47.4467	, 108	, 1
27.1525	, 36.9685	, 108	, 1
23.2976	, 19.6017	, 108	, 1
19.832	, 11.186	, 108	, 1
12.7107	, 2.5924	, 108	, 1
5.5457	, −0.4150	, 108	, 1
−0.01007	, −0.04313	, 108	, 1
41.0213	, 48.1632	, 162	, 1
39.6319	, 39.2661	, 162	, 1
38.6344	, 30.4192	, 162	, 1
33.8422	, 16.8768	, 162	, 1
28.2826	, 6.96425	, 162	, 1
18.2607	, −1.0973	, 162	, 1
4.4469	, 0.2564	, 162	, 1
0.1344	, 0.01421	, 162	, 1
40.4748	, 47.8315	, 216	, 1
41.1403	, 43.5986	, 216	, 1
40.9666	, 30.6183	, 216	, 1
41.4111	, 14.9213	, 216	, 1
34.093	, 0.2635	, 216	, 1
16.9322	, 0.9311	, 216	, 1
5.55319	, 0.167384	, 216	, 1
0.06208	, −0.07885	, 216	, 1
40.536	, 47.9986	, 270	, 1
40.8065	, 41.4721	, 270	, 1
39.8169	, 33.6058	, 270	, 1
41.8009	, 13.1977	, 270	, 1
37.0837	, 0.3062	, 270	, 1
13.1546	, 1.2999	, 270	, 1
7.0730	, −0.2726	, 270	, 1
0.07475	, −0.04795	, 270	, 1

Problems B

Because we very much learn by doing, a number of problems are included here. Problems generally attempt to confirm or extend a concept presented in the text, or to provide computational experience with a technique. They generally are focused on a single aspect of the material. They may or may not require programming. Problems are grouped by chapter.

Chapter 2

2.1 Determine the Bézier curve using position vectors

$$B_0 [0 \quad 0], \ B_1 [1 \quad 1], \ B_2 [2 \quad -1], \ B_3 [3 \quad 0]$$

as the control polygon. Calculate results for parametric values of 0, $\frac{1}{3}$, $\frac{2}{3}$, 1.

2.2 Determine the position vector B_2 that gives tangent vector continuity across the join between the two Bézier curve segments otherwise defined by

$$B_0 [0 \quad 0 \quad 0], \ B_1 [2 \quad 2 \quad -2], \ B_3 [4 \quad 0 \quad 0]$$

and $\quad Q_0 [4 \quad 0 \quad 0], \ Q_1 [6 \quad -2 \quad 1], \ Q_2 [8 \quad -3 \quad 2], \ Q_3 [10 \quad 0 \quad 1]$

2.3 For the Bézier curve defined by the control polygon in Ex. 2.1, determine the control polygon required to generate the sixth-degree Bézier curve equivalent to the fourth-degree curve of Ex. 2.1. Hint: Raise the degree in successive steps.

2.4 Determine the control polygon vertices that subdivide the Bézier curve defined in Ex. 2.1 into two cubic Bézier curves.

2.5 Apply the Bézier curve subdivision technique successively to the Bézier curve and its control polygon vertices of Ex. 2.1, and show by example that the control polygon and the curve converge.

Chapter 3

3.1 Repeat Ex. 3.3 for the knot vector $[0 \ \ 0 \ \ 0 \ \ 2 \ \ 2 \ \ 3 \ \ 3 \ \ 3]$. The results are shown in Fig. 3.7e. Compare these results with those of Ex. 3.3 and Fig. 3.7d.

3.2 Determine algebraic relations for the nonuniform basis functions obtained with knot vectors $[0 \ \ 0 \ \ 0 \ \ 0.4 \ \ 2.6 \ \ 3 \ \ 3 \ \ 3]$ and $[0 \ \ 0 \ \ 0 \ \ 1.8 \ \ 2.2 \ \ 3 \ \ 3 \ \ 3]$. The results are shown in Figs. 3.7b and 3.7c. Compare the results with each other and with those of Figs. 3.7d and 3.7e.

3.3 Illustrate the dependencies of the B-spline basis functions for curves of orders 4 and 5 defined by six polygon vertices. Use a technique similar to that in Sec. 3.4.

3.4 Determine the fourth-order B-spline curve for the control polygon

$$B_1 [0 \ \ 0], \ B_2 [1 \ \ 1], \ B_3 [4 \ \ 3], \ B_4 [3 \ \ 1]$$

Compare the results to the Bézier curve calculated in Prob. 2.1.

3.5 Determine the third-order B-spline curve using the control polygon defined in Prob. 3.4. Calculate the points on the curve for parameter values of 0, $1/2$, 1, $3/2$, 2.

3.6 Using the chord length approximation discussed in Sec. 3.6, determine the fourth-order open B-spline curve for the control polygon given in Ex. 3.5. Compare the results to those given in Ex. 3.5.

3.7 Using the chord length approximation discussed in Sec. 3.6, determine the third-order periodic B-spline curve for the control polygon given in Ex. 3.5. Compare the results to those given in Ex. 3.5.

3.8 Using the chord length approximation discussed in Sec. 3.6, determine the fourth-order periodic B-spline curve for the control polygon given in Ex. 3.5. Compare the results to those given in Ex. 3.5 and in Prob. 3.6.

3.9 For the control polygon given in Ex. 3.6, determine the pseudovertices necessary to make the end points of the periodic B-spline curve coincide with B_1 and B_4, respectively. Compare the results with those shown in Fig. 3.22.

3.10 For the control polygon given in Ex. 3.6, determine the pseudovertices necessary to make the tangent vectors at the ends of the curve $[-1 \ \ 1]$ and $[1 \ \ -1]$, respectively. Also, calculate the start and end points of the curve. Compare the results with those shown in Fig. 3.22.

3.11 Show that the two B-spline curves defined in Ex. 3.15 by the control polygon

$$B_1 \begin{bmatrix} 0 & 0 \end{bmatrix}, \; B_2 \begin{bmatrix} 1 & 1 \end{bmatrix}, \; B_3 \begin{bmatrix} 2 & 1 \end{bmatrix}, \; B_4 \begin{bmatrix} 3 & 0 \end{bmatrix}$$

with alternate knot vectors defined by

$$[X'] = [0 \quad 0 \quad 0 \quad 1 \quad 2 \quad 2 \quad 2]$$

and

$$[X] = [0 \quad 0 \quad 0 \quad 2 \quad 4 \quad 4 \quad 4]$$

are identical. Hint: Calculate a number of points on the first curve $0 \le t' \le 2$ and on the second curve $0 \le t = 2t' \le 4$, and compare the results.

3.12 Show that the subdivided B-spline curve in Ex. 3.15 is the same as the original curve. Hint: Calculate several points on the two curves, and plot them to the same scale.

3.13 Show that the subdivided B-spline curve in Ex. 3.16 is the same as the original curve. Hint: Calculate several points on the two curves, and plot them to the same scale.

3.14 Show that if, after the original curve in Ex. 3.16 is subdivided, the new polygon vertex C_3 is moved to coincide with C_2, then the resulting curve has a sharp corner at $C_2 = C_3$.

3.15 To obtain a better understanding of the nature of a vector-valued function such as $P(t) = [x(t) \quad y(t)]$, plot graphs of $x(t)$ versus t, $y(t)$ versus t and $y(t)$ versus $x(t)$ for the fourth-order ($k = 4$) B-spline curve defined by

$$B_1 \begin{bmatrix} 0 & 0 \end{bmatrix}, \; B_2 \begin{bmatrix} 2 & 2 \end{bmatrix}, \; B_3 \begin{bmatrix} 4 & 2 \end{bmatrix}, \; B_4 \begin{bmatrix} 6 & 0 \end{bmatrix}$$

with the open knot vector

$$[0 \quad 0 \quad 0 \quad 0 \quad 1 \quad 1 \quad 1 \quad 1]$$

Repeat for the third-order ($k = 3$) B-spline curve with the open knot vector

$$[0 \quad 0 \quad 0 \quad 1 \quad 2 \quad 2 \quad 2]$$

3.16 Consider the fourth-order (cubic) B-spline curve ($k = 4$) defined by the control polygon

$$B_1 \begin{bmatrix} 0 & 0 \end{bmatrix}, \; B_2 \begin{bmatrix} 1 & 1 \end{bmatrix}, \; B_3 \begin{bmatrix} 2 & 1 \end{bmatrix}, \; B_4 \begin{bmatrix} 3 & 0 \end{bmatrix},$$
$$B_5 \begin{bmatrix} 4 & -1 \end{bmatrix}, \; B_6 \begin{bmatrix} 5 & 0 \end{bmatrix}, \; B_7 \begin{bmatrix} 6 & 0 \end{bmatrix}$$

Raise the degree of the curve from 3 to 4, i.e., from fourth order to fifth order ($k = 5$). What are the new knot vector and the new control polygon?

3.17 Consider the fifth-order (quartic) B-spline curve ($k = 5$) defined by the control polygon

$$B_1 \begin{bmatrix} 0 & 0 \end{bmatrix}, \; B_2 \begin{bmatrix} 3/4 & 3/4 \end{bmatrix}, \; B_3 \begin{bmatrix} 5/4 & 1 \end{bmatrix}, \; B_4 \begin{bmatrix} 47/24 & 11/12 \end{bmatrix},$$

$$B_5 \left[^5\!/_2 \quad ^1\!/_2 \right], \; B_6 \left[3 \quad 0 \right], \; B_7 \left[^7\!/_2 \quad -^1\!/_2 \right], \; B_8 \left[^{97}\!/_{24} \quad -^{19}\!/_{24} \right],$$

$$B_9 \left[^{19}\!/_4 \quad -^1\!/_4 \right], \; B_{10} \left[^{21}\!/_4 \quad 0 \right], \; B_{11} \left[6 \quad 0 \right]$$

defined on an open knot vector given by

$$\left[0 \quad 0 \quad 0 \quad 0 \quad 0 \quad 1 \quad 2 \quad 3 \quad 4 \quad 5 \quad 6 \quad 7 \quad 8 \quad 8 \quad 8 \quad 8 \right]$$

Reduce the degree of the curve to cubic ($k = 4$). Hint: Reduce the curve to Bézier segments by inserting multiple knot values at each of the internal knots. Reduce the degree of each Bézier segment, and then remove any unnecessary knot values.

3.18 Reparameterize the third-order B-spline curve defined by the control polygon

$$B_1 \left[0 \quad 0 \right], \; B_2 \left[1 \quad 1 \right], \; B_3 \left[2 \quad 0 \right], \; B_4 \left[3 \quad -1 \right], \; B_5 \left[4 \quad 0 \right]$$

and the knot vector

$$\left[X \right] = \left[0 \quad 0 \quad 0 \quad 2 \quad 2 \quad 3 \quad 3 \quad 3 \right]$$

to have an equal number of points on the curve in the intervals 0–2 and 2–3.

Chapter 4

4.1 Determine the analytical expressions for the second derivative along a rational B-spline curve. Evaluate the results for $t = 0$ and $t = n + k - 2$.

4.2 Do Ex. 4.1 for $k = 4$.

4.3 Generate the rational B-spline curves for the control polygon

$$B_1 \left[0 \quad 0 \right], \; B_2 \left[1 \quad 2 \right], \; B_3 \left[^5\!/_2 \quad 0 \right], \; B_4 \left[^5\!/_2 \quad 0 \right],$$

$$B_5 \left[^5\!/_2 \quad 0 \right], \; B_6 \left[4 \quad 2 \right], \; B_7 \left[5 \quad 0 \right]$$

with $\qquad \left[H \right] = \left[1 \quad 1 \quad h_3 \quad h_4 \quad h_5 \quad 1 \quad 1 \right]$

for values of $h_3 = h_4 = h_5 = 0$, $^1\!/_4$, 1, 5. Compare the results to Fig. 4.10.

4.4 Determine the first and second derivatives at $t = 0$ and $t = 3$ for the control polygon in Ex. 4.1.

4.5 Determine the first and second derivatives at $t = 0$ and $t = 2$ for $k = 4$ for the control polygon in Ex. 4.1.

Chapter 5

5.1 For a 4×4 bicubic Bézier surface, show that for $u = w = 0$

$$Q_{uw}(0,0) = 9 \left[(B_{1,1} - B_{0,1}) - (B_{1,0} - B_{0,0}) \right]$$

5.2 Determine the 4×4 Bézier control polygon that yields the bicubic Coons surface patch defined by the position vectors

$$P(0,0) = [-100 \quad 0 \quad 100], \quad P(0,1) = [-100 \quad -100 \quad -100]$$

$$P(1,0) = [100 \quad -100 \quad 100], \quad P(1,1) = [100 \quad 0 \quad -100]$$

The tangent vectors are

$$P_u(0,0) = [100 \quad 100 \quad 0], \quad P_u(0,1) = [1 \quad 1 \quad 0], \quad P_u(1,0) = [1 \quad -1 \quad 0],$$

$$P_u(1,1) = [1 \quad -1 \quad 0], \quad P_w(0,0) = [0 \quad 10 \quad -10], \quad P_w(0,1) = [0 \quad -1 \quad -1],$$

$$P_w(1,0) = [0 \quad 1 \quad -1], \quad P_w(1,1) = [0 \quad -1 \quad -1]$$

The twist vectors are

$$P_{uw}(0,0) = [0 \quad 0 \quad 0], \quad P_{uw}(0,1) = [0.1 \quad 0.1 \quad 0.1],$$

$$P_{uw}(1,0) = [0.1 \quad -0.1 \quad -0.1], \quad P_{uw}(1,1) = [0 \quad 0 \quad 0]$$

As a check, the point at $u = w = 1/2$ in the Coons bicubic surface is $Q(1/2, 1/2) = [6.18 \quad -42.75 \quad -0.56]$.

5.3 Generate the Bézier surface of Ex. 5.3 without using matrix methods.

Chapter 6

6.1 Compute the fourth-order B-spline surface for the 4×5 control net given by

$B_{1,1}[0 \quad 0 \quad 100]$	$B_{2,1}[25 \quad 0 \quad 150]$	$B_{3,1}[50 \quad 0 \quad 100]$
	$B_{4,1}[75 \quad 0 \quad 50]$	$B_{5,1}[100 \quad 0 \quad 100]$
$B_{1,2}[0 \quad 33 \quad 150]$	$B_{2,2}[25 \quad 33 \quad 200]$	$B_{3,2}[50 \quad 33 \quad 100]$
	$B_{4,2}[75 \quad 33 \quad 50]$	$B_{5,2}[100 \quad 33 \quad 50]$
$B_{1,3}[0 \quad 66 \quad 50]$	$B_{2,3}[25 \quad 66 \quad 25]$	$B_{3,3}[50 \quad 66 \quad 100]$
	$B_{4,3}[75 \quad 66 \quad 150]$	$B_{5,3}[100 \quad 66 \quad 150]$
$B_{1,4}[0 \quad 100 \quad 100]$	$B_{2,4}[25 \quad 100 \quad 50]$	$B_{3,4}[50 \quad 100 \quad 100]$
	$B_{4,4}[75 \quad 100 \quad 150]$	$B_{5,4}[100 \quad 100 \quad 100]$

Use an open knot vector. Determine by hand calculation the point in the center of an 11×15 parametric surface net.

Write a program to compute the two diagonal parametric lines $u = 2w$ and $u = 2(1 - w)$. List the points from $(0, 0)$ to $(2, 1)$ for $u = 2w$ and from $(0, 1)$ to $(2, 0)$ for $u = 2(1 - w)$. List 11 values for each diagonal.

Compute and display the 11×15 parametric surface. List 15 u and 11 w values. Use an appropriate viewing transformation (see [Roge90a]).

6.2 Generate the closed periodic B-spline surfaces shown in Fig. 6.5.

6.3 Generate the combined open and periodic B-spline surface shown in Fig. 6.6.

6.4 Generate the closed periodic B-spline toroidal surface shown in Fig. 6.7.

6.5 Determine the Gaussian curvature at $u = w = 1/2$ for the surfaces described in Ex. 5.3 and shown in Figs. 5.7a to 5.7d. Compare the results. Display the results in a form similar to that of Fig. 7.7c.

6.6 Determine the Gaussian curvature for the fourth-order B-spline surface defined by

$B_{1,1}[-1000 \quad 0 \quad 1000]$ $\qquad$ $B_{1,2}[-500 \quad 0 \quad 1000]$ $\qquad$ $B_{1,3}[0 \quad 0 \quad 1000]$
$B_{1,4}[0 \quad 0 \quad 1000]$ $\qquad$ $B_{1,5}[0 \quad 0 \quad 1000]$ $\qquad$ $B_{1,6}[500 \quad 0 \quad 1000]$
$B_{1,7}[1000 \quad 0 \quad 1000]$

$B_{2,1}[-1000 \quad 0 \quad 500]$ $\qquad$ $B_{2,2}[-500 \quad 125 \quad 500]$ $\qquad$ $B_{2,3}[0 \quad 125 \quad 500]$
$B_{2,4}[0 \quad 125 \quad 500]$ $\qquad$ $B_{2,5}[0 \quad 125 \quad 500]$ $\qquad$ $B_{2,6}[500 \quad 125 \quad 500]$
$B_{2,7}[1000 \quad 0 \quad 500]$

$B_{3,1}[-1000 \quad 0 \quad 0]$ $\qquad$ $B_{3,2}[-500 \quad 125 \quad 0]$ $\qquad$ $B_{3,3}[0 \quad 300 \quad 0]$
$B_{3,4}[0 \quad 300 \quad 0]$ $\qquad$ $B_{3,5}[0 \quad 300 \quad 0]$ $\qquad$ $B_{3,6}[500 \quad 125 \quad 0]$
$B_{3,7}[1000 \quad 0 \quad 0]$

$B_{4,1}[-1000 \quad 0 \quad 0]$ $\qquad$ $B_{4,2}[-500 \quad 125 \quad 0]$ $\qquad$ $B_{4,3}[0 \quad 300 \quad 0]$
$B_{4,4}[0 \quad 300 \quad 0]$ $\qquad$ $B_{4,5}[0 \quad 300 \quad 0]$ $\qquad$ $B_{4,6}[500 \quad 125 \quad 0]$
$B_{4,7}[1000 \quad 0 \quad 0]$

$B_{5,1}[-1000 \quad 0 \quad 0]$ $\qquad$ $B_{5,2}[-500 \quad 125 \quad 0]$ $\qquad$ $B_{5,3}[0 \quad 300 \quad 0]$
$B_{5,4}[0 \quad 300 \quad 0]$ $\qquad$ $B_{5,5}[0 \quad 300 \quad 0]$ $\qquad$ $B_{5,6}[500 \quad 125 \quad 0]$
$B_{5,7}[1000 \quad 0 \quad 0]$

$B_{6,1}[-1000 \quad 0 \quad -500]$ $\qquad$ $B_{6,2}[-500 \quad 125 \quad -500]$ $\qquad$ $B_{6,3}[0 \quad 125 \quad -500]$
$B_{6,4}[0 \quad 125 \quad -500]$ $\qquad$ $B_{6,5}[0 \quad 125 \quad -500]$ $\qquad$ $B_{6,6}[500 \quad 125 \quad -500]$
$B_{6,7}[1000 \quad 0 \quad -500]$

$B_{7,1}[-1000 \quad 0 \quad -1000]$ $\qquad$ $B_{7,2}[-500 \quad 0 \quad -1000]$ $\qquad$ $B_{7,3}[0 \quad 0 \quad -1000]$
$B_{7,4}[0 \quad 0 \quad -1000]$ $\qquad$ $B_{7,5}[0 \quad 0 \quad -1000]$ $\qquad$ $B_{7,6}[500 \quad 0 \quad -1000]$
$B_{7,7}[1000 \quad 0 \quad -1000]$

Display the result in a form similar to that of Fig. 7.7c.

Chapter 7

7.1 Generate a torus as a rational B-spline surface by rotating the circle of radius 1 centered at $x = 5$, $z = 1$ about the z-axis. (See Fig. 7.17.)

7.2 Generate a sphere of radius 1 as a rational B-spline surface by rotating the semicircle of radius 1 centered at $x = 0$, $z = 1$ about the z-axis. (See Fig. 7.18.)

7.3 Generate the complete ruled surface shown in Fig. 7.14. Is the complete surface developable? Is part of the surface developable? If yes, what part?

Initially, use the control polygon for $P(0, w)$ as

$$B_1 \begin{bmatrix} 0 & 0 & 0 \end{bmatrix}, \; B_2 \begin{bmatrix} 1 & 1 & 0 \end{bmatrix}, \; B_3 \begin{bmatrix} 1 & 1 & 0 \end{bmatrix}, \; B_4 \begin{bmatrix} 2 & 1 & 0 \end{bmatrix}, \; B_5 \begin{bmatrix} 3 & 0 & 0 \end{bmatrix}$$

with $h_1 = h_2 = h_3 = h_4 = h_5 = 1$ and $k = 3$. The control polygon for $P(1, w)$ is

$$\bar{B}_1 \begin{bmatrix} 0 & 0 & 6 \end{bmatrix}, \; \bar{B}_2 \begin{bmatrix} 1 & 1 & 6 \end{bmatrix}, \; \bar{B}_3 \begin{bmatrix} 2 & 1 & 6 \end{bmatrix}, \; \bar{B}_4 \begin{bmatrix} 3 & 0 & 6 \end{bmatrix}$$

with $\bar{h}_1 = \bar{h}_2 = \bar{h}_3 = \bar{h}_4 = 1$ and $k = 3$.

Modify the control polygon for $P(0, w)$ to

$$B_1 \begin{bmatrix} 0 & 0 & 0 \end{bmatrix}, \; B_2 \begin{bmatrix} 1 & 1 & 0 \end{bmatrix}, \; B_3 \begin{bmatrix} 1 & 1 & 0 \end{bmatrix}, \; B_4 \begin{bmatrix} 3 & 0 & 0 \end{bmatrix}$$

with $h_1 = h_2 = h_4 = 1$ and $h_3 = 5, 50$. Compare the results.

Algorithms C

Gathered here are a number of useful algorithms. The algorithms are presented using pseudocode on pedagogical grounds. Presentation using pseudocode requires that the algorithms be translated into a 'real' programming language. Hopefully, this process increases the understanding of the algorithms and hence of the underlying mathematics. The algorithms are available in C through a link at *www.mkp.com/NURBS/nurbs.html*.

The pseudocode versions of the algorithms were algorithmically derived from working code. Hopefully, this process resulted in more accurate algorithms. However, errors may have been introduced in the typesetting process. Consequently, implementors should carefully check the algorithms against the mathematics presented in the text.

The algorithms are designed to be educational, i.e., they are intended to support the mathematical techniques discussed in the text. They are *not* intended to be the *most* efficient implementations possible. Frequently, computational inefficiencies are accepted if the resulting algorithm more closely follows the discussion in the text. An example is the B-spline surface algorithm **bsplsurf**. In the pseudocode algorithm given below, the B-spline basis functions for each parameter value are calculated inside the main loop. This reduces memory requirements. However, it is computationally more efficient to calculate all of the basis functions externally to the main loop, form their products and store them in a large array. Appropriate elements of the array are then used within the main loop to calculate position vectors on the surface. A few minutes' thought shows that, for reasonably complex surfaces, the array size becomes quite large. However, the algorithm runs several times faster than the pseudocode algorithm presented. When implementing the pseudocode algorithms, it is suggested that the algorithm first be implemented as given. The algorithms are grouped by chapter and alphabetically by name within each chapter.

Chapter 2

bezier

Subroutine to calculate a Bézier curve (see Eq. (2.1)).

$b(,)$	=	*array containing the control polygon vertices*
		b(,1) contains the x component of the vertex
		b(,2) contains the y component of the vertex
		b(,3) contains the z component of the vertex
Basis	=	*function to calculate the Bernstein basis value (see Eq. (2.2))*
cpts	=	*number of points to be calculated on the curve*
Factrl	=	*function to calculate the factorial of a number*
$j(,)$	=	*Bernstein basis function*
Ni	=	*factorial function for the Bernstein basis*
npts	=	*number of control polygon vertices*
$p(,)$	=	*array containing the curve points*
		p(,1) contains the x component of the point
		p(,2) contains the y component of the point
		p(,3) contains the z component of the point
t	=	*parameter value $0 \le t \le 1$*

subroutine bezier(npts,b(,),cpts; p(,))

def **Ni**(n,i) = **Factrl**(n)/(**Factrl**(i)***Factrl**(n−i))   *factorial function*
def **Basis**(n,i,t) = **Ni**(n,i)*(t^i)*((1−t)^(n−i))   *Bernstein basis function*

dimension j(1,20)   *allows for 20 polygon vertices*
dimension temp(1,3), temp1(1,3), temp2(1,3)
icount = 0
Mat j = **Zer**(1,npts)
for t = 0 **to** 1 **step** 1/(cpts−1)
    icount = icount+1
    determine the Bernstein basis function (see Eq. (2.2))

```
    for i = 1 to npts
        j(1,i) = Basis(npts−1,i−1,t)
    next i
    determine a point on the curve
    Mat temp = j*b
    place in array
    for i = 1 to 3
        p(icount,i) = temp(1,i)
    next i
next t
return
```

dbezier

Subroutine to calculate a Bézier curve and its first and second derivatives (see Eqs. (2.1), (2.11) and (2.12))

$b(,)$ = *array containing the control polygon vertices*
   b(,1) contains the x component of the vertex
   b(,2) contains the y component of the vertex
   b(,3) contains the z component of the vertex
$Basis$ = *function to calculate the Bernstein basis value*
$cpts$ = *number of points to be calculated on the curve*
$d1(,)$ = *array containing the first derivative of the curve*
   d1(,1) contains the x component of the derivative
   d1(,2) contains the y component of the derivative
   d1(,3) contains the z component of the derivative
$d2(,)$ = *array containing the second derivative of the curve*
   d2(,1) contains the x component of the derivative
   d2(,2) contains the y component of the derivative
   d2(,3) contains the z component of the derivative
$Factrl$ = *function to calculate the factorial of a number*
$j(,)$ = *Bernstein basis function*
$j1(,)$ = *first derivative of the Bernstein basis function*
$j2(,)$ = *second derivative of the Bernstein basis function*
Ni = *factorial function for the Bernstein basis*
$npts$ = *number of control polygon vertices*
$p(,)$ = *array containing the curve points*
   p(,1) contains the x component of the point
   p(,2) contains the y component of the point
   p(,3) contains the z component of the point
t = *parameter value $0 \leq t \leq 1$*

subroutine dbezier(npts,b(,),cpts; p(,),d1(,),d2(,))

def **Ni**(n,i) = **Factrl**(n)/(**Factrl**(i)***Factrl**(n−i))   *factorial function*
def **Basis**(n,i,t) = **Ni**(n,i)*(t^i)*((1−t)^(n−i))   *Bernstein basis function*

dimension j(1,20), j1(1,20), j2(1,20)   *allows for 20 polygon vertics*
dimension temp(1,3),temp1(1,3),temp2(1,3)

zero and redimension matrices

Mat j = **Zer**(1,npts)
Mat j1 = **Zer**(1,npts)
Mat j2 = **Zer**(1,npts)

for t = 0 **to** 1 **step** 1/(cpts−1)
    icount = icount+1
    if icount = cpts **then** t = 1   *necessary to handle incremental calculation of t*

    determine the Bernstein basis function and its first and second derivative
    (see Eqs. (2.2), (2.13) and (2.14))

    for i = 1 **to** npts
      j(1,i) = **Basis**(npts−1,i−1,t)
      if t ≠ 0 and t ≠ 1 **then**   *handle the end points specially*
        j1(1,i) = (((i−1)−(npts−1)*t)/(t*(1−t)))*j(1,i)
        j2(1,i) = ((i−1)−(npts−1)*t)^2 − (npts−1)*t*t − (i−1)*(1−2*t)
        j2(1,i) = j(1,i)*j2(1,i)/(t*t*(1−t)*(1−t))
      end if
    next i

    determine a point on the curve

    Mat temp = j*b

    determine the curve first and second derivatives (see Eqs. (2.1), (2.11) and (2.12))

    if t <> 0 and t ≠ 1 **then**   *handle the end points specially*
      Mat temp1 = j1*b
      Mat temp2 = j2*b
    else
      if t = 0 **then**
        temp1(1,1) = (npts−1)*(b(2,1)−b(1,1))
        temp1(1,2) = (npts−1)*(b(2,2)−b(1,2))
      end if
      if t = 0 **then**
        temp2(1,1) = (npts−1)*(npts−2)*(b(1,1)−2*b(2,1)+b(3,1))
        temp2(1,2) = (npts−1)*(npts−2)*(b(1,2)−2*b(2,2)+b(3,2))
      end if
      if t = 1 **then**
        temp1(1,1) = (npts−1)*(b(npts,1)−b(npts−1,1))
        temp1(1,2) = (npts−1)*(b(npts,2)−b(npts−1,2))
      end if
      if t = 1 **then**
        temp2(1,1) = (b(npts,1)−2*b(npts−1,1)+b(npts−2,1))
        temp2(1,1) = (npts−1)*(npts−2)*temp2(1,1)
        temp2(1,2) = (b(npts,2)−2*b(npts−1,2)+b(npts−2,2))
        temp2(1,2) = (npts−1)*(npts−2)*temp2(1,2)

```
        end if
      end if
```
place in arrays
```
      for i = 1 to 3
         p(icount, i) = temp(1,i)
         d1(icount, i) = temp1(1,i)
         d2(icount, i) = temp2(1,i)
      next i
   next t
   return
```

Chapter 3

basis

Subroutine to generate B-spline basis functions for open uniform knot vectors (see Eqs. (3.2)).

c	=	*order of the B-spline basis function*
d	=	*first term of the basis function recursion relation*
e	=	*second term of the basis function recursion relation*
npts	=	*number of control polygon vertices*
$n(,)$	=	*array containing the basis functions*
		$n(1,1)$ contains the basis function associated with B_1 etc.
nplusc	=	*constant npts + c, maximum number of knot values*
t	=	*parameter value*
$temp()$	=	*temporary array*
$x()$	=	*knot vector*

subroutine basis(c,t,npts,x(); n(,))

dimension temp(20)   *allows for 20 polygon vertices*

nplusc = npts+c

calculate the first-order basis functions $N_{i,1}$ (see Eq. (3.2a))

```
for i = 1 to nplusc−1
   if t >= x(i) and t < x(i+1) then
      temp(i) = 1
   else
      temp(i) = 0
   end if
next i
```

calculate the higher-order basis functions (see Eq. (3.2b))

```
for k = 2 to c
   for i = 1 to nplusc−k
      if temp(i) ≠ 0 then          if basis function is zero skip the calculation
         d = ((t−x(i))*temp(i))/(x(i+k−1)−x(i))
```

```
        else
            d = 0
        end if
        if temp(i+1) ≠ 0 then          if basis function is zero skip the calculation
            e = ((x(i+k)−t)*temp(i+1))/(x(i+k)−x(i+1))
        else
            e = 0
        end if
        temp(i) = d + e
    next i
next k
if t = x(nplusc) then temp(npts) = 1                    pick up last point
put in n array
for i = 1 to npts
    n(1,i) = temp(i)
next i
if t = x(nplusc) then n(1,npts) = 1                     pick up last point
return
```

bsplfit

Subroutine to fit a B-spline curve using an open uniform knot vector (see Eq. (3.35)).

$b(,)$ = array containing the control polygon vertices
    $b(\ ,1)$ contains the x component of the vertex
    $b(\ ,2)$ contains the y component of the vertex
    $b(\ ,3)$ contains the z component of the vertex
$dpts$ = number of data points
$d(,)$ = array containing the data points
    $d(\ ,1)$ contains the x component of the data point
    $d(\ ,2)$ contains the y component of the data point
    $d(\ ,3)$ contains the z component of the data point
k = order of the B-spline basis function
n = matrix of basis function
$nbasis$ = array containing the basis functions for a single value of t
$ninv$ = inverse of $trn(n) \times n$
$nplusc$ = number of knot values
$npts$ = number of control polygon vertices
$ntemp$ = temporary matrix to hold $trn(n) \times n$
$ntmp$ = temporary matrix to hold inverse of $trn(n) \times n \times d$
$ntrn$ = transpose of the n matrix
t = parameter value $0 \le t \le 1$
$tpar()$ = array containing the chordwise approximation to the parameter values
$x()$ = array containing the knot vector

subroutine bsplfit(dpts,d(,),npts,k; b(,))

dimension nbasis(1,20),x(30),n(20,20),temp(1,3)   *allow for 20 data points*
dimension tpar(20),ninv(20,20),ntrn(20,20),ntemp(20,20),ntmp(20,3)

zero and redimension the matrices

Mat nbasis = **Zer**(1,npts)
Mat x = **Zer**(npts+k)
Mat n = **Zer**(dpts,npts)
Mat ntrn = **Zer**(npts,dpts)
Mat ntemp = **Zer**(npts,npts)
Mat ntmp = **Zer**(npts,2)
Mat ninv = **Zer**(npts,npts)
Mat tpar = **Zer**(dpts)

call knot(npts,k; x())

call param(dpts,d; tpar)

nplusc = npts+k

generate the matrix of basis functions

for i = 1 **to** dpts
    t = tpar(i)*x(nplusc)   *calculate the parameter value for one row*
    call basis(k,t,npts,x; nbasis)   *calculate the basis function for one row*
    for j = 1 **to** npts
        n(i,j) = nbasis(1,j)   *build the matrix row by row*
    next j
next i

generate the control polygon vertices using the least squares technique

Mat ntrn = trn(n)   *find the transpose of the matrix of basis functions*
Mat ntemp = ntrn*n   *$trn(n) \times n$*
Mat ninv = **Inv**(ntemp)   *inverse of $trn(n) \times n$*
Mat ntmp = ntrn*d   *inverse of $trn(n) \times n \times d$*
Mat b = ninv*ntmp   *calculate the control polygon vertices*

return

bspline

Subroutine to generate a B-spline curve using an open uniform knot vector (see Eq. (3.1)).

$b(,)$ = *array containing the control polygon vertices*
            $b(,1)$ contains the x component of the vertex
            $b(,2)$ contains the y component of the vertex
            $b(,3)$ contains the z component of the vertex
k = *order of the B-spline basis function*
$nbasis$ = *array containing the basis functions for a single value of t*
$nplusc$ = *number of knot values*
$npts$ = *number of control polygon vertices*
$p(,)$ = *array containing the curve points*

p(,1) contains the x component of the point
p(,2) contains the y component of the point
p(,3) contains the z component of the point

p1 = *number of points to be calculated on the curve*
t = *parameter value $0 \leq t \leq 1$*
x() = *array containing the knot vector*

subroutine bspline(npts,k,p1,b(,); p(,))

dimension nbasis(1,20),x(30),temp(1,3)   *up to 20 polygon vertices and order 5*
nplusc = npts+k

zero and redimension the knot vector and the basis array

Mat nbasis = **Zer**(1,npts)
Mat x = **Zer**(nplusc)

generate the uniform open knot vector

call knot(npts,k; x)

icount = 0

calculate the points on the B-spline curve

for t = 0 **to** x(npts+k) **step** x(npts+k)/(p1−1)
 icount = icount+1
 call basis(k,t,npts,x; nbasis)   *generate the basis function for this value of t*
 Mat temp = nbasis∗b   *generate the point on the curve*
 p(icount,1) = temp(1,1)   *assign the current value of the point on the curve*
 p(icount,2) = temp(1,2)   *to the curve array*
 p(icount,3) = temp(1,3)
next t

return

bsplineu

Subroutine to generate a B-spline curve using a periodic uniform knot vector (see Eq. (3.1)).

b(,) = *array containing the control polygon vertices*
   b(,1) contains the x component of the vertex
   b(,2) contains the y component of the vertex
   b(,3) contains the z component of the vertex
k = *order of the B-spline basis function*
nbasis = *array containing the basis functions for a single value of t*
nplusc = *number of knot values*
npts = *number of control polygon vertices*
p(,) = *array containing the curve points*
   p(,1) contains the x component of the point
   p(,2) contains the y component of the point
   p(,3) contains the z component of the point
p1 = *number of points to be calculated on the curve*

t = *parameter value $0 \leq t \leq 1$*
$x()$ = *array containing the knot vector*

subroutine bsplineu(npts,k,p1,b(,); p(,))

dimension nbasis(1,20),x(30),temp(1,3)   *up to 20 polygon vertices and order 5*

zero and redimension the knot vector and the basis array

Mat nbasis = **Zer**(1,npts)
Mat x = **Zer**(npts+k)

nplusc = npts+k

generate the uniform periodic knot vector

call knotu(npts,k; x)

icount = 0

calculate the points on the B-spline curve

for t = (k−1) **to** (npts−1+1) **step** ((npts−1+1)−(k−1))/(p1−1)
        icount = icount+1
        call basis(k,t,npts,x; nbasis)   *generate the basis function for this value of t*
        Mat temp = nbasis*b   *generate the point on the curve*
        p(icount,1) = temp(1,1)   *assign the current value of the point on the curve*
        p(icount,2) = temp(1,2)   *to the curve array*
next t

return

dbasis

Subroutine to generate B-spline basis functions and their derivatives for uniform open knot vectors (see Eqs. (3.2) and (3.29)–(3.32)).

$b1$ = *first term of the basis function*
$b2$ = *second term of the basis function*
c = *order of the B-spline basis function*
$d1(,)$ = *array containing the derivative of the basis functions*
                 $d1(1,1)$ contains the derivative of the basis function for B_1 etc.
$d2(,)$ = *array containing the derivative of the basis functions*
                 $d2(1,1)$ contains the derivative of the basis function for B_1 etc.
$f1$ = *first term of the first derivative of the basis function*
$f2$ = *second term of the first derivative of the basis function*
$f3$ = *third term of the first derivative of the basis function*
$f4$ = *fourth term of the first derivative of the basis function*
$npts$ = *number of control polygon vertices*
$n(,)$ = *array containing the basis functions*
                 $n(1,1)$ contains the basis function for B_1 etc.
$nplusc$ = *constant npts + c, maximum knot value*
$s1$ = *first term of the second derivative of the basis function*
$s2$ = *second term of the second derivative of the basis function*
$s3$ = *third term of the second derivative of the basis function*

$s4$	=	*fourth term of the second derivative of the basis function*
t	=	*parameter value*
$temp()$	=	*temporary array*
$x()$	=	*knot vector*

subroutine dbasis(c,t,npts,x(); n(,),d1(,),d2(,))

dimension temp(20),temp1(20),temp2(20)   *up to 20 control polygon vertices*

nplusc = npts+c

zero the temporary arrays

Mat temp = **Zer**(npts+c)
Mat temp1 = **Zer**(npts+c)
Mat temp2 = **Zer**(npts+c)

calculate the first-order basis functions $n(i,1)$ (see Eq. (3.2a))

for i = 1 **to** nplusc−1
   if t ≥ x(i) **and** t < x(i+1) **then**
      temp(i) = 1
   else
      temp(i) = 0
   end if
next i

if t = x(nplusc) **then** temp(npts) = 1   *handle the end specially*

calculate higher-order basis functions and their derivatives
(see Eqs. (3.2b) and (3.29)–(3.32))

for k = 2 **to** c
   for i = 1 **to** nplusc−k

      calculate basis function

      if temp(i) ≠ 0 **then**   *if basis function is zero, skip the calculation*
         b1 = ((t−x(i))∗temp(i))/(x(i+k−1)−x(i))
      else
         b1 = 0
      end if

      if temp(i+1) ≠ 0 **then**   *if basis function is zero, skip the calculation*
         b2 = ((x(i+k)−t)∗temp(i+1))/(x(i+k)−x(i+1))
      else
         b2 = 0
      end if

      calculate first derivative

      if temp(i) ≠ 0 **then**   *if basis function is zero, skip the calculation*
         f1 = temp(i)/(x(i+k−1)−x(i))
      else
         f1 = 0
      end if
      if temp(i+1) ≠ 0 **then**   *if basis function is zero, skip the calculation*

```
        f2 = −temp(i+1)/(x(i+k)−x(i+1))
    else
        f2 = 0
    end if
    if temp1(i) ≠ 0 then              if basis function is zero, skip the calculation
        f3 = (t−x(i))*temp1(i)/(x(i+k−1)−x(i))
    else
        f3 = 0
    end if
    if temp1(i+1) ≠ 0 then            if basis function is zero, skip the calculation
        f4 = (x(i+k)−t)*temp1(i+1)/(x(i+k)−x(i+1))
    else
        f4 = 0
    end if

    calculate second derivative

    if temp1(i) ≠ 0 then              if basis function is zero, skip the calculation
        s1 = 2*temp1(i)/(x(i+k−1)−x(i))
    else
        s1 = 0
    end if
    if temp1(i+1) ≠ 0 then            if basis function is zero, skip the calculation
        s2 = −2*temp1(i+1)/(x(i+k)−x(i+1))
    else
        s2 = 0
    end if
    if temp2(i) ≠ 0 then              if basis function is zero, skip the calculation
        s3 = (t−x(i))*temp2(i)/(x(i+k−1)−x(i))
    else
        s3 = 0
    end if
    if temp2(i+1) ≠ 0 then            if basis function is zero, skip the calculation
        s4 = (x(i+k)−t)*temp2(i+1)/(x(i+k)−x(i+1))
    else
        s4 = 0
    end if
    temp(i) = b1 + b2
    temp1(i) = f1 + f2 + f3 + f4
    temp2(i) = s1 + s2 + s3 + s4
  next i
next k

put in arrays

for i = 1 to npts
    n(1,i) = temp(i)
    d1(1,i) = temp1(i)
    d2(1,i) = temp2(i)
```

next i

return

dbasisu

Subroutine to generate B-spline basis functions and their derivatives for uniform periodic knot vectors (see Eqs. (3.2) and (3.29)–(3.32)).

$b1$ $=$ *first term of the basis function*
$b2$ $=$ *second term of the basis function*
c $=$ *order of the B-spline basis function*
$d1(,)$ $=$ *array containing the derivative of the basis functions*
    $d1(1,1)$ contains the derivative of the basis function for B_1 etc.
$d2(,)$ $=$ *array containing the derivative of the basis functions*
    $d2(1,1)$ contains the derivative of the basis function for B_1 etc.
$f1$ $=$ *first term of the first derivative of the basis function*
$f2$ $=$ *second term of the first derivative of the basis function*
$f3$ $=$ *third term of the first derivative of the basis function*
$f4$ $=$ *fourth term of the first derivative of the basis function*
$npts$ $=$ *number of control polygon vertices*
$n(,)$ $=$ *array containing the basis functions*
    $n(1,1)$ contains the basis function for B_1 etc.
$nplusc$ $=$ *constant npts + c, maximum knot value*
$s1$ $=$ *first term of the second derivative of the basis function*
$s2$ $=$ *second term of the second derivative of the basis function*
$s3$ $=$ *third term of the second derivative of the basis function*
$s4$ $=$ *fourth term of the second derivative of the basis function*
t $=$ *parameter value*
$temp()$ $=$ *temporary array*
$x()$ $=$ *knot vector*

subroutine dbasisu(c,t,npts,x(); n(,),d1(,),d2(,))

dimension temp(20),temp1(20),temp2(20)   *up to 20 control polygon vertices*

nplusc = npts+c

zero the temporary arrays

Mat temp = **Zer**(nplusc)
Mat temp1 = **Zer**(nplusc)
Mat temp2 = **Zer**(nplusc)

calculate the first-order basis functions $N_{i,1}$ (see Eq. (3.2a))

for i = 1 **to** nplusc−1
    if t ≥ x(i) **and** t < x(i+1) **then**
        temp(i) = 1
    else
        temp(i) = 0

    end if
next i

if t = x(npts+1) **then**   *handle the end specially by resetting the*
    temp(npts) = 1   *first-order basis functions.*
    temp(npts+1) = 0
end if

calculate higher-order basis functions and their derivatives
(see Eqs. (3.2b) and (3.29)–(3.32))

for k = 2 **to** c
    for i = 1 **to** nplusc−k

        calculate basis function

        if temp(i) $\neq$ 0 **then**   *if basis function is zero, skip the calculation*
          b1 = ((t−x(i))*temp(i))/(x(i+k−1)−x(i))
        else
          b1 = 0
        end if

        if temp(i+1) $\neq$ 0 **then**   *if basis function is zero, skip the calculation*
          b2 = ((x(i+k)−t)*temp(i+1))/(x(i+k)−x(i+1))
        else
          b2 = 0
        end if

        calculate first derivative

        if temp(i) $\neq$ 0 **then**   *if basis function is zero, skip the calculation*
          f1 = temp(i)/(x(i+k−1)−x(i))
        else
          f1 = 0
        end if
        if temp(i+1) $\neq$ 0 **then**   *if basis function is zero, skip the calculation*
          f2 = −temp(i+1)/(x(i+k)−x(i+1))
        else
          f2 = 0
        end if
        if temp1(i) $\neq$ 0 **then**   *if basis function is zero, skip the calculation*
          f3 = (t−x(i))*temp1(i)/(x(i+k−1)−x(i))
        else
          f3 = 0
        end if
        if temp1(i+1) $\neq$ 0 **then**   *if basis function is zero, skip the calculation*
          f4 = (x(i+k)−t)*temp1(i+1)/(x(i+k)−x(i+1))
        else
          f4 = 0
        end if

        calculate second derivative

        if temp1(i) $\neq$ 0 **then**   *if basis function is zero, skip the calculation*
          s1 = 2*temp1(i)/(x(i+k−1)−x(i))
        else
          s1 = 0
        end if
        if temp1(i+1) $\neq$ 0 **then**   *if basis function is zero, skip the calculation*
          s2 = −2*temp1(i+1)/(x(i+k)−x(i+1))
        else
          s2 = 0
        end if
        if temp2(i) $\neq$ 0 **then**   *if basis function is zero, skip the calculation*
          s3 = (t−x(i))*temp2(i)/(x(i+k−1)−x(i))
        else
          s3 = 0
        end if
        if temp2(i+1) $\neq$ 0 **then**   *if basis function is zero, skip the calculation*
          s4 = (x(i+k)−t)*temp2(i+1)/(x(i+k)−x(i+1))
        else
          s4 = 0
        end if
        temp(i) = b1 + b2
        temp1(i) = f1 + f2 + f3 + f4
        temp2(i) = s1 + s2 + s3 + s4
     next i
   next k

   put in arrays

   for i = 1 **to** npts
     n(1,i) = temp(i)
     d1(1,i) = temp1(i)
     d2(1,i) = temp2(i)
   next i

   return

dbspline

Subroutine to generate a B-spline curve and its derivatives using an open uniform knot vector (see Eqs. (3.1), (3.27) and (3.28)).

b(,)   = *array containing the control polygon vertices*
           b(,1) contains the x component of the vertex
           b(,2) contains the y component of the vertex
           b(,3) contains the z component of the vertex
d1(,)   = *array containing the first derivative of the curve*
           d1(,1) contains the x component
           d1(,2) contains the y component

		d1(,3) contains the z component
d2(,)	=	*array containing the second derivative of the curve*
		d2(,1) contains the x component
		d2(,2) contains the y component
		d2(,3) contains the z component
d1nbasis(,)	=	*first derivative of the basis functions for a single value of t*
d2nbasis(,)	=	*second derivative of the basis functions for a single value of t*
k	=	*order of the B-spline basis function*
nbasis	=	*array containing the basis functions for a single value of t*
nplusc	=	*number of knot values*
npts	=	*number of control polygon vertices*
p(,)	=	*array containing the curve points*
		p(,1) contains the x component of the point
		p(,2) contains the y component of the point
		p(,3) contains the z component of the point
p1	=	*number of points to be calculated on the curve*
t	=	*parameter value $0 \leq t \leq 1$*
x()	=	*array containing the knot vector*

subroutine dbspline(npts,k,p1,b(,); p(,),d1(,),d2(,))

allows for 20 polygon vertices with basis function of order 5

dimension x(30),nbasis(1,20),d1nbasis(1,20),d2nbasis(1,20)
dimension temp(1,3),temp1(1,3),temp2(1,3)
zero and redimension the knot vector, basis, curve and derivative arrays

Mat p = **Zer**(p1,3)
Mat d1 = **Zer**(p1,3)
Mat d2 = **Zer**(p1,3)
Mat nbasis = **Zer**(1,npts)
Mat d1nbasis = **Zer**(1,npts)
Mat d2nbasis = **Zer**(1,npts)
Mat x = **Zer**(npts+k)

nplusc = npts+k

generate the uniform open knot vector

call knot(npts,k; x)

icount = 0

calculate the points on the B-spline curve and their first and second derivatives

for t = 0 **to** x(nplusc) **step** x(nplusc)/(p1−1)
    icount = icount+1
    if icount = p1 **then** t = x(nplusc)   *compensate for incremental calculation of t*

    generate the basis function and its derivatives for this value of t
    (see Eqs. (3.2) and (3.29)–(3.32))

    call dbasis(k,t,npts,x; nbasis,d1nbasis,d2nbasis)
    Mat temp = nbasis*b   *generate the point on the curve*

Mat temp1 = d1nbasis∗b	*first derivative at that point on the curve*
Mat temp2 = d2nbasis∗b	*second derivative at that point on the curve*

p(icount,1) = temp(1,1)	*assign the current value of the point on the curve*
p(icount,2) = temp(1,2)	*to the curve array*
d1(icount,1) = temp1(1,1)	*assign the current value of the derivative at that*
d1(icount,2) = temp1(1,2)	*point on the curve to the derivative array*
d2(icount,1) = temp2(1,1)	*assign the current value of the derivative at that*
d2(icount,2) = temp2(1,2)	*point on the curve to the derivative array*

next t

return

dbsplineu

Subroutine to generate a B-spline curve and its derivatives using an open uniform knot vector (see Eqs. (3.1), (3.27) and (3.28)).

$b(,)$	=	*array containing the control polygon vertices*
		b(,1) contains the x component of the vertex
		b(,2) contains the y component of the vertex
		b(,3) contains the z component of the vertex
$d1(,)$	=	*array containing the first derivative of the curve*
		d1(,1) contains the x component
		d1(,2) contains the y component
		d1(,3) contains the z component
$d2(,)$	=	*array containing the second derivative of the curve*
		d2(,1) contains the x component
		d2(,2) contains the y component
		d2(,3) contains the z component
$d1nbasis(,)$	=	*first derivative of the basis functions for a single value of t*
$d2nbasis(,)$	=	*second derivative of the basis functions for a single value of t*
k	=	*order of the B-spline basis function*
$nbasis$	=	*array containing the basis functions for a single value of t*
$nplusc$	=	*number of knot values*
$npts$	=	*number of control polygon vertices*
$p(,)$	=	*array containing the curve points*
		p(,1) contains the x component of the point
		p(,2) contains the y component of the point
		p(,3) contains the z component of the point
$p1$	=	*number of points to be calculated on the curve*
t	=	*parameter value $0 \leq t \leq 1$*
$x()$	=	*array containing the knot vector*

subroutine dbsplineu(npts,k,p1,b(,); p(,),d1(,),d2(,))

allows for 20 polygon vertices with basis function of order 5

dimension x(30),nbasis(1,20),d1nbasis(1,20),d2nbasis(1,20)
dimension temp(1,3),temp1(1,3),temp2(1,3)

zero and redimension the knot vector, basis, curve and derivative arrays

Mat p = **Zer**(p1,3)
Mat d1 = **Zer**(p1,3)
Mat d2 = **Zer**(p1,3)
Mat nbasis = **Zer**(1,npts)
Mat d1nbasis = **Zer**(1,npts)
Mat d2nbasis = **Zer**(1,npts)
Mat x = **Zer**(npts+k)

nplusc = npts+k

generate the open uniform knot vector

call knotu(npts,k; x)

icount = 0

calculate the points on the B-spline curve and their first and second derivatives
(see Eqs. (3.2), (3.11) and (3.12))

for t = (k−1) **to** npts **step** (npts−(k−1))/(p1−1)
    icount = icount+1
    if icount = p1 **then** t = npts   *compensate for incremental calculation of t*

    generate the basis function and its derivatives for this value of t

    call dbasisu(k,t,npts,x; nbasis,d1nbasis,d2nbasis)
    Mat temp = nbasis*b   *generate the point on the curve*
    Mat temp1 = d1nbasis*b   *first derivative at that point on the curve*
    Mat temp2 = d2nbasis*b   *second derivative at that point on the curve*

    p(icount,1) = temp(1,1)   *assign the current value of the point on the curve*
    p(icount,2) = temp(1,2)   *to the curve array*
    d1(icount,1) = temp1(1,1)   *assign the current value of the derivative at that*
    d1(icount,2) = temp1(1,2)   *point on the curve to the derivative array*
    d2(icount,1) = temp2(1,1)   *assign the current value of the derivative at that*
    d2(icount,2) = temp2(1,2)   *point on the curve to the derivative array*

next t

return

knot

Subroutine to generate a B-spline open knot vector with multiplicity k at the ends (see Sec. 3.3).

c   = *order of the basis function*
n   = *the number of control polygon vertices*
nplus2   = *index of x() for the first occurence of the maximum knot vector value*
nplusc = *maximum value of the knot vector* $n + c$
x()   = *array containing the knot vector*

subroutine knot(n,c; x())

nplusc = n+c

```
nplus2 = n+2
x(1) = 0
for i = 2 to nplusc
    if i > c and i < nplus2 then
        x(i) = x(i−1) + 1
    else
        x(i) = x(i−1)
    end if
next i

return
```

knotc

Subroutine to generate a nonuniform open knot vector proportional to the chord lengths between control polygon vertices (see Eq. (3.4)).

$b(,)$	=	*array containing the control polygon vertices*
		$b(,1)$ *contains the x component of the vertex*
		$b(,2)$ *contains the y component of the vertex*
		$b(,3)$ *contains the z component of the vertex*
c	=	*order of the basis function*
chord	=	*chord distance between control polygon vertices*
csum	=	*accumulated sum of the chord distances*
maxchord	=	*sum of the chord distances between control polygon vertices*
npts	=	*the number of control polygon vertices*
nplusc	=	*maximum value of the knot vector* $n + c$
numerator	=	*numerator of Eq. (3.4)*
$x()$	=	*array containing the knot vector*
xchord	=	*x component of the distance between control polygon vertices*
ychord	=	*y component of the distance between control polygon vertices*

subroutine knotc(npts,c,b(,); x())

dimension chord(20)

```
nplusc = npts+c
n = npts−1
```

zero and redimension the knot vector and chord values

Mat chord=**Zer**(n)

determine chord distance between control polygon vertices and their sum

```
maxchord = 0
for i = 2 to npts
    xchord = b(i,1) − b(i−1,1)
    ychord = b(i,2) − b(i−1,2)
    chord(i−1) = Sqrt(xchord∗xchord + ychord∗ychord)
    maxchord = maxchord + chord(i−1)
next i
```

multiplicity of k zeros at the beginning of the open knot vector

```
for i = 1 to c
    x(i)=0
next i
```

generate the internal knot values

```
for i = 1 to n−c+1
    csum = 0
    for j = 1 to i
        csum = csum+chord(j)
    next j
    numerator = (i/(n−c+2))*chord(i+1) + csum
    x(c+i) = (numerator/maxchord)*(n−c+2)
next i
```

multiplicity of k zeros at the end of the open knot vector

```
for i = n+2 to nplusc
    x(i) = n−c+2
next i
return
```

knotu

Subroutine to generate a B-spline periodic uniform knot vector (see Sec. 3.3).

c =   *order of the basis function*
n =   *the number of control polygon vertices*
nplus2 =   *index of $x()$ for the occurrence of the maximum knot vector value*
nplusc =   *maximum value of the knot vector $n + c$*
$x()$ =   *array containing the knot vector*

subroutine knotu(n,c; x())

```
nplusc = n+c
nplus2 = n+2

for i = 1 to nplusc
    x(i) = i−1
next i

return
```

matpbspl

Subroutine to generate a B-spline curve using matrix methods and a periodic uniform knot vector (see Eq. (3.11)).

$b(,)$ =   *array containing the control polygon vertices in the sliding window*
                b(,1) contains the x component of the vertex in the sliding window
                b(,2) contains the y component of the vertex in the sliding window
                b(,3) contains the z component of the vertex in the sliding window
$d(,)$ =   *array containing the control polygon vertices*

$d(\ ,1)$ *contains the x component of the vertex*
$d(\ ,2)$ *contains the y component of the vertex*
$d(\ ,3)$ *contains the z component of the vertex*

fcoeff	=	*coefficient for the integer $[N^*]$ matrix*
k	=	*order of the B-spline basis function*
nbasis	=	*array containing the basis functions for a single value of t*
nplusc	=	*number of knot values*
npts	=	*number of control polygon vertices*
p(,)	=	*array containing the curve points*

$p(\ ,1)$ *contains the x component of the point*
$p(\ ,2)$ *contains the y component of the point*
$p(\ ,3)$ *contains the z component of the point*

p1	=	*number of points to be calculated on the span of the curve*
ptemp(,)	=	*temporary matrix containing a single curve point t∗n∗b*
t(,)	=	*parameter matrix*
temp(,)	=	*temporary matrix t∗n*
u	=	*normalized parameter value $0 \leq u \leq 1$*

subroutine matpbspl(k,npts,p1,d(,); p(,))

dimension t(1,9),b(9,3),n(9,9),temp(1,9),ptemp(1,3)   *allows for ninth order*

zero and redimension matrices

Mat b = **Zer**(k,3)
Mat n = **Zer**(k,k)
Mat t = **Zer**(1,k)
Mat temp = **Zer**(1,k)

set up the $[N]$ *matrix*

call nmatrix(k; fcoeff,n)

set up the sliding polygon vertex matrix and calculate the points

icount = 0

for j = 0 **to** npts   *set up sliding polygon vertex matrix*

    for l = 0 **to** k−1
      b(l+1,1)=d(mod(j+l,npts)+1,1)
      b(l+1,2)=d(mod(j+l,npts)+1,2)
      b(l+1,3)=d(mod(j+l,npts)+1,3)
    next l

    for u = 0 **to** 1 −(1/(p1−1)) **step** 1/(p1−1)
      icount = icount+1
      for i = 1 **to** k   *set up the parameter matrix*
        t(1,i) = u^(k−i)
      next i
      Mat t = fcoeff∗t   *calculate the points on this segment*
      Mat temp = t∗n
      Mat ptemp = temp∗b

$$p(icount,1) = ptemp(1,1)$$
$$p(icount,2) = ptemp(1,2)$$
$$p(icount,3) = ptemp(1,3)$$

assign the current value of the point on the curve to the curve array

next u

next j

return

nmatrix

Subroutine to calculate the general B-spline periodic basis matrix (see Eq. (3.9)).

$Factrl$ = *function that calculates the factorial of a number*
$fcoeff$ = *coefficient of the integer matrix* $1/(k-1)!$
k = *order of the periodic basis function*
$n(,)$ = *integer form of the* $[N^*]$ *matrix*
$Ni(n,i)$ = *function that calculates* $\binom{n}{i}$

subroutine nmatrix(k; fcoeff,n(,))

def **Ni**(n,i) = **Factrl**(n)/(**Factrl**(i)∗**Factrl**(n−i))

zero and redimension the $[N]$ *matrix*

Mat n = **Zer**(k,k)

fcoeff = 1/**Factrl**(k−1)   *calculate the constant multiplicative factor*

set up the matrix

for i = 0 **to** k−1
    temp = **Ni**(k−1,i)
    for j = 0 **to** k−1
        sum = 0
        for l = j **to** k−1
            sum1 = (k −(l+1))∧i
            sum2 = (−1)∧(l−j)
            sum3 = **Ni**(k,l−j)
            sum = sum + sum1∗sum2∗sum3
        next l
        n(i+1,j+1) = temp∗sum
    next j
next i

return

param

Subroutine to calculate parameter values based on chord distances.

$d(,)$ = *array containing the data points*
$dpts$ = *number of data points*

isum   =   *incremental sum of the chord distances*
sum   =   *sum of all the chord distances*
tparm() =   *array containing the parameter values*

subroutine param(dpts,d(,); tparm())

sum = 0
isum = 0
tparm(1) = 0

calculate the sum of the chord distances for all the data points

for i = 2 **to** dpts
    sum = sum + **Sqrt**((d(i,1)−d(i−1,1))^2 + (d(i,2)−d(i−1,2))^2)
next i

calculate the parameter values

for i = 2 **to** dpts
    isum = isum + **Sqrt**((d(i,1)−d(i−1,1))^2 + (d(i,2)−d(i−1,2))^2)
    tparm(i) = isum/sum
next i

return

Chapter 4

rbasis

Subroutine to generate a rational B-spline basis function using an open knot vector (see Eq. (4.3)).

c =   *order of the B-spline basis function*
d =   *first term of the basis function recursion relation*
e =   *second term of the basis function recursion relation*
$h()$ =   *array containing the homogeneous coordinate weighting factors*
npts   =   *number of control polygon vertices*
nplusc =   *constant npts + c, maximum number of knot values*
$r(,)$ =   *array containing the basis functions*
            $r(1,1)$ contains the basis function associated with B_1 etc.
sum   =   *sum of the products of the nonrational basis functions and the*
            homogeneous coordinate weighting factors
t =   *parameter value*
temp() =   *temporary array*
$x()$ =   *knot vector*

subroutine rbasis(c,t,npts,x(),h(); r(,))

dimension temp(20)   *allows for 20 polygon vertices*

nplusc = npts+c

calculate the first-order nonrational basis functions $N_{i,1}$ (see Eq. (3.2a))

```
for i = 1 to nplusc−1
    if t ≥ x(i) and t < x(i+1) then
        temp(i) = 1
    else
        temp(i) = 0
    end if
next i
```

calculate the higher-order nonrational basis functions (see Eq. (3.2b))

```
for k = 2 to c
    for i = 1 to nplusc−k
        if temp(i) ≠ 0 then                          if zero skip the calculation
            d = ((t−x(i))*temp(i))/(x(i+k−1)−x(i))
        else
            d = 0
        end if
        if temp(i+1) ≠ 0 then                        if zero skip the calculation
            e = ((x(i+k)−t)*temp(i+1))/(x(i+k)−x(i+1))
        else
            e = 0
        end if
        temp(i) = d + e
    next i
next k
if t = x(nplusc) then temp(npts) = 1                 pick up last point
```

calculate sum for denominator of rational basis functions (see Eq. (4.3))

```
sum = 0
for i = 1 to npts
    sum = sum + temp(i)*h(i)
next i
```

form rational basis functions and put in r vector (see Eq. (4.3))

```
for i = 1 to npts
    if sum ≠ 0 then
        r(1,i) = temp(i)*h(i)/sum
    else
        r(1,i) = 0
    end if
next i
return
```

rbspline

Subroutine to generate a rational B-spline curve using an open uniform knot vector (see Eqs. (4.2) and (4.4)).

$b(,)$ = *array containing the control polygon vertices*
    b(,1) contains the x component of the vertex
    b(,2) contains the y component of the vertex
    b(,3) contains the z component of the vertex
$h()$ = *array containing the homogeneous coordinate weighting factors*
k = *order of the B-spline basis function*
$nbasis$ = *array containing the rational basis functions for a single value of t*
$nplusc$ = *number of knot values*
$npts$ = *number of control polygon vertices*
$p(,)$ = *array containing the curve points*
    p(,1) contains the x component of the point
    p(,2) contains the y component of the point
    p(,3) contains the z component of the point
$p1$ = *number of points to be calculated on the curve*
t = *parameter value $0 \leq t \leq 1$*
$x()$ = *array containing the knot vector*

subroutine rbspline(npts,k,p1,b(,),h(); p(,))

dimension nbasis(1,20),x(30),temp(1,3)   *allows for 20 data points with basis*
                                                    function of order 5

nplusc = npts+k

zero and redimension the knot vector and the basis array

Mat nbasis = **Zer**(1,npts)
Mat x = **Zer**(nplusc)

generate the open uniform knot vector

call knot(npts,k; x)

icount = 0

calculate the points on the rational B-spline curve

for t = 0 **to** x(npts+k) **step** x(npts+k)/(p1−1)
    icount = icount+1
    call rbasis(k,t,npts,x,h; nbasis)   *rational basis functions for this value of t*
    Mat temp = nbasis∗b   *generate the point on the curve*
    p(icount,1) = temp(1,1)   *assign the current value of the point on the curve*
    p(icount,2) = temp(1,2)   *to the curve array*
    p(icount,3) = temp(1,3)
next t

return

rbsplinu

Subroutine to generate a rational B-spline curve using a periodic uniform knot vector
(see Eqs. (4.3) and (4.4)).

$b(,)$ = *array containing the control polygon vertices*
    b(,1) contains the x component of the vertex

                    b(,2) contains the y component of the vertex
                    b(,3) contains the z component of the vertex

$h()$	=	*array containing the homogeneous coordinate weighting factors*
k	=	*order of the B-spline basis function*
nbasis	=	*array containing the rational basis functions for a single value of t*
nplusc	=	*number of knot values*
npts	=	*number of control polygon vertices*
$p(,)$	=	*array containing the curve points*

                    p(,1) contains the x component of the point
                    p(,2) contains the y component of the point
                    p(,3) contains the z component of the point

$p1$	=	*number of points to be calculated on the curve*
t	=	*parameter value $0 \leq t \leq 1$*
$x()$	=	*array containing the knot vector*

subroutine rbsplinu(npts,k,p1,b(,),h(); p(,))

dimension nbasis(1,20),x(30),temp(1,3)   *allows for 20 data points with basis*
                                               function of order 5

nplusc = npts+k

zero and redimension the knot vector and the basis array

Mat nbasis = **Zer**(1,npts)
Mat x = **Zer**(nplusc)

generate the open uniform knot vector

call knotu(npts,k; x)

icount = 0

calculate the points on the rational B-spline curve

for t = (k−1) **to** (npts−1+1) **step** ((npts−1+1)−(k−1))/(p1−1)
    icount = icount+1
    call rbasis(k,t,npts,x,h; nbasis)   *rational basis functions for this value of t*
    Mat temp = nbasis*b   *generate the point on the curve*
    p(icount,1) = temp(1,1)   *assign the current value of the point on the curve*
    p(icount,2) = temp(1,2)   *to the curve array*
    p(icount,3) = temp(1,3)

next t

return

Chapter 5

bezsurf

Subroutine to calculate a Bézier surface (see Eq. (5.3)).

$b(,)$	=	*array containing the control net vertices*

                    b(,1) contains the x component of the vertex

$b(\ ,2)$ *contains the y component of the vertex*
$b(\ ,3)$ *contains the z component of the vertex*
Note: $B_{i,j} = b(,)$ has dimensions of $n*m \times 3$, with j varying fastest

$Basis$	=	*function to calculate the Bernstein basis value*
$Factrl$	=	*function to calculate the factorial of a number*
jin	=	*Bernstein basis function in the u direction (see Eq. (2.2))*
kjm	=	*Bernstein basis function in the w direction (see Eq. (2.2))*
m	=	*one less than the number of control net vertices in w direction*
n	=	*one less than the number of control net vertices in u direction*
Ni	=	*factorial function for the Bernstein basis*
$p1$	=	*number of parametric lines in the u direction*
$p2$	=	*number of parametric lines in the w direction*
$q(,)$	=	*position vectors for points on the surface*

$q(\ ,1)$ *contains the x component of the vector*
$q(\ ,2)$ *contains the y component of the vector*
$q(\ ,3)$ *contains the z component of the vector*
for a fixed value of u the next m elements contain
the values for the curve $q(u_i, w)$ q has dimensions
of $p1*p2 \times 3$

subroutine bezsurf(b(,),n,m,p1,p2; q(,))

def **Ni**(n,i) = **Factrl**(n)/(**Factrl**(i)∗**Factrl**(n−i))
def **Basis**(n,i,t) = **Ni**(n,i)∗(t^i)∗((1−t)^(n−i))

icount = 0

for u = 0 **to** 1 **step** 1/(p1−1)   *for fixed u calculate various values of w*
   for w = 0 **to** 1 **step** 1/(p2−1)
      icount = icount+1
      for i = 0 **to** n
      jin = **Basis**(n,i,u)   *Bernstein basis function in the u direction*
         for j = 0 **to** m
         j1 = (m+1)∗i + (j+1)
         kjm = **Basis**(m,j,w)   *Bernstein basis function in the w direction*
           for k = 1 **to** 3
             q(icount,k) = q(icount,k) + b(j1,k)∗jin∗kjm   *calculate surface point*
           next k
         next j
      next i
   next w
next u

return

mbezsurf

Subroutine to calculate a Bézier surface using matrix methods (see Eq. 5.4).

$b(,)$ = *array containing the control net vertices*

$b(\ ,1)$ *contains the x component of the vertex*
$b(\ ,2)$ *contains the y component of the vertex*
$b(\ ,3)$ *contains the z component of the vertex*
Note: $B_{i,j} = b(,)$ has dimensions of $n*m \times 3$ j varies fastest

jin	=	*Bernstein basis function in the u direction (see Eq. (2.2))*
kjm	=	*Bernstein basis function in the w direction (see Eq. (2.2))*
m(,)	=	*the* $[\mathrm{M}]$ *matrix (see Eq. (5.4))*
m1	=	*one less than the number of control vertices in w direction*
n1	=	*one less than the number of control vertices in u direction*
Factrl	=	*function that calculates the factorial of a number*
n(,)	=	*the* $[\mathrm{N}]$ *matrix (see Eq. (5.4))*
Ni(n,i)	=	*function that calculates* $\binom{n}{i}$ *(see Eq. (2.3))*
p1	=	*number of parametric lines in the u direction*
p2	=	*number of parametric lines in the w direction*
q(,)	=	*position vectors for points on the surface*

$q(\ ,1)$ *contains the x component of the vector*
$q(\ ,2)$ *contains the y component of the vector*
$q(\ ,3)$ *contains the z component of the vector*
for a fixed value of u the next m elements contain
the values for the curve $q(u_i, w)$, q has dimensions
of $p1*p2 \times 3$

u(,)	=	$[\mathrm{U}]$ *parameter matrix (see Eq. (5.4))*
w(,)	=	$[\mathrm{W}]$ *parameter matrix (see Eq. (5.4))*

subroutine mbezsurf(b(,),n1,m1,p1,p2; q(,))

allows for a 10 × 10 Bézier net

dimension x(10,10),y(10,10),z(10,10),g(10,10)
dimension n(10,10),m(10,10),u(1,10),w(10,1)
dimension temp1(10,10),temp2(10,10),temp3(1,10),temp4(1,1)

def **Ni**(n,i) = **Factrl**(n)/(**Factrl**(i)∗**Factrl**(n−i))

redimension matrices and fill with zeros

Mat n = **Zer**(n1+1,n1+1)
Mat m = **Zer**(m1+1,m1+1)
Mat x = **Zer**(n1+1,m1+1)
Mat y = **Zer**(n1+1,m1+1)
Mat z = **Zer**(n1+1,m1+1)
Mat g = **Zer**(n1+1,m1+1)
Mat u = **Zer**(1,n1+1)
Mat w = **Zer**(m1+1,1)
Mat temp1 = **Zer**(n1+1,m1+1)
Mat temp2 = **Zer**(n1+1,m1+1)
Mat temp3 = **Zer**(1,m1+1)
Mat temp4 = **Zer**(1,1)

set up the x,y,z matrices, i.e., the components of $[\mathrm{B}]$

for i = 1 **to** n1+1

```
    for j = 1 to m1+1
        ij = (m1+1)*(i−1) + j
        x(i,j) = b(ij, 1)
        y(i,j) = b(ij, 2)
        z(i,j) = b(ij, 3)
    next j
next i
```

set up the [N] *and* [M] *matrices*

```
for i = 0 to n1
    for j = 0 to n1
        if i+j <= n1 then
            n(i+1,j+1) = Ni(n1,j)*Ni(n1−j, n1−i−j)*(−1)^(n1−i−j)
        else
            n(i+1,j+1) = 0
        end if
    next j
next i

for i = 0 to m1
    for j = 0 to m1
        if i+j <= m1 then
            m(i+1,j+1) = Ni(m1,j)*Ni(m1−j, m1−i−j)*(−1)^(m1−i−j)
        else
            m(i+1,j+1) = 0
        end if
    next j
next i

Mat m = Trn(m)                          transpose of [M] for later use

for k = 1 to 3
    icount = 0                              reset the surface point counter

    if k = 1 then Mat g = x      assign each component of [B] in turn to [G]
    if k = 2 then Mat g = y
    if k = 3 then Mat g = z

    set up the unchanging [N][B][M] matrix for each pass (recall [M] = [M]ᵀ)
    Mat temp1 = g*m                                          [B][M]ᵀ
    Mat temp2 = n*temp1                                   [N][B][M]ᵀ
    for t = 0 to 1 step 1/(p1−1)                     set up the u matrix
        for i = 0 to n1
            u(1,i+1) = t^(n1−i)
        next i

    Mat temp3 = u*temp2      [U][N][B][M]ᵀ    constant for this u value
        for s = 0 to 1 step 1/(p2−1)             set up the w matrix
            icount = icount+1
```

```
                for i = 0 to m1
                    w(i+1,1) = s^(m1−i)
                next i
                Mat temp4 = temp3*w                    calculate the surface point
                q(icount,k) = temp4(1,1)              assign the point to the q array
            next s
        next t
    next k

    return
```

Chapter 6

bsplsurf

Subroutine to calculate a Cartesian product B-spline surface using open uniform knot vectors (see Eq. (5.3)).

$b()$ = *array containing the control net vertices*
  b(,1) contains the x component of the vertex
  b(,2) contains the y component of the vertex
  b(,3) contains the z component of the vertex
  Note: $B_{i,j} = b(,)$ has dimensions of $n*m \times 3$ with j varying fastest
  The polygon net is $n \times m$
k = *order in the u direction*
l = *order in the w direction*
$mbasis(,)$ = *nonrational basis functions for one value of w (see Eqs. (3.2))*
$mpts$ = *the number of control net vertices in w direction*
$nbasis(,)$ = *nonrational basis functions for one value of u (see Eqs. (3.2))*
$npts$ = *the number of control net vertices in u direction*
$p1$ = *number of parametric lines in the u direction*
$p2$ = *number of parametric lines in the w direction*
$q()$ = *array containing the resulting surface*
  q(,1) contains the x component of the vector
  q(,2) contains the y component of the vector
  q(,3) contains the z component of the vector
  for a fixed value of u the next m elements contain
  the values for the curve $q(u_i, w)$, q has dimensions
  of $p1*p2 \times 3$; the display surface is $p1 \times p2$

subroutine bsplsurf(b(,),k,l,npts,mpts,p1,p2; q(,))

allows for 20 data points with basis function of order 5

dimension x(30),y(30),nbasis(1,20),mbasis(1,20)

zero and redimension the arrays

Mat x = **Zer**(npts+k)
Mat y = **Zer**(mpts+l)
Mat nbasis = **Zer**(1,npts)

Mat mbasis = **Zer**(1, mpts)
Mat q = **Zer**(p1∗p2,3)

generate the open uniform knot vectors

call knot(npts,k; x())   *calculate u knot vector*
call knot(mpts,l; y())   *calculate w knot vector*

nplusc = npts+k
mplusc = mpts+l

icount = 0

calculate the points on the B-spline surface

for u = 0 **to** x(nplusc) **step** x(nplusc)/(p1−1)
    call basis(k,u,npts,x; nbasis)   *basis function for this value of u*
    for w = 0 **to** y(mplusc) **step** y(mplusc)/(p2−1)
        call basis(l,w,mpts,y; mbasis)   *basis function for this value of w*
    icount = icount + 1
    for i = 1 **to** npts
        for j = 1 **to** mpts
            j1 = mpts∗(i−1) + j
            for s = 1 **to** 3
                q(icount,s) = q(icount,s) + b(j1,s)∗nbasis(1,i)∗mbasis(1,j)
            next s
        next j
    next i
    next w
next u
return

bspsurfu

Subroutine to calculate a Cartesian product B-spline surface using periodic uniform knot vectors (see Eq. (5.3)).

$b()$ =   *array containing the control net vertices*
               b(,1) contains the x component of the vertex
               b(,2) contains the y component of the vertex
               b(,3) contains the z component of the vertex
               Note: $B_{i,j} = b(,)$ has dimensions of n∗m × 3 with j varying fastest
               The control net is n × m
$q()$ =   *array containing the resulting surface*
               q(,1) contains the x component of the vector
               q(,2) contains the y component of the vector
               q(,3) contains the z component of the vector
               for a fixed value of u the next m elements contain
               the values for the curve $q(u_i, w)$, q has dimensions
               of p1∗p2 × 3; the display surface is p1 × p2

k	=	*order in the u direction*
l	=	*order in the w direction*
mbasis(,)	=	*nonrational basis functions for one value of w (see Eqs. (3.2))*
mpts	=	*the number of control net vertices in w direction*
nbasis(,)	=	*nonrational basis functions for one value of u (see Eqs. (3.2))*
npts	=	*the number of control net vertices in u direction*
p1	=	*number of parametric lines in the u direction*
p2	=	*number of parametric lines in the w direction*

subroutine bspsurfu(b(,),k,l,npts,mpts,p1,p2; q(,))

allows for 20 data points with basis function of order 5

dimension x(30),y(30),nbasis(1,20),mbasis(1,20)

zero and redimension the arrays

Mat x = **Zer**(npts+k)
Mat y = **Zer**(mpts+l)
Mat nbasis = **Zer**(1,npts)
Mat mbasis = **Zer**(1,mpts)
Mat q = **Zer**(p1*p2,3)

generate the periodic uniform knot vectors

call knotu(npts,k; x())   *calculate u knot vector*
call knotu(mpts,l; y())   *calculate w knot vector*

nplusc = npts+k
mplusc = mpts+l

icount = 0

calculate the points on the B-spline surface

for u = (k−1) **to** (npts−1+1) **step** ((npts−1+1)−(k−1))/(p1−1)
    call basis(k,u,npts,x; nbasis)   *basis function for this value of u*
    for w = (l−1) **to** (mpts−1+1) **step** ((mpts−1+1)−(l−1))/(p2−1)
      call basis(l,w,mpts,y; mbasis)   *basis function for this value of w*

      icount = icount+1

      for i = 1 **to** npts
        for j = 1 **to** mpts
          for s = 1 **to** 3
          j1 = mpts*(i−1)+j
          q(icount,s) = q(icount,s) + b(j1,s)*nbasis(1,i)*mbasis(1,j)
          next s
        next j
      next i
    next w
next u

return

dbsurf

Subroutine to calculate a Cartesian product B-spline surface and its derivatives using open uniform knot vectors (see Eq. (5.3) and Eqs. (5.7) to (5.11)).

$b()$	=	*array containing the control net vertices*
		$b(\ ,1)$ *contains the x component of the vertex*
		$b(\ ,2)$ *contains the y component of the vertex*
		$b(\ ,3)$ *contains the z component of the vertex*
		Note: $Bi, j = b(,)$ has dimensions of $n*m \times 3$, j varies fastest
		the polygon net is $n \times m$
$d1mbasis(,)$	=	*first derivative of the basis functions for w (see Eq. (3.29))*
$d1nbasis(,)$	=	*first derivative of the basis functions for u (see Eq. (3.29))*
$d2mbasis(,)$	=	*second derivative of the basis functions for w (see Eq. (3.31))*
$d2nbasis(,)$	=	*second derivative of the basis functions for u (see Eq. (3.31))*
k	=	*order in the u direction*
l	=	*order in the w direction*
$mbasis(,)$	=	*basis functions for w (see Eqs. (3.2))*
$mpts$	=	*the number of control net vertices in w direction (see Eq. (3.1))*
$nbasis(,)$	=	*basis functions for u (see Eqs. (3.2))*
$npts$	=	*the number of control net vertices in u direction (see Eq. (3.1))*
$p1$	=	*number of parametric lines in the u direction*
$p2$	=	*number of parametric lines in the w direction*
$q()$	=	*resulting surface (see Eq. (5.3))*
		$q(\ ,1)$ *contains the x component of the vector*
		$q(\ ,2)$ *contains the y component of the vector*
		$q(\ ,3)$ *contains the z component of the vector*
		for a fixed value of u the next m elements contain
		the values for the curve $q(u(sub\ i),w)$, q has dimensions
		of $p1*p2 \times 3$; the display surface is $p1 \times p2$
$qu(,)$	=	*u derivative vectors for the*
		B-spline surface, has dimensions of $p1*p2 \times 3$ (see Eq. (5.7))
$qw(,)$	=	*w derivative vectors for the*
		B-spline surface, has dimensions of $p1*p2 \times 3$ (see Eq. (5.8))
$quu(,)$	=	*uu derivative vectors for the*
		B-spline surface, has dimensions of $p1*p2 \times 3$ (see Eq. (5.9))
$quw(,)$	=	*uw derivative vectors for the*
		B-spline surface, has dimensions of $p1*p2 \times 3$ (see Eq. (5.10))
$qww(,)$	=	*ww derivative vectors for the*
		B-spline surface, has dimensions of $p1*p2 \times 3$ (see Eq. (5.11))

subroutine dbsurf(b(,),k,l,npts,mpts,p1,p2; q(,),qu(,),qw(,),quw(,),quu(,),qww(,))

allows for 20 data points with basis function of order 5

dimension x(30),y(30)
dimension nbasis(1,20),mbasis(1,20)
dimension d1nbasis(1,20),d1mbasis(1,20)
dimension d2nbasis(1,20),d2mbasis(1,20)

zero and redimension the arrays

Mat x = **Zer**(npts+k)
Mat y = **Zer**(mpts+l)
Mat nbasis = **Zer**(1,npts)
Mat mbasis = **Zer**(1,mpts)
Mat d1nbasis = **Zer**(1,npts)
Mat d1mbasis = **Zer**(1,mpts)
Mat d2nbasis = **Zer**(1,npts)
Mat d2mbasis = **Zer**(1,mpts)
Mat q = **Zer**(p1*p2,3)
Mat qu = **Zer**(p1*p2,3)
Mat qw = **Zer**(p1*p2,3)
Mat quw = **Zer**(p1*p2,3)
Mat quu = **Zer**(p1*p2,3)
Mat qww = **Zer**(p1*p2,3)

generate the open uniform knot vectors

call knot(npts,k; x())   *calculate u knot vector*
call knot(mpts,l; y())   *calculate w knot vector*

nplusc = npts+k
mplusc = mpts+l

icount = 0

calculate the points on the B-spline surface

for u = 0 **to** x(nplusc) **step** x(nplusc)/(p1−1)
    call dbasis(k,u,npts,x; nbasis,d1nbasis,d2nbasis)   *basis function & derivatives*
    for w = 0 **to** y(mplusc) **step** y(mplusc)/(p2−1)
        call dbasis (l,w,mpts,y; mbasis,d1mbasis,d2mbasis)

    icount = icount+1

    for i = 1 **to** npts
        for j = 1 **to** mpts
            for s = 1 **to** 3
            j1 = mpts*(i−1) + j
            q(icount,s) = q(icount,s) + b(j1,s)*nbasis(1,i)*mbasis(1,j)
            qu(icount,s) = qu(icount,s) + b(j1,s)*d1nbasis(1,i)*mbasis(1,j)
            qw(icount,s) = qw(icount,s) + b(j1,s)*nbasis(1,i)*d1mbasis(1,j)
            quw(icount,s) = quw(icount,s) + b(j1,s)*d1nbasis(1,i)*d1mbasis(1,j)
            quu(icount,s) = quu(icount,s) + b(j1,s)*d2nbasis(1,i)*mbasis(1,j)
            qww(icount,s) = qww(icount,s) + b(j1,s)*nbasis(1,i)*d2mbasis(1,j)
            next s
        next j
    next i
    next w
next u
return

Chapter 7

rbspsurf

Subroutine to calculate a Cartesian product rational B-spline surface using an open uniform knot vector (see Eq. (7.1)).

$b()$ = *array containing the control net vertices*
         $b(\ ,1)$ contains the x component of the vertex
         $b(\ ,2)$ contains the y component of the vertex
         $b(\ ,3)$ contains the z component of the vertex
         $b(\ ,4)$ contains the homogeneous coordinate weighting factor
         Note: $B_{i,j} = b(,)$ has dimensions of $n*m \times 4$ with j varying fastest
         The polygon net is $n \times m$
k = *order in the u direction*
l = *order in the w direction*
$mbasis(,)$ = *array containing the nonrational basis functions for w (see Eqs. (3.2))*
$mpts$ = *the number of control net vertices in w direction*
$nbasis(,)$ = *array containing the nonrational basis functions for u (see Eqs. (3.2))*
$npts$ = *the number of control net vertices in u direction*
$p1$ = *number of parametric lines in the u direction*
$p2$ = *number of parametric lines in the w direction*
$q()$ = *array containing the resulting surface*
         $q(\ ,1)$ contains the x component of the vector
         $q(\ ,2)$ contains the y component of the vector
         $q(\ ,3)$ contains the z component of the vector
         for a fixed value of u the next m elements contain
         the values for the curve $q(u_i, w)$, q has dimensions
         of $p1*p2 \times 3$; the display surface is $p1 \times p2$
sum = *summation of the rational surface basis functions*

subroutine rbspsurf(b(,),k,l,npts,mpts,p1,p2; q(,))

allows for 20 data points with basis function of order 5

dimension $x(30), y(30), nbasis(1,20), mbasis(1,20)$

zero and redimension the arrays

Mat x = **Zer**(npts+k)
Mat y = **Zer**(mpts+l)
Mat nbasis = **Zer**(1,npts)
Mat mbasis = **Zer**(1,mpts)
Mat q = **Zer**(p1*p2,3)

generate the open uniform knot vectors

call knot(npts,k; x())   *calculate u knot vector*
call knot(mpts,l; y())   *calculate w knot vector*

nplusc = npts+k
mplusc = mpts+l

icount = 0

calculate the points on the B-spline surface

for u = 0 **to** x(nplusc) **step** x(nplusc)/(p1−1)

    call basis(k,u,npts,x; nbasis)   *nonrational basis function for u*

    for w = 0 **to** y(mplusc) **step** y(mplusc)/(p2−1)

      call basis(l,w,mpts,y; mbasis)   *nonrational basis function for w*

      call sumrbas(b,nbasis,mbasis,npts,mpts; sum)   *sum of basis functions*

      icount = icount+1

      for i = 1 **to** npts

        for j = 1 **to** mpts

          for s = 1 **to** 3

            j1 = mpts*(i−1) + j

            qtemp = b(j1,4)*b(j1,s)*nbasis(1,i)*mbasis(1,j)/sum   *surface point*

            q(icount, s) = q(icount, s) + qtemp   *assign to surface array*

          next s

        next j

      next i

    next w

next u

return

sumrbas

Subroutine to calculate the sum of the nonrational basis functions (see Eq. (7.3)).

$b()$ = *array containing the control net vertices*

           b(,1) contains the x component of the vertex

           b(,2) contains the y component of the vertex

           b(,3) contains the z component of the vertex

           b(,4) contains the homogeneous coordinate weighting factor

           *Note: $B_{i,j} = b(,)$ has dimensions of n*m × 4, j varies fastest*

           the polygon net is n × m

$mbasis(,)$ = *the nonrational basis functions for w*

$mpts$ = *the number of control net vertices in w direction*

$nbasis(,)$ = *the nonrational basis functions for u*

$npts$ = *the number of control net vertices in u direction*

sum = *sum of the basis functions*

subroutine sumrbas(b(,),nbasis(,),mbasis(,),npts,mpts; sum)

sum = 0

for i = 1 **to** npts

    for j = 1 **to** mpts

      j1 = mpts*(i−1) + j

      sum = sum + b(j1,4)*nbasis(1,i)*mbasis(1,j)   *calculate the sum*

    next j

next i

return

References

[Ball77] Ball, A.A., Consurf I–III, *CAD*, Vol. 6, pp. 243–249, 1974; Vol. 7, pp. 237–242, 1975; Vol. 9, pp. 9–12, 1977.

[Bars80] Barsky, B.A., and Greenberg, D.P., Determining a set of B-spline control vertices to generate an interpolating surface, *Comput. Graph. and Image Process.*, Vol. 14, pp. 203–226, 1980.

[Bars82] Barsky, B.A., End conditions and boundary conditions for uniform B-spline curve and surface representations, *Comp. in Indus.*, Vol. 3, pp. 17–29, 1982.

[Bars85] Barsky, B.A., Arbitrary subdivision of Bézier curves, TR UCB/CSD 85/265, Comp. Sci. Div., University of California, Berkeley, November 1985.

[Bart87] Bartels, R.H., Beatty, J.C., and Barsky, B.A., *Splines for Use in Computer Graphics & Geometric Modeling*, Morgan Kaufmann, San Francisco, 1987.

[Bezi68] Bézier, P.E., How Renault uses numerical control for car body design and tooling, SAE paper 680010, Soc. Automotive Engineers' Congress, Detroit, MI, 1968.

[Bezi70] Bézier, P.E., *Emploi des Machines à Commande Numerique*, Masson et Cie, Paris, 1970.

[Bezi71] Bézier, P.E., Example of an existing system in the motor industry: The Unisurf system, *Proc. Roy. Soc. London Ser. A*, Vol. 321, pp. 207–218, 1971.

[Bezi72] Bézier, P.E., *Emploi des Machines à Commande Numerique*, Masson et Cie, Paris, 1970; transl. Forrest, A.R., and Pankhurst, A.F., as Bézier, P.E., *Numerical Control Mathematics and Applications*, John Wiley & Sons, London, 1972.

[Bezi86] Bézier, P.E., *The Mathematical Basis of the Unisurf CAD System*, Butterworth, London, 1986.

[Bloo97] Bloomenthal, Jules, Ed., *Introduction to Implicit Surfaces*, Morgan Kaufmann, San Francisco, 1997.

[Boeh80] Boehm, W., Inserting new knots into B-spline curves, *CAD*, Vol. 12, pp. 199–201, 1980.

[Boeh82] Boehm, W., On cubics: A survey, *Comput. Graph. and Image Process.*, Vol. 19, pp. 201–226, 1982.

[Boeh85] Boehm, W., and Prautzsch, H., The insertion algorithm, *CAD*, Vol. 17, pp. 58–59, 1985.

[Clar74] Clark, J.H., 3-D design of free form B-spline surfaces, NTIS, Dept. of Commerce, AD/A-002 736, September 1974.

[Cohe80] Cohen, E., Lyche, T., and Riesenfeld, R.F., Discrete B-splines and subdivision techniques in computer aided geometric design and computer graphics, *Comput. Graph. and Image Process.*, Vol. 14, pp. 87–111, 1980.

[Cohe82] Cohen, E., and Riesenfeld, R.F., General matrix representations for Bézier and B-spline curves, *Comp. in Indus.*, Vol. 3, pp. 9–15, 1982.

[Cohe83] Cohen, E., Some mathematical tools for a modeler's bench, *IEEE Comput. Graph. and Appl.*, Vol. 3, No. 7, pp. 63–66, October 1983.

[Cohe85] Cohen, E., Lyche, T., and Schumacher, L.L., Algorithms for degree-raising of splines, *ACM TOG*, Vol. 4, pp. 171–181, 1985.

[Coon67] Coons, S., Surfaces for computer-aided design of spaceforms, MIT Proj. MAC, MAC–TR–41, June 1967. (Also as AD 663 504).

[Cox71]   Cox, M.G., The numerical evaluation of B-splines, National Physical Laboratory DNAC 4, August 1971.

[Dann85] Dannenberg, L., and Nowacki, H., Approximate conversion of surface representations with polynomial bases, *Comput. Aid. Geom. Des.*, Vol. 2, pp. 123–132, 1985.

[deBo72] de Boor, C., On calculation with B-splines, *Jour. Approx. Theory*, Vol. 6, pp. 50–62, 1972.

[Dill81] Dill, J.C., An application of color graphics to the display of surface curvature, *Comput. Graph.*, Vol. 15, pp. 153–161, 1981 (SIGGRAPH 81).

[Dill82] Dill, J.C., and Rogers, D.F., Color graphics and ship hull surface curvature, *Proc. of the Fourth International Conference on Computer Applications in the Automation of Shipyard Operation and Ship Design* (ICCAS 82), 7–10 June 1982, Annapolis, MD, pp. 197–205, North Holland, 1982.

[Eck93]   Eck, M., Degree reduction of Bézier curves, *Comput. Aid. Geom. Des.*, Vol. 10, pp. 237–251, 1993.

[Fari93] Farin, G.E., *Curves and Surfaces for Computer Aided Geometric Design—A Practical Guide*, 3rd ed., Academic Press, Boston, 1993.

[Faro85] Farouki, R., and Hinds, J., A hierarchy of geometric forms, *IEEE Comput. Graph. and Appl.*, Vol. 5, No. 5, pp. 51–78, 1985.

[Faux79] Faux, I.D., and Pratt, M.J., *Computational Geometry for Design and Manufacture*, Ellis Horwood, Chichester (John Wiley & Sons, New York), 1979.

[Forr68] Forrest, A.R., "Curves and Surfaces for Computer-aided Design," Ph.D. dissertation, Cambridge University, 1968.

[Forr72] Forrest, A.R., Interactive interpolation and approximation by Bézier polynomials, *Comp. J.*, Vol. 15, pp. 71–79, 1972.

[Forr79] Forrest, A.R., On the rendering of surfaces, *Comput. Graph.*, Vol. 13, pp. 253–259, 1979 (SIGGRAPH 79).

[Forr80] Forrest, A.R., The twisted cubic curve: A computer aided geometric design approach, *CAD*, Vol. 12, pp. 165–172, 1980.

[Gord74] Gordon, W.J., and Riesenfeld, R.F., Bernstein-Bézier methods for the computer aided design of free-form curves and surfaces, *J. ACM*, Vol. 21, pp. 293–310, 1974.

[Hart78] Hartley, P.J., and Judd, C.J., Parameterization of Bézier type B-spline curves and surfaces, *CAD*, Vol. 10, pp. 130–134, 1978.

[IGES86] IGES "Initial Graphics Exchange Specifications, Version 3.0," Doc. No. NBSIR 86-3359 Nat. Bur. of Stds., Gaithersburg, MD, 1986.

[Lach88] Lachance, M.A., Chebyshev economization for parametric surfaces, *Comput. Aid. Geom. Des.*, Vol. 5, pp. 195–208, 1988.

[Lee86] Lee, E., Rational Bézier representation for conics, in *Geometric Modeling*, Farin, G., Ed., SIAM, pp. 3–27, 1986.

[Munc79] Munchmeyer, F.C., Schubert, C., and Nowacki, H., Interactive design of fair hull surfaces using B-splines, *Proc. of the Third International Conference on Computer Applications in the Automation of Shipyard Operation and Ship Design* (ICCAS 79), 18–21 June 1979, University of Strathclyde, Glasgow, Scotland, pp. 67–76, North Holland, 1979.

[Munc80] Munchmeyer, F.C., The Gaussian curvature of Coons biquintic patches, *Proc. ASME Century 2 Inter. Comp. Tech. Conf.*, Honolulu, HI, 12–15 August 1980.

[Pete73] Peters, G.J., Interactive computer graphics application of the bicubic parametric surface to engineering design problems, McDonnell Douglas Automation Company, St. Louis, MO, presented at SIAM 1973 National Meeting, Hampton, VA, 18–21 June 1973.

[Pieg86] Piegl, L., A geometric investigation of the rational Bézier scheme of computer aided design, *Comp. in Indus.*, Vol. 7, pp. 401–410, 1986.

[Pieg87] Piegl, L., and Tiller, W., Curve and surface constructions using rational B-splines, *CAD*, Vol. 19, pp. 485–498, 1987.

[Pieg94] Piegl, L., and Tiller, W., Software engineering approach to degree elevation of B-spline curves, *CAD*, Vol. 26, No. 1, pp. 17–28, 1994.

[Pieg95] Piegl, L., and Tiller, W., Algorithm for degree reduction of B-spline curves, *CAD*, Vol. 27, No. 2, pp. 101–110, 1995.

[Pieg97] Piegl, L., and Tiller, W., *The NURBS Book*, 2nd ed., Springer, Berlin, 1997.

[Prau84a] Prautzsch, H., A short proof of the Oslo algorithm, *Comput. Aid. Geom. Des.*, Vol. 1, pp. 95–96, 1984.

[Prau84b] Prautzsch, H., Degree elevation of B-spline curves, *Comput. Aid. Geom. Des.*, Vol. 1, No. 1, pp. 193–198, 1984.

[Prau91] Prautzsch, H., and Piper, B., A fast algorithm to raise the degree of spline curves, *Comput. Aid. Geom. Des.*, Vol. 8, pp. 253–265, 1991.

[Ries73]   Riesenfeld, R.F., "Application of B-spline Approximation to Geometric Problems of Computer Aided Design," Ph.D. dissertation, Syracuse University, Syracuse, NY, 1972. Also available as University of Utah UTEC-CSc-73-126, March 1973.

[Roge77]   Rogers, D.F., B-spline curves and surfaces for ship hull design, *Proc. of SNAME, SCAHD 77, First International Symposium on Computer Aided Hull Surface Definition*, Annapolis, MD, 26–27 September 1977.

[Roge79]   Rogers, D.F., Rodriguez, F., and Satterfield, S.G., Computer aided ship design and the numerically controlled production of towing tank models, *Proc. of 16th Des. Auto. Conf.*, San Diego, CA, 24–27 June 1979.

[Roge80]   Rogers, D.F., and Satterfield, S.G., B-spline surfaces for ship hull design, *Comput. Graph.*, Vol. 14, pp. 211–217, 1980 (SIGGRAPH 80).

[Roge82]   Rogers, D.F., and Satterfield, S.G., Dynamic B-spline surfaces, *Proc. of the Fourth International Conference on Computer Applications in the Automation of Shipyard Operation and Ship Design* (ICCAS 82), 7–10 June 1982, Annapolis, MD, pp. 189–196, North Holland, 1982.

[Roge89]   Rogers, D.F., and Fog, N.G., Constrained B-spline curve and surface fitting, *CAD*, Vol. 21, pp. 641–648, 1989.

[Roge90a]   Rogers, D.F., and Adams, J.A., *Mathematical Elements for Computer Graphics*, 2nd ed., McGraw-Hill, New York, 1990.

[Roge90b]   Rogers, D.F., and Adlum, L., Dynamic rational and nonrational B-spline surface for display and manipulation, *CAD*, Vol. 22, pp. 609–616, 1990.

[Sabi71]   Sabin, M.A., An existing system in the aircraft industry. The British Aircraft Corporation numerical master geometry system, *Proc. Roy. Soc. London Ser. A*, Vol. 321, pp. 197–205, 1971.

[Scho46]   Schoenberg, I.J., Contributions to the problem of approximation of equidistant data by analytic functions, *Q. Appl. Math.*, Vol. 4, pp. 45–99; pp. 112–141, 1946.

[Shan88]   Shantz, M., and Chang, S., Rendering trimmed NURBS with adaptive forward differencing, *Comput. Graph.*, Vol. 22, pp. 189–198, 1988 (SIGGRAPH 88).

[Till83]   Tiller, W., Rational B-splines for curve and surface representation, *IEEE Comput. Graph. and Appl.*, Vol. 3, No. 6, pp. 61–69, September 1983.

[Till92]   Tiller, W., Knot-removal algorithms for NURBS curves and surfaces, *CAD*, Vol. 24, No. 8, pp. 445–453, 1992.

[Vers75]   Versprille, K.J., "Computer-aided Design Applications of the Rational B-spline Approximation Form," Ph.D. dissertation, Syracuse University, Syracuse, NY, February, 1975.

[Watk88]   Watkins, M.A., and Worsey, A.J., Degree reduction of Bézier curves, *CAD*, Vol. 20, No. 7, pp. 398–405, 1988.

[Wein92]   Weinstein, S.E., and Xu, Y., Degree reduction of Bézier curves by approximation and interpolation, in *Approximation Theory*, Anastassiou, G.A., Ed., Dekker, New York, 1992, pp. 503–512.

Index

Boldface entries in the index refer to pseudocode algorithms.

About the Author

Dave Rogers is the author of the computer graphics classics, *Mathematical Elements for Computer Graphics* and *Procedural Elements for Computer Graphics*. He is also the coeditor of four books from the state-of-the-art series on computer graphics and has published two fluid dynamics texts. His books have been translated into six foreign languages.

Dr. Rogers was founder and former director of the Computer Aided Design/Interactive Graphics Group at the United States Naval Academy. His early classic work in the use of B-splines and NURBS for dynamic real-time manipulation of ship hull surfaces spawned both commercial and research programs.

He was series editor for the Springer-Verlag series "Monographs in Visualization" and a founding editor of the journal *Computers & Education*. He is also a member of the editorial boards of *The Visual Computer* and *Computer Aided Design*. He frequently serves on the organizing and technical program committees of computer graphics conferences worldwide, including SIGGRAPH and Computer Graphics International.

He was the Fujitsu Scholar at the Royal Melbourne Institute of Technology and a Visiting Professor at the University of New South Wales in Australia. He was an Honorary Research Fellow at University College London in England, where he studied naval architecture with the Royal Corps of Naval Constructors.

Professor Rogers was one of the original faculty who established the Aerospace Engineering Department at the United States Naval Academy in 1964. He is currently Director of Aeronautics, Director of the Fluid Dynamics Laboratories and Head of the Supercomputer and Scientific Visualization Group at the Academy.

Kevin Sharer, CEO of Amgen and former student of Professor Rogers, recently endowed the David F. Rogers Chair of Aerospace Engineering at the United States Naval Academy in his honor.

Dave Rogers has both an experimental and a theoretical research background. His research interests include highly interactive graphics, computer aided design and manufacturing, numerical control, computer aided education, hypersonic viscous flow, boundary layer theory, computational fluid mechanics and flight dynamics.

He is an active pilot and holds an ATP (Air Transport Pilot) rating. He is chief pilot for the flight test course at the Academy. He has flown extensively throughout the Canadian High Arctic, including to Alert at 82 degrees 30 minutes north; across the North Atlantic to Iceland, Norway, Scotland and Ireland; to Alaska; and throughout the Bahamas and the Caribbean. His photographs of the Canadian High Arctic have been featured in a photography art show. Dave frequently flies his Bonanza to SIGGRAPH. He holds a Ph.D. in aeronautical engineering from Rensselaer Polytechnic Institute.